Holidays of the World
Cookbook for Students

Holidays of the World Cookbook for Students

by Lois Sinaiko Webb

ORYX PRESS

1995

The rare Arabian Oryx is believed to have inspired the myth of the unicorn. This desert antelope became virtually extinct in the early 1960s. At that time several groups of international conservationists arranged to have 9 animals sent to the Phoenix Zoo to be the nucleus of a captive breeding herd. Today the Oryx population is over 1000, and over 500 have been returned to the Middle East.

Children should always have adult supervision when working in the kitchen. Please see "Getting Started" on page xix for more information

Published simultaneously in Canada

Printed and Bound in the United States of America

∞ The paper used in this publication meets the minimum requirements of American National Standard for Information Science—Permanence of Paper for Printed Library Materials, ANSI Z39.48, 1984.

Library of Congress Cataloging-in-Publication Data

Webb, Lois Sinaiko.
    Holidays of the world cookbook for students / by Lois Sinaiko Webb.
       p. cm.
    Includes bibliographical references and index.
    Summary: A collection of 388 recipes from more than 136 countries plus an introduction describing local holidays, customs, and foods that are part of the holiday tradition in each country.
    ISBN 0-89774-884-0
    1. Holiday cookery—Juvenile literature. 2. Holidays—Juvenile literature. 3. Fasts and feasts—Juvenile literature. [1. Holiday cookery. 2. Holidays. 3. Cookery, International.] I. Title.
TX739.W43 1995   95-26019
641.5'68—dc20   CIP
                                                       AC

To my daughter
Josie Wilson Belsky

Contents

Middle East 47

Europe 73

Preface

A great way to learn about different cultures is through the foods people eat. That was the goal of *The Multicultural Cookbook for Students,* which I coauthored. Writing a cookbook about holidays requires a slightly different focus. In addition to providing recipes, I have tried to explain different rituals and traditions and how they relate to foods. As a food writer, I want to mention that this book is not meant to explain the religions of the world, but because holidays and religions are often intertwined, I have included some background material about the religious nature of many holidays.

Holidays of the World Cookbook for Students describes interesting celebrations observed by people thoughout the world. In some countries I have described official national holidays, while in others I have listed seasonal or regional holidays. The holiday celebrations for each country were selected because they are either the most important or the most interesting and unique to a country. Whenever possible, the history or legend of the holiday is included along with reasons why it is celebrated and how it is observed. The background information describes the eating habits and customs of the people, the rituals connected with the celebration, and the recipes served for the holiday feast or eaten during the holiday season. These foods and traditions are wide ranging: cookie-making traditions in the Netherlands and Germany, candies in Muslim and Hindu countries, and *tamales,* as eaten in Mexico and other countries in Latin America.

Celebrations reveal a great deal about the lives and history of the population. Holidays are not the whole of life, but they do show how people are attached to their roots and emphasize the importance of ancestors and family. Although the customs and rituals described for each country are current, many appear directly connected with those of ancient times. An example of this phenomenon is the Yule log tradition of many European countries. Today the burning of the Yule log is associated with Christmas, but the tradition originated as part of pagan rituals celebrating the winter solstice, the burning log symbolically chasing away winter.

This book contains 388 recipes from more than 136 countries. Also included are 6 regional celebrations in the United States, with more than 10 regional recipes.

Besides their holiday relevancy, the recipes were selected because they could be simplified and made with inexpensive and readily available ingredients. Whenever possible, the recipe choice was discussed with people from the country or region. The recipes are typical of the many side dishes, desserts, and baked goods that help make holiday feasts special and complete. In many countries, roast meat is the centerpiece of the holiday feast, and this practice is mentioned. In most cases, however, the meat recipe was not included because of expense and difficulty in preparation, particularly for recipes from those countries where traditions include spit-roasting whole animals.

The section of recipes for each continent or region begins with an introduction giving general information about the people and their predominant religions, establishing what holidays are observed by each country.

Each country has an average of three recipes. We have provided more recipes for some countries, and fewer for a couple. Each recipe includes the following:

- Yield, stating how many people the recipe will serve.

- Ingredients, listing how much of which food items you need to make the recipe.

- Equipment, listing cooking equipment, such as pans, bowls, spoons, etc.

- Instructions, telling you exactly how to make the recipe.

In addition, many recipes have terms that are printed in boldface type. Any word that is in boldface type is defined in "The Glossary of Food Terms," starting on page xxiii.

All recipes have been tested by the author and other food writers, grandmothers, and mothers and/or fathers with children in the Houston, Texas, area.

ACKNOWLEDGEMENTS

A special thanks to my dear friend and special consultant Mary Kegg, journalist and food writer.

I wish to thank my sisters and friends, both professional and amateur cooks, from around the world, who shared their kind help and insight: Frank Camera, Ning Yu, Billy Wong, Guangde Wong, Fred Clayton, Janice Clayton, Maureen Crowley, Penelope Michel-Paro, Jean Seltzer, Bea Marlowe, Esther Cohn, and Ruth Max.

Getting Started

SAFETY TIPS

To make cooking an enjoyable experience it's a good idea to 1) cook safely; 2) think before you act, using common sense; and 3) make sure that you, your cooking tools, and your kitchen are clean. All experienced cooks know the importance of these few simple rules.

Don't Cook Alone. Have Adult Help. Even apprentice chefs in restaurants never cook alone; an experienced cook is always present to teach food preparation and explain cooking equipment.

Keep Food at Proper Temperature at All Times. Cold food must be kept cold and hot food must be kept hot. Never cover food while it is cooling to room temperature, because it takes longer to cool down and there is a chance of bacteria forming. Cover to refrigerate or freeze. It is very important not to use spoiled food. If you think something may have spoiled, ask an adult if it should be discarded.

Prevent Fire Accidents. The kitchen's most dangerous equipment are stove-top burners, where most home accidents occur. Always keep a fire extinguisher (designed for stove fires) within easy reach and in working condition. To prevent stove-top accidents follow a few simple rules:

Never turn your back on or walk away from a skillet or pan of hot cooking oil. Always have the necessary utensils and ingredients ready to go before heating the oil.

If the oil should begin to smoke or seems too hot, quickly turn off the heat. *Do not* move the pan, and *do not* throw water in the pan. Allow it to cool down and begin again.

Never leave food that is cooking unattended, unless you are making a soup or stew with plenty of liquid and cooking on low heat. Even a soup or stew must be checked from time to time while it cooks to make sure it's not drying out, sticking, or burning. If the phone rings or there are other distractions while cooking, turn off the heat, and, using a potholder, slide the pan to a cold burner. If the pot is too heavy, ask an adult to do it. Double-check the burner to make sure you turned it *off*. (A common mistake is to turn it up, thinking you have turned it to *off*.) When you return to the kitchen, if it hasn't been more than a few minutes, continue cooking where you left off.

When you finish cooking, before leaving the kitchen, make sure the oven and stove-top burners are *off*.

Keep dry, heatproof oven mitts or pot holders handy. All metal spoons and handles get hot. Use wooden mixing spoons or plastic-handled metal spoons instead. Do not use all-plastic spoons or other cooking tools for mixing hot food, because they will melt. Never transfer very hot food to plastic containers or plastic bags; some are not made to hold hot food and might melt.

When lifting the lid off a pan of hot food always direct the open lid away from you so that the steam does not come toward your face.

Accidents do happen, however, and it is a good idea to have a first aid kit with burn and cut medication on hand.

Adjust the Cooking Time. Please note that the recommended cooking time given for each recipe is approximate. This time can vary, based on thickness of the pan, thickness of the ingredients, and differing heat controls on stoves.

Keep Knives Sharp. Dull knives can be dangerous, even more so than sharp knives. A dull knife can slip off food, causing accidents. Always cut food on a cutting board, and always have an adult standing by to help. Always carry a knife by the handle with the blade pointing toward the floor; never pass a knife to another person blade first, and do not put utility knives in a dishwasher or in a sink full of soapy water. It is not only dangerous, but it is also not good for the knives. Wash knives by hand, and keep them in a safe place away from small children.

Use Caution When Working with Hot Peppers. Cover hands with gloves or plastic baggies to prevent burning. Do not touch your eyes or face as you are working; if you do, splash with cold running water.

Be Extremely Careful When Working Around Hot Grease. Always have an adult help you when cooking with hot grease or oil. When you finish using the deep fryer or other pans with grease, immediately turn off the heat or unplug the pan. Double-check to make sure the burners are *off*, not turned to high, which is a very serious and common mistake many people make. *Do not move the pan of hot grease until it is cool.* Keep a kitchen fire extinguisher in working order and handy at all times. Accidents do happen, so be prepared.

CLEANLINESS IN THE KITCHEN

1. Tie your hair back or wear something on your head, such as a bandanna.

2. Roll up your sleeves and wear an apron or some protection to keep your clothes clean.

3. Do not touch any food or cooking equipment unless you have first washed and dried your hands. Wash your hands frequently while handling food to prevent cross-contamination. Raw chicken and raw eggs are two foods that can easily become infected by bacteria called salmonella. Raw chicken must be kept at a cold temperature (below 45° F.) at all times. It is best to thaw frozen chicken in the refrigerator (this can take a day or so, depending on the size) or more quickly under cold, running water. When preparing the chicken, keep the work area and all utensils sanitized (*sanitize* means to kill disease-causing bacteria by cleaning). Also, immediately after the chicken has been prepared and before any other food preparation, sanitize the work surface, utensils, and equipment again to prevent cross-contamination. Eggs keep well at 36° F. When buying eggs, look for the freshness date on the container, and check each egg to be sure there are no cracks.

4. Wash all fresh fruits and vegetables before cutting.

5. Have all the utensils and equipment clean, ready, and in good working order before beginning to cook.

6. Wipe up spills and drips at once. Good cooks clean up after themselves and always leave the kitchen spotless.

EQUIPMENT AND METHODS YOU NEED TO KNOW ABOUT

Almost every recipe you will use from this book will require the following basic equipment:

- ◆ A set of **measuring cups**. You will probably need nested cups in different sizes for measuring dry items such as flour, and you will probably need a liquid measuring cup with lines drawn on the sides to tell you how much liquid you have.

- ◆ A set of **measuring spoons** for measuring small amounts of liquid and dry items.

- ◆ A **work surface**, such as a counter top or table top, where you can put all of your equipment as you prepare your food.

- ◆ A set of **sharp knives** for cutting and dicing ingredients.

Each recipe will tell you what other equipment you will need—such as bowls, pans, or spoons—to make the food described.

Glossary of Food Terms

Asian fish sauces: The primary flavoring used in Asian cooking. Fish sauces are extracted from fermented fish or seafood. Every Asian country has its own sauce. These sauces, such as the Filipino *patis* and the Vietnamese *nuoc mam,* tend to be very salty and have a fairly strong smell.

Basmati rice: Long-grained and nonglutinous rice (each grain cooks separately from the other).

Baste: To moisten food with melted fat, meat drippings, stock, water, or sauce to improve flavor and to prevent drying out during cooking. Basting is done by using a **bulb baster** or spoon.

Bean curd: see **Tofu**

Bias slice: To slice at an angle. It is a typical way of slicing vegetables for Asian food preparation.

Blanch nuts: To blanch nuts, cover them with boiling water and let them stand for five minutes. Drain, and when cool enough to handle, skins will easily peel off.

Blanch vegetables: To blanch vegetables, fill a saucepan with 4 cups of water for every 1 cup of vegetables to be blanched. Bring water to boil over high heat, and add vegetables. Bring water back to a boil for 1 minute. Remove at once from heat, drain vegetables in **colander**, and rinse them under cold running water to stop the cooking action. Blanching is done to make peeling off the skin easier, to set color, to slightly soften the vegetables, and to remove the raw flavor.

Blend: To mix two or more ingredients together completely into one.

Blender: An appliance with whirling blades that quickly crushes and blends food.

Bulb baster: A kitchen utensil used for moistening meat or fowl while it is baking. A bulb baster has a clear plastic or metal shaft with a heavy rubber bulb at one end. To operate, place the shaft opening in the pan drippings and squeeze the rubber bulb. By releasing the bulb, the air comes back into the bulb, drawing the liquid from the pan up into the shaft. Squeeze the bulb again to wet the surface of the meat or fowl.

Candy or cooking thermometer: An instrument that registers the temperature of a cooking mixture. To properly use the thermometer, the bottom end should be immersed below the surface of the cooking mixture, but not touching the pan bottom. These thermometers are available at most supermarkets and in the kitchen gadget sections of many stores.

Cassava (also called manioc): An edible root, almost pure starch, easily digestible and nutritious. Cassava comes from tropical yucca plants. There are two kinds: sweet cassava, eaten as a vegetable; and bitter cassava, which is made into tapioca and manioc, a meal used in cooking. Tapioca is used for thickening soups and in puddings. Manioc flour is used extensively in South American cooking. Brazil is the world's largest grower of cassava. It is available in some supermarkets and all Latin American food stores. Although cassava is native to South America, since its introduction from Brazil, probably by slave ships, it has become a staple in African cooking as well.

Chicken (doneness): To check whether chicken is done cooking, pierce the thickest part of chicken with fork tines or knife. If the juices that trickle out are clear, instead of pinkish, the chicken is done.

Chick-peas: Also called garbanzo beans, chick-peas are round legumes (beans), available dried or canned.

Christmas crackers: Colorful crepe-paper-covered, tube-shaped party favors, about 5 inches long by 1 inch wide, with tabs at each end. Each person at the table gets one and when the tabs are pulled, the cracker makes a popping noise. Inside the tube there is either a limerick or a toy. Christmas crackers are an English Christmas dinner tradition and are also popular in Australia.

Cilantro: The Spanish name for coriander (see **Coriander**).

Cinnamon sugar: To make cinnamon sugar, mix 3 tablespoons sugar with 1 teaspoon ground cinnamon.

Citron: A fruit of the citrus family resembling a large, lumpy lemon, cultivated for its thick rind, which is candied. Candied citron is available at most supermarkets in the fruit and nut section, especially available during the Christmas season.

Coarsely chop: To cut into large, bite-size pieces, about ½ to 1 inch square. See also **Finely Chop**.

Colander: A metal or plastic bowl with holes used for draining liquid from solid food.

Cookie cutters: Decoratively shaped plastic or metal cutters (available at some supermarkets and in the kitchen gadget section of many stores) used for cutting rolled-out cookie dough. The rim of a water glass or lid of an aerosol spray can are good substitutes for cutting round cookies. Both are about 3 inches in diameter.

Cookie gun (also called **Cookie press**): A kitchen tool with decorative tips used for pressing out cookie dough in decorative shapes (available in the kitchen gadget section of many stores).

Cookie press: see **Cookie gun**

Coriander: Also known as **cilantro**, it is found in either fresh leaf form, which is an herb, or as dried seeds, a spice.

Core: To cut out the innermost part of a fruit or vegetable that contains the seeds and sometimes membrane.

Coucous: A granule-like grain made of durum wheat semolina. Couscous is also the name of the national dish of Morocco made with the couscous grain.

Crush: To grind or mash to a paste or into tiny bits.

Cube: To cut something into small (about ½-inch) squares; compare to **Dice**.

Dashi: An all-purpose soup stock made of dried kelp and dried fish flakes. The prepared dried mix (available at all Asian food stores) is very easy to make; just add water.

Deep fry: To quickly cook food by frying it in oil at a very high temperature. If oil is not hot enough, the food becomes oily and soggy.

1. Fry at 350° to 375° F. To check proper heat if you don't have a cooking thermometer a) dip the end of a wooden spoon handle or wooden skewer or chopstick in oil. When tiny bubbles appear around immersed wood, oil is hot enough for frying food; or b) oil is hot enough when a 1-inch cube of white bread browns in 1 minute.

2. Fry in small batches; overloading fryer basket lowers oil temperature.

Deep fryer: A special container with a built-in thermostat used for quickly frying food. A wok, deep skillet, or saucepan with a cooking thermometer can be made into a deep fryer. A wok is ideal for deep frying. Its sloping sides enable one to decrease the amount of oil normally used for deep frying. Use only vegetable oil and fry only small amounts of food at one time. Some woks come with a semi-circular wire rack that may be placed above the oil for draining foods. After the food is fried, place it on the rack so that oil drips into the wok to drain; then drain on paper towels. To remove food from wok, use either a slotted metal spoon, tongs, or spatula. (See **Wok.**)

Degrease: To remove grease from liquid, such as pan juices, using **bulb baster** or spoon. It is easy to degrease by placing cooled liquid in freezer for about 2 hours. Grease will rise to the surface and can be skimmed off.

Devein: To remove visible black (sometimes white) vein running down the back of peeled shrimp. It is easy to remove by cutting thin membrane while rinsing shrimp under cold running water. Remove vein, using either the tip of a fingernail or point of a knife, and discard.

Dice: To cut into very small (about ¼-inch) pieces; compare to **Cube.**

Dollop: A small amount or blob.

Double boiler: Two pans made to fit together with one resting partway inside the other; it usually comes with a cover that fits either pan. **Simmering** water in the lower pan gently heats the upper pan and its contents. A double boiler is used when the food must not cook over direct heat, such as when melting chocolate or making some cream sauces. The amount of water in the bottom pan is important; it must be enough to cook the food and not boil away, but if it is too full, it can boil over and be dangerous. A double boiler can be devised by fitting a shallow pan or heatproof bowl with rounded sides into a bottom pan that is deep enough to fill at least halfway with water. Be sure the top pan or bowl fits securely on top of the bottom pan so there is no danger of it slipping off.

Drizzle: Is to lightly pour a liquid or sauce in fine lines over a surface. This is done when only a little liquid or sauce is needed, usually as a decorative touch. An easy way to drizzle is to put the liquid or sauce into a squirt bottle with a small hole in the nozzle.

Dutch oven: A cast iron pot with a tight-fitting, domed lid that is used for slow cooking soups, stews, and cobblers.

Egg Glaze: To prepare, use 1 egg and 1 tablespoon water, mix together, and brush over pastry.

Egg whites: see **Eggs, separated**

Egg yolks: see **Eggs, separated**

Eggs, separated: Means that the egg yolk has been put in one container and the white in another. *How to crack and separate eggs:* Wash and dry your hands.

1. Have three bowls ready: one for the yolks (the yellow part), one for whites, and one to crack the eggs over.

2. Hold the egg in one hand; crack it with one light, sharp blow against the rim of the bowl, or crack lightly with the dull side of a table knife. Try to make an even, crosswise break in the shell.

3. Hold the cracked egg over an empty bowl; take it in both hands, with the crack on the upper side, and pull the crack open with your thumbs, breaking it apart into halves. As you do this, some of the egg white will drip into the bowl underneath it. Hold the yolk-filled half shell upright so it cups the yolk. Empty any remaining egg white in the other half shell into the bowl.

4. Hold the yolk-filled half over the bowl, and carefully, so the yolk doesn't break, pass it back and forth from one half shell to the other. As you do this, more egg white drips into the bowl. When the yolk is free of egg white put it into a separate bowl and continue cracking remaining eggs the same way.

If an egg is spoiled, it can easily be discarded when cracked into a separate bowl. Make sure no yolk (yellow part) gets in the white because the slightest fat from the yolk will keep the whites from whipping.

Finely chop: To cut into very tiny pieces. It is the same as to **mince**. See also **Coarsely chop.**

Florets: Tender, edible tops of cauliflower or broccoli, distinguishing tops from stalks (stems).

Fold in: Gently and slowly mixing (using a whisk or mixing spoon) in a rotating, top to bottom motion, allowing air to be incorporated into the mixture.

Food mill: A hand-cranking kitchen tool that mashes food through tiny holes, removing fibers, skin, and seeds.

Food processor: An electric machine with rapidly whirling blades in the bottom of the container to soften, beat, mix, **blend**, shred, and slice ingredients.

Froth: To make foamy by adding air to the mixture; this is done by vigorously beating or whipping.

Garnish: To put something on or around food, either to make more colorful, such as adding a sprig of parsley, or to make it more flavorful, such as adding syrup or icing.

Ginger root: Used as a spice either fresh, preserved, or dried and ground. Buy fresh ginger with smooth skin, not wrinkled and dry. Fresh ginger is juicy; when old it is fibrous and dry.

Glutinous rice: Called *no-mi* in China, it is used in rice porridge and for dessert dishes. Glutinous rice is polished whole kernels of a short-grain variety; it is slightly sweet and extremely sticky.

Grater: A metal kitchen utensil used for grating, shredding, and slicing. Graters are found in flat, cylindrical, or box shapes, and some have a handle across the top for a firm grip. The surface used for grating is perforated with rough-edged round holes that stick out forming a rasp-like surface. There are usually two grating surfaces, one for finely grating things such as spices, and a larger rasp-like surface for coarse grating things such as cheese and for making bread crumbs. The shredder sur-

face is perforated with ¼-inch round holes that have a raised cutting edge along the bottom side of each hole. The slicing surface has several parallel slits with a raised cutting edge along the bottom side of each slit.

Grill: Cooking over heat on a perforated rack. The grill can be gas, electric, charcoal, wood, or a combination. The food takes on a distinct grilled flavor, especially over a wood fire.

Ground: When referring to peanuts or ground nuts, ground means finely crushed.

Groundnuts: Another name for peanuts.

Hibachi: A small Japanese table-top charcoal grill.

Knead: To work a dough until smooth and elastic, preferably with the hands. It is especially important in bread making. Shape the dough into a ball. Push the "heels" of your hands against the dough, fold the upper half over, and turn it a little bit. Then push in the heels of your hands against the dough and repeat the whole procedure many times until dough is very smooth.

Jellyroll pan: A jellyroll pan is used for making a cake that must be thin enough to roll up. A standard jellyroll pan is 12 x 7 x ¾ inches. A cookie sheet of comparable size and with a raised edge can also be used to make the thin, flat cake.

Lemon grass: A lemon-like flavoring used in Asian cooking. It is used in everything from soups to desserts. In some parts of the world it is called sorrel.

Manioc: see **Cassava**

Marinade: The sauce in which food is marinated.

Marinate: To soak food, especially meat, in a sauce made up of seasonings and liquids.

Millet: The name for several different plant species that are grown as grain for human food in different parts of the world, such as Africa, Asia, and India. It seems to grow where nothing else can and has been cultivated in dry, poor soil for over a thousand years as an important high-protein food staple. To this day millet nourishes about one-third of the world's population and is said to equal rice in food value. Millet is available at most health food stores either in the form of meal, groats, or flour. Millet is a "nonglutinous" grain. Gluten gives the elasticity to wheat flour needed in bread baking. Adding some millet to wheat flour makes excellent tasting bread. Millet has an important place in the U.S. economy even though it is not a popular food grain. In the United States, it is cultivated mostly as a forage grass and poultry feed, especially suitable for chicks and pet birds.

Mince: see **Finely chop**

Mortar and pestle: Used for mashing or crushing. The mortar is the hard stone or wood bowl, and the pestle is the hand-held tool used to mash an ingredient to release its essence and make it smooth and lump-free.

Opaque: Refers to food with a solid-appearing texture. The flesh of fish and seafood, such as shrimp, have an almost translucent (clear) grayish color when raw. As they cook, the flesh color changes to an opaque white or whitish-pink.

Oxtail: The tail of any beef-producing animal. Ox simply means steer or beef. Any bone-in beef can be substituted.

Pastry brush: Used for applying glazes to foods. It can be a 1-inch paint brush, but it should be soft and of good quality so the bristles do not come out.

Peel (vegetables and fruits): To remove the skin or rind of vegetables and fruits. This is done with a vegetable peeler or paring knife by carefully removing the outer surface without cutting into the edible flesh part.

Peel (shrimp): To remove the hard shell that covers the edible flesh of the shrimp. This is done by holding the shrimp between the thumb and index finger of one hand and carefully pulling the tiny legs under the shrimp

apart with fingers of the other hand. The shell should easily peel off.

Peel (tomatoes): To peel tomatoes, drop in boiling water for about 1 or 2 minutes. Remove with **slotted spoon** and rinse under cold water to cool to handle. If the skin does not crack open, poke tomato with a small knife and the skin easily peels off.

Phyllo pastry sheets: Used in Greek and Middle Eastern cooking. Available in one-pound box, containing 22 paper-thin sheets, each 14 x 18 inches in size (available in the freezer section of most supermarkets, brand name Fillo). Thaw in refrigerator overnight—do not thaw at room temperature and do not refreeze; store in refrigerator. Once the package is opened, keep covered with damp towel to prevent drying out.

Pilaf, pilav, pilaw, pilau, pulaos: Depending on the language, this word means "cooked through." It is rice or grain briefly fried, then steamed or cooked in liquid. Turks, Syrians, Arabs, Iranians, and Mongols each claim it as their national dish.

Pith: The spongy tissue between the skin and flesh of fruits such as oranges, lemons, and grapefruit.

Plantains: Called "cooking bananas." They are either baked, fried, or boiled. Plantains of different sizes and shapes are eaten at every stage of ripeness. Black-skinned plantains are sweetest. Ripe plantains peel easily, but peeling green plantains is more difficult because the skin clings to the edible fruit. To peel, first slice off about 1 inch at each end, and cut the plantain in half, crosswise. Cut lengthwise slits in skin and unwrap a strip at a time, crosswise rather then peeling it lengthwise, as you would a banana.

Punch down: An action performed in bread making. When the prepared yeast mixture is added to flour, it begins to ferment and gases (carbon dioxide) develop, causing the dough to rise. The gases are forced out of the dough by a process known as punching down; this helps to relax the gluten and equalizes the temperature of the dough. To punch down, take your fist and flatten the dough against the bowl. The best time to punch down the dough is when it has doubled in size through fermentation. After the dough is punched, it must rise a second time before it can be made into bread or rolls.

Rehydrate: To restore to former condition by adding water or other liquid to reconstitute.

Render: Releasing fat from meat by heating, such as frying bacon.

Rolling boil: To boil over medium to medium-high heat.

Rolling pin: A cylindrical tool, held at each end, used for rolling out pastry dough on a flat surface.

Scald or scalded: To heat just to boiling point, when small bubbles appear around edges of pan, but not boiling.

Seed or seeded: To remove and discard seeds, usually in fruit or vegetables.

Segment: To cut out edible fruit sections from the **pith**.

Self-rising flour: This type of flour contains leavening agents and salt for convenience.

Serrated knife: A knife that has saw-like notches along the cutting edge, such as on a bread knife.

Sesame seeds: Used for flavoring in Middle Eastern and Asian cooking. Toast sesame seeds in skillet by cooking over medium heat, tossing frequently, until lightly browned, about 5 minutes. Spread out on a plate to cool. The best places to buy sesame seeds are health food and Middle Eastern food stores.

Shred: To cut into small strips, strings, or pieces.

Sift: To shake a dry, powdered substance (such as flour, baking powder, etc.) through a strainer/sifter to make it smooth and lump-free (see **Sifter**).

Sifter: Such as a flour sifter, is a container with strainer bottom used for sifting (see **Sift**).

Simmer: To slowly cook food just below the boiling point.

Simple syrup: Mix 1 cup sugar and 2 cups water in small saucepan over medium heat, until sugar dissolves. Bring to a boil, without mixing, and let boil for 1 minute. Remove from heat. Cool to room temperature and keep refrigerated. Makes about 2½ cups.

Slotted spoon: A spoon with small holes or slots, used to drain liquid from solid food.

Spatula: The spatula with a long, narrow, flexible metal blade with a rounded end is used for spreading icing on cakes and for mixing and scraping bowls. Spatulas with a broad, flexible rubber or plastic head are used for gently stirring (**folding**) ingredients together and for scraping bowls. Metal spatulas have a long handle and a broad, flexible blade with either a square or rounded head. They are also called pancake turners. They are used for turning or removing hot food from hot containers. A slotted metal spatula allows grease or liquid to drain off the food before it is transferred from one container to another. *Use only a metal spatula when handling hot food. Plastic and rubber spatulas can melt from the heat.*

Springform pan: A two-part, round baking pan. The sides of the pan are a ring, held in place around the bottom plate by a spring clamp.

Steamer pan: A two-part pan with a tight-fitting cover. The upper pan is perforated and sits above simmering water in the lower pan. Items placed in the upper pan cook by steam. A steamer pan can be made with a metal **colander** fitted into a large-size saucepan with cover. The pan must be large enough so that the **simmering** water does not touch the upper container. The steamer basket (upper container) can be propped up with something heat-proof, such as a wad of foil or clean, empty cans placed in water.

Stem: To cut off the stem end of a vegetable or fruit; it is the spot where the vegetable or fruit was connected to the vine.

Stir-Fry: To continually mix, in a tossing motion, while quickly cooking food, in very little oil, over high heat. This is usually done in a **Wok**.

Sweetened condensed milk (homemade): To make this in a **food processor** or **blender**, combine 1 cup instant nonfat dry milk with ⅓ cup boiling water. Add ⅔ cup confectioners' sugar and 3 tablespoons butter or margarine; mix until thickened. Yield: about 1¼ cups. Cover and refrigerate, up to one month.

Toasted sesame seeds: See **Sesame seeds**

Tofu (also called **Bean curd**): Made from soybeans, it is high in protein and easily digestible. It comes in two popular forms, firm and soft. Firm tofu comes in blocks that can be sliced and fried or cubed, used mostly as a meat substitute. Soft tofu is crumbled and added to stews, soups, and drinks.

Trim: For fruits and vegetables, it means to remove the stem, core, and any tough, inedible parts, brown spots, or discoloration. To

trim meat means to remove fat, gristle, or silver skin.

Tube pan: A ring-shaped cake pan with high sides and a central tube to promote rapid rising and even baking. The standard size for tube pans is 10 inches across.

Turmeric: A spice, used more for its yellow color than flavor. It is used to color curries, pickles, margarine, and cloth.

Vegetable brush: A small brush with bristles that are soft enough to not bruise fruits or vegetables while cleaning them, yet firm enough to clean off the dirt.

Whisk: Beating in a fast, circular motion, giving the mixture a lighter texture by beating in air. This mixing is done with a kitchen mixing tool with a bulbous end made of fine wires held together by a long handle, also called a **whisk**.

Wok: A Chinese, rounded-bottom metal pan with sloping sides. Its shape allows heat to spread evenly and food to cook quickly over high heat while constantly being stirred (see **Stir-Fry**). It is also used for deep-frying and steaming.

Introduction

Holidays and celebrations bring people together to share successes and remembrances. They can be related to country, region, city, village, church, or family. Religious celebrations give people the opportunity to renew their faith and beliefs. The rite of passage rituals celebrate life-changing events, such as marriages, births, deaths, graduations, and anniversaries.

For every celebration, from a national event observed by millions of people to a simple marriage with only a justice of the peace, there are ancient rituals, folklore, legends, customs, superstitions, symbols, and myths that people follow. Many of these holiday rituals are thousands of years old, and in many cases, their origins have been completely lost over time or, at best, are only vague memories.

For many holiday feasts, various foods are symbolic reminders of the act or deed being celebrated. One such example is bread, either church-blessed in Christian Easter observances or the challah, blessed at the dinner table in Jewish homes for special occasions such as Sabbath and holiday dinners.

These symbolic foods keep people connected to their roots. When people emigrate, over generations some traditions such as clothing and language may be forgotten, but that is not true of food, especially the memorable holiday cooking. For centuries in the United States, families retained their identity by following the cooking traditions of their homelands: Germans in Milwaukee, Norwegians in Minnesota, Mexicans in the Southwest, Chinese in San Francisco, Dutch in Pennsylvania, and Jews, regardless of where they settled.

When we learn about other cultures and religions, the doors of understanding and compassion open. I hope that through the common language of food, this cookbook about world holiday celebrations, rituals, and feasting will help us learn even more about those with whom we share this planet.

WORLD CALENDARS

Many of the holidays described in this book fall on different days in different years. The dates of these holidays change each year because various cultures and religions use different calendars. As discussed later in this section, these calendars differ because they are based on alternate ways of measuring time— some using the sun, and others the moon.

In prehistoric times the calendar was based simply on the cycles of nature as observed by primitive people. Because people depended upon the growing season to survive, the year would begin, and still does in many cultures, with either the first signs of spring or around the time of the harvest. One example is the Iranian New Year, *Nou Ruz*, which begins with the spring planting. As a symbolic reminder, Iranians place seeds in bowls of water so they will grow to be green shoots for the first day of spring.

These ancient farmers also celebrated on the summer solstice (the longest day), and on the winter solstice (the shortest day) each year.

Lunar Calendar

As people gained knowledge, they calculated the year according to the phases of the moon. The moon's cycle was interpreted thousands of years ago by astrologers and religious leaders in different parts of the world. The monthly full moon, with its beautiful light, has long been a favored time for religious ceremonies, and many religions have developed lunar calendars. The phases of the moon are used to measure the months throughout Asia and the Middle East. The lunar year is 354 days, 8 hours, 48 minutes, and 34 seconds. The solar year is 365 days, 5 hours, 48 minutes, and 46 seconds. Most lunar calendars make up the 11-day difference between the two with extra days or months added to the lunar year, so festivals will remain in customary seasons. Others do not, however. The Islamic calendar, for example, does not add extra days, and so all Islamic holidays eventually are celebrated in every month of the Western (Gregorian) calendar.

Gregorian Calendar

The solar cycle of 365.25 days is what the Western world follows. It begins on January 1 and ends on December 31. It was established by Julius Caesar in 46 B.C., and so it was referred to as the Julian calendar. This system was later improved by Pope Gregory in 1582, and it is now known as the Gregorian calendar. An ordinary year has 365 days, and every fourth year (leap year) is one day longer. The Gregorian calendar is used, at least for business, in most countries of the world.

Christian Calendar

The Christian calendar (ecclesiastical calendar) is a cycle of seasons and days that commemorate the life of Jesus and the history of the Christian church. Within Christianity, there are several different church traditions, and the calendars differ also. In the Western Christian churches, the year begins four Sundays before Christmas, called Advent. Christian Eastern Orthodox churches begin the year either on September 1 or 14. Easter is the most important holiday of the year for all Christians, but which other holidays are celebrated, and how they are celebrated, vary according to the beliefs and traditions of each church. The Eastern Orthodox church, for instance, has 12 major holidays in addition to Easter, and the Roman Catholic church designates certain "holy days" when all must attend mass. Anglican, Lutheran, and most Protestant groups observe fewer holidays than either the Catholic or Orthodox traditions dictate.

Hebrew Calendar

The Hebrew calendar calculates its years by the sun and its months by the moon. The 12 months alternate between 29 and 30 days with 2 of them varying in length. A 13th leap month, *Adar* II (also known as *Veadar*), is added seven times to the lunar calendar, the 3rd, 6th, 8th, 11th, 14th, 17th, and 19th years, in a fixed 19-year cycle.

In the Hebrew calendar, each day begins after the sunset on the preceding day and lasts until the following sunset. All religious observations begin just after sundown on the day prior to the designated holiday date. This way of reckoning days is quite different from the Western calendar, where a day runs from midnight to midnight.

An interesting fact about the Hebrew calendar is that it has four New Year's observations. The New Year was originally celebrated in the month of *Nissan* (March-April), when the first crops were harvested, according to the civil calendar of the ancient Jewish nation. Later the rabbis specified *Rosh Hashana*, in the fall, as the calendrical New Year, the anniversary of the creation of the world. *Rosh Hashana* literally means "head of the year" or "beginning of the year," and it is the most widely celebrated New Year. The next New Year is the first of *Elul* for the tithing of animals, which refers to the ancient tradition of pledging one-tenth of your flock or crops to support the temple. The fourth New Year is *Tu B'Shevat*, also known as "New Year for Trees" on *Shevat* 15, a one-day festival coinciding with the blossoming of trees in Israel. In Israel saplings are planted on this day to mark the occasion, and all sorts of fruits are eaten.

Islamic Calendar

The Islamic calendar is a lunar calendar. The first day of the first year of the Islamic calendar is figured from the date Muhammad the Prophet fled Mecca and went to Medina, July 16, A.D. 622, according to the Western calendar. Today, unless you are a scholar in Muslim studies, pinpointing exact dates can be very difficult. The Islamic lunar calendar is calculated in every Muslim country, and the different calendars often don't agree with one another. Special people, called *muezzin*, are selected to watch for the rising of the new moon at sunset on the 29th day of each lunar month. Whether a month has 29 or 30 days depends on the moon, or rather, when it is sighted. If the moon is not visible when the sun has gone down on the 29th day, the month will have 30 days. Two 29-day or two 30-day months might thus occur in succession, but not necessarily in all the Muslim countries. This calendar is used to determine religious festivals only; for commerce and international business, the Western calendar is followed in most Muslim countries.

The Islamic calendar is completely lunar, with only 354 days, and falls short 11 days every solar year. Following the phases of the moon, holidays fall during different seasons of the year, and sooner or later all Islamic holidays fall in every month of the Western (Gregorian) calendar year. (The cycle takes 32½ years to complete itself.)

Just as with the Hebrew calendar, each day begins after the sunset on the preceding day and lasts until the following sunset. Therefore holiday celebrations begin on the evening before the holiday date.

Hindu Calendar

Hinduism is one of the oldest religions in existence. It ranks as the world's third largest religion, behind Christianity and Islam. The majority of Hindus live in India, where the religion first began, but there are large numbers of Hindus in countries throughout the world, including the United States.

There are several Hindu calendars, but most of them have 12 months of 27 to 31 days. Extra days are added every three years. Each month is measured from full moon to full moon, and the month is divided in halves, the dark half (waning moon) and the bright half (waxing moon). Festival dates are determined by their position in the dark or bright half of a month. Some parts of India, which is largely Hindu, celebrate the solar New Year (as many Asians do) when the sun enters the sign of Aries, varying by a few days in mid-April. Some begin the new year with the Festival of Lights, *Diwali*.

Diwali is in the Hindu month of *Kartika* (October-November), and by happy coincidence, *Diwali* also marks the end of autumn and the beginning of the winter season in India. The celebration lasts for at least two days, but in some areas it may last up to ten. The origins of *Diwali* are obscured in folklore and legend, but for most Hindus, it heralds the New Year. Houses and courtyards are illuminated with hundreds of tiny oil lamps called *dipa* to symbolize the renewal of life. Today many people use strings of white Christmas tree lights instead.

Buddhist Calendar

Most Southeast Asians follow the Buddhist calendar, which calculates the New Year by the sun's position in the sky and the months by the moon, based on a Hindu calendar. The solar New Year is based on the position of the sun in relation to the 12 segments of the heavens, each named for a sign in the zodiac. The new year begins when the sun enters the segment called Aries, usually between April 13th and 18th.

In Thailand and most Buddhist countries, year one is 543 B.C. except in Laos. According to the Laotian Buddhist calendar, year one is 638 B.C.

The dates of Buddhist festivals are based on the lunar months and vary a great deal from the Gregorian calendar. In Cambodia, Laos, and Thailand months are referred to by number; in Sri Lanka each month has its own name.

Chinese Calendar

At some period during China's ancient beginning more than five thousand years ago, Chinese astronomers discovered the regularity of the moon's movements and developed the lunar calendar. According to the lunar calendar, the first day of each month begins with the new moon. Twelve moon cycles add up to 354 days, which make a lunar year. In order to create compatibility with the solar calendar, an extra month is added every few years—seven out of every 19 years have 13 months. The calendar begins with the first day of the first month, which falls in January/February. In Chinese tradition, everyone has a birthday on New Year's Day and becomes a year older, rather than advancing his or her age on the actual day of birth.

Another difference between the Chinese and Western calendars is how the passing years and birth dates are remembered. For thousands of years, the Chinese followed the Buddhist teachings. The monks had to find an easy way for everyone to remember at least the exact year, if not the exact month and day, of birth and other special events in history. They named each year for an animal, and there are twelve of them: rat, ox, tiger, rabbit, dragon, snake, horse, ram, monkey, rooster, dog, and pig. Twelve animals represent a cycle, and after the year of the pig, which represents the twelfth year of a cycle, it begins again with the year of the rat. The lunar months are numbered.

Bibliography

Abercrombie, Thomas J. "Saudi Arabia." *National Geographic* (January 1966).

Africa News Service Inc., edited by Tami Hultman. *The Africa News Cookbook* (New York: Penguin Books, 1985).

Copage, Eric V. *U.S. Kwanzaa* (New York: William Morrow & Co, Inc., 1991).

Devillers, Carole. "Haiti's Voodoo Pilgrimages." *National Geographic* (March 1985).

Fulton, M. *Encyclopedia of Food & Cookery* (New York: W. H. Smith, 1985).

Grigson, Jane, ed. *World Atlas of Food* (New York: Simon & Schuster, 1974).

Grosvenor, Donna K., and Gilbert M. Grosvenor. "Ceylon, the Resplendent Land." *National Geographic* (April 1966).

Hodgson, Bryan. "Time and Again in Burma." *National Geographic* (July 1984).

Iny, Daisy. *The Best of Baghdad Cooking* (Toronto, Canada: Clarke, Irwin & Co., 1976).

Jolly, Alison. "Man against Nature: Madagascar." *National Geographic* (February 1987).

Krohn, Norman Odya. *Menu Mystique* (Middle Village, NY: Jonathan David Inc., 1983).

New York Public Library Desk Reference, 2d ed. (New York: Prentice Hall General Reference, 1993).

Office of Public Communication, Bureau of Public Affairs, U.S. Department of State. *Background Notes* (Washington DC: U.S. Government Printing Office). To obtain *Background Notes* write to Superintendent of Documents, U.S. Government Printing Office, Washington, DC 20402.

Ojakangas, Beatrice A. *The Finnish Cookbook* (New York: Crown Publishers, 1964).

Riely, Elizabeth. *The Chef's Companion* (New York: Van Nostrand Reinhold, 1986).

Sarvis, Shirley. *A Taste of Portugal* (New York: Charles Scribner's Sons, 1967).

Sheraton, Mimi. *From My Mother's Kitchen* (New York: HarperCollins, 1979).

———. *Visions of Sugarplums* (New York: Harper & Row, 1981).

Stager, Curt. "Cameroon's Killer Lake." *National Geographic* (September 1987).

Time-Life Books. *Foods of the World Series* (New York: Time-Life).

    Bailey, Adrian. *The Cooking of the British Isles*, 1969.

    Feibleman, Peter S. *The Cooking of Spain and Portugal*, 1969.

    Field, Frances, and Michael Field. *A Quintet of Cuisines*, 1970.

    Hahn, Emily. *The Cooking of China*, 1968.

    Hazelton, Nika Standen. *The Cooking of Germany*, 1969.

    Nickles, Harry G. *Middle Eastern Cooking*, 1969.

    Papashvily, Helen. *Russian Cooking*, 1969.

    Shenton, James P., et al. *American Cooking: The Melting Pot*, 1971.

    Steinberg, Rafael. *The Cooking of Japan*, 1976.

    ———. *Pacific and Southeast Asian Cooking*, 1970.

Van Straalen, Alice. *The Book of Holidays Around the World* (New York: E. P. Dutton, 1986).

Wernecke, Herbert H. *Christmas: Customs around the World* (Philadelphia: Westminster Press, 1959).

White, Peter T. "Vietnam, Hard Road to Peace." *National Geographic* (November 1989).

Young, Gordon. "Paraguay." *National Geographic* (August 1982).

Holidays of the World Cookbook for Students

Africa

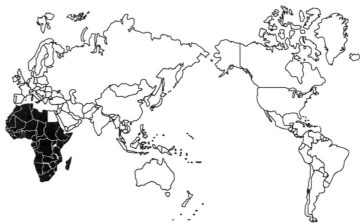

Africa is a large, varied continent filled with diverse people and diverse lands. There are hundreds of ethnic groups in Africa. Because most Africans engage in farming many communal festivals celebrate agrarian events. The worship of ancestors through gods, spirits, and sorcery is also an important part of African life. Many of these celebrations incorporate masks, costumes, headdresses, dances, and drums in ritual performances that tell a story which the people understand. Every step, prance, and movement of the performers is done with a purpose, and every beat of the drum or other instrument has meaning. The performers are well versed in the legends they are dramatizing because these traditions have been handed down from generation to generation. African Christians combine their traditional worship of the rain, sun, and ancestors with the beliefs of Christianity, and most African Muslims blend agrarian and ancestral worship with Islamic beliefs.

African holiday feasts vary according to several things: The importance of the celebration, religious dietary restrictions, and what is affordable or available from the hunt, garden, or market. For the most important holidays in Africa, the highlight of the feast is spit-roasted meat, usually lamb, goat, or wild game. (Cattle are considered a form of wealth in most African countries and are slaughtered only on the rarest occasions.)

For many Africans roasted meat is a rare treat, reserved for special feast days, including agrarian and harvest festivals, the Muslim celebration of the end of *Ramadan*, *Eid al-Fitr*, and the Christian Christmas or Easter.

Even when meat is used, it is more often a flavoring agent than the central item in a meal. Meat is added to dishes made from **millet** and other grains, yams and other root and vine vegetables, rice, and greens. Fruits and vegetables are almost always fresh and naturally ripened, and so what is eaten varies with the seasons.

The following recipe for African Porridge is typical of what is eaten every day as well as at most holiday feasts.

African porridge is made with water or milk and cornmeal. It is called *nsima* in Malawi and Zambia, *ugali* in Kenya and Tanzania, *oshifima* in Namibia, *bidia* in Zaire, and *mealie-meal* or *putu* among the English- or Zulu-speaking South Africans. Large kettles of this cornmeal mush are prepared along with the meat, vegetables, and fresh fruit served at community feasts. Each family eats from a container they bring from home, usually a large hollowed out calabash (gourd) or plastic tub. The food is eaten with the right hand only. Throughout Africa and the Middle East, it is considered rude to touch food with the left hand, which is used for personal grooming.

In Africa the traditional way to eat cornmeal mush is to pull off a chunk, press a hole in it with your thumb, and then use it to scoop up stew or sauce.

African Porridge   Cornmeal Mush

Yield: 4 to 6
- 1 cup milk
- 1¼ cups cornmeal
- 1 cup water

Equipment: Small bowl, wooden mixing spoon, medium saucepan, rubber **spatula**, greased medium bowl

1. Pour milk into small bowl, and slowly add ¾ cup cornmeal to the milk. Beat constantly until mixture forms a smooth paste.

2. Bring water to a boil in medium saucepan over high heat. Add cornmeal mixture from step 1 to boiling water, and, stirring constantly, reduce heat to medium. Cook for 3 minutes, stirring constantly, while adding the remaining ½ cup cornmeal. Continue stirring until mixture is lump-free and smooth. When mixture begins to pull away from sides of pan and sticks together, remove from heat.

3. Pour cornmeal mixture into greased medium bowl and set aside to cool.

Serve at room temperature with other food.

Tanzania

Most of the population of Tanzania are Bantu-speaking Africans, but there is also smatterings of Asians, Arabs, Hindus, and Europeans. There are more than 120 ethnic groups in Tanzania, among them the San (Bushmen) and Khoikhoi (Hottentot) people. The official language is Kiswahili, although English is widely spoken. About a third of the people follow traditional religious practices, including animist beliefs (all things have a soul). The rest of the population is equally divided between those who follow Muslim and Christian religions.

Expatriates, tourists, and natives freely observe holidays according to the traditions of their religion or in the style of their homeland. The holiday feast could include anything from East African soups to giant Indian Ocean lobster, shrimp, Indian curries, Italian pizzas, Chinese *dim sum*, milk shakes, ice cream, and lots of fruit.

The following soup recipe is more typical of what most Tanzanians, who engage in subsistence farming (growing just enough food to survive), would be able to afford. It is a flavorful and nourishing soup for holiday feasts like *Eid al-Fitr* (the feast ending the fasting month of *Ramadan*), especially when eaten with *wali na samaki* and *kashata* (recipes follow).

Supu Ya Ndizi — East African Plantain Soup

Yield: serves 4 to 6

- 2 or 3 (1 pound) green **plantains, peeled**
- 6 cups chicken broth, homemade (recipe page 52) or canned
- salt and pepper to taste

Equipment: Electric **blender** or **food processor**, rubber **spatula**, **Dutch oven** or large saucepan with cover, mixing spoon

1. Finely slice peeled plantains and put into blender or food processor with 1 cup chicken broth. Blend until smooth and lump-free.

2. Pour remaining 5 cups chicken broth into Dutch oven or large saucepan, add plantain mixture, and stir. Cover and cook over medium heat, stirring occasionally, until soup is thickened, about 45 minutes. Add salt and pepper to taste.

Serve warm in individual soup bowls.

Most Tanzanians love fish, and their country has great lakes, rivers, and coastal waters for fishing. Regardless of their religious beliefs, the holiday feast for most Tanzanians would be fish instead of meat. The popular fish dish listed next would be eaten for *Eid al-Fitr*, *Eid al-Adha*, Easter, or Christmas. For tribal ceremonial gatherings, this dish would be prepared in large communal kettles.

Most Tanzanian cooking is fiery hot and spicy. The following recipe has been adjusted for milder flavor.

Wali na Samaki — Rice with Fish

Yield: serves 6

- 2 green bell peppers, **cored, seeded**, and **coarsely chopped**
- 1 onion, coarsely chopped

2 cups (16-ounce can) whole tomatoes, coarsely chopped

2 cups water

juice of 1 lemon

1 teaspoon **grated** lemon rind

½ teaspoon **crushed** red pepper, more or less to taste

3 bay leaves

salt and pepper to taste

1 cup all-purpose flour

2½ to 3 pounds skinless fish fillets: red snapper, halibut, cod, or other firm-flesh fish, cut into 2-inch chunks

4 tablespoons vegetable oil, more or less as needed

5 to 6 cups cooked rice (keep warm for serving)

Equipment: **Dutch oven** or large saucepan with cover, mixing spoon, pie pan, large skillet, **slotted spoon**, metal **spatula**, grater, oven mitts, 9-inch baking pan

1. Prepare sauce: In Dutch oven or large saucepan, add green peppers, onion, tomatoes, water, lemon juice, lemon rind, ¼ teaspoon red pepper (more or less to taste), bay leaves, and salt and pepper to taste, and stir. Bring to a boil over high heat, and stir. Reduce heat to **simmer**, cover, and cook for about 30 minutes, until flavors are blended. Remove bay leaves and discard before serving. Keep warm until ready to serve.

Preheat oven to 200° F.

2. Prepare and fry fish: Put flour in pie pan. Coat fish with flour, shake off excess.

3. Heat 2 tablespoons oil in large skillet over medium-high heat. Carefully add fish pieces, a few at a time, sprinkle with salt and pepper to taste, and fry for about 3 to 5 minutes on each side until golden brown and cooked through. Drain well and transfer fish to baking pan. Keep warm in oven until serving time. Add more oil if necessary. Continue frying in batches. Lower heat to prevent burning.

To serve, mound rice on a serving platter, arrange fish over it, and cover with vegetable sauce.

Coconut Balls are an easy-to-make, between-meal snack. They are eaten during *Eid al-Fitr*, served to guests during *Eid al-Adha* or Christian holidays, and eaten by children at tribal ceremonial gatherings.

Kashata   Coconut Balls

Yield: serves 4

1 cup sugar

1 teaspoon ground cinnamon

1 cup unsweetened **grated** coconut, fresh, homemade (recipe page 193) or canned

Equipment: Medium saucepan, **grater**, wooden mixing spoon, cookie sheet, aluminum foil

1. Melt sugar in medium saucepan over medium-low heat, about 5 minutes. Add cinnamon and coconut, and, stirring frequently, cook for about 3 minutes, until sugar browns. Remove from heat and cool to warm.

2. Cover cookie sheet with foil. Using wet hands, form coconut mixture into ping-pong-size balls and place on foil. Refrigerate for 1 hour to set.

Serve as a sweet snack.

Kenya

The major cities in Kenya are among the most modern in Africa with the latest conveniences, but, at the same time, most Kenyans engage in subsistence farming (growing just enough food to survive) in rural areas. Kenya has no one predominant religion or official language, although most people follow traditional religious customs.

England colonized Kenya, and a very large Christian population remains there. Christmas for Kenyans of British origin is typically English, except without the cold weather, hot toddies, and flaming puddings of the homeland. Tropical Kenyan weather and beautiful beaches along the Indian Ocean bring many visitors to the tourist resorts during the holiday season.

Christmas dinner is more likely to be freshly caught fish or cold cuts with vegetables and fruits than an elaborate hot meal of roast beef, goose, or ham. The fruit would probably be pineapple, which is one of Kenya's cash crops.

Fillet of Beef with Pineapple

Yield: serves 6

6 to 8 (¼-inch-thick) slices prepared roast beef (available at the deli section of most supermarkets)

6 to 8 slices canned pineapple rings; reserve juice

1 cup chicken broth, homemade (recipe page 52) or canned

1 teaspoon curry powder

1 tablespoon cornstarch

2 **egg yolks**, beaten

1 tablespoon vegetable oil

1 onion, **finely chopped**

½ cup *each* peanuts, chopped green onion, seedless raisins, and chutney, homemade (recipe follows) or commercial, for serving

Equipment: Medium serving platter, plastic wrap, small bowl, medium skillet, mixing spoon

1. Place a roast beef slice to one side of serving platter. Arrange a pineapple ring on top so that it partially overlaps the beef. Continue alternating beef slices and pineapple, covering the platter. Cover with plastic wrap and refrigerate until ready to serve.

2. Prepare sauce: Pour chicken broth into small bowl, and add curry powder, cornstarch, egg yolks, and pineapple juice (add water to juice to make ½ cup, if necessary). Stir until smooth.

3. Heat oil in medium skillet over medium-high heat. Add onion, and, stirring continually, fry until soft, about 3 minutes.

4. Add broth mixture to onions, stirring constantly until mixture thickens, about 3 minutes.

To serve, drizzle sauce over platter of beef and pineapple and serve at room temperature. Serve with little side dishes of condiments: peanuts, chopped green onion, raisins, and chutney. To eat, add a little of each condiment to each bite of beef and pineapple.

Peach Chutney

Yield: about 2½ cups

1 tablespoon vegetable oil

1 onion, **finely chopped**

½ cup seedless raisins

1 tablespoon mustard seeds

1 cup peach marmalade (the chunkier the better)

½ cup white vinegar

½ cup brown sugar

Equipment: Medium saucepan, wooden mixing spoon

1. Heat oil in medium saucepan over medium-high heat. Add onion, and fry, stirring continually, until soft, about 3 minutes. Add raisins, mustard

seeds, marmalade, vinegar, and brown sugar, and stir.

2. Reduce heat to medium-low and cook until mixture thickens, about 10 minutes.

3. Remove from heat, and cool to room temperature. Refrigerate until ready to serve.

Serve as a condiment with curry dishes and beef slices (recipe precedes).

Somalia

The people in most other African countries have retained their ethnic and religious diversity, but in Somalia an overwhelming portion of the population is Sunni Muslim, and Islam is the state religion. Islamic laws and rituals are followed to the letter.

The ancient tradition of animal sacrifice is observed for Muslim feasts such as *Eid al-Fitr* and *Eid al-Adha*. If families can afford it, the husband slaughters the animal, and his wife, or wives, skins and cooks it to share with the extended family, neighbors, and friends.

For most Somalis, sacrificing an animal is far too expensive. Roasted meat is a luxury, and a little goes a long way when made into a stew. *Skudahkharis*, the one-dish meal of rice with a little lamb, would be more typical of what most Somalis eat to celebrate the ending of *Ramadan, Eid al-Fitr,* or other Islamic holidays.

Skudahkharis   Lamb and Rice

Yield: serves 4

  2 tablespoons vegetable oil
  1 onion, **finely chopped**
  1 clove garlic, finely chopped, or ½ teaspoon garlic granules
  1 pound boneless lamb, cut into bite-size pieces
  2 tomatoes, **stemmed** and **coarsely chopped**
  1 teaspoon ground cumin
  ½ teaspoon ground cloves
  1 teaspoon ground cinnamon
  ½ cup canned tomato paste
  5 cups water
  2 cups brown rice, uncooked
  salt and pepper to taste

Equipment: **Dutch oven** or large saucepan with cover, mixing spoon

1. Heat 2 tablespoons oil in Dutch oven or large saucepan over medium-high heat. Add onion, garlic, and lamb, and, stirring constantly, cook until meat is browned on all sides, about 5 minutes.

2. Add tomatoes, cumin, cloves, cinnamon, tomato paste, and water, and stir. Bring to a boil over high heat, add rice and salt and pepper to taste, and stir. Reduce heat to **simmer**, cover, and cook for about 30 minutes, or until rice has absorbed most of the water. Remove from heat and keep covered for 5 minutes.

Serve warm in a bowl. Guests help themselves, eating with the fingers of the right hand.

Ethiopia

Most Ethiopians are either Coptic Christians or Muslims. The Ethiopian Church observes all traditional Christian holidays as well as a few of its own. The most important is *Maskal*, the "Finding of the Cross." According to legend, Queen Helena, mother of the Emperor Constantine, made a pilgrimage to Jerusalem in the fourth century to find the cross on which Christ was crucified as well as other Christian relics. As the story goes, she found the cross, and to proclaim her success and ward off evil spirits, she had towering bonfires built.

The *Maskal* (also spelled *Meskal*) festival begins with parades, complete with brass bands, marching soldiers, and hundreds of people carrying lighted crosses. At night, fireworks and towering bonfires light up the sky, and people rejoice by singing and dancing. There are great banquets with feasts of roasting lambs, rich stews, and stacks of flat bread, called *injera*.

The spicy stews, called *wats*, are the national dish of Ethiopia. When they are made less spicy and without peppers they're called *alecha*.

Alecha — Lamb and Chicken Stew

Yield: serves 6 to 8

- 2 tablespoons vegetable oil
- 2 large onions, **finely chopped**
- 3 cloves garlic, finely chopped, or 1 teaspoon garlic granules
- 1½ pounds boneless lamb cut into 1-inch chunks
- ½ cup lemon juice
- 3 cups water, more or less as needed
- 1 teaspoon ground allspice
- 1 tablespoon ground **ginger**
- 1 teaspoon paprika
- salt and pepper to taste
- 2 to 3 pounds chicken, cut into serving-size pieces
- 4 large carrots, **trimmed** and cut into 2-inch chunks
- 1 (16-ounce) can of stewed tomatoes, including juice
- 6 hard-cooked eggs, shelled
- *injera* (recipe follows) (for serving)
- 6 cups cooked rice (keep warm for serving)
- 1 cup plain yogurt (for serving)

Equipment: **Dutch oven** or large saucepan with cover, mixing spoon, fork

1. In Dutch oven or large saucepan, heat oil over medium heat. Add onions and garlic, stir, and fry until soft, about 3 minutes. Add lamb, lemon juice, and 2 cups water, stir, and bring to a boil. Reduce heat to **simmer**, cover, and cook for 30 minutes.

2. Add remaining 1 cup water, allspice, ginger, paprika, salt and pepper to taste, and stir well. Layer chicken pieces, carrots, and tomatoes with juice on top, cover, and simmer about 40 minutes, basting frequently, or until chicken is tender. If the stew seems too dry, add a little more hot water. (It should not be soupy.)

3. Poke the hard-cooked eggs in several places with a fork, and add to stew. Cover and heat through, about 5 minutes.

Serve the stew in a deep platter placed in the middle of the table and have everyone help themselves. Serve with injera bread (recipe follows), rice, and yogurt.

Injera   Ethiopian Flat Bread

Yield: serves 6 to 8
- 3 cups warm water
- 2½ cups **self-rising** flour
- 3 tablespoons club soda

Equipment: Nonstick 10- to 12-inch electric skillet, **blender** or **food processor**, mixing spoon, medium mixing bowl, kitchen towel, clean work surface, 4-ounce ladle, metal **spatula** or tongs

Preheat nonstick electric frying pan to 400° F.

1. Pour warm water into blender or food processor, add self-rising flour, cover, and blend on low for about 10 seconds. Increase blender speed to high, and blend for about 30 seconds until smooth and lump-free.

2. Pour batter into medium mixing bowl, add club soda, and mix. The batter should be the consistency of heavy cream.

3. Prepare to fry: Spread towel on work surface. Using a 4-ounce ladle, pour batter to one side in electric skillet and quickly tilt pan to spread batter evenly over bottom. Small bubbles will immediately appear on the surface, and edges will curl away from sides of skillet. In about 1 minute, use metal spatula or tongs to pick up *injera* by the edges to remove from pan. Spread out on towel to cool. The finished *injera* is pliable and folds easily. (If *injera* is brown and crisp, it is overdone.) Fold in quarters and stack, slightly overlapping on plate.

To serve injera *the Ethiopian way, pass it around and have each person take one. The trick is to use only the right hand to tear it apart and use the pieces to transport the food to your mouth. As in many other countries, the right hand is the only one used to handle food in Ethiopia. This is because the left hand is used for personal grooming and toiletry, and using it to handle food would be offensive.*

Many vegetarian dishes are served by Ethiopian Christians as a main dish during days the Coptic Church forbids eating meat; they are also served as side dishes at other times.

Yemiser Selatta   Lentil Salad

Yield: serves 6 to 8
- 1½ cups dried lentils (cooked in water until tender, not mushy)
- 1 onion, **finely chopped**
- 2 tablespoons vinegar
- 6 tablespoons peanut oil, olive oil, or blend
- 3 cloves garlic, finely chopped, or 1 teaspoon garlic granules
- ½ teaspoon red pepper flakes, more or less to taste
- salt and pepper to taste

Equipment: **Colander**, medium mixing bowl, mixing spoon

1. Place colander in sink, and add cooked lentils to drain.

2. In medium mixing bowl, combine onion, vinegar, oil, garlic, and ½ teaspoon red pepper flakes. Add drained lentils and salt and pepper to taste. Stir and set aside at room temperature for about 1 hour before serving; stir frequently to blend flavors.

Serve at room temperature.

SHORTCUT COOKING TIP FOR THE PREVIOUS RECIPE: Transfer drained, cooked lentils to medium mixing bowl, and add 1 finely chopped onion and ½ cup of your favorite prepared Italian salad dressing. Season with salt and pepper to taste and stir; serve at room temperature.

Uganda

More than half the Ugandan population is Christian, although a large number are animists (who believe that everything has a soul), and a small number are Muslim. English is the official language of the country, but Swahili and Luganda are widely spoken. Roman Catholic and Protestant communities observe all traditional Christian holidays.

In Uganda, holiday celebrations are communal. The Christian church takes part in tribal festivals, and tribal leaders join with priests on Christian holidays. At both tribal and Christian festivals, there is dancing, music, singing, and chanting. The Christian clergy leads the people in prayer, followed by dancers who communicate with spirits and ancestors to help them with their problems. Every festival includes a feast. The type of food served depends upon the importance of the festival.

Most holiday or special-occasion meals call for fish, which most likely comes out of one of the many lakes in Uganda.

Engege Apolo

Ugandan-Style Fried Fish

Yield: serves 4 to 6

4 to 6 (6- to 8-ounce-each) fillets of fish, such as trout, red snapper, or sea bass, with skin left on

salt to taste

2 teaspoons ground curry powder, more or less to taste

2 tablespoons vegetable oil, more if necessary

2 onions, thinly sliced

4 tomatoes, thinly sliced

2 green bell peppers, **cored**, **trimmed**, and thinly sliced

juice of 2 limes

2 limes, cut into wedges, for **garnish**

Equipment: Wax paper, work surface, large skillet, metal **spatula**, 13- x 9-inch baking pan, aluminum foil, oven mitts

1. Place fish fillets side by side on wax-paper-covered work surface, and sprinkle both sides with salt and curry powder to taste. Set aside at room temperature for 30 minutes.

2. Heat 2 tablespoons oil in large skillet over medium-high heat. Add fillets, in batches, and fry for about 3 to 5 minutes on each side. Add more oil, if necessary, to prevent sticking. Using metal spatula, transfer fish to baking pan.

Preheat oven to 350° F.

3. After frying all the fish fillets, return large skillet with pan drippings to medium-high heat, adding more oil if necessary. Add onions, tomatoes, bell peppers, and lime juice, and, stirring constantly, cook for about 3 minutes until onions are soft. Remove from heat and spread mixture over

fish. Cover with foil, and bake in oven for 10 minutes.

To serve transfer to serving platter and garnish with lime wedges.

Mozambique

Mozambique, located on the east coast of Africa, was colonized by the Portuguese, who brought their language, cooking, and Catholicism. Although subjected to the influences of Portugal and Islamic coastal traders, most Mozambicans have retained their own culture and follow traditional African customs. About 15 percent of the population are Christians, most of whom live in large cities. In addition, about 30 percent of the people are Muslims. The rest of the population is influenced by traditional beliefs.

Seafood is almost always included in the holiday feasts of Mozambicans living along the coast, regardless of their religion. This simple shrimp recipe reflects the Portuguese flair for cooking with lots of garlic and hot peppers. Quantities have been greatly reduced from the original recipe.

Camarao Grelhado Piri Piri

Garlic Shrimp

Yield: serves 4

- 4 tablespoons vegetable oil
- 2 cloves garlic, **finely chopped**, or ½ teaspoon garlic granules
- ⅛ teaspoon **ground** red pepper, more or less to taste
- salt to taste
- ¼ cup lemon or lime juice
- 1 pound (about 30) headless shrimp, **peeled** and **deveined** (rinsed and drained)
- 4 cups cooked rice (keep warm for serving)

Equipment: Medium mixing bowl with cover or large baggie, mixing spoon, large skillet

1. In medium mixing bowl or large baggie, combine oil, garlic, ¼ teaspoon red pepper (more or less to taste), salt to taste, and lemon or lime juice, and stir well. Add shrimp and stir to coat with mixture. Cover bowl or seal baggie and refrigerate for at least 1 hour, stirring or turning frequently.

2. Transfer shrimp with oil mixture to large skillet and cook over medium-high heat, stirring constantly, until cooked through (shrimp become **opaque** white), about 5 to 8 minutes.

Serve shrimp while hot right from the skillet with a side dish of rice.

Cashew nuts are among Mozambique's leading exports, and the following cake is a holiday favorite.

Bolo Polana   Nuts and Potato Cake

Yield: serves 8 to 10

- 1¾ cups butter or margarine, at room temperature, more as needed
- 1¾ cups cake flour, more or less as needed
- 2 cups sugar

4 **eggs, separated**

1 cup mashed potatoes, homemade or prepared instant mashed potatoes (follow directions on package)

1 cup **ground**, unsalted cashew nuts

grated rind of lemon

½ cup heavy cream

1 teaspoon vanilla extract

Equipment: 9-inch **springform pan**, large mixing bowl, mixing spoon or electric mixer, flour **sifter**, medium mixing bowl, rubber **spatula**, **grater**, oven mitts, toothpick

Preheat oven to 350° F.

1. Prepare springform pan by spreading 2 tablespoons butter or margarine over bottom and sides of pan. Sprinkle with 2 tablespoons flour, tilting pan from side to side to coat well. Invert over sink and tap out excess flour. Set aside.

2. In large mixing bowl, using mixing spoon or electric mixer, beat 1½ cups butter or margarine; add sugar, a little at a time, until light and fluffy, about 3 minutes. Mixing constantly, add egg yolks (one at a time), mashed potatoes, cashews, lemon rind, cream, and vanilla. **Sift** in 1½ cups flour, a little at a time, and mix well.

3. In medium mixing bowl, using clean beaters, beat egg whites until stiff peaks form.

4. Using rubber spatula, **fold** egg whites into potato mixture. Pour into prepared springform pan.

5. Bake in oven for about 1½ hours or until top is golden and toothpick inserted in middle of cake comes out clean. Cool for about 10 minutes, and remove sides of springform pan.

Serve warm or at room temperature, cut into wedges.

Madagascar

Madagascar, located in the Indian Ocean off the coast of east Africa, is the fourth largest island in the world. The two largest population groups there are of Indonesian (Malagasy) and Black African descent. The Malagasy are descendants of Indonesian seafarers who first settled in Madagascar about two thousand years ago. Further Asian, African, and Arab migrations consolidated the original mixture, which was transformed even farther by the French colonists.

Most Malagasy combine animism (the belief that all things have a soul) with ancestor worship. They believe that when family members die, they join other long-dead ancestors to watch over living descendants. The spiritual communion with the dead, called *Famadihana* or "turning over the dead," is very profound.

A large number of Malagasy are Christian (about 40 percent), and Easter is their most important holiday. The Malagasy Christians incorporate the ancient cult of the dead ritual, *Famadihana,* with their religious beliefs.

Crusty French bread, a remnant of French colonial days, and rice are eaten at every meal.

Both are included in the Easter and *Famadihana* feasts, which may also include stuffed eggs, fish and other seafood, fresh vegetables, and bowls of fresh fruit.

Curried rice (recipe follows) is a typical holiday dish.

Curried Rice with Raisins and Nuts

Yield: serves 6

4 cups water

2 cups rice, (preferably **basmati)**

2 tablespoons vegetable oil

1 large onion, **finely chopped**

½ cup seedless raisins

½ cup **coarsely chopped** nuts: almonds, walnuts, pecans, or peanuts

2 teaspoons curry powder

1 cup chicken broth homemade (recipe page 52) or canned

salt to taste

Equipment: **Dutch oven** or medium saucepan with cover, mixing spoon, medium skillet

1. Bring water to a boil in Dutch oven or medium saucepan over high heat. Add rice, and stir. Reduce heat to simmer, cover, and cook for 20 minutes, or until rice is tender and all the water has been absorbed. Keep covered and set aside.

2. Heat 2 tablespoons oil in medium skillet over medium-high heat. Add onion, and, stirring constantly, fry until soft, about 3 minutes. Add raisins, nuts, curry powder, and chicken broth. Reduce heat to **simmer**, and, stirring frequently, cook for about 3 minutes.

3. Add onion mixture and salt to taste to rice, and stir well.

Serve as a side dish with chicken, meat, or fish.

The waters surrounding Madagascar are full of shrimp and other seafood, making them plentiful and cheap. Shrimp are prepared in many ways and for every occasion, among them, *Famadihana,* Christmas Eve supper, and Holy Week.

Shrimp in Coconut Milk

Yield: serves 4

½ cup butter or margarine

3 cloves garlic, **finely chopped**, or 1 teaspoon garlic granules

½ cup lime or lemon juice

1 to 1½ pounds (about 26 to 30) headless shrimp, **peeled** and **deveined**

1 cup coconut milk, homemade (recipe page 194) or canned

salt and white pepper to taste

3 to 4 cups cooked rice (keep warm for serving)

Equipment: Large skillet, mixing spoon

Melt butter or margarine in large skillet over medium heat, add garlic and juice, and stir well. Add shrimp and toss to coat. Add coconut milk and salt and white pepper to taste. Cook both sides of shrimp until **opaque** white and cooked through, about 5 minutes.

To serve, spoon shrimp with coconut sauce over bed of rice.

South Africa

In South Africa, Christians make up more than 70 percent of the population. There are also large Hindu, Muslim, and Jewish communities, as well as a great number of people following traditional tribal beliefs. All faiths freely celebrate their religious holidays.

The majority of Christians in South Africa are Protestants, but there are vast differences among the wide range of Protestant churches in ritual, doctrine, and organization. The churches people belong to depend, in part, on their ethnic backgrounds and their social outlook. In South Africa, that has traditionally meant racial segregation in churches. Most native (Black) Christians either belong to the churches European and North American missionaries started many years ago or to the numerous independent churches that have provided an opportunity for leadership among the Blacks.

For decades, South Africa was in the hands of the ruling Afrikaners (white Africans of primarily Dutch, German, and French descent) who imposed "apartheid" (in their language it means "apartness"). In 1948 apartheid laws were enacted that violated the human rights of Blacks and made them second-class citizens in the eyes of the law. Anti-apartheid action fostered many years of civil conflict. Boycotts and pressure imposed by people in other countries, especially the United States, and constant pressure from Black leaders in South Africa, some of whom were imprisoned for many years, finally led to some changes. In 1990 reforms came about while Frederik Willem de Klerk was president of South Africa. For the first time, Blacks were able to vote, and on May 10, 1994, the head of the African National Congress and longtime Black leader, Nelson Mandela, was sworn in as president of South Africa. Since Mandela's election, anti-apartheid changes are slowly coming about; the Blacks have a voice in their government, and a multiracial democratic society has become a reality.

In South Africa, Christmas is the most important Christian holiday, but there is no one unique way to celebrate it. Many white settlers observe the traditions of their ancestral homeland exactly as they remember them. Among the Black South Africans, new celebrations mix the myths and spirit worship of their ancestors with the Christian traditions brought by the missionaries and European settlers.

Almost all Christian South Africans have Christmas parties and family gatherings; they love to shop, bake cookies, decorate their homes, exchange gifts and attend church, sing Christmas songs, and enjoy holiday feasts. Many churches sponsor covered-dish suppers during the holiday season to bring people together with music, good food, and fellowship.

Besides Christmas, South African national holidays are New Year's Day, January 1; Founder's Day, April 6; Good Friday; Easter Monday; Ascension Day; Labor Day; Republic Day; Kruger Day, October 10; Day of the Vow, December 16; and Day of Good Will, December 26, when gifts are given to the disadvantaged.

Corn, called *mealie* in South Africa, is a favorite food, and it is included in holiday feasts along with the traditional roast.

Baked Mealies and Tomatoes

Corn and Tomato Casserole

Yield: serves 6

  2 cups corn kernels, fresh, canned, or frozen, thawed and drained

  16-ounce can whole tomatoes, **coarsely chopped**

  2 eggs, lightly beaten

  ¼ cup light brown sugar, firmly packed

  1 cup lightly toasted white bread, cut into 1-inch cubes

  salt and pepper, to taste

½ cup bread crumbs

¼ cup melted butter or margarine

Equipment: Large mixing bowl, mixing spoon, greased 1½ quart oven-proof casserole, oven mitts

Preheat oven to 325° F.

1. In large mixing bowl, combine corn, tomatoes, eggs, brown sugar, toasted bread cubes, and salt and pepper to taste, and stir. Transfer mixture to greased casserole and smooth the top.

2. Sprinkle bread crumbs over top, and **drizzle** with melted butter or margarine. Bake in oven for 45 minutes or until top is golden brown.

Serve in casserole as side dish with Christmas dinner.

South African Christmas baking reflects Dutch, French, and English influences, and cookies are an indispensable part of the holiday season. Number and letter shapes are especially popular.

Krakelinge   Dutch Figure-Eight Cookies

Yield: about 24 cookies

½ cup butter or margarine, at room temperature

½ cup sugar, more as needed

1 egg, lightly beaten

1½ cups all-purpose flour

1 teaspoon baking powder

1 teaspoon ground cinnamon

⅛ teaspoon salt

4 tablespoons confectioners' sugar, more or less, for **garnish**

Equipment: Large mixing bowl, mixing spoon or electric mixer, flour **sifter**, lightly floured work surface, ruler, wide **spatula**, buttered or nonstick cookie sheet, wax paper, oven mitts

1. In large mixing bowl, use mixing spoon or electric mixer to mix butter or margarine and ½ cup sugar until light and fluffy, about 3 minutes. Add egg, and mix well.

2. Put flour, baking powder, cinnamon, and salt in flour sifter, and sift into egg mixture, a little at a time. Mix constantly until a blended and smooth dough forms. Using clean hands, **knead** dough into a firm ball.

3. Divide dough into 2 pieces. On lightly floured work surface, using floured hands, flatten one piece into a 6-inch square about ½ inch thick. Cut the square into 12 (½ inch wide) strips. Roll a strip of dough between the palms of your hands into a rope about ¼ inch thick and about 8 inches long. Place on work surface and shape into a figure eight or any other shape you like. Lightly brush the ends with water and pinch together. Using a wide spatula, place cookies side-by-side on buttered or nonstick cookie sheet; allow about 1 inch between cookies. Refrigerate the cookies on the cookie sheet for about 30 minutes to firm up before baking in oven.

Preheat oven to 400° F.

4. Bake in oven for about 12 minutes until lightly browned. Repeat making cookies, chilling, and baking in batches.

Using wide spatula, transfer cookies to wax-paper-covered work surface, to cool to room temperature. Sprinkle with confectioners' sugar.

Serve cookies as a sweet snack.

These twice-baked biscuits, *karringmelkbeskuit*, are very popular in South Africa. They are often made during the Christmas season and are used for dunking into milk, hot chocolate, tea, or coffee.

Karringmelkbeskuit   Buttermilk Rusk

Yield: about 4 dozen

1½ cups unbleached flour

1 cup whole wheat flour

¼ cup sugar

½ tablespoon baking powder

¼ pound cold butter or margarine

1 egg, beaten
1 cup buttermilk, more as needed

Equipment: Large mixing bowl, knife, greased or nonstick baking sheet, toothpick, oven mitts

Preheat oven to 350° F.

1. In large mixing bowl, combine unbleached and whole wheat flours with sugar and baking powder.

2. Cut the cold butter or margarine into pea-size pieces, add pieces to flour mixture, and quickly blend them with your fingertips. (The texture should be gritty.) Add the egg and 1 cup of buttermilk, a little at a time, until the batter is just moist enough to hold together. Add a little more buttermilk if necessary.

3. Using floured hands, pinch off ping-pongball size pieces of dough, and roll them into balls. Place on greased baking sheet, about 1 inch apart.

4. Bake in oven for about 20 minutes, until golden brown, or until toothpick inserted in center comes out clean. Remove cookie sheet from oven but do not remove biscuits from cookie sheet.

Reduce oven heat to 200° F.

5. Return biscuits on the cookie sheet to cooled oven to dry out. Leave in the oven for about 4 hours.

Serve for dunking into hot beverages. Store in airtight container.

Lesotho

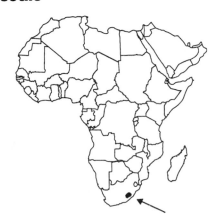

In Lesotho most city dwellers are Roman Catholic, while the people living in rural areas follow native beliefs. Lesotho is totally landlocked by South Africa, and more than 100,000 Sotho work in South African mines. Besides the economic ties, Lesotho and South Africa share many foods and Christian holidays.

The one thing they do not share is *Moshoeshoe Day*, March 12th. This important civic holiday honors the nineteenth-century chief who established the kingdom of Lesotho. On this day of remembrance the people celebrate with sports events, parades, music, dancing, family gatherings, and community festivals. In communal villages there is usually a feast of goat or lamb.

Cabbage is a favorite vegetable, and it is always served with meat, which is reserved for special occasions such as *Moshoeshoe Day*.

Cabbage and Bacon

Yield: serves 6
  6 slices lean bacon, **finely chopped**
  1½ to 2 pound cabbage, **cored**, coarsely **shredded, blanched**
  2 cooking apples, **peeled**, cored, and finely chopped
  salt and pepper to taste
  ½ cup hot water, more or less, if necessary

Equipment: Large skillet with cover, mixing spoon

1. Fry bacon pieces in large skillet over medium-high heat. Stir constantly until bacon is **rendered**, about 3 minutes. Add cabbage, apples, and salt and pepper to taste, and toss to mix.

2. Reduce heat to medium-low, cover, and cook for 30 minutes or until cabbage is tender. Stir frequently. If too dry, add just enough hot water to prevent sticking.

Serve cabbage as a side dish.

Cornmeal cakes are served at almost every meal in Lesotho, including holiday occasions. They are broken into pieces used to scoop up sauces and stews.

Mealie-Meal   Cornmeal Cakes

Yield: about 20 cakes
 1 cup yellow cornmeal
 2 tablespoons sugar
 1 teaspoon salt
 1 tablespoon vegetable oil
 2¼ cups boiling water
 2 **eggs, separated**

Equipment: Medium saucepan, mixing spoon, cup, small mixing bowl, egg beater or electric mixer, rubber **spatula**, greased or nonstick baking sheet, metal spatula, oven mitts

 1. In medium saucepan, mix cornmeal, sugar, salt, and oil. Add boiling water and blend well. Cook over low heat, stirring frequently, until thickened, about 10 minutes. Cool to warm.

 Preheat oven to 400° F.

 2. Beat egg yolks in cup and add to mixture. Stir well.

 3. In small bowl, using egg beater or electric mixer, beat egg whites until stiff. **Fold** whites into cornmeal mixture using rubber spatula.

 4. Drop tablespoonfuls of batter onto baking sheet, making 2-inch patties about ¼ inch thick. Bake in oven for about 30 minutes, or until browned and puffed.

Serve warm for best flavor.

Zimbabwe

When England colonized Zimbabwe, the English settlers brought their language and religion with them. Today, however, only a small number of the native Zimbabweans, almost all city dwellers, profess to be Christians. The majority of the population practices tribal religious beliefs, although some aspects of Christianity have trickled into their ancient rituals. According to traditional beliefs, spirit guardians, or elders, known as *midzimu*, guard families. The lion spirit, *mhondoro*, guards leaders and the country. Families often have *midzimu* shrines at their homes. If sickness or misfortune befalls them, they believe the spirits are upset and try to appease them with offerings of home-brewed millet beer set on the shrine. The *mhondoro* spirits deal with plagues, epidemics, and war. When villagers need to contact spirits such as *mhondoro,* there are great ceremonial festivities. Crowds of people partake in activities, which include ritual music, spiritual dancing, parades, sporting matches, and feasting.

 Chicken and beef are rarities in everyday life and are only eaten at special occasions. Stews, such as the one that follows, are very common at these feasts.

Huku ne Dovi — Chicken and Groundnut (Peanut) Stew

Yield: serves 6 to 8

2 to 4 tablespoons vegetable oil, more if
  necessary
2½ to 3 pounds chicken, cut into serving-size
  pieces
2 onions, **finely chopped**
1 cup peanut butter
4 cups water
1 (16-ounce) can stewed whole tomatoes
salt and pepper to taste
½ teaspoon ground red pepper, more or less to
  taste (optional)
2 cups finely chopped cabbage
3 sweet potatoes, **coarsely chopped**
3 carrots, **trimmed, peeled**, and coarsely
  chopped
2 turnips, trimmed, peeled, and coarsely
  chopped
12 fresh whole okra, or frozen, thawed

Equipment: **Dutch oven** or large saucepan with
cover, baking pan, **slotted spoon** or metal tongs,
oven mitts

Preheat oven to 200° F.

1. Heat 2 tablespoons oil in Dutch oven or large
saucepan over medium-high heat. Carefully add
chicken pieces, a few at a time, and fry on each
side until golden brown, about 5 minutes. (Add
more oil if necessary to prevent sticking.) Transfer chicken pieces to baking pan with slotted spoon
or tongs, and keep warm in oven. Continue until
all chicken pieces are fried.

2. Add 2 tablespoons oil, if necessary, to same
Dutch oven or large saucepan used in step 1. Add
onions, and, stirring constantly, fry for 3 minutes,
until soft. Reduce heat to medium, add peanut
butter and 1 cup water, and stir well. Add remaining 3 cups water, stewed tomatoes, salt and pepper to taste, and ½ teaspoon ground red pepper
(more or less to taste), and stir well. Add the

chicken pieces warming in the oven, cover, and
cook for about 30 minutes.

3. Stir in cabbage, sweet potatoes, carrots, turnips, and okra. Cover and cook for another 25
minutes until tender.

*Serve stew right from the pot as they do in Africa.
Everyone eats with the fingers of the right hand.
The reason for using only the right hand is that in
many countries the left hand is used for personal
grooming and toiletry and is thus considered un-
clean.*

In Zimbabwe, cornmeal mush, called *sadza,*
and vegetable stew, *usavi,* are eaten at almost
every meal including holiday feasts. The stews
are made with whatever vegetables are available from the garden or market. The vegetables
are **coarsely chopped** and tossed into a pot
with a little water to simmer slowly for several hours.

Sadza — Cornmeal Mush, Fried

Yield: serves 6

4 cups water
1 cup coarsely ground yellow cornmeal
1 teaspoon salt
4 tablespoons all-purpose flour, more or less as
  needed
2 to 4 tablespoons butter or margarine, more as
  needed

Equipment: Small mixing bowl, mixing spoon,
medium saucepan, rubber **spatula**, greased or nonstick 8- x 4-inch loaf pan, knife, pie pan, large skillet, metal spatula

1. In small bowl, mix 1 cup water, cornmeal,
and salt.

2. Put remaining 3 cups water in medium saucepan and bring to a boil over high heat. Slowly add
cornmeal mixture to boiling water while stirring
constantly. Reduce heat to low, and, stirring fre-

quently, cook until mixture pulls away from the sides of pan, about 10 minutes.

3. Transfer cornmeal to greased or nonstick loaf pan, cool to room temperature, and then refrigerate until firm.

4. When cornmeal mixture is cold, take out of refrigerator and cut into ½-inch thick slices.

5. Put 4 tablespoons flour into pie pan. Melt 2 tablespoons butter or margarine in skillet over medium heat. Coat both sides of corn meal slice with flour in pie pan, and fry for about 5 minutes on each side, until crisp and browned. Continue frying in batches, adding more butter or margarine as needed.

Serve sadza *warm, and use it to sop up soup or stew.*

Botswana

The official language of Botswana is English (although Setswana is widely spoken), and nearly half of the people in Botswana are Christians. Although most of the population are farmers and nomadic herders, only about 40 percent still follow native beliefs.

An important holiday for the Christians is Christmas. Chiefs, other leaders, and the clergy preside over the elaborate celebration which combines ancestral and agrarian rituals with holiday traditions brought to Botswana by missionaries, British colonists, and other European settlers. At the official festival grounds huge kettles of food are served to the throngs of people.

Historically, cattle raising dominates Botswana economy and social structure. Botswana has the largest slaughterhouse in Africa, with most of the meat prepared for export. Beef is used for every feast, even if it's only the innards made into stew or the bones used for soup.

Botswana is subtropical and extremely warm most of the time. Cold beef curry is ideal for the Christmas dinner.

Cold Beef Curry

Yield: serves 8
  2 to 4 tablespoons butter or margarine
  2 onions, **finely chopped**
  ½ tablespoon curry powder, more or less to taste
  2 tomatoes, **peeled,** and **coarsely chopped**
  2 tablespoons all-purpose flour
  2 cups beef broth
  6 cups coarsely chopped, cooked beef
  2 cups cold cooked rice
  4 hard-cooked eggs, shelled and quartered, for **garnish**

Equipment: **Dutch oven** or large saucepan, mixing spoon, cup

1. Melt 2 tablespoons butter or margarine in Dutch oven or large saucepan over medium-high heat. Add onions, and, stirring constantly, fry until soft, about 3 minutes. Reduce heat to medium, and add ½ tablespoon curry powder, more or less to taste, and tomatoes.

2. In cup, mix flour with about ½ cup beef broth to make a lump-free paste. Stirring constantly, add paste to onion mixture. Add remaining beef broth and stir until thickened, about 3 minutes. Add chopped beef, stir, and cook for 10 minutes. Cool to room temperature and refrigerate to chill through, about 2 hours.

To serve, mound cold rice on serving platter and cover with cold beef curry. Decorate with wedges of hard-cooked eggs.

Namibia

The urbanized eastern and southern parts of Namibia have a large English-speaking, Christian population. Most people belong to the Lutheran church, which was first brought by Finnish missionaries and later by German colonizers. The city dwellers celebrate Christmas and Easter according to the traditions of their church and their ancestral homeland (see Germany, Portugal, Netherlands, and South Africa). In northeastern Namibia, farmers and their herds stay pretty much to themselves. The holidays they observe either come from ancient tribal beliefs that celebrate agrarian events like the solstice (when the sun is at its northernmost or southernmost position, which signals either the beginning of summer or winter) or else they relate to ancestral worship.

In the Christian parts of Namibia, the children set out their shoes on Christmas Eve to be filled with candy and gifts by Saint Nicholas, and he has no trouble traveling around. Relative to the size of its population, Namibia may have one of the most highly developed infrastructures in Africa, with more than 38,999 kilometers (23,000 miles) of roads, a very good railroad system, and a domestic airline.

Kejenou is a festival dish served by West African Christians for Easter and Christmas dinner. It is especially popular with those living along the coast, where shrimp are plentiful.

Kejenou   Chicken and Shrimp Stew

Yield: serves 4 to 6

2 to 4 tablespoons vegetable oil, more if needed

1 chicken, cut into serving-size pieces

3 cloves garlic, **finely chopped,** or 1 teaspoon garlic granules

2 teaspoons paprika

2 onions, finely chopped

4 tomatoes, **stemmed, peeled,** and finely chopped, or 2 cups canned stewed tomatoes

1½ cups rice

1 teaspoon each ground cinnamon and nutmeg

4 cups water

salt and pepper to taste

8 to 12 large (about ½ pound) headless shrimp, peeled, **deveined,** rinsed, and drained

Equipment: **Dutch oven** or large saucepan with cover, metal tongs or metal **spatula,** medium heat-proof bowl

1. Heat 2 tablespoons oil in Dutch oven or large saucepan over medium-high heat. Carefully add chicken pieces and fry about 8 minutes on each side until well browned. Put finished chicken pieces in medium, heat-proof bowl, and continue frying in batches. Add more oil as needed.

2. In same Dutch oven or large saucepan, add 2 tablespoons oil to pan drippings, and heat over medium heat. Add garlic and paprika, and stir. Add onions, and fry until soft, about 3 minutes. Add tomatoes, rice, cinnamon, nutmeg, water, and salt and pepper to taste, and stir well. Add chicken pieces to rice mixture and lay on top. Increase heat to high, and bring to boil. After it boils, reduce heat to **simmer,** cover, and cook for 20 minutes. Add shrimp, and, using metal tongs or metal

spatula, gently push down into rice mixture. Cover and continue cooking for about 10 minutes more, or until shrimp are cooked through and chicken is tender.

To serve, place the pan of kejenou *in the center of the table and serve with* mealie-meal *(recipe page 16). Have the guests eat the* kejenou *by scooping it onto the* mealie-meal.

Angola

Angola was colonized in the fifteenth century by the Portuguese, who brought their language and Catholicism with them. In the cities, religious holidays are observed according to Portuguese traditions, while traditional beliefs and celebrations remain strong in the villages and countryside. When Angola gained independence in 1975, it became a Marxist communist state, and most of the Europeans left the country. The ruling government discourages all religious observances, and December 25, for instance, is celebrated as Family Day, not as Christmas. The only national holidays allowed are connected to the Popular Movement for the Liberation of Angola (MPLA), the ruling party in Angola.

The Portuguese way of seasoning food with garlic and hot pepper has been adopted by Angolans. The seasonings in this recipe have been reduced. This gumbo is eaten for the Family Day Feast on December 25.

Nyeleng   Peanut and Beef Gumbo

Yield: serves 4 to 6

　1½ pounds lean beef, cut into about 1-inch chunks
　½ teaspoon salt
　5 cups water
　1 pound okra, **trimmed** and each cut into 3 pieces
　1 cup chunky-style peanut butter
　1 onion, **finely chopped**
　¼ teaspoon ground red pepper, more or less to taste
　steamed **millet** or cornmeal mush, cooked according to directions on package (keep warm, for serving)

Equipment: **Dutch oven** or large saucepan with cover, mixing spoon

1. Put meat and salt in Dutch oven or large saucepan. Add water, and bring to a boil over high heat. Reduce heat to **simmer** for about 1 hour; skim and discard froth from surface.

2. Add okra, peanut butter, onion, and ¼ teaspoon red pepper. Stir, cover, and cook 1 hour longer.

Serve over millet or cornmeal mush.

Zaire/Zambia

Located in central Africa, both Zaire (in black) and Zambia (in grey) are largely populated by Bantu-speaking Africans. Although many people follow traditional tribal religions, both Zaire and Zambia have large Roman Catholic communities as well as independent African Protestant churches. Holiday celebrations often blend Christian rituals with ancient tribal practices. The Christian church takes part in tribal festivals, and tribal leaders join with priests on Christian holidays. At all festivals the dancers are masked and dressed in the ritual costumes to fit the occasion. For instance, after a regional disaster, a massive memorial service was held. The Christian clergy led the people in prayer, followed by dancers, wearing huge buffalo masks symbolizing strength, who danced for the dead. Every festival includes a feast. The type of food served depends upon the importance of the festival. Meat is reserved for the most important occasions. Other than the choice and amount of meat available, holiday food is often no different from the daily diet.

In this recipe pinto beans are combined with manioc (also called **cassava**); since manioc is not easily available in the United States, potatoes are a good substitute. This dish accompanies roasted meat at a communal Easter or harvest feast.

Pinto Beans with Potatoes

Yield: serves 6

2 tablespoons vegetable oil, more if necessary

1 onion, **finely chopped**

2 celery stalks, washed, **trimmed**, and finely chopped

4 cups cooked pinto beans, homemade (prepared according to directions on package) or canned, drained

3 potatoes, boiled, **peeled,** and **coarsely chopped**

4 to 6 cups cooked rice (keep warm for serving)

Equipment: Large saucepan, mixing spoon, **colander**

1. Heat 2 tablespoons oil in large saucepan over medium-high heat. Add onion and celery, and, stirring constantly, fry until soft, about 3 minutes.

2. Reduce heat to medium, add cooked beans and more oil if necessary to prevent sticking, and heat through. Stir in potatoes and heat through, about 5 minutes.

Serve this recipe warm, over rice.

Rwanda/Burundi

Rwanda (in black) and Burundi (in grey) are two tiny countries wedged in between Zaire, Tanzania, and Uganda. In both countries, the predominant ethnic groups are the indigenous Hutus, who account for 85 percent of the population, and Tutsis, who account for 14 percent. The Tutsis came to the region to raise cattle about five hundred years ago, and since that time they have been in control of the area, subjugating the Hutu people to serfdom. The conflict between the Tutsis and Hutus is largely responsible for current troubles in this region, which have caused thousands of people to flee to the neighboring countries to escape the horrific death and destruction.

Rwanda is a country without villages; parents, children, aunts, uncles, cousins, and grandparents live within self-contained compounds. This traditional way of life is still maintained throughout much of rural Rwanda. If the family does not join others for a community feast, they prepare their own, and they have plenty of holidays from which to choose.

It was the Belgian missionaries who converted the majority of Rwandans and Burundi (more than 70 percent of the people in each country) to Christianity. Besides agrarian and ancestral feasts, almost every Christian celebration is a national holiday: Easter Monday, Ascension Day, Pentecost Monday, Assumption Day, All Saints' Day, and Christmas Day. Easter is the most important holiday, and it is the custom for family members who have moved away to return home for the occasion.

The few urban communities center around government administrative centers. In Burundi, most people live on family farms, where they remain throughout their lives.

In both countries, owning cattle is a very important indication of wealth, and cattle are rarely slaughtered for feasting. Chicken, such as in the following recipe, is eaten by the more fortunate, but the holiday feast for most people is meatless porridge. (See next recipe.)

Kuku na Nazi Chicken in Coconut Milk

Yield: serves 4 to 6

2 tablespoons vegetable oil, more if necessary
1 (3-pound) chicken, cut into serving size pieces
1 onion, **finely chopped**
1 teaspoon ground **ginger**
3 cloves garlic, finely chopped, or 1 teaspoon garlic granules
½ teaspoon ground red pepper, more or less to taste
2 cups coconut milk, homemade (recipe page 194) or canned
4 cups cooked rice (keep warm for serving)

Equipment: **Dutch oven** or large skillet, **slotted spoon** or tongs, medium baking pan

1. Heat 2 tablespoons oil in Dutch oven or large skillet over medium-high heat. Carefully add chicken pieces, and fry for about 8 minutes on each side until golden brown. Transfer to medium baking pan and continue frying in batches. Add more oil, if necessary, to prevent sticking.

2. Add 1 tablespoon oil to skillet, and heat over medium heat. Add onion, ginger, garlic, and ½ teaspoon red pepper, more or less to taste. Stir and fry until onion is soft, about 3 minutes. Return chicken pieces to pan with onions, and add coconut milk. Cover and cook over low heat for about 45 minutes, or until chicken is tender.

Serve chicken over rice.

Split-Pea and Banana Porridge

Yield: serves 4

3 cups water
1 cup dried split peas, rinsed and drained
salt and pepper to taste
2 ripe bananas
2 tablespoons vegetable oil
1 onion, thinly sliced

Equipment: Medium saucepan with cover, wooden mixing spoon, small skillet

1. Pour water into medium saucepan. Add peas, bring to boil over high heat for 1 minute, and stir. Reduce heat to **simmer**, cover, and cook for about 45 minutes, or until tender. Add salt and pepper to taste, and stir well.

2. Peel bananas and lay them whole on top of peas without mixing. Cover and continue cooking for about 10 minutes, or until bananas are mushy.

3. Heat oil in small skillet over medium-high heat. Add onion, and fry, stirring constantly, until browned, about 3 minutes. Season with salt and pepper, and stir. Spread onion and pan drippings over bananas and serve.

Serve from the pan while still warm.

Central African Republic

In the Central African Republic about half the population, including mostly French expatriates, observes Christian holidays. Many people in this country combine animist beliefs (everything has a soul) with Christianity. There are 80 ethnic groups living in rural areas, and most still follow ancestral tribal beliefs. Communal holiday celebrations are held to honor the spirits of the harvest, rainfall, death, and illness.

One of the high points in Central African celebrations is the Christmas mass. The Catholic priests and tribal chiefs, dressed in their finest regalia, oversee the blessings of the land, good spirits, ancestors, and food. Thousands join in the celebrations; dancers wearing elaborate costumes and headdresses chant and step to the beat of "talking drums." Each beat of the drums sends a message to the listening crowd.

Preparing the holiday feast is a communal project; the men and boys hunt, and the women dress and prepare the meat, usually spit-roasted wild game.

Many African recipes are one-dish meals that combine greens with rice, beans, or grains. This recipe is a typical African dish. For special holiday occasions, if hunting was good or the budget allowed, a little meat would be added.

Greens and Rice

Yield: serves 6

- 2 cups rice
- 1 pound spinach, fresh, washed, **trimmed**, and **finely chopped**, or frozen, thawed and finely chopped
- 1 onion, finely chopped
- 2 tomatoes, **stemmed** and quartered
- 1 cup finely chopped cooked chicken, ham, or lamb (optional)
- 4½ cups water
- ½ teaspoon ground red pepper, more or less to taste
- salt and pepper to taste

Equipment: **Dutch oven** or large saucepan with cover, mixing spoon

1. In Dutch oven or large saucepan, mix rice; spinach; onion; tomatoes; cooked chicken, ham or lamb; and water. Bring to a boil over high heat, stir, and reduce heat to **simmer**.

2. Cover and cook for about 30 minutes, or until rice is tender. Add ½ teaspoon red pepper, more or less to taste, and salt and pepper to taste; stir well.

Serve immediately while warm, right from the pan as a one-pot meal.

Cameroon

The United Republic of Cameroon is located in western Africa, and its population is very diverse, with more than two hundred ethnic groups. Most of the people still follow traditional religious beliefs, but there are large minority populations of Muslims and Christians. Muslims live in northern Cameroon, and the Christians live in the south.

Neither Christians nor Muslims strictly adhere to their religious doctrines, and they often alter the traditional practices and add ancestral tribal beliefs to many celebrations. For instance, Muslims observe Islamic holidays via transistor radio from Cairo. At the end of the holy month of *Ramadan*, when the news reports a sliver of new moon is sighted in the Egyptian sky, *Ramadan* is officially over for the Muslims of Cameroon, even though the new moon won't be seen in Cameroon for several hours. For all Muslims the sighting of the new moon brings an end to the month-long fasting, and in Cameroon festivities begin early in the day.

The Christian holidays in Cameroon, such as Easter, are elaborate celebrations combining Christian beliefs with local customs. Thousands of people gather for Catholic mass followed by speeches from government officials, clergy, and tribal leaders. Feasting and ritual dances fill the rest of the afternoon. Among the activities are masked *juju* dancers who tell a story with every leap, as they stamp their rattle-draped feet to the rhythm of the drums and gongs. Their presence keeps evil spirits away. For the communal feast, one large bowl is brought from home and filled; the family members then share the food.

For Muslims of Cameroon, the most important holiday meal is the feast at the end of *Ramadan*, *Eid al-Fitr*, and for Christians it is the Easter feast. *Poulet au yassa*, a chicken stew, is a favorite holiday feast for both Christians and Muslims in all West African countries. Most cooks have their own versions of this dish.

Poulet au Yassa — Chicken Stew

Yield: serves 6

- 3 onions, **finely chopped**
- 6 cloves garlic, finely chopped, or 2 teaspoons garlic granules
- ground red pepper, to taste (optional)
- 2 teaspoons **grated** fresh **ginger** or 1 teaspoon ground ginger
- ½ cup lime or lemon juice
- salt and pepper to taste
- 2 to 4 tablespoons vegetable oil, more or less as needed
- 2½ to 3 pounds chicken, cut into serving-size pieces
- 1 cup chicken broth, homemade (recipe page 52) or canned
- 4 to 6 cups cooked rice, **millet**, or **couscous** (keep warm for serving)

Equipment: Small mixing bowl, **grater**, mixing spoon, rubber gloves or plastic baggies, large mixing bowl with cover, **Dutch oven** or large skillet with cover, metal tongs

1. In small mixing bowl, combine onions, garlic, red pepper to taste, ginger, lime or lemon juice, salt and pepper to taste, and 2 tablespoons oil; stir well. Cover your hands with rubber gloves or plastic baggies, rub mixture on chicken pieces, and place them in large mixing bowl. Pour remaining mixture over chicken, cover, and refrigerate for about 2 hours, turning chicken 2 or 3 times in **marinade**.

2. Heat 2 tablespoons oil in Dutch oven or large skillet over medium-high heat. Add chicken pieces and fry on each side for about 5 minutes, or until golden brown. Fry in batches, adding more oil as needed. Keep warm.

3. Add chicken broth and remaining marinade to the same pan used for frying the chicken. Reduce heat to medium, stir, and return chicken pieces to pan. Cover and cook for about 30 min-

utes, or until tender. Test whether chicken is done, as discussed in the glossary on page xxiv.

To serve, arrange the chicken around a mound of rice, couscous, or millet and spoon pan drippings over it.

A large variety of cooked vegetables and grains are served for holiday feasts. Along with roasted meat or *poulet au yassa,* a millet dish is served, which is a staple in Africa.

Fried Millet

Yield: serves 4

4–6 tablespoons butter or margarine

2 onions, **finely chopped**

1 cup **millet** (available at most health food stores)

3 cups chicken broth, homemade (recipe page 52) or canned

½ cup **shredded** Swiss or cheddar cheese

salt and pepper to taste

Equipment: Medium skillet with cover, mixing spoon

1. Melt 4 tablespoons butter or margarine in medium skillet over medium-high heat, add onions, and cook until soft, about 3 minutes. Add millet, and, stirring constantly, cook for 3 minutes.

2. Stir in broth, and bring to a boil. Reduce heat to **simmer**, cover, and, stirring frequently, cook for about 20 minutes, or until millet is tender. Remove from heat, and add remaining 2 tablespoons butter or margarine, cheese, and salt and pepper to taste. Stir, cover, and let stand for about 10 minutes. Stir well before serving.

Serve millet while warm as a side dish with meat or fowl.

Sudan

Sudan has two distinct cultures—the Arabic-speaking Sunni Muslims, who live in the northern region and in most cities, and the southern Sudanese, who follow traditional tribal beliefs, although some have converted to Christianity. Despite the Sudanese presence in the south, Arabic is the official language of the country, and Islamic law is the law of the land. Resolving differences between the Sudanese and Muslims is a major problem within the country.

One of the most important Muslim holidays is *Eid al-Adha.* According to the Islamic holy book, the Koran, God instructed Ibrahim to kill his son Ishmael as an offering to Him and as a show of faith. Ibrahim was about to kill the boy when God told him to stop and instead to sacrifice a ram. (This event may sound familiar to Jewish and Christian readers as it is an important story in the Bible as well, the story of Abraham and Isaac.) In memory of Ibrahim's faith, many Muslims slaughter a cow, ram, or lamb for the "Feast of Sacrifice" (*Eid al-Adha*). As part of the tradition, they must give a portion of the sacrifice to the poor.

There are many side dishes served with the beef or lamb, such as the following salad.

Eggplant and Peanut Salad

Yield: serves 4 to 6

    1 to 1½ pounds eggplant, **peeled** and **coarsely chopped**
    1 teaspoon salt, more if necessary
    juice of 2 lemons
    1 clove garlic, **finely chopped,** or ½ teaspoon garlic granules
    3 tablespoons olive oil
    ½ cup coarsely chopped peanuts
    pepper to taste

Equipment: **Colander**, paper towels, medium salad bowl, salad mixing tools, medium skillet, **slotted spoon**

1. Put eggplant pieces in colander, sprinkle with 1 teaspoon salt, and let sit for 10 minutes. Rinse under running water, and, using clean hands, squeeze eggplant to remove excess moisture. Pat dry with paper towels.

2. In salad bowl, mix lemon juice and garlic, and set aside.

3. Heat 2 tablespoons oil in medium skillet over medium-high heat. Carefully add eggplant, and, stirring constantly, fry until tender and golden, about 3 minutes. Remove fried eggplant with slotted spoon, and drain on several layers of paper towels.

4. Add eggplant and peanuts to lemon-oil mixture and mix to coat. Add salt and pepper to taste. Refrigerate until ready to serve. Toss again before serving.

Serve as a side dish at room temperature for best flavor.

Chad

In Chad the population is made up of two distinct groups. In the north and east regions, the majority of people are from nomadic or seminomadic Muslim tribes. Through their long religious and commercial relationships with bordering Sudan and Egypt, the tribes have become more or less "Arabized," speaking Arabic and engaging in many other Arab cultural practices as well. In the southern portions of Chad, the native people took more readily to the European culture of the French colonists. Many Chadians in the south became Christians, although most people in this region are animists (believing that all things have a soul). The large community of French expatriates in Chad observes all Christian holidays. The climate of Chad is very hot, and so the French tradition of a blazing yule log in the fireplace at Christmas is replaced with the yule log (recipe page 102) on the dinner table.

For the Muslims of Chad, the feast after *Ramadan, Eid al-Fitr,* is their most important holiday.

In the following recipe, any vegetables can be added to the stew, but Chadians grow great quantities of sweet potatoes and peanuts. Adding meat to this stew would make it a special holiday meal. The ideal for Chadians, however, is to serve this as a side dish with spit-roasted meat.

Mtedza-Malawi Peanut Vegetable Stew

Yield: serves 6

- 2 tablespoons vegetable oil
- 1 onion, **finely chopped**
- 1 cup water
- 2 sweet potatoes (leave skins on), washed, **trimmed**, and thinly sliced
- 3 carrots, washed, trimmed, and coarsely sliced
- 16-ounce can of stewed tomatoes
- ½ teaspoon ground red pepper, more or less to taste
- salt and pepper to taste
- 1 cup corn, fresh; or frozen, thawed; or canned, with juice
- 1 cup **coarsely chopped** roasted peanuts
- 6 hard-cooked eggs, shelled and left whole (for serving)
- 4 to 6 cups cooked rice (for serving)

Equipment: **Dutch oven** or large skillet with cover, mixing spoon

1. Heat oil in Dutch oven or large skillet over medium-high heat. Add onion and fry until soft, about 3 minutes.

2. Add water, potatoes, carrots, tomatoes, ½ teaspoon red pepper (more or less to taste), and salt and pepper to taste. Stir and bring to a boil. Reduce heat to **simmer**, cover, and cook for 20 minutes.

3. Add corn and peanuts and stir well. Top with hard-cooked eggs, cover, and cook for 5 minutes to heat through.

Serve hot stew directly from the pot and spoon over rice. The whole eggs may be decoratively arranged over the top.

Niger

Many remnants of French colonization remain in Niger, including the French language, which is still the official language. Despite the fact that most of the population is Muslim, the people of Niger maintain a special relationship with France. Most Christians who call Niger home are originally from France.

Niger is predominantly a country of small villages, populated by farmers and nomadic herders. Muslim and tribal harvest feasts include roast lamb or goat and side dishes of yams and rice.

Joffof is a West African specialty, and there are as many ways to make it as there are people to cook it. The following recipe is typical of what might be served at *Eid al-Fitr*, the Muslim feast after *Ramadan*.

Joffof Rice with Lamb

Yield: serves 6

- 2 tablespoons vegetable oil
- 1 pound lean, boneless lamb, cut into bite-size pieces
- 2 onions, **finely chopped**

3 cloves garlic, finely chopped, or 1 teaspoon
  garlic granules
2 cups water
4 cups canned stewed tomatoes
½ cup tomato paste
4 cups **coarsely chopped** mixed vegetables,
  such as zucchini, carrots, broccoli, squash,
  yams, or sweet potatoes
¼ teaspoon ground red pepper (optional)
salt and pepper to taste
4 cups cooked rice (keep warm for serving)

Equipment: **Dutch oven** or large saucepan with
cover, mixing spoon

1. Heat oil in Dutch oven or large saucepan over
medium-high heat. Add meat, onions, and garlic,
and, stirring constantly, fry for about 5 minutes
until meat is browned. Add water, stewed tomatoes, and tomato paste, and stir. Bring to a boil,
and then reduce heat to **simmer**. Cover and cook
for 30 minutes.

2. Stir in mixed vegetables, red pepper, and salt
and pepper to taste. Cover and cook for 30 minutes, stirring frequently.

*To serve, mound rice in a serving bowl and cover
with vegetable mixture.*

Nigeria

Nigeria has a rich diversity of people with
more than 250 ethnic groups. The dominant
ethnic group in the northern two-thirds of the
country is the Hausa-Fulani, most of whom
are Muslims. The Yoruba people live mainly
in the southwest; about half are Christians and
half Muslim, making almost half of the total
population of Nigeria Muslim. The Catholic
Ibos mostly reside in the southeast. With all
their diversification, most Nigerians speak
English.

Many Nigerians combine tribal worship
with Muslim or Christian teachings, while
others practice a wide range of traditional religions, including sorcery and worship of ancestral spirits.

National holidays are New Year's Day, January 1; Good Friday; Muhammad's Birthday,
called *Mouloud*; National Day, October 1;
Easter Monday; 2 days each for the Muslim
holidays, *Eid al-Fitr*, the end of *Ramadan*; *Eid
al-Adha*, the feast of the sacrifice also known
as *Idal-Kebir*; Christmas Day, December 25;
and Boxing Day, December 26.

The feast after *Ramadan, Eid al-Fitr,* is the
most important Muslim holiday. The day begins with men praying at the mosque, and afterwards each city has a festival. The *emir*
(local ruler) leads a procession of elaborately
dressed horsemen to his palace, accompanied
by costumed marchers wielding swords and
spears, and musicians beating drums and
blowing long silver horns. Wrestlers, acrobats,
snake charmers, jugglers, and camel racers
entertain the crowds on the palace grounds.
The day-long festivities include a community
feast of spit-roasted lambs and goats served
with a variety of side dishes, such as the following chick-pea recipe.

Boiled Brown Bean or Chick-Pea Salad

Yield: serves 6

4 cups canned brown beans or **chick-peas** (also
  called garbanzos), including liquid (available
  at most supermarkets and Latin American
  food stores)

1 tablespoon olive oil

1 onion, **finely chopped**

1 cup mild or hot salsa (available at most
supermarkets)

salt and pepper to taste

Equipment: Medium mixing bowl, mixing spoon

Put beans with liquid into medium mixing bowl.
Add olive oil, onion, salsa, salt and pepper to taste.
Stir well and refrigerate until ready to serve.

Serve cold or at room temperature as a side dish.

Every festival—Muslim, Christian, or tribal—
includes feasts of roasted meat accompanied
with platters of fritters and one-dish stews.
The groundnut patties listed below can be
made into balls and **deep-fried**.

Kuli Kuli   Groundnut Patties

CAUTION: HOT OIL USED

Yield: serves 6

1 cup vegetable oil, more or less as needed

1 onion, **finely chopped**

1 egg, beaten

1 (12-ounce) can **chick-peas**, drained and
mashed

½ cup smooth or chunky peanut butter

2 tablespoons all-purpose flour

¼ teaspoon baking powder

¼ teaspoon ground red pepper, more or less to
taste

salt to taste

Equipment: Small skillet, mixing spoon, medium
mixing bowl, wax paper, work surface, large skillet, metal **spatula**, paper towels

1. Heat 1 tablespoon oil in small skillet over
medium high heat. Add onion, stir, and fry until
soft, about 3 minutes.

2. In medium mixing bowl, mix fried onions,
egg, mashed chick-peas, peanut butter, flour, baking powder, ¼ teaspoon red pepper (more or less

to taste), and salt to taste. Using clean hands, shape
dough into 2-inch patties about ½ inch thick. Place
patties on wax-paper-covered work surface.

3. Have an adult help you heat ¼ inch oil in large
skillet over medium-high heat. Carefully fry patties on each side for about 5 minutes, until browned
and crispy. Drain well on paper towels and keep
warm until ready to serve. Continue frying in
batches.

*Serve patties warm or cold. In Africa, it is custom-
ary to use the patties to scoop up food from the
communal bowl.*

In Nigeria, the *Iri-Ji* festival celebrates the new
harvest. *Ji*, meaning yam, is a staple crop,
symbolic of life. When the yams are harvested,
celebration and thanksgiving are in order. The
festival also demonstrates the link between the
living and their ancestors. At the *Iri-Ji* festival there are traditional tribal dances and music everywhere. Large pots of *futari*, a yam
and squash dish, are cooked at the official gathering place. Plastic tubs or calabash bowls are
brought from home, and each is filled with
enough food for families to share.

Futari   Yams and Squash

Yield: serves 6 to 8

2 tablespoons vegetable oil

1 onion, **finely chopped**

1 pound Hubbard squash, cut into 1-inch pieces
(discard seeds)

2 (about ¾ pounds) yams or sweet potatoes,
peeled and cut into 1-inch pieces

1 cup coconut milk, fresh homemade (recipe
page 194) or canned

½ teaspoon salt

½ teaspoon ground cinnamon

¼ teaspoon ground cloves

Equipment: **Dutch oven** or large saucepan with
cover, mixing spoon

1. Heat oil in Dutch oven or large saucepan over medium-high heat. Add onion, and, stirring constantly, fry until soft, about 3 minutes.

2. Add squash, yams or sweet potatoes, coconut milk, salt, cinnamon and cloves, and stir. Bring to a boil, and then reduce heat to **simmer**. Cover and simmer for 10 minutes. Uncover and cook, stirring occasionally, until vegetables are tender, about 5 minutes.

Serve in bowls while still hot.

Ghana

In Ghana, there are a large number of Christians (about 40 percent of the population). There is a sizable Muslim population, mostly in the north, and more than 50 ethnic groups living in rural areas who follow ancient communal tribal beliefs. The largest of these tribal groups are the Akan, Mole-Dagbani, Ewe, and Ga-Adangbe.

In rural Ghana, the Ga people celebrate the *Homowo* festival, which means "Hooting at Hunger," during the month of August. It seems many years ago they suffered a severe famine, and every year since, when the harvest is good, they celebrate by scorning and hooting at the hunger that had made them suffer. The Ga feast includes milled corn (recipe African Porridge, page 2) and fish in honor of their ancestors' suffering. The chiefs sprinkle cornmeal and palm oil around houses, while singing and chanting villagers do ritual dances to the beating drums.

The following month, at the end of September, begins the Yam festival, a seven-day harvest festival offering thanks to the gods who have blessed the land with crops; it is also a tribal gathering that celebrates the unity of the Ga-Adangbe people. The celebration is like New Year's and Thanksgiving in one. There is ritual dancing, chanting, drumming, and merrymaking. During the week-long festivities, farmers bring in the new crops of yams, **millet**, and other vegetables and grains, and once the harvest is complete, the New Year has officially begun.

West African holiday feasts include a variety of stews, spit-roasted lamb or goat, and *fufu*. *Fufu* is a staple served with every meal. It is made by boiling starchy foods, such as **cassava**, yams, **plantains**, or rice, and pounding them into a glutinous mass.

Fufu   Yam or Sweet Potato Loaf or Balls

Yield: serves 6
  1½ pounds yams or sweet potatoes, boiled with
    skins on and cooled to room temperature
  1 teaspoon ground nutmeg
  salt and pepper to taste

Equipment: Knife, medium mixing bowl, potato masher or electric **food processor**

1. Peel boiled yams or sweet potatoes, and cut into small-size chunks. Using potato masher or electric food processor, mash until smooth and lump-free. Add nutmeg and salt and pepper to taste.

2. Using wet, clean hands, shape mixture into a rounded loaf or into golf-ball-size balls.

Serve fufu loaf or balls on a serving plate. Each person pinches off a handful or takes a ball and eats it along with other foods. Fufu balls are also placed on top of stews or in soups and eaten as dumplings.

Chicken and vegetable one-pot stews, such as the following recipe for *hkatenkwan*, are favorites on feast days. *Fufu* (recipe precedes) is eaten with the stew. In Africa, families sit on the ground around the pot of food, and everyone, using only the right hand, digs in. The *fufu* is used as a scoop to collect the pan juices. (The left hand is never placed on the table; it is used only for personal grooming.)

Hkatenkwan One-Pot Meal with Ginger Chicken and Okra

Yield: serves 6

    1 chicken cut into serving-size pieces
    1 tablespoon **peeled** and **finely chopped** fresh **ginger** or 1 teaspoon ground ginger
    1 onion, finely chopped
    8 cups water
    2 tablespoons tomato paste
    1 tomato, **trimmed** and **coarsely chopped** or 1 cup canned stewed tomatoes
    1 cup chunky peanut butter
    ½ teaspoon ground red pepper
    1 cup eggplant, peeled and cut into ½-inch pieces
    12 whole okras, fresh or frozen, **trimmed**
    salt and pepper to taste

Equipment: **Dutch oven** or large saucepan with cover, **slotted spoon**, medium bowl

1. Put chicken pieces, ginger, onion, and water into Dutch oven or large saucepan. Bring to boil over high heat, stir, and reduce heat to **simmer**. Cover and cook for about 1 hour, or until chicken is tender. Using slotted spoon, remove chicken pieces and place in medium bowl.

2. Add tomato paste, tomato or stewed tomatoes, peanut butter, red pepper, eggplant, okra, and salt and pepper to taste to liquid in pan. Stir, cover, and cook for 15 minutes over medium heat.

3. Return chicken to pan, laying the pieces on top of vegetables. Cover, and cook to heat through, about 10 minutes.

To serve, set the saucepan in the middle of the table and have the guests help themselves.

Côte d' Ivoire (Ivory Coast)

In Côte d'Ivoire, over half the people are Muslims and about 12 percent are Christians. Called the Paris of West Africa, the country is a paradox. Large cities have modern skyscrapers, fine shops, traffic jams, and expert medical facilities, while the people of 60 ethnic groups in rural areas still live in traditional ways and practice tribal religions.

Most of the French-speaking Christians live in the cities and follow French holiday traditions. *Réveillon*, the Christmas Eve supper served after midnight mass, is the most important meal of the year. The centerpiece on the dinner table is the yule log (recipe page 102), which is eaten for dessert.

Plantains and bananas are prepared in many different ways throughout West Africa. *Aloco* are eaten like candy or cookies and are served at festive occasions, including the Muslim holiday *Eid al-Fitr.*

Aloco
Fried Plantain Slices

CAUTION: HOT OIL USED

Yield: serves 6

- 1 cup vegetable oil, more if needed
- 8 firm, ripe **plantains, peeled**, cut crosswise into ¼-inch slices
- 2 tablespoons sugar, more or less as needed, for **garnish**

Equipment: Baking sheet, paper towels, large skillet, wooden spoon, **slotted metal spoon**

1. Cover baking sheet with several layers of paper towels.

2. Have an adult help you heat 1 cup of oil in large skillet over medium-high heat. Oil is hot enough for frying when small bubbles appear around a wooden spoon handle when it is dipped in the oil.

3. Carefully add plantain slices, a few at a time, and fry for about 3 minutes on each side, or until golden brown. (The centers will be soft.) Remove with slotted spoon and drain on paper towels. Sprinkle with sugar and keep warm until ready to serve.

Serve aloco while warm and eat as a sweet snack.

When it's avocado season in West Africa, avocados are cheap and plentiful. Most people in West Africa eat the avocado right out of the shell with just salt and hot pepper sauce. Many people living in the cities, however, have a very contemporary lifestyle. They enjoy inviting family and friends to Christmas dinner, for example, and setting a pretty table. This recipe is a very popular way to serve avocados at holiday feasts.

Avocat Épicé
Avocado Boat

Yield: serves 4

- 2 ripe avocados, cut in half lengthwise, pits removed
- 1 onion, **finely chopped**
- 1 tomato, **cored** and finely chopped
- 2 or 3 drops liquid hot sauce, more or less to taste (optional)
- juice of 1 lime
- salt and pepper to taste

Equipment: Spoon, small mixing bowl, fork

1. Using a spoon, scoop out the avocados. Leave the shell intact to refill later. Put the avocado pulp in the small bowl, and mash smooth using the fork.

2. Add onion, tomato, 2 or 3 drops liquid hot sauce (optional, more or less to taste), lime juice, salt and pepper to taste, and mix well. Spoon the avocado mixture equally into each shell.

Serve each person a filled shell. The mashed avocado can be eaten with a fork, spoon, or scooped out with crackers, slice of cucumber, or carrot or celery sticks.

Sierra Leone/Liberia

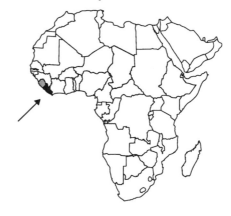

English is the official language in both Sierra Leone (in grey) and Liberia (in black), although tribal languages are widely spoken in both countries. In Sierra Leone, the two most prominent ethnic groups are the Mende and Temne, and about 60 percent of the people are Muslims. Almost everyone else follows traditional tribal beliefs, except for a small Christian minority group.

The most important national holiday in Sierra Leone is Independence Day, April 27, commemorating the date the country gained independence from England in 1961. Each community or town has an all-day celebration with ritual dances, chanting, drumming, and feasting.

Other festivals celebrate ancestors, the harvest, and Muslim feast days, such as *Eid al-Fitr,* the feast after the holy month of *Ramadan.* The festive celebrations are similar, with dancing, singing, and community foods. What makes the celebrations unique are the different cloths, masks, and headdresses worn by the dancers for specific occasions. The movements of the dancers also change according to the celebration, and they convey a recognizable message and meaning to the participants and onlookers.

In Liberia, Muslims and Christians are in the minority. Most citizens prefer to preserve the agrarian tribal rituals of their ancestors. Many life-sustaining and life-threatening acts of nature are the basis of the festivals. The ceremonial feasts are always communal, and all the women and young girls are expected to pitch in to prepare the meal for everyone. Rice is eaten at almost every meal, and in some tribes fish is added as a good omen.

Celebrations in Liberia are similar to those in Sierra Leone. There is drumming, dancing, and feasting. Dancing is a dramatic expression of life itself; to the people of Liberia it is as important as language and can convey the entire gamut of emotions. Drumming and singing accompany the dancers, setting the scene and creating the mood.

In both countries the communal feast for most festivals includes rice and cornmeal mush, colored orange from palm oil and steamed. It is served in huge mounds and consumed with fish or meat cooked in groundnut stew. The amount of fish or meat in the sauce is dictated by the wealth of the community. Every feast includes great quantities of man-

goes, watermelons, pineapples, pawpaws, oranges, and bananas; fresh fruit juices are also widely consumed.

Families eat together out of a tub or bowl they have brought from home and pick up the food with the right hand. It is rude to eat with the left hand, as it is used only for personal grooming.

The following recipe is a popular dish served on feast days in many West African countries. The colorful dish gets its name, black beauty and ponkie rice, from the eggplant, which is called "black beauty," and the pumpkin, which is called "ponkie" in this region of Africa.

Black Beauty and Ponkie Rice
Eggplant and Pumpkin Rice

Yield: serves 4

1 pound eggplant
1 teaspoon salt
2 tablespoons vegetable oil
1 onion, **finely chopped**
1 pound chopped, lean meat
½ cup canned pumpkin
1 tomato, **coarsely chopped**
2 green peppers, **cored**, **seeded**, and coarsely chopped
¼ teaspoon ground red pepper, more or less to taste
2 teaspoons paprika
4 cups cooked rice (keep warm for serving)

Equipment: Work surface, knife, **colander**, paper towels, large skillet, mixing spoon

1. **Trim** stem from eggplant, leaving skin on. Cut into bite-size pieces. Place in colander, sprinkle with salt, and toss to coat. Place in sink to drain for 30 minutes. Rinse under running water, and drain. Squeeze out any excess moisture with your hands. Pat dry with paper towels.

2. Heat oil in large skillet over medium-high heat. Add onion and meat, and, stirring constantly, fry until browned, about 5 minutes.

3. Add drained eggplant, pumpkin, tomato, green peppers, ¼ teaspoon ground red pepper (more or less to taste), and paprika. Stir and reduce heat to medium-low. Cover and cook for about 10 minutes. Remove cover, stir, and cook for 5 minutes more.

Serve over rice.

Throughout most of Africa, adding meat or chicken to the pot, such as in the next recipe, makes the meal a special luxury reserved for festive occasions.

Rice with Chicken

Yield: serves 6 to 8
  2½ to 3 pounds chicken, cut into serving-size pieces
  2 onions, **coarsely chopped**
  3 cloves garlic, **finely chopped,** or 1 teaspoon garlic granules
  6 cups water
  1 (16-ounce) can stewed whole tomatoes
  1½ cups rice, uncooked
  2 cups coarsely chopped cabbage
  1 medium eggplant with skin on, washed and coarsely chopped
  2 acorn squash with skins on, washed, **seeded, trimmed**, and cut into bite-size chunks
  salt and pepper to taste
  ¼ teaspoon ground red pepper to taste (optional)

Equipment: **Dutch oven** or large saucepan with cover, mixing spoon

1. Put chicken, onions, garlic, water, and tomatoes in Dutch oven or large saucepan. Bring to a boil over high heat. Reduce heat to **simmer**, cover, and cook for 30 minutes.

2. Stir in rice, cabbage, eggplant, squash, salt and pepper to taste, and red pepper to taste. Bring to a boil over high heat, reduce heat to simmer, cover, and cook for 25 minutes, or until vegetables are tender. Remove from heat and keep covered for about 15 minutes before serving.

Serve this one-dish meal from the pot and have guests help themselves. In most of Africa it is customary to eat with the fingers of the right hand. The left hand never touches food.

Guinea

Guinea was colonized by the French, but today only a small French community and the language remain. Muslims are in the majority, and all Islamic observances are national holidays. The most important Muslim holiday in Guinea is the *Eid al-Fitr,* the feast after the month of fasting, *Ramadan.* (See page 47.)

Traditionally, lambs or goats are roasted for the holiday feasts. Bean cakes, called *elele,* are served not only at every feast but also at every meal. They are used to scoop up sauces and stews.

Elele
Bean Cakes

CAUTION: HOT OIL USED

Yield: serves 4

- 2 cups canned black-eyed peas, drained and mashed
- 1 onion, **finely chopped**
- 1 egg, beaten
- 4 to 5 tablespoons all-purpose flour, more if needed
- 1 teaspoon ground **ginger**
- salt and pepper to taste
- 1 cup vegetable oil, more or less as needed, for frying

Equipment: Medium mixing bowl, mixing spoon or electric mixer, large skillet, wooden spoon, slotted metal **spatula**, baking sheet, paper towels

1. In medium mixing bowl, use mixing spoon or electric mixer to mix black-eyed peas, onion, egg, 4 tablespoons flour, ginger, and salt and pepper to taste. Continue mixing until well blended. Refrigerate mixture for at least 30 minutes. The mixture should be firm enough to hold together during frying. Add remaining 1 tablespoon flour or more, if necessary.

2. To prepare for frying, have an adult help you cover bottom of large skillet with ¼ inch oil and heat over medium-high heat. Oil is hot enough for frying when small bubbles appear around the wooden spoon handle when dipped into the oil. Place several layers of paper towels on baking sheet.

3. Carefully drop heaping tablespoonfuls of batter into oil and flatten slightly with back of spoon into 2-inch patties, about ¼ inch thick. Fry for about 3 minutes on each side, until browned. Remove with slotted metal spatula and drain on paper towels. Continue frying in batches, adding more oil, if necessary. Keep patties warm until ready to serve.

Serve patties warm or cold. Like most Muslims, Guineans eat with their right hand only; the left hand is used for personal grooming and toiletry. The patties are used to scoop up food.

Senegal

Senegal is a former French colony, but today less than 5 percent of the people are French Christians, most of whom live in the larger cities. The majority (about 90 percent) are Muslims who observe Islamic rituals. Ethnic groups in rural areas still follow ancient tribal beliefs.

The Muslim elite of Senegal usually has whole roasted lamb for religious feasts, such as the feast after *Ramadan, Eid al-Fitr,* and other important family gatherings. The lamb is stuffed with **couscous** and raisins. The innards of the lamb are made into a stew called *mafé.*

The *mafé* is a one-dish meal served with rice or **millet**. It is more typical of what most people can afford to eat for religious and agrarian feasts. It can be made with beef, chicken, lamb, fish, vegetables, or any combination. The stew is thickened with peanut butter. For homemade natural peanut butter try the recipe after the stew.

Mafé of Senegal
Groundnut Stew

Yield: serves 4 to 6

- 2 tablespoons vegetable oil
- 1 onion, **finely chopped**
- 1½ pounds lean, boneless beef or lamb, cut into 2-inch chunks

½ cup smooth peanut butter, store bought or homemade (recipe follows)
½ cup canned tomato paste
2 cups water, more if necessary
ground red pepper, to taste (optional)
salt and pepper to taste
3 carrots, cut into 1-inch slices
2 small white turnips, **coarsely chopped**
½ pound spinach, washed, **trimmed**, and coarsely chopped
4 to 6 cups cooked rice or **millet** (keep warm for serving)

Equipment: **Dutch oven** or large saucepan with cover, mixing spoon, small mixing bowl

1. Heat oil in Dutch oven or large saucepan over medium-high heat. Add onion, and, stirring constantly, fry until soft, about 3 minutes. Add meat and cook until lightly browned, about 8 minutes.

2. In small mixing bowl, mix peanut butter and tomato paste, adding 2 cups water, a little at a time, until smooth. Add ground red pepper to taste and salt and pepper to taste, mix well, and pour over meat in saucepan. Layer carrots, turnips, and spinach over meat, cover, and simmer for about 45 minutes, until meat is tender. Check liquid during cooking, and, if necessary, add more water to prevent sticking. The mixture, however, should not be soupy.

To serve mafé, *spoon over rice or millet in a serving bowl.*

Peanut Butter

Yield: about 1 cup
3 to 5 tablespoons safflower or vegetable oil
2 cups unsalted, dry-roasted peanuts (with shells removed)

Equipment: Electric **blender** or food **processor**, rubber **spatula**

Pour 3 tablespoons oil in blender or food processor, add peanuts, and process until smooth and creamy, adding more oil, a little at a time, if necessary.

Serve as spread or add to mafé *(recipe precedes). Peanut butter keeps well if covered and refrigerated.*

Burkina Faso

Most Burkinabè (the people of Burkina Faso) are farmers and migrant workers who adhere to ancient African tribal beliefs and hold agrarian festivals worshipping the sun, rain, and earth. In addition to the large population following tribal beliefs, more than two million people are Muslims and celebrate all Islamic holidays.

There are many agrarian and ancestral worship festivals in Burkina Faso, but none is more important than the *Bobo Masquerade*, honoring the god Wuro. According to legend, he created perfect balance between the sun, earth, and rain, but the people upset this perfect ecosystem when they began farming. Wuro appointed the god Dwo to act as mediator between the people and the natural order. The legend is retold by costumed dancers representing the god Dwo. They wear huge painted masks, high headdresses, and shaggy costumes and step to the beat of drums. Through the ritual language of dance, they chase away the year's evil, restoring order and bringing rain for the crops.

Peanuts, called **groundnuts**, are a staple crop in many areas of West Africa, and they are used extensively in cooking. This recipe is a typical feast day dish using locally grown peanuts. In Africa there is a large variety of leafy greens that are used for this recipe. Spinach is a good substitute.

African Greens in Peanut Sauce

Yield: serves 6
- 1 tablespoon vegetable oil
- 1 onion, **finely chopped**
- 1 green pepper, **cored**, **seeded**, and finely chopped
- 1 pound fresh spinach or frozen, thawed
- 1 tomato, finely chopped
- ¼ cup peanut butter (either creamy or chunky)
- salt and pepper to taste
- 4 cups cooked rice (keep warm for serving)

Equipment: Medium saucepan with cover, mixing spoon

1. Heat oil in medium saucepan over medium-high heat. Add onion and green pepper, stir, and fry until onion is soft, about 3 minutes. Add spinach and tomato, and stir.

2. Reduce heat to medium, cover, and cook until spinach is tender, about 5 minutes. Add peanut butter and salt and pepper to taste, stir, and heat just until hot.

Serve as a side dish or over rice.

To get in the Christmas spirit, French city dwellers bake cookies and make candy for the holiday season. Peanuts, called **groundnuts** in Africa, are a cash crop in Burkina Faso, and the French put them to good use, as in the following recipe.

Groundnut Cookies   Peanut Cookies

Yield: about 3 dozen
- 3 cups (14 ounces) **finely chopped,** salted peanuts
- 3 eggs
- 1 cup brown sugar, firmly packed
- 3 tablespoons all-purpose flour
- ¼ teaspoon baking powder

Equipment: Medium mixing bowl, mixing spoon or electric mixer, tablespoon, ungreased or nonstick cookie sheet, oven mitts, metal **spatula**

Preheat oven to 350° F.

1. In medium mixing bowl, combine chopped peanuts, eggs, brown sugar, flour, and baking powder, and, using mixing spoon or electric mixer, mix until well blended.

2. Drop dough by tablespoonfuls onto baking sheet, about 1 inch apart, and bake in oven for about 10 minutes until lightly browned.

Serve as a sweet snack and store in covered jar.

Groundnut Truffles   Peanut Candy

Yield: about 24 pieces
- ¼ cup chunky peanut butter
- 1 teaspoon vanilla
- 1 cup **shredded,** sweetened coconut

Equipment: Medium mixing bowl, mixing spoon, wax paper, baking sheet

1. In medium mixing bowl, mix peanut butter and vanilla. Add coconut and mix into a paste.

2. Using clean hands, shape into 1-inch balls. Place, side by side, on wax-paper-covered baking sheet. Cover loosely with wax paper and refrigerate overnight, or until very firm.

Serve as a sweet snack during the holiday season.

Mali/Mauritania

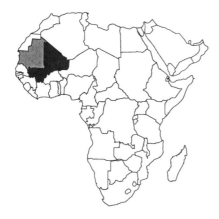

The majority of people living in Mali (in black) and neighboring Mauritania (in grey) are Muslims, and both countries observe all Islamic holidays. There are some basic differences between the two countries, however. In Mali, the official language is French, and the government is an independent republic. In Mauritania the official language is Arabic, and Islam is the state religion. Rigid Islamic laws govern the country.

The most important holiday for both countries is the *Eid al-Fitr*, the feast at the end of *Ramadan*. (See page 47 for a description of *Ramadan*.) The food prepared for Muslim feasts in Mali and Mauritania is similar to that of their northern neighbor, Algeria, a combination of North African and European flavors.

Most North African Muslims feast on lamb, goat, or camel meat stews with **couscous**. (See the following recipe.) Muslim women, who do almost all of the food preparation in these countries, believe preparing the holiday food is as much a part of the feasting ritual as the eating. The following recipe for lamb stew is typical of the food served for *Eid al-Fitr*.

Lamb Stew

Yield: serves 6 to 8
  2 tablespoons olive oil
  2 pounds lean, boneless lamb, cut into bite-size pieces
  2 cups water
  2 onions, **finely chopped**
  3 cloves garlic, finely chopped, or 1 teaspoon garlic granules
  3 zucchini, **trimmed** and cut into ¼-inch disks
  4 carrots, trimmed and finely sliced
  3 potatoes, **coarsely chopped**
  1 cup coarsely chopped cabbage
  2 cups canned stewed tomatoes
  cooked **couscous** (recipe follows) for serving

Equipment: **Dutch oven** or large saucepan with cover, mixing spoon

1. Heat oil in Dutch oven or large saucepan over medium-high heat, add meat, and, stirring constantly, fry until browned, about 5 minutes.

2. Stir in water, onions, garlic, zucchini, carrots, potatoes, cabbage, and stewed tomatoes. Bring to a boil, reduce heat to low, cover, and cook for about 45 minutes or until meat is tender. Stir frequently to prevent sticking.

Serve stew over sweet couscous *(recipe follows).*

For Muslim women, cooking shortcuts are unthinkable, and cooking **couscous**, as they do in Africa, is very labor-intensive. We're lucky to have packaged foods that make cooking easier and quicker.

Sweet Couscous

Yield: serves 6 or 8
  1½ cups (10-ounce package) semolina **couscous** (available at some supermarkets

and all health food and Middle East food stores)

1 cup dates, pitted and chopped (cut with wet scissors)

½ cup raisins

1 cup cooked **chick-peas,** dried, homemade (cook according to directions on the package) or canned, drained

salt to taste

Equipment: Medium saucepan with cover, scissors, mixing spoon

1. In medium saucepan, prepare couscous (according to directions on package).

2. Remove from heat, and add dates, raisins, chick-peas and salt to taste. Mix, cover, and keep warm until ready to serve.

Serve with the preceding lamb stew recipe.

Libya

In Libya all aspects of life are controlled by Islamic law. The government takes severe measures to restrict citizen contact with non-Islamic and non-Arabic influences. Both the religious and civil courts uphold Islamic law.

Libyans observe all Muslim holidays with extreme devotion and solidarity. No celebration is more important than the Islamic holy month of *Ramadan,* the ninth month of the Islamic calendar. (See page xxxiii for discussion of Islamic calendar.) At the end of that month everyone eagerly waits for the sighting of the new moon, signaling that *Ramadan* is over and the feast of *Eid al-Fitr* can begin. Ancient Islamic rituals are followed to the letter by Libyans as they prepare the holiday feast. Most dishes have remained unchanged for centuries.

Stuffing vegetables, such as in the following recipe, makes them easy to eat without utensils, which is certainly handy for a massive feast like *Eid al-Fitr.*

Stuffed Tomatoes

Yield: serves 4

4 large tomatoes

4 tablespoons butter or margarine

1 onion, **finely chopped**

½ cup *each* seedless raisins and **coarsely chopped, blanched** almonds

½ cup *each* finely chopped dried apple slices and dried apricots (cover with warm water, soak for 30 minutes, and drain)

4 cups cooked rice

½ cup orange marmalade

2 teaspoons cinnamon

4 tablespoons honey

salt and pepper to taste

Equipment: Sharp knife, teaspoon, small bowl, paper towels, work surface, large skillet, mixing spoon, greased or nonstick 9-inch baking pan, aluminum foil, oven mitts

Preheat oven to 350° F.

1. Using sharp knife, cut ¾ inch off top of each tomato. Using teaspoon, scoop pulp out of tomatoes into a small bowl. Place several layers of paper towels on work surface, and turn tomato shells upside down to drain on paper towels. **Trim** and finely chop tomato tops.

2. Melt butter or margarine in large skillet over medium heat, and add onion, tomato pulp, chopped tomato tops, raisins, almonds, and drained fruit.

Fry for about 3 minutes, stirring continually. Remove from heat, and add cooked rice, 2 tablespoons marmalade, 1 teaspoon cinnamon, 2 tablespoons honey, and salt and pepper to taste. Stir well.

3. Pack rice mixture into tomato shells and spread remaining mixture evenly over bottom of greased or nonstick 9-inch baking pan. Place stuffed tomatoes on top of rice mixture.

4. In small bowl, mix remaining marmalade, 1 teaspoon cinnamon, and 2 tablespoons honey, and drizzle over tomatoes. Cover pan tightly with foil and bake in oven for 20 minutes. Remove foil and bake uncovered for 5 minutes.

Serve either warm or cold as a side dish with lamb or fowl.

Sweets are an important part of *Eid al-Fitr,* also known as the "Candy Holiday," and almost all Muslim children love *semesmyah.* It is very healthy, quick and easy to make with only 3 ingredients, and keeps well without refrigeration.

Semesmyah   Sesame Candy

Yield: 16 pieces
  3 tablespoons *each* brown sugar and honey
  1 cup sesame seeds (they are inexpensive at
    health food stores)
  vegetable oil cooking spray

Equipment: Small saucepan, wooden mixing spoon, 2 (12-inch each) squares aluminum foil, baking sheet, **rolling pin**, knife

1. In small saucepan, combine brown sugar and honey. Cook over low heat, stirring constantly, until sugar dissolves, about 3 minutes. Add sesame seeds, stir well, and remove from heat.

2. Place one piece of foil on baking sheet and spray with cooking spray. Pour sesame mixture onto foil, and, using back of wooden spoon, spread out into a square-shape, about ½-inch thick.

3. Spray one side of the remaining piece of foil with cooking spray. Place it sprayed-side-down on top of the sesame mixture. Use either the flat of your hand or a rolling pin, press down on the top piece of foil, and evenly flatten the sesame mixture to about ¼ inch thick. Remove top foil, and cut sesame mixture into 1-inch squares. Replace the piece of foil (sprayed-side-down) and refrigerate overnight, or until set.

Serve as a sweet snack. The flavor of sesame candy improves with age.

North Africa

Algeria, Morocco, and Tunisia in northwestern Africa became known as the *Maghreb,* "go to the unknown," by Arab invaders in the seventh century. The Arabic holy wars were successful, and most North Africans, regardless of their origin or mother tongue, converted to Islam and absorbed the Arab culture. Today the people are known as North African Muslims, with a history and culture of their own that is neither Arab nor Berber. (The Berbers are native nomads who have an ancient history in the *Maghreb.*)

For Muslims, the meal after *Ramadan, Eid al-Fitr* (also known as *Aid-es-Seghir*), is the most important feast. It always begins with soup or stew to satisfy the empty stomach and restore strength after the daily fasting during *Ramadan.*

The most famous of soups throughout North Africa is *Ramadan* soup. Except for beans, rice, egg, and lemon juice, which are mandatory, you can add just about anything you like to the following recipe.

Harira Souiria
(also spelled H'rira) Ramadan Soup

Yield: serves 6 to 8

1 onion, **coarsely chopped**

½ to 1 pound lean lamb or beef, cut into ½-inch chunks

1 cup dried **chick-peas**, soaked overnight and drained or 2 cups canned chick-peas, including juice (also called garbanzos)

8 cups water

¼ cup brown lentils

½ cup rice

1 cup canned stewed tomatoes, including juice

½ cup fresh, chopped parsley or ¼ cup dried parsley flakes

1 egg, beaten

¼ cup lemon juice, more or less to taste

salt and pepper to taste

Equipment: **Dutch oven** or large saucepan with cover, wooden mixing spoon

1. In Dutch oven or large saucepan, combine onion, meat, chick-peas (if using canned chick-peas, add later), and water, and stir well. Bring to a boil over high heat, and stir. Reduce heat to simmer, cover, and cook for 25 minutes.

2. Stir in lentils, rice, tomatoes, and parsley, and bring to a boil over high heat. Reduce heat to simmer, cover, and cook for 20 minutes.

3. If using canned chick-peas, add now. Stirring constantly, add egg, ¼ cup lemon juice, and salt and pepper to taste. Simmer, uncovered, for 10 minutes.

To serve, ladle warm soup into individual bowls. In Algeria and Tunisia the soup is served with chunks of French bread for sopping, and in Morocco Arab flat bread (recipe page 69) is preferred.

In most Muslim countries *Ras el Am*, New Year's Day, is a quiet family observance. Some North African communities prefer to spend the day in prayer, mourning their dead.

There are other North Africans who choose to observe *Ras el Am* as a happy occasion. There are festivals, folk dancing, singing, community feasts, and giant bonfires or firework displays.

Algeria

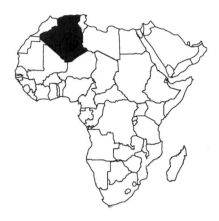

Along the Algerian coast, fish are plentiful and are included in Muslim feasts, such as *Eid al-Fitr*.

Fish with Cumin

Yield: serves 4

½ cup olive oil, vegetable oil, or blend of both, more if needed

½ cup **finely chopped** parsley or ¼ cup dried parsley flakes

3 cloves garlic, **crushed**, or 1 teaspoon garlic granules

1 teaspoon paprika

2 tablespoons ground cumin

salt and pepper to taste

4 (6- to 8-ounce-each) fish fillets with skins on: trout, red snapper, or sea bass, rinsed and patted dry with paper towels

lemon wedges, for **garnish**

Equipment: Small bowl, mixing spoon, greased 13-x 9-inch baking pan, aluminum foil, oven mitts

Preheat oven to 350° F.

1. In small bowl, combine ½ cup oil, parsley, garlic, paprika, cumin, and salt and pepper to taste, and mix into a paste.

2. Place fillets, flesh-side up, in baking pan and spread cumin paste over each. Cover with foil and bake in oven for 20 minutes. Remove foil and bake for 10 minutes more. Fish is fully cooked when flesh is **opaque** white and flakes easily when poked with a fork.

To serve, transfer fish to serving platter and surround with lemon wedges for garnish and for squeezing over the fish.

In most Algerian homes a bowl of fresh fruit is placed on the table at the end of a meal. While seated around the table, it is customary for each person to **peel** and cut their selected fruit. For holiday feasts, such as *Aid-es-Seghir* (*Eid al-Fitr*) or *Ras el Am*, the cook will often present the fruit, already peeled, sliced, mixed, and flavored such as in this recipe.

Chlada Fakya   Fresh Fruit Medley

Yield: serves 6

  ½ cantaloupe, **peeled**, **seeded**, and cut into bite-size pieces

  ½ honeydew melon, peeled, seeded, and cut into bite-size pieces

  1 cup strawberries, cut in half, **stemmed**, and washed

  2 bananas, peeled and thinly sliced

  5 seedless oranges, peeled and segmented

  ½ cup orange juice

  juice of 2 lemons

  2 tablespoons sugar

  1 teaspoon vanilla extract

  1 teaspoon cinnamon

Equipment: Medium serving bowl, mixing spoon, small mixing bowl

1. In medium serving bowl, carefully toss cantaloupe, honeydew melon, strawberries, bananas, and oranges.

2. In small bowl, mix orange and lemon juice, sugar, vanilla, and cinnamon, and then pour over fruit. Toss gently, and refrigerate until ready to serve. Toss before serving.

Serve in individual bowls at the end of the holiday feast.

Morocco

In Morocco *Aid-es-Seghir* (*Eid al-Fitr*) marks the end of *Ramadan*. It is a family holiday where toys and candy gifts are given to children. Moroccans take great care in preparing the holiday feast. A dish called *bisteeya*, usually made with pigeons, is the grandest meal anyone can be served. It takes several cooks many hours to prepare it. *Bisteeya* is made in a special pan that is at least two feet across. To serve 12 people, the traditional recipe calls for 8 pigeons, 1 pound sugar, 3 pounds butter, 30 eggs, 4 pounds of flour, 1 pound of almonds, cinnamon, ginger, pimentos, onions, saffron, and coriander. The ingredients are placed between more than 100 layers of paper-thin pastry.

The following recipe is a streamlined version. For the paper-thin pastry use **phyllo** dough.

Bisteeya
(also Bastela or Bstila)
Chicken Pie

Yield: serves 6 to 8

2 tablespoons vegetable oil

3 cloves garlic, **crushed**, or 1 teaspoon garlic granules

2 large onions, **grated**

½ cup sliced almonds

1 cup **finely chopped** fresh parsley or ½ cup dried parsley flakes

2 teaspoons ground **ginger**

3 teaspoons ground cinnamon, more as needed

5 cups boneless, skinless chicken, cooked and cut into bite-size chunks

salt and pepper to taste

1 cup butter or margarine, more or less as needed

5 eggs, beaten until frothy

¼ cup sugar

1-pound package frozen **phyllo** dough, thawed (available in freezer section of most super-markets—thaw according to directions on package)

2 teaspoons confectioners' sugar, more or less as needed

Equipment: **Grater**; large skillet; wooden mixing spoon; medium skillet; small saucepan; work surface; pastry brush; buttered, deep, 9-inch Pyrex pie pan; kitchen towel; oven mitts

1. In large skillet, heat oil over medium-high heat. Add garlic, onions, almonds, parsley, ginger, and 2 teaspoons cinnamon. Stirring constantly, fry until onions are soft, about 3 minutes.

2. Remove from heat, add cooked chicken and salt and pepper to taste, and stir well. Set aside.

3. Melt 2 tablespoons butter or margarine in medium skillet over medium heat. Add eggs, sugar, and 1 teaspoon ground cinnamon, and stir well. Adding more butter or margarine if necessary to prevent sticking, stir constantly until eggs are soft scrambled, about 5 minutes. Add to chicken mixture and lightly toss together.

Preheat oven to 350° F.

4. Melt ½ cup butter or margarine in small sauce-pan. Brush bottom and sides of pie pan with melted butter or margarine. Remove sheets of phyllo from package and unfold (according to directions on package); keep covered with clean towel.

5. Center one phyllo sheet in buttered pie pan, and gently press into the pan, allowing for a gen-erous overhang all around the top edge. (It is okay to have wrinkles, folds, and overlapping sheets of dough. If sheets tear, simply pinch together and brush with melted butter or margarine.) Brush the first sheet generously with melted butter or mar-garine. Repeat layering 5 more sheets of phyllo, brushing each with melted butter or margarine.

6. Fill crust with chicken mixture and cover with 3 layers of phyllo, brushing each with melted but-ter or margarine. Roll overhanging edges together and tuck inside of rim of pie pan. Brush top and edges with remaining melted butter or margarine. (The edge of pie will be thick.) Using fork tines, poke about 8 steam vents into top crust.

7. Bake in oven for about 20 minutes, or until golden brown. Remove from oven and sprinkle top with confectioners' sugar and cinnamon.

To serve, cut the warm pie into wedges and place it in the middle of the table. In Morocco, everyone first washes their hands at the table. Using only the right hand, guests help themselves to a wedge of pie.

The national drink, enjoyed by rich and poor alike, is hot green tea flavored with fresh mint. Hot tea soothes the soul, mint freshens the mouth, and the sugar renews one's energy af-ter a day of fasting during *Ramadan.*

Moroccan Mint Tea

Yield: 6 cups

8 cups boiling water, more or less as needed

1 tablespoon green tea (available at many supermarkets and all Middle East food stores)

½ cup sugar, more or less to taste

¼ cup fresh spearmint leaves, more or less to taste

Equipment: 6-cup teapot with cover, tablespoon

1. Pour 2 cups hot water into the teapot, swirl it around to warm the teapot, and throw the water away.

2. Put green tea, ¼ cup sugar, and ¼ cup spearmint leaves in warmed teapot. Add 6 cups hot water, cover, and allow to "steep" (blend favors) for at least 3 minutes. Before serving, stir and add sugar to taste.

To serve the tea hot in a cup or as they do in Morocco, use heat-proof, juice-size glasses and slowly sip the tea.

The following very rich, candy-like cake made from dates is cut into very small pieces and served as an energy booster at feasts, weddings, and other festive occasions. In date-growing regions of the world like Morocco, dates are often referred to as "the candy that grows on trees."

Mescouta — Date Bars

Yield: 27 pieces

2 eggs, well beaten

1 cup sugar

1 teaspoon vanilla extract

½ cup melted butter or margarine

¾ cup all-purpose flour

½ teaspoon baking powder

1 cup pitted dates, chopped (cut with wet scissors)

1 cup **finely chopped** walnuts or almonds

¹/₃ cup seedless raisins

confectioners' sugar, for **garnish**

Equipment: Large mixing bowl, egg beater or electric mixer, mixing spoon, rubber **spatula**, scissors, greased 9-inch-square cake pan, oven mitts, toothpick, small dish

Preheat oven to 350° F.

1. In large mixing bowl, mix eggs, sugar, vanilla, and melted butter or margarine with egg beater or electric mixer until well blended, about 3 minutes. Mixing constantly, add flour, a little at a time, and baking powder.

2. Using rubber spatula, fold in dates, nuts, and raisins, and mix well. Pour mixture into greased 9-inch-square cake pan.

3. Bake in oven for about 30 minutes, or until a toothpick inserted in the center comes out clean. While still warm, cut into bars about an inch wide and 3 inches long.

4. Put 3 tablespoons confectioners' sugar into a small dish. Roll each bar in confectioners' sugar.

Store bars in box, with wax paper between layers. Serve as a sweet snack.

Tunisia

Tunisian sand cookies, *sablés*, are melt-in-your-mouth delicious. They can be made into different shapes: coins (for wealth), crescents (for health), and rings (for love).

Sablés
Sand Cookies

Yield: about 2 to 3 dozen
- 4 hard-cooked **egg yolks**
- 6 tablespoons butter (for best results use only butter), at room temperature
- 6 tablespoons sugar
- **grated** rind of ½ lemon
- ¼ teaspoon salt
- 1 cup all-purpose flour
- ¼ cup confectioners' sugar, more or less as needed, for **garnish**

Equipment: Medium mixing bowl, fork, mixing spoon, **grater**, floured work surface, lightly greased or nonstick cookie sheet, oven mitts, metal **spatula**

1. In medium mixing bowl, mash yolks using back of fork. Add butter, sugar, lemon rind, and salt. Mix into a smooth paste. Add flour, a little at a time, to form a smooth dough. Refrigerate dough for 4 hours.

Preheat oven to 350° F.

2. On lightly floured work surface, **knead** dough until soft, about 3 minutes. Pinch off walnut-size pieces, and make them into coin, crescent, or ring shapes; slightly flatten each cookie with your hand. Place cookies about an inch apart on lightly greased or nonstick cookie sheet.

3. Bake in oven for about 15 minutes, or until cookies are light golden on bottom. While cookies are still warm, sprinkle them with confectioners' sugar.

Serve cookies with tea or glass of milk.

Sweet rice pudding, such as the recipe that follows for *mhalbya*, is eaten as part of the main meal, not as dessert. Tunisians eat only fresh fruit at the end of a meal.

Mhalbya
Tunisian Rice Pudding

Yield: serves 4 to 6
- 4 cups cooked rice
- ½ cup confectioners' sugar
- 3 cups milk
- 2 eggs, slightly beaten
- ½ cup seedless raisins
- 4 tablespoons butter or margarine
- ½ cup sliced almonds
- 2 tablespoons sugar
- ½ teaspoon cinnamon

Equipment: Medium mixing bowl, wooden mixing spoon, buttered medium casserole, small skillet, oven mitts

Preheat oven to 350° F.

1. In medium mixing bowl, combine cooked rice, confectioners' sugar, milk, eggs, and raisins. Mix well, and transfer to buttered medium casserole. Smooth top, and bake in oven for 45 minutes.

2. Melt butter or margarine in small skillet over medium heat. Add almonds, sugar, and cinnamon, and stir. Cook to dissolve sugar, about 2 minutes, and remove from heat.

3. Using oven mitts, remove rice casserole from oven, and spread almond mixture over top. Return to oven for 10 minutes, until lightly browned.

Serve rice pudding warm or at room temperature for best flavor.

Stuffed Dates with Fondant

Yield: about 3 dozen
- 2 tablespoons cream or milk
- 1 teaspoon vanilla
- 2¼ cups (about ½ pound) confectioners' sugar
- 1 **egg white**
- 1 pound large, whole pitted dates
- 36 walnut or pecan halves, for **garnish**

½ cup granulated sugar, more or less as needed, for garnish

Equipment: Medium mixing bowl, wooden mixing spoon, aluminum foil, cookie sheet

1. Make fondant: In medium mixing bowl, mix cream or milk, vanilla, 1½ cups confectioners' sugar, and egg white until smooth. Add remaining ¾ cup confectioners' sugar, and mix until firm and smooth, about 5 minutes. Cover with foil, and refrigerate for 4 hours.

2. Assemble: Stuff each date with about 1 teaspoon fondant, and press a nut into each one, for garnish. Roll in granulated sugar, and place side by side on cookie sheet. Roll each piece a second time in sugar. Place dates back on cookie sheet, cover with foil, and refrigerate.

Serve as a sweet treat or pack in a box or tin and give as a holiday gift.

Middle East

Historians, politicians and geographers have never agreed exactly on where the Middle East begins and ends. For the purposes of this book, however, the Middle East begins with the countries that border the eastern end of the Mediterranean Sea and extends east through Iran. The northern boundary includes Turkey and runs south to the Indian Ocean.

The majority of people living in the Middle East are Muslims, although there are some Christian communities and the Jewish state of Israel. Because of its concentration of Muslims, this region is often known as the Islamic Realm. Muslims follow traditions and practices that have remained unchanged for over a thousand years. Islam is their guiding force, dictating civil laws, monitoring their lifestyles, and requiring prayer five times a day.

The Muslim observances are a time for religious devotion and respect for the laws of Islam. Holiday celebrations are a time of community and family solidarity. The Muslims' depth of faith is unwavering, especially during the most sacred and pious holiday, the month-long fasting of *Ramadan*.

During *Ramadan*, Muslims are not permitted to eat or drink from sunup to sundown, but according to the Koran, they may eat and drink once the sun has set.

Ramadan commemorates the revelation of the Koran to the Arabian Prophet Muhammad, founder of the faith, in the seventh century A.D. The Koran is the holy book containing all the Islamic rules and laws.

The timing of *Ramadan* varies, because in the Islamic lunar calendar the holidays move through the seasons in 33-year cycles. Fasting, and especially not having anything to drink, is difficult for farmers and laborers when *Ramadan* falls in the summertime, but few fail to observe the rigid law of Islam.

Additional rulings from the Koran require that Muslims must not eat any meat from a pig, and the meat they do eat must be slaughtered according to the Koran. Another holiday, the Feast of Sacrifice known in Arabic as *Eid al-Adha*, celebrates the decree that all Muslims must share with the less fortunate. According to the Koran, the more one gives to the needy, the more worthy one will be in heaven.

Muslim holiday feasts often bring family and friends together for a hearty meal. Roasted lamb is the favorite meat with many side dishes, including stuffed vegetables, bean salad, rice and lentils, and, of course, flat bread. Flat bread is an important part of every meal. Using only the fingers of the right hand, the bread is torn apart, and the pieces are used as a scoop to transport the food from the bowl to one's mouth.

Most Muslims living in the Islamic Realm eat from a low table while sitting on a carpet or floor pillows. No one must eat until the pre-meal hand-washing ritual is completed. No forks, knives, or spoons are provided, and only the right hand is used for eating. The left hand must not touch food, as it is used for personal grooming and toiletry.

Religious leaders have always acted as mentors and advisors to their people, not only in matters of faith and morality, but also with regard to food and drink. This is true for both Israelis and Muslims. Despite vast cultural, political, and geographical differences, there are some similarities between Israelis and Muslims. For both, their lives are governed by religious dietary restrictions regarding the acceptance and preparation of food; lamb is the basic meat, wheat is a staple grain, eggplant is a favorite vegetable, and almost everyone loves yogurt. Neither Israelis nor Muslims are allow to eat pork, and each has strict rules about butchering and preparing the meat they do eat.

Food gives strength and sustains life; the Muslim and Jewish dietary laws are meant to teach reverence for life. To show compassion for all living things and to avoid cruelty to animals, special humane methods of slaughter are required.

Egypt

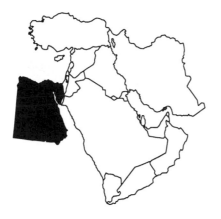

Most Egyptians are Muslims, although about 10 percent of the people belong to the Egyptian Coptic Christian Church. All Muslim observances are national holidays. *Sham al-Nessim*, "smell the spring day," is a national holiday celebrating the arrival of spring. This celebration dates back to the time of the Pharaohs. Ancient Egyptians believed that on this spring day, which falls on the first Monday after the Coptic Easter, the earth was born. Schools and businesses close, and all Egyptian families, no matter what religion, spend the day in the park or countryside. Special symbolic foods are packed in the picnic basket. Beautifully colored hard-cooked eggs, symbolizing life, are always included. (In fact, the tradition of coloring Easter eggs may have its roots in this spring festival.) Fish is added to prevent illness, and lentils, such as in the following recipe, bring good fortune. All meals end with fresh fruit, and a sweet snack is brought along for nourishment during the day-long outing. (The recipe for *basboosa*, an almond cake, is an example of the type of sweet that might be served.)

Koushry   Lentils and Rice

Yield: serves 4 to 6
   4 tablespoons vegetable oil
   3 onions, **finely chopped**
   4 cups cooked brown lentils (cook according to directions on package and keep warm)
   4 cups cooked rice, keep warm
   salt and pepper to taste

Equipment: Small skillet, mixing spoon, medium mixing bowl with cover

1. Heat oil in small skillet over medium-high heat. Add onions, and, stirring constantly, fry until soft, about 3 minutes.

2. In medium mixing bowl, stir cooked lentils and rice. Add fried onions with pan drippings, and stir well.

Serve warm or at room temperature.

In Egypt, cake is usually eaten as a between-meal-snack, not dessert.

Basboosa   Almond Cake with Lemon Syrup

Yield: serves 10 to 12
   6 **eggs, separated**
   1 cup sugar
   1 cup **ground** almonds
   1 cup farina (Cream of Wheat may be used)
   1 teaspoon baking powder
   1 teaspoon almond extract
   18 to 20 whole **blanched** almonds
   lemon syrup (recipe follows), for **garnish**

Equipment: Large mixing bowl, egg beater or electric mixer, mixing spoon and rubber **spatula**, medium mixing bowl, buttered and floured or nonstick 9-inch **springform pan**, oven mitts, knife

Preheat oven to 350° F.

1. Put egg yolks and sugar in large mixing bowl, and use egg beater or electric mixer to mix them until light and creamy. Add ground almonds, farina (Cream of Wheat), baking powder, and almond extract; mix well.

2. Put egg whites in medium mixing bowl, and, using clean, dry egg beater or electric mixer, beat until stiff. Using mixing spoon or rubber spatula, **fold** egg whites into farina mixture. Transfer mixture to buttered and floured or nonstick springform pan.

3. Bake in oven for about 60 minutes or until golden. Remove from oven and cool for about 10 minutes.

4. Using a knife, mark cake into thin serving-size wedges, and garnish each slice with a whole almond at the wide end. Pour warm lemon syrup over cake. Use only enough syrup to moisten cake; do not make it soggy.

Serve cake at room temperature.

Lemon Syrup

Yield: about 1 cup
    1½ cups water
    ½ cup sugar
    juice of 1 lemon

Equipment: Small saucepan, mixing spoon, **candy thermometer**

Pour water into small saucepan, and add sugar and lemon juice. Bring to a boil over high heat, and, stirring constantly, boil until sugar dissolves. Reduce heat to simmer and cook until mixture registers 220° on candy thermometer. Cool to warm.

Use as mentioned in previous recipe for basboosa.

Maulid al-Nabi is the Muslim national feast day commemorating the birthday of the prophet Muhammad, who was born in Mecca around A.D. 570. The day is devoted to prayer, and at night the mosques are lit up in celebration. In some communities, families get together in the evening for a covered-dish feast. Each family brings a favorite dish to share with others, such as this recipe, *chirkasia.*

Chirkasia

Chicken with Rice in Nut Sauce

Yield: serves 6
    6 cups water
    1 onion, **finely chopped**
    3 bay leaves
    1 teaspoon ground cardamom
    6 boneless chicken breasts
    salt and pepper to taste
    3 slices white bread, crusts removed
    4 tablespoons butter or margarine
    3 cloves garlic, **finely chopped,** or 1 teaspoon garlic granules
    1 teaspoon paprika
    2 cups finely chopped nuts: walnuts, almonds, or pistachios
    6 cups cooked rice (keep warm for serving)

Equipment: Large saucepan, **slotted spoon,** medium baking pan with cover, **colander,** large skillet, oven mitts

Preheat oven to 200° F.

1. Pour water into large saucepan, and add onion, bay leaves, cardamom, chicken breasts, and salt and pepper (to taste). Bring to a boil over high heat, and then reduce heat to simmer. Cook for about 35 minutes, until chicken is tender.

2. Using slotted spoon, transfer chicken to medium baking pan, cover, and keep in warm oven. Remove bay leaves and discard. Save 3 cups of broth. Any remaining broth can be refrigerated to use at another time.

3. Prepare sauce: Put bread in colander and wet under running water. Using clean hands, squeeze out water.

4. Heat butter or margarine in large skillet over medium-high heat. Add garlic, paprika, nuts, and salt and pepper (to taste), and, stirring constantly, fry for about 3 minutes, until nuts are golden. Reduce heat to medium, and crumble bread into pan, using your clean hands. Add the 3 cups of broth saved in step 2, and, stirring frequently, cook un-

til blended and heated through, about 5 minutes.

To serve, mound rice on deep-rimmed serving platter, arrange chicken breasts on top of rice, and cover with sauce.

Israel

Most Israelis are Jewish, and one of their most important holidays is Passover. The eight-day spring festival commemorates the freeing of Jews from Egyptian bondage thousands of years ago. Many Jewish households use special cooking utensils, plates, and cutlery for this observance. Designated food vendors provide Passover foods under the supervision of a recognized Rabbinate (Jewish religious leaders with the authority to approve selected food).

On the first two nights of Passover, there is the ritualistic Passover feast, called the Seder (meaning order or procedure). When the family and guests are seated around the table, they read aloud from the *Haggadah* (the narration of the Exodus). The sacred story from the Old Testament tells of the suffering endured by the Jews while enslaved by the Egyptians. It tells of how God instructed Moses, a shepherd, to go to the pharaoh and demand freedom for his people. Moses was ignored, so to get the pharaoh's attention, God responded

with a series of terrible plagues. It was not until the last plague, the slaying of the first born in every Egyptian house, that the pharaoh freed the Jews, who had marked their doors with lamb's blood so that the Angel of Death would "pass over" them; thus the name Passover.

At Passover, each year, the narrative is retold and the symbols of the Passover meal are explained to each generation. Three or four ceremonial *matzos* are placed, one on top of another, under a napkin. The Seder plate holds the symbolic foods: A roasted shank bone of lamb represents the sacrifice of the lamb; bitter herbs, such as horseradish, symbolize the bitterness of slavery; *charoset* (recipe follows) represents the mortar the Israelites used to make bricks while enslaved in Egypt; parsley and hard-boiled eggs suggest the greenery and renewal of life in the springtime; and saltwater represents the tears of the Israelite slaves. (Before eating, the parsley and egg are dipped in the saltwater). In a set order, each person takes a taste of each thing on the Seder plate, as an explanation of its meaning is said aloud.

A festive meal is eaten in the middle of the Seder, usually beginning with *matzo* ball soup (recipe follows in this section). The main course consists of roast chicken or lamb or beef pot roast and many vegetable dishes. It is customary for the adults to drink four glasses of wine with appropriate blessings.

An extra place is set at the table and a wine glass is filled for the spirit of the prophet Elijah, who is always invited. Everyone at the Seder hopes that someday he will arrive with the Messiah. Setting a place for Elijah symbolizes man's faith in God and hope for peace among all mankind.

The following recipe is for *charoset*, one of the symbolic foods placed on the Passover Seder plate.

Charoset

Yield: about 2 cups

   1 cup chopped nuts (walnuts, pecans, almonds, or combination)

   5 apples, quartered, **cored**, and **finely chopped**

   1 teaspoon **grated** lemon peel

   3 tablespoons lemon juice

   1½ tablespoons sugar

   1 tablespoon ground cinnamon

   ¼ teaspoon ground **ginger**

Equipment: Medium bowl with cover, mixing spoon, **grater**

In medium mixing bowl, use mixing spoon to toss nuts, apples, lemon peel, lemon juice, sugar, cinnamon, and ginger. Cover and refrigerate.

About ½ to 1 cup of charoset *is placed in a mound on the Passover Seder plate.*

With the pharaoh chasing them, Moses and his people had no time to properly bake their bread by allowing it to rise. Therefore, the Jews baked unleavened bread. *Matzo* is the symbolic unleavened bread. Commercially baked *matzo* is available at most supermarkets and kosher stores during the Passover season. You can also try the following recipe.

Matzo   Unleavened Bread

Yield: about 4 pieces

   2 cups unbleached flour, more if necessary

   ½ cup cold water, more if necessary

Equipment: Large mixing bowl, fork, kitchen towel, floured work surface, floured **rolling pin**, ungreased baking sheet, oven mitts, wide metal **spatula**

Preheat oven to 500° F.

1. Put 2 cups flour in large mixing bowl. Make a well in the center of flour and add ½ cup water. Using clean hands or a fork, add flour to water in the well, a little at a time, making a soft, pliable dough. If dough is too sticky, add flour, a little at a time, or if too dry, add a little water. Divide dough into 4 equal-size pieces and cover with towel.

2. On floured work surface, **knead** 1 piece of dough for about 2 minutes. Using floured rolling pin, roll piece into a round or square shape about ⅛ inch thick. Sprinkle dough with flour if it is sticky. Roll out only enough dough to bake at one time.

3. Using fork tines, pierce through dough, completely covering matzo with tiny holes. (The holes prevent matzo from buckling while it bakes.) Roll dough around floured rolling pin, transfer it to ungreased baking sheet, and lay it flat.

4. Bake in oven for about 10 minutes, until browned edges curl and brown spots appear on surface. Remove baking sheet from oven, and, using wide metal spatula, turn bread over. Return to oven, and bake on second side for about 8 minutes, or until golden brown. (Brown spots on the surface add to the flavor.) Remove from oven and cool *matzo* on rack.

To eat matzo, *spread with butter, jam, or peanut butter.*

The traditional Passover dinner begins with chicken soup, usually served with *matzo* balls (recipe follows).

Chicken Soup

Yield: serves 6 or 8

   3 to 4 pounds chicken, cut into serving-size pieces

   10 cups water

   2 bay leaves

   2 carrots, **trimmed**, **peeled**, and coarsely sliced

   1 onion, **coarsely chopped**

   4 celery ribs, washed, trimmed, and coarsely sliced

   salt and pepper to taste

   matzo-ball dumplings (recipe follows), for serving (optional)

Equipment: Large saucepan with cover, mixing spoon, metal tongs or **slotted spoon**, large heat-proof serving platter

1. Put chicken in large saucepan, and cover it with water. Add bay leaves, carrots, onion, celery, and salt and pepper to taste, and bring to a boil over high heat. Reduce heat to **simmer**, cover, and cook for about 1 hour, until chicken is very tender.

2. Using tongs or slotted spoon, remove chicken, and transfer to heat-proof serving platter; keep in warm place. Before serving soup, remove bay leaves and discard.

To serve, the boiled chicken can be pulled off the bones, coarsely chopped, and added to the soup or served separately. Add 1 or 2 matzo *dumplings (recipe follows) to each bowl of soup.*

Matzo meal products are available all year long, but during Passover the package must say "for Passover."

Knaidlach   Matzo-Ball Dumplings

Yield: 8 to 10 balls
  2 tablespoons vegetable oil
  2 eggs, beaten
  ½ cup *matzo* meal (available at most supermarkets and all kosher markets)
  1 teaspoon salt, more or less to taste
  2 tablespoons water, more as needed

Equipment: Medium mixing bowl, mixing spoon, large saucepan with cover, **slotted spoon**

1. In medium mixing bowl, mix oil and eggs until well blended, about 2 minutes. Add *matzo* meal, ½ teaspoon salt, more or less to taste, and 2 tablespoons water; mix well. Refrigerate for about 15 minutes.

2. Prepare to cook dumplings: Fill large saucepan half full with water. Add ½ teaspoon salt, and bring to a boil over high heat. Reduce heat until water reaches a **rolling boil**.

3. Using clean hands, form batter into golf-ball-size balls. Drop balls, one by one, into water and bring back to rolling boil. Reduce heat to **simmer**, cover, and cook for 30 minutes. (If necessary, cook in batches.) Remove *matzo* balls with slotted spoon and keep warm.

To serve, add one or two matzo *balls to each bowl of hot chicken soup.*

Boobelach   Fried Matzo Meal Cakes

CAUTION: HOT OIL USED
Yield: about 6 to 8
  3 eggs
  1 cup water, more if necessary
  ½ teaspoon salt
  1 cup fine *matzo* meal (available at most supermarkets and all kosher markets)
  2 to 4 tablespoons vegetable oil, more if necessary
  2 teaspoons **cinnamon sugar,** for serving

Equipment: Medium mixing bowl, mixing spoon, large skillet, metal **spatula**, paper towels

1. In medium mixing bowl, mix eggs, 1 cup water, and salt. Stirring constantly, add *matzo* meal, a little at a time, to make a thick batter. Add more water, if necessary.

2. Heat 2 tablespoons oil in large skillet over medium-high heat. Drop tablespoonfuls of batter into 3-inch pancakes, each about ¼ inch thick. Reduce heat to medium, and fry on each side for about 5 minutes, until browned and crispy. Transfer to paper towels to drain. Keep finished patties in warm place, and continue frying the rest of the batter in batches, adding more oil, if necessary.

Serve boobelach *warm, sprinkled with cinnamon sugar.*

Israelis grow wonderful citrus fruit, which is especially enjoyed during Passover. The following lemon-flavored cake is a typical Passover dessert.

Passover Lemon Sponge Cake

Yield: serves 8 to 10

8 **eggs, separated**

1½ cups sugar

½ teaspoon salt

juice and **grated** rind of ½ lemon

1 cup *matzo meal*

4 to 5 cups fruit, for serving (optional—strawberries, raspberries, sliced bananas, or peaches)

quipment: 2 large mixing bowls, egg beater or .lectric mixer, **grater**, **whisk** or rubber **spatula**, ungreased 10-inch **tube pan**, oven mitts, toothpick

Preheat oven to 350° F.

1. Put egg whites in large mixing bowl, and use egg beater or electric mixer to beat them until stiff but not dry. Set aside.

2. In the other large mixing bowl, beat egg yolks until light, about 1 minute. Add sugar, and beat until creamy, about 3 minutes. Add salt, lemon juice, rind, and *matzo meal*, and beat well.

3. Using whisk or spatula, **fold** egg whites into yolk mixture. Pour mixture into tube pan, and bake in oven for about 45 minutes or until toothpick inserted in center comes out clean. Remove from oven. Invert cake (still in the pan) on rack to cool.

Cut cake into wedges, and serve with fruit, such as strawberries, raspberries, sliced bananas, or peaches.

Hanukkah, the Festival of Lights, marks the rededication by the Jews of the holy temple in Jerusalem after its desecration by the Syrian King Antiochus IV, who forced the Jews to worship the Greek gods. The Jews rebelled and fought off the Syrians. After they rebuilt the temple, and they were about to rededicate it, they found they only had enough oil for the lamp in the temple to burn for one day. Miraculously, it burned for eight days. During the eight-day midwinter festival, one candle is lit in a candelabra, the *menorah*, on the first night. On each of the next seven nights an additional candle is lit until eight are lit on the last night. During the week, school and work continue as usual, but evenings are filled with gift-giving, singing, and games.

A popular *Hanukkah* dish is potato pancakes called *latkes*. The reason for eating them at *Hanukkah* is somewhat of a mystery. One popular legend is that the oil in which the *latkes* are fried is a reminder of the ancient oil lamps in the holy temple that burned for eight days and nights.

Latkes   Potato Pancakes

CAUTION: HOT OIL USED

Yield: serves 4 to 6

4 large potatoes (about 2 pounds), **peeled** and finely **grated**

2 eggs

2 tablespoons **self-rising** flour

salt and pepper to taste

4 tablespoons vegetable oil, more or less as needed

1 cup *each* sour cream and applesauce, for serving

Equipment: **Grater**, large mixing bowl, mixing spoon, large skillet, metal **spatula**, oven mitts, 13- x 9-inch baking pan

Preheat oven to 200° F.

1. Squeeze handfuls of grated potatoes to make as dry as possible, discarding juice into the sink. Place potatoes in large mixing bowl, and add eggs, flour, and salt and pepper to taste; mix well.

2. Heat 2 tablespoons oil in large skillet over medium-high heat. Carefully spoon potato mixture into skillet, making pancakes about 3 inches across and about ¼ inch thick. Fry potato cakes 3 to 5 minutes on each side, until browned and edges are crispy. Adjust burner heat if necessary to prevent burning. Transfer to baking pan, and keep warm in oven until ready to serve. Repeat frying in batches, adding more oil as needed.

Serve warm with side dishes of sour cream and applesauce.

Lebanon/Syria

Lebanon (in black), which has been the site of much unrest and fighting, has large Christian and Muslim communities. Christians were in Lebanon centuries before the arrival of Muslims. Today there are nearly equal numbers of Christians and Muslims, although there are more Muslims. To keep the balance of power, a national mandate requires both religious groups to have equal government representation, and both Muslim and Christian observances are national holidays.

In Arabic-speaking Syria (in grey), the majority of the population is Muslim, and only about 13 percent is Christian. Only Muslim observances are national holidays.

In both countries, one of the most important Muslim holidays is *Eid al-Adha*, the Feast of Sacrifice. According to the Koran, Allah instructed Ibrahim to kill his son Ishmael. Just as Ibrahim was about to swing the ax to kill his son, a voice from Heaven stopped him. Ibrahim sacrificed a lamb instead, and now it is a tradition for families to slaughter a lamb and spit-roast it. (This story also appears in the Old Testament as the story of Abraham and Isaac and is part of the Jewish and Christian tradition.) This roast lamb, eaten with rice or other grains, is the highlight of a Muslim feast. Most people, however, have to settle for meat stew that is made with lamb, camel, or goat.

Yogurt cheese is a favorite of both Christians, who spread it on Easter bread, and Muslims, who eat it as an appetizer on toasted Arab flat bread (recipe page 69).

Labna
(also Labneh or Labanee)   **Yogurt Cheese**

Yield: about 1 cup
    2 cups plain yogurt
    salt to taste

Equipment: Strainer, cloth dinner napkin or cheesecloth, medium bowl, mixing spoon

1. Set strainer over medium bowl, and line it with cloth dinner napkin or double thickness of cheesecloth. Pour yogurt into cloth and set in refrigerator for at least 8 hours to drain until firm.

2. Discard drained liquid. Transfer cheese to small mixing bowl. Add salt to taste, and mix. Cover and refrigerate.

Serve labna *as a spread, or sprinkle with sugar and serve a dollop with fresh fruit for dessert.*

In Lebanon, cookie baking is an important part of Easter festivities. *Kâk bi halvîb* and *ma' amoul* (recipe page 64) are two favorites.

Kâk bi Halvîb   Easter Milk Cookies

Yield: about 24

    4 cups flour
    1 (¼-ounce) package active dry yeast
    ½ teaspoon ground anise
    ¼ teaspoon ground marjoram
    2 tablespoons olive oil
    7 tablespoons melted butter or margarine
    ¾ cup milk, more or less as needed
    1 cup sugar
    1 teaspoon almond extract

Equipment: Large mixing bowl, mixing spoon, small saucepan, kitchen towel, floured work surface, 3-inch **cookie cutter** or glass rim, lightly greased or nonstick baking sheet, oven mitts

1. In large mixing bowl, combine flour, yeast, anise, and marjoram. Continue stirring and slowly add oil and butter or margarine, a little at a time. Set aside.

2. Warm ¾ cup milk in small saucepan over low heat. Add sugar and stir until dissolved, about 1 minute. Remove from heat. Add almond extract, mix, and pour milk mixture into flour mixture. Using clean hands, form into a soft dough. Cover with towel and set dough in warm place for about 2 hours.

Preheat oven to 400° F.

3. Using palm of your hand, flatten dough to about ½ to ¾ inches thick on floured work surface. Using cookie cutter or rim of glass, press out disks and place them about 1½ inches apart on greased or nonstick baking sheet.

4. Put in oven and immediately reduce heat to 350°. Bake for 15 minutes until browned.

Serve cookies as a sweet treat with milk or tea.

During Muslim holidays like *Eid al-Fitr* and *Eid al-Adha*, it is a tradition for people to wear new clothes and visit with friends and relatives. Most like to bring small gifts, which very often are sweets like *teen mihshee*, stuffed figs.

Teen Mihshee   Stuffed Figs

Yield: makes 18 to 24

    1 cup orange juice
    juice of 1 lemon
    1 (12-ounce) package large dried figs (about
        18-24 to package)
    1 cup fondant (recipe page 45)
    18 to 24 walnut halves
    1 cup sugar

Equipment: Medium saucepan, **slotted spoon, colander**, paring knife, wax paper, baking sheet

1. In medium saucepan, mix orange and lemon juice. Add figs, and cook over medium heat until soft, about 30 minutes; stir frequently. Drain in colander and cool. Discard juice.

2. With paring knife, remove stems from dates and split open lengthwise down one side.

3. Stuff each fig with 1 teaspoon *fondant* and a walnut half. Use fingers to reshape fig. Roll in sugar and place side by side on wax-paper-covered baking sheet to dry out.

Serve stuffed figs as a sweet treat, or pack in a pretty box or tin and give as a holiday gift.

Jordan

The majority of Jordanians are Arabs, and most other ethnic groups who live in Jordan have adapted the Arab culture. One exception is Jordan's small Christian community, which makes up 5 percent of the population. All Muslim holidays are observed by Jordanians, and *Eid al-Fitr*, the feast at the end of month-long *Ramadan,* is the most joyous.

Yalanchi is a typical Middle Eastern stuffing for grape leaves, zucchini, eggplant, bell peppers, and tomatoes. Vegetables are always included in holiday feasts, along with dishes like Saudi Arabia's *tabbouleh* (recipe page 59) and Lebanon's yogurt cheese (recipe 55). To complete the feast, *yalanchi* is served with roasted lamb, salads, eggplant, custard sprinkled with almonds, and folded sheets of flat bread (recipe page 69).

Yalanchi   Stuffing for Tomatoes

Yield: serves 6

6 medium firm tomatoes
2 tablespoons olive oil, more or less as needed
1 medium onion, **finely chopped**
½ cup seedless raisins, soaked in warm water for 10 minutes and drained
½ cup pine nuts or finely chopped walnuts
1 tablespoon finely chopped fresh parsley or 1 teaspoon dried parsley flakes
½ teaspoon *each* ground allspice and ground cinnamon
1 tablespoon sugar
juice of 1 lemon
1 cup cooked rice
salt and pepper to taste

Equipment: Sharp knife, teaspoon, paper towels, work surface, large skillet, greased 9- to 12-inch baking pan

1. Slice about ½ inch off tops of tomatoes. Using teaspoon, scoop out pulp (discard or save for another use). Place 2 or 3 layers of paper towels on work surface. Turn tomatoes upside down on towels to drain.

2. Heat 2 tablespoons oil in large skillet over medium-high heat. Add onion, and, stirring con-

stantly, fry for about 3 minutes, until soft. Add raisins, nuts, parsley, allspice, cinnamon, sugar, and lemon juice, stir, and fry for 2 minutes. (Add more oil, if needed, to prevent sticking.) Add cooked rice and salt and pepper to taste. Mix well, and heat through, about 3 minutes. Remove from heat.

Preheat oven to 350° F.

3. Rub skin of tomatoes with olive oil and fill with rice mixture. Place filled tomatoes side by side in baking pan; any remaining filling can be spooned between tomatoes. Bake in oven for about 30 minutes, until tomatoes are tender but still firm.

Serve at room temperature for best flavor. This is an excellent dish to take on a picnic.

Saudi Arabia

The Islamic religion is the guiding force of Saudi Arabia, dictating the country's civil laws and monitoring its customs. Most laws and regulations have remained unchanged for hundreds of years.

Muslims have five duties, called the five pillars of Islam. First, they must believe and recite the creed, the *shahadah,* "There is no god but Allah, and Muhammad is his Prophet." The second duty is daily prayer, at least five times a day, facing toward Mecca. The third is giving money for the needy, called the *zakat.* The fourth is fasting during the month of *Ramadan.* The fifth duty is that all Muslims are expected to make the pilgrimage to Mecca once in their lifetime.

Mecca, in Saudi Arabia, is the Muslims' most sacred city. According to the Koran, the Islamic holy book, there is no more meaningful experience during a Muslim's lifetime than to make the pilgrimage to the Grand Mosque in Mecca and pray to Allah (God). Thousands of Muslims from all over the world come to Saudi Arabia for the yearly pilgrimage, called the *Hajj*. Men and women must separate and remain apart until the journey is completed. All pilgrims, from the poorest soul to the king, wear the *ihraam*, simple white robes, as a show of Muslim unity and that all men are equal in the eyes of Allah. Shoes are removed and feet washed before entering the mosque. Once inside, the pilgrims circle the *Ka'ba*, the cubic building surrounding the black stone, seven times, and they attempt to touch or kiss it as a symbol of loyalty to Allah, thus achieving the goal of a lifetime. The black stone represents the original House of God. Muslims believe it was built by Ibrahim and his son Ishmael.

After Mecca, the pilgrims go to the city of Miná, a short distance away, where they throw stones at the devil pillars. This is the place where Muslims believe the devil tried to tempt Ibrahim to refuse to sacrifice his son as God had commanded. In the end, God gave Ibrahim a ram to sacrifice instead.

The memory of that sacrifice survives in tradition, and during the pilgrimage the *hadjis* (pilgrims) visit other meaningful places in Muhammad's life. Part of the ritual is having a goat, sheep, camel, or cow butchered at the official slaughterhouse in Miná and giving the meat to the poor. This event is re-enacted by Muslims throughout the world in the Islamic festival of the *Eid al-Adha*.

After visiting the mosque and Miná, most pilgrims return to wearing their normal clothes, and they go on to Medina, Arabia's second holy city. The prophet Muhammad spent the last ten years of his life there after

idol worshipers, alarmed at his rising popularity, drove him and a handful of followers from his native Mecca. The Muslim calendar dates begin from the year of his *Hegira* (flight) in A.D. 622.

In the Middle East, thick soups are eaten at most holiday celebrations. During the *Hajj*, many pilgrims make a meal of *shobat bazeela* (recipe follows), *tabbouleh* (recipe follows), and *kimaje*, Arab flat bread (recipe page 69). They often wash it down with a glass of *lassi* (recipe page 70).

Shobat Bazeela — Vegetable and Lentil Soup

Yield: serves 4 to 6

- 6 cups water
- 1¼ cups dried lentils (any color can be used)
- 1 onion, **finely chopped**
- 3 cloves garlic, finely chopped, or 1 teaspoon garlic granules
- 2 potatoes, **peeled**, and cut into bite-size pieces
- 1 rib celery, finely chopped
- 2 zucchini, cut into ½-inch slices
- 1 teaspoon ground cumin
- salt and pepper to taste
- 2 lemons, cut into wedges, for serving

Equipment: **Dutch oven** or medium saucepan with cover, mixing spoon

1. Pour water into Dutch oven or medium saucepan. Add lentils, onion, and garlic, stir, and bring to a boil over high heat. Reduce heat to simmer, cover, and cook for 15 minutes.

2. Stir in potatoes, celery, zucchini, cumin, and salt and pepper (to taste). Cook uncovered for about 20 minutes until potatoes and lentils are tender.

To serve, ladle into individual soup bowls and sprinkle with lemon juice.

Bulgur is a nutty-textured, parboiled cereal. Some form of bulgur is eaten in all holiday feasts, including this recipe for *tabbouleh*, a bulgur (cracked wheat) salad.

Tabbouleh   Cracked Wheat Salad

Yield: serves 6

- 1½ cups fresh parsley, stems removed, washed and drained
- 1 cup bulgur (cracked wheat—available at most supermarkets and all Middle East and health food stores)
- 2 cups boiling water
- ½ cup chopped, **trimmed**, and washed green onions
- 3 tomatoes, trimmed and **finely chopped**
- 2 teaspoons crushed dried mint leaves
- ½ cup fresh lemon juice
- ¼ cup olive oil, more or less as needed
- salt and pepper to taste

Equipment: Sharp knife, or scissors, work surface, medium mixing bowl, small mixing bowl, strainer, mixing spoon

1. Finely chop parsley on work surface or finely cut with a scissors. Place chopped parsley in medium mixing bowl.

2. Place bulgur in small mixing bowl, cover with boiling water, and soak for 30 minutes. Drain bulgur in strainer, and, using clean hands, squeeze out excess water and add to parsley in medium mixing bowl.

3. Add onions, tomatoes, mint, lemon juice, ¼ cup oil, and salt and pepper (to taste) to bulgur mixture. Toss well, and add more oil, if necessary, to coat mixture. Cover and refrigerate for at least 1 hour.

Serve as a salad or side dish. The flavor is best when served at room temperature.

Iraq

Two ethnic groups, the Arabs and Kurds, make up Iraq's large Muslim population, although the Kurds are vastly outnumbered. Only about 5 percent of the people are Christians. The Muslims devoutly observe all religious holidays; the feast after the month of fasting for *Ramadan, Eid al-Fitr,* is the biggest celebration.

The foods that might be served at *Eid al-Fitr* are similar to those eaten throughout the Middle East for important occasions. For instance, almost every family would include dishes such as Egypt's *koushry* (lentils and rice, recipe page 49), Jordan's *yalanchi* (stuffed vegetables, recipe page 57), and, of course, the Arabian Peninsula's *hummus bi tahina* (**chick-pea** spread, recipe page 68).

Many households keep pastries, desserts, and candies on hand as an energy-boosting snack, to satisfy a sweet tooth, to eat at teatime, or to give as a gift when visiting friends. Only fruits, never sweets, are eaten at the end of a meal. Candied orange, lemon, or grapefruit peels (recipe page 137) are very popular throughout the Middle East. In Iraq, candied orange peel is called *g'shur purtaghal.* Another popular candy in Iraq is *locum,* Turkish delight (recipe page 66).

This recipe for *shirini,* a Kurdish pumpkin pudding, is a typical Middle Eastern treat, sweet and syrupy. If fresh pumpkin isn't available, squash or yams can be used instead.

Shirini   Kurdish Pumpkin Pudding

Yield: serves 4 to 6
- 1½ cups sugar
- 1 cup water
- ½ teaspoon ground **ginger**
- ½ teaspoon ground cinnamon
- 3 to 4 cups bite-size pieces **peeled** and **seeded** fresh pumpkin, or squash, or peeled yams
- ½ cup **coarsely chopped** walnuts, for **garnish**
- 1 cup thawed, frozen whipped topping, or yogurt, for garnish

Equipment: Medium saucepan with cover, wooden mixing spoon

In medium saucepan, combine sugar, water, ginger, and cinnamon. Bring to a boil over high heat, add pumpkin or squash or yams, and stir. Reduce heat to low, cover, and cook for about 20 minutes. Remove cover, and cook for about 10 minutes, until almost all the syrup is absorbed and pumpkin or squash or yams is tender. Stir frequently to prevent sticking.

To serve, spoon into individual bowls and sprinkle with chopped walnuts. Garnish with a dollop of whipped topping or yogurt.

The Iraqis take great pride in their children, especially the child's reading of the Koran (the Islamic holy book). Muslim children begin reading the Koran at a very early age, and when they are ready for the *Al' Khatma* (the reading), it is a very solemn ceremony; the boys read to the men, and the girls read to the women. The children who read without error earn the title of *Haftz*. After the readings, the men have a special luncheon for the boys, and the women have a tea for the girls. The afternoon is spent honoring the *Haftz* (children who read the Koran perfectly) with gifts and

money. There are singing and games as well as plenty to eat, such as fresh fruit and sweets, among them *tamur ou rashi* (recipe follows) and *locum* (recipe on page 66).

Dates are called the "candy that grows on trees." This simple recipe, *tamur ou rashi*, is popular throughout the Middle East.

Tamur ou Rashi Tahini with Dates

Yield: serves 4 to 6
- 2 to 3 dozen pitted dates
- 1 cup *tahini*, homemade (recipe page 68), or bottled (available at Middle East food stores)

Serve tahini in a small bowl with a dish of pitted dates. The dates are dipped into the tahini before popping into your mouth.

Iran

Most Iranians are Muslims belonging to the Shiite branch of Islam. It is the official state religion, and it dominates all aspects of life. All the Islamic holidays are national holidays in Iran, and religious customs are followed very carefully.

For all Muslims, Friday is the day of the Sabbath and a day of rest. If you invite friends and relatives for lunch, they start arriving right after breakfast, and many will stay six or seven hours. They remove their shoes when they enter the house, and it is traditional for hosts to have all sizes of pajamas to give guests so that they can be comfortable.

Iranian meals are traditionally served on a *sofreh*, a cotton cover embroidered with prayers and poems. It is spread over a Persian carpet around which everyone sits while eating. Iranians eat with their right hand, since the left must never touch food, as it is used for personal grooming.

Hot tea is prepared early each morning in the *samovar* (a metal urn to heat tea) and stays on all day. The sabbath lunch would probably be *kateh* and *salata* with *taratoor* (recipes follow) or *yalanchi* (recipe page 57). Flat bread like *kimaje* (recipe page 69) is served with every meal.

After lunch, everyone has sweet hot tea, and then the men usually nap for an hour or so. When they wake, they have tea and start eating the leftovers from lunch. The Sabbath supper is similar to lunch, but people eat late in the evening, about 9 P.M.

One holiday celebration that predates the introduction of Islam is *Nou Ruz*, the Iranian New Year. The holiday, unique to Iran, begins at the moment the sun reaches the sign of Aries in the zodiac. It is the custom for Iranian families to wait for that moment gathered around the *Haft Sen* or Seven Ss; the *Haft Sen* is a table adorned with food and symbols appropriate to the occasion (in Persian, the names of the seven symbolic foods begin with the letter S or Sen—*sabayeh*, sprouted seeds; *sonbul*, hyacinth; *samanook*, sweet wheat pudding; *serkeh*, vinegar; *sumac*, powdered leaves; *seeb*, apples; and *senjed*, olives). They also place several eggs on a mirror which, according to legend, jiggles at the instant the new year arrives. According to an ancient Persian myth, the earth is supported on one horn of a bull, and every year the bull tosses the burden to its other horn to gain a little relief from the weight of the world. When the eggs respond to the mighty toss of the bull's horn, the earth moves and the new year begins. *Nou Ruz* lasts for 13 days; schools are closed, gifts and greetings are exchanged, and mountains of sweets are eaten. The nationwide party traditionally ends in day-long picnics on the last day of *Nou Ruz*.

Rice is eaten at almost every meal, and golden rice cakes, called *kateh*, are ideal to pack in the picnic basket.

Kateh   Golden Rice Cake

Yield: serves 6 to 8
  2½ cups water
  1 cup milk
  2 cups rice
  1 teaspoon salt
  2 tablespoons butter or margarine

Equipment: Medium saucepan with cover, mixing spoon, 10-inch skillet with cover (preferably nonstick), wide metal **spatula**

1. Pour water and milk into medium saucepan, and bring to a boil over high heat. Stir in rice and salt, and bring back to boil. Reduce heat to **simmer**, cover, and cook for 20 minutes. Remove pan from heat, but keep covered for 10 minutes.

2. Melt 2 tablespoons butter or margarine in 10-inch skillet over medium heat, and add cooked rice. Using backside of metal spatula, press down on rice to fill pan; smooth top and make as compact as possible. Cover and cook over medium-low heat for about 1 hour, or until rice is firm and a golden brown crust has formed on the bottom side. Using spatula, press down on rice occasionally while it is cooking. The top edges of rice will lightly brown.

3. Uncover rice and cool to warm. Invert serving platter over skillet, and, holding both tightly together, flip over so that cake drops onto platter.

To serve, warm in oven or microwave or serve cold. To eat, cut into wedges.

Salads are popular with all meals, and they are always included in holiday feasts. The next two recipes for a salad and dressing are typical Iranian recipes.

Taratoor   Salad Dressing

Yield: about 1¼ cups
- juice of 2 lemons, strained
- ½ cup *tahini,* homemade (recipe page 68) or bottled (available at some supermarkets and all Middle East stores)
- 3 cloves garlic, **finely chopped** or 1 teaspoon garlic granules
- ¼ cup water
- ½ teaspoon ground cumin
- salt to taste

Equipment: Medium mixing bowl, egg beater or electric mixer

Put lemon juice in medium mixing bowl, and add *tahini,* garlic, water, and cumin. Using egg beater or electric mixer, mix until smooth and well blended. Add salt to taste, and mix well.

Serve as salad dressing and toss with fresh vegetable salad (recipe follows). Taratoor *keeps for several weeks if covered and refrigerated.*

Salata   Mixed Vegetable Salad

Yield: serves 6
- 4 tomatoes, **peeled, cored,** and cut each into 6 wedges
- 1 cucumber, peeled and thinly sliced
- 1 onion, thinly sliced
- 1 green pepper, cored, **seeded,** and finely sliced into strips
- ½ cup *taratoor* dressing, more if necessary (recipe precedes)
- salt and pepper to taste

Equipment: Medium salad bowl, salad mixing tools

1. In medium salad bowl, combine tomatoes, cucumber, onion, and green pepper.

2. Mix *taratoor* dressing before adding to salad. Add salt and pepper to taste, and, using salad tools, gently toss to coat vegetables with ½ cup dressing. Add a little more dressing, if necessary.

Serve salad at room temperature for best flavor.

Cyprus

The overwhelming majority of people calling Cyprus home are of Greek and Turkish origin. The Greek and Turkish Cypriots share many customs, but they maintain distinct identities based on religion, language, and close ties with their respective motherland. More than 80 percent of all Cypriots are Greek, and they observe all Greek Orthodox holidays. The Turkish Cypriot community celebrates Muslim holidays.

In 1983, the Turkish Cypriots declared their independence by forming the Turkish Republic of Northern Cyprus. This arrangement is recognized only by Turkey, and the differences between the Turkish and Greek Cypriots are still unresolved. In the last few years, United Nations negotiations have been taking place to work out a suitable agreement between both communities.

For the Muslims, *Seker Bayrami*, the "Festival of Sugar," also called *Ramazan Bayrami*, is a three-day national holiday after the month-long fasting of *Ramadan*. (*Seker Bayrami* is what Turkish people call *Eid al-Fitr*; see section on Turkey for more recipes.) Children are given gifts of candy and money. Greeting cards are exchanged, and families gather for the holiday feast.

In the Greek Orthodox Church, Easter is the most important holiday, and the traditional feast is always whole roasted lamb. The Easter soup that is traditionally served is a complicated recipe made with the liver, brain, intestines, and head of the lamb to be roasted. This recipe is a simplified version that uses lamb bones and lean meat.

Mayeritsa   Easter Soup

Yield: serves 4 to 6
  2 small meaty lamb bones (about ½ to ¾ pound)
  1 pound lean lamb, **coarsely chopped**
  8 cups water
  1 onion, **finely chopped**
  3 celery ribs, **trimmed** and finely chopped
  ¼ cup finely chopped fresh parsley or dried parsley
  ½ cup rice
  3 **egg yolks**, beaten
  1 tablespoon cornstarch
  1 cup milk
  juice of ½ lemon
  salt and pepper to taste

Equipment: Large saucepan with cover, mixing spoon, small bowl

1. Put lamb bones and meat in large saucepan, and cover with water. Add onion and celery, and bring to a boil over high heat. Stir and reduce heat to simmer. Cover and cook for about 1 hour. (Occasionally skim **froth** and fat from surface during cooking and discard.)

2. Add parsley and rice, stir, cover, and cook for about 25 minutes until rice is tender.

3. In small bowl, mix egg yolks, cornstarch, and milk until smooth and lump-free. Stirring constantly, slowly add mixture to lamb soup, and cook uncovered for about 5 minutes. Remove soup from heat, and add lemon juice and salt and pepper to taste. Stir and serve.

To serve, ladle hot soup into individual soup bowls.

Greek and Turkish Cypriots love bread, and a feast without bread is no feast at all. The following recipe for Turkish bread rings, called *simi,* is easy to make using frozen bread dough.

Simi   Turkish Bread Rings

Yield: 3 rings
  1 (1-pound) loaf of frozen white bread dough (thaw according to directions on package)
  1 egg
  2 tablespoons water
  ¼ cup sesame seeds

Equipment: 2 greased or nonstick baking sheets, small bowl, fork, **pastry brush**, kitchen towel, oven mitts

1. Divide thawed loaf into 3 pieces. Roll and pull a piece between the palms of your floured hands into a 15-inch rope. Moisten ends and pinch together into a ring (about 5 inches across). Place ring on greased or nonstick baking sheet. Continue making 2 more rings, and place side by side on second baking sheet; allow about 2 inches between rings.

2. In small bowl, mix the egg and water with a fork. Brush egg mixture on tops of bread rings, and sprinkle with sesame seeds. Cover with towel, and set in warm place to double in size, about 30 minutes.

Preheat oven to 375° F.

3. Bake in oven for about 30 minutes, until golden brown.

Serve with the holiday feast. Simi are especially good for breaking into chunks and dunking into soup.

Ma'amoul is one of the rich pastries made famous by the Turks, and almost every Middle Eastern baker prepares them for the holidays. These cookies are also a Greek Easter specialty.

Ma'amoul — Filled Cookies

Yield: about 20 pieces

½ cup **finely chopped** nuts, such as walnuts, almonds, or pistachios

½ cup sugar

1 teaspoon ground cinnamon

2 cups all-purpose flour, more if necessary

½ cup melted butter or margarine

1 teaspoon vanilla extract

3 tablespoons water, more if necessary

2 to 3 tablespoons confectioners' sugar, for **garnish**

Equipment: Small mixing bowl, mixing spoon, flour **sifter**, large mixing bowl with cover, knife, lightly greased or nonstick cookie sheet, oven mitts

1. Prepare filling: In small mixing bowl, mix nuts, sugar, and cinnamon; set aside.

2. Prepare dough: **Sift** 2 cups flour into large mixing bowl. Make a well in the center of the flour, and add melted butter or margarine, vanilla, and 3 tablespoons water. Using clean hands, mix into a smooth dough that holds together. If dough doesn't hold together, add a little more water. If dough is sticky, add a little more flour. Cover and refrigerate for 1 hour.

Preheat oven to 325° F.

3. Assemble: Pinch off golf-ball-size pieces of dough. Holding the ball in the palm of one hand, use fingers of the other hand to form the dough into a cup-shape. Fill cup with about 1 teaspoon nut mixture. Enclose filling, rub a damp finger over edges of cookie dough, and seal closed. After filling and sealing a cookie ball, flatten slightly and place seam-side down on lightly greased or nonstick cookie sheet. Repeat until all cookies are made.

4. Bake in oven for about 25 minutes until golden, but **not** brown. Cool to room temperature. (The cookies harden as they cool.) Sprinkle warm cookies with confectioners' sugar.

Serve cookies as a sweet treat during the holidays or wrap in waxed tissue and pack in box or tin to give as a holiday gift.

Turkey

Turkey sits at the crossroads of two continents, Europe and Asia, where Western and Eastern, and new and old cultures mesh together. For example, in many Turkish cities the newest hi-tech public-address systems call Muslims to prayer throughout the day. Business and civic holidays are in sync with the Western world, while religious observances follow ancient Islamic traditions.

The majority of Turks are Muslims, and one of their most important holidays is the Sacrificial Feast, *Kurban Bayrami*, known as *Eid al-Adha* elsewhere in the Islamic world. The celebration is often compared to Christmas with parties and the exchange of greeting cards.

The holiday commemorates Ibrahim's (Abraham's) near-sacrifice of his son Ishmael (Isaac) to God. At the last moment God told Ibrahim to sacrifice a ram instead. (This is the same story that appears in the Old Testament.) Many Turkish families follow the ancient ritual of slaughtering a goat or lamb and then sharing the meat with the poor.

No one goes away hungry from a Turkish feast, which includes a hearty soup such as the following recipe *domatesli mercimek corbasi*, a lentil soup.

Domatesli Mercimek Corbasi

Turkish Lentil Soup

Yield: serves 6 to 8
  1 cup dried lentils
  7 cups canned beef broth
  3 cups canned tomato juice
  1 onion, **finely chopped**
  3 cloves garlic, finely chopped, or 1 teaspoon garlic granules
  2 tablespoons finely chopped fresh parsley or 1 tablespoon dried parsley flakes
  3 bay leaves
  salt and pepper to taste

Equipment: **Dutch oven** or large saucepan with cover, mixing spoon

1. In Dutch oven or large saucepan, combine lentils, beef broth, tomato juice, onion, garlic, parsley, and bay leaves. Bring to a boil over high heat, and stir. Reduce heat to **simmer** and cover.

2. Cook until lentils are tender, about 40 minutes. Add salt and pepper to taste, stir, and remove from heat. Remove and discard bay leaves before serving.

Serve hot soup in individual bowls with chunks of crusty bread for sopping.

Along with the roast lamb, **pilafs** are popular and served as side dishes at most holiday feasts.

Bulgur Pilavi

Cracked Wheat Pilaf

Yield: serves 4 to 6
  4 tablespoons butter or margarine
  1 onion, **finely chopped**
  1 cup bulgur (cracked wheat—available at most supermarkets and health food stores and all Middle East food stores)
  3 cups water or canned beef broth
  salt to taste

Equipment: Large skillet with cover, mixing spoon

1. Melt 2 tablespoons butter or margarine in large skillet over medium-high heat. Add onion, and, stirring constantly, fry until soft, about 3 minutes. Add bulgur and remaining 2 tablespoons butter or margarine, and fry for another minute, stirring constantly to coat well.

2. Stir in water or broth, and bring to a boil. Reduce heat to **simmer**, cover, and cook for about 25 minutes until bulgur is tender. Add salt to taste, and stir well.

Serve in a bowl while warm.

As a rule, Turkish cooks add spices and seasonings with a heavy hand, and a salad such as *cacik* is very refreshing. *Cacik* is served at holidays like *Kurban Bayrami* and *Seker Bayrami*.

Cacik

Turkish Cucumber Salad

Yield: serves 4
  1 cup plain yogurt
  2 tablespoons **finely chopped** fresh mint leaves or 1 teaspoon dried mint leaves
  juice of ½ lemon

1 clove garlic, finely chopped, or ½ teaspoon
    garlic granules
¼ teaspoon salt
1 cucumber, **peeled** and finely sliced

Equipment: Medium mixing bowl, mixing spoon

1. In medium mixing bowl, mix yogurt, mint leaves, lemon juice, garlic, and salt until well blended.

2. Add cucumber slices, toss to coat, and refrigerate until ready to serve.

Serve cold, as a side dish at the holiday feast.

The Muslim holiday *Eid al-Fitr* is called *Seker Bayrami* in Turkey, meaning the "Festival of Sugar." Children are the focus of this family celebration, and they are given money and candy such as *locum. Locum* is a popular Turkish candy that has been enjoyed throughout the Middle East for generations.

Locum   Turkish Delight Candy

Yield: about 60 pieces
    3 envelopes unflavored gelatin
    1½ cups water
    2 cups sugar
    3 tablespoons white corn syrup
    ¾ cup cornstarch
    juice of 1 lemon
    1 cup **coarsely chopped** nuts: pistachio,
        almonds, or walnuts
    ¾ cup confectioners' sugar, more or less as
        needed, for coating

Equipment: Cup, medium saucepan, wooden mixing spoon, **candy thermometer** (optional), 8-inch-square cake pan, aluminum foil, knife, small bowl

1. Sprinkle gelatin into ½ cup water, and set aside to soften for about 5 minutes.

2. Pour another ½ cup water into medium saucepan, and bring to a boil over medium-high heat.

Add sugar and corn syrup, and stir until sugar dissolves, about 1 minute. Continue cooking until mixture reaches 240° F. on candy thermometer, or until it forms a soft ball when ½ teaspoon of mixture is dropped into a cup of cold water. Reduce heat to medium.

3. Dissolve cornstarch in remaining ½ cup water, and mix well. Add to sugar mixture, and, stirring constantly, **simmer** slowly until very thick, about 3 minutes; remove from heat. Add lemon juice and gelatin mixture, and stir until gelatin dissolves. Add nuts and stir thoroughly.

4. Line bottom and sides of 8-inch cake pan with foil. Sprinkle with thick layer of confectioners' sugar. Pour in candy, and do not move for about 4 hours, until jelled. Sprinkle with confectioners' sugar, and refrigerate at least 4 more hours, or until firm.

5. Cut into 1-inch squares, and roll each piece in confectioners' sugar to coat all sides.

Serve as a sweet treat or give as a gift, packed in box or tin. Place candies in layers, with pieces of wax paper, lightly dusted with confectioners' sugar, between layers.

Arabian Peninsula

Kuwait, Oman, Qatar, the United Arab Emirates, and Yemen are tiny countries on the Arabian peninsula, and all share borders with Saudi Arabia. Although each country is a separate entity, they share a cultural heritage, including food.

Kuwait

The majority of people living in Kuwait are Muslim, although there is a very small Christian community. All Muslim holidays are observed, including the feast after *Ramadan*, *Eid al-Fitr*.

Oman

The official language in Oman is Arabic, and more than 75 percent of the people are Muslim. There are, however, a great many Hindu expatriates who came as workers from India, Pakistan, Bangladesh, and Sri Lanka. The Hindu holidays are observed in solemn prayer and with family gatherings. Every family prepares *ghee* (recipe page 160) to cook with and to burn in the *dipa* lamps during the joyous holiday, *Diwali*. (See India, page 159.)

Qatar

In Qatar, more than 40 percent of the population is Arab, 36 percent is of Indian/Pakistani origin, and there is a sizable Iranian (Persian) community. More than 95 percent of the people are Muslims and observe all Islamic holidays.

United Arab Emirates

Ninety percent of the people living in the United Arab Emirates are Muslims, although only about 20 percent of the population are Emiri citizens. Among the remaining 10 percent are Catholics from the Philippines and Hindus from Pakistan and India. Each group observes its religious holidays in solemn prayer and family gatherings, with no showy processions or pageantry.

Yemen

In Yemen the overwhelming number of people are Arabs, and Arabic is universally spoken. For hundreds of years there has been little change. Most families live in the same villages and towns as their ancestors, and every aspect of life is dominated by the Muslim religion. Following tradition, a lamb is slaughtered for Muslim holidays and is eaten with grains or rice. As in many Muslim countries, one of the most important holidays in Yemen is *Eid al-Fitr*, the feast after *Ramadan*.

The next two recipes, *tahini* and *hummus bi tahina,* are important staples found in the kitchens of homes throughout the Middle East. *Tahini* is used in many recipes, such as sauces and spreads. It is a basic ingredient in *hummus bi tahina,* which is a spread used in the same way as butter or margarine is in the Western world. A dish of *hummus bi tahina* is always on the dinner table for important Muslim feasts, among them *Eid al-Fitr* and *Eid al-Adha,* the Feast of Sacrifice.

A good quality *tahini* is available at all Middle Eastern food stores, but you may want to try the following recipe.

Tahini   Sesame Paste

Yield: about 1 cup
　½ cup sesame seeds (available at Middle
　　Eastern and health food stores)
　2 teaspoons lemon juice
　1 teaspoon vegetable oil
　2 tablespoons water
　2 tablespoons olive oil, more or less as needed,
　　for **garnish** (optional)

Equipment: Electric **blender** or nut grinder, rubber **spatula** or mixing spoon, small bowl

1. Put sesame seeds in electric blender or nut grinder and grind until smooth and lump-free.

2. Transfer to small bowl, and add lemon juice, vegetable oil, and water; mix to a smooth paste. Cover and refrigerate.

To serve tahini, *mound on a small plate and* **drizzle** *with olive oil. It can be used as a spread for crackers or a dip for raw vegetables.*

Tahini *is also added to many Middle Eastern recipes. Covered and refrigerated,* tahini *keeps well for several months.*

In this next recipe, a **food processor** works best, but the ingredients can be mashed using a **mortar and pestle**, **food mill**, fork, or a strainer.

Hummus bi Tahina

Yield: about 2 cups
　2 cups cooked **chick-peas**, homemade or
　　canned, drained (save liquid)
　3 cloves garlic, **finely chopped,** or 1 teaspoon
　　garlic granules
　3 tablespoons *tahini* (sesame paste), homemade
　　(recipe precedes) or bottled (available at
　　some supermarkets and all Middle East food
　　stores)
　juice of 2 lemons
　salt to taste
　¼ teaspoon paprika, for **garnish**
　2 tablespoons fresh parsley, finely chopped, or
　　1 tablespoon dried parsley flakes, for garnish

Equipment: **Mortar and pestle**, electric **blender**, or **food processor**; rubber **spatula**, small plastic container with cover

1. Mash chick-peas, using mortar and pestle, blender, or food processor until smooth and lump-free, adding just enough reserved liquid (about ¼ to ½ cup) to make the mixture resemble the texture of mashed potatoes.

2. Continue mashing, add garlic, *tahini,* lemon juice, and salt to taste. Blend well. Transfer to small

plastic container, cover, and refrigerate until ready to serve.

To serve, mound hummus *on a small plate, and sprinkle with paprika and parsley, for garnish.*

The Arabic word for flat bread, *kimaje,* means "open bread." *Kimaje* or similar flat bread is served with almost every meal. The bread is torn apart, and the pieces are used as a scoop to transport the food from the bowl to one's mouth. The bread is eaten not only at every meal, but also for all Muslim feast days, among them *Eid al-Fitr,* the feast after *Ramadam,* and *Eid al-Adha,* the Feast of the Sacrifice. A favorite way to eat *kimaje* is to scoop up a little *hummus bi tahina* on it.

Kimaje   Arab Flat Bread

Yield: 6 pieces of bread
- 1 package active dry yeast
- 1¼ cups lukewarm water, more as needed
- 1 tablespoon vegetable oil
- ½ teaspoon sugar
- ½ teaspoon salt
- 3½ cups all-purpose flour, more or less as needed

Equipment: Large mixing bowl, mixing spoon, lightly floured work surface, 3 kitchen towels, lightly floured **rolling pin**, 3 cookie sheets, oven mitts

1. In large mixing bowl, dissolve yeast in 1¼ cups warm water. Add oil, sugar, salt, and 2 cups flour, and beat with mixing spoon until smooth. Add just enough of remaining 1½ cups flour to make a nonsticky, easy-to-handle dough.

2. Transfer dough to lightly floured work surface, and **knead** until smooth and elastic, about 10 minutes.

3. Transfer dough to lightly oiled, large mixing bowl, and move dough around bowl to grease all sides. Cover bowl with towel, and set in warm place until dough doubles in size, about 1 hour. (Dough is ready when the indention from a finger poke remains.)

4. **Punch down** dough, transfer to floured work surface, and divide into 6 equal-size balls. Place balls side by side on work surface, cover with towel, and let rise for 30 more minutes.

5. Using lightly floured rolling pin or palm of hand, flatten each ball into a 6-inch disk, about ⅛-inch thick. Using 3 cookie sheets, place 2 disks on each, allowing space between them so they can rise without touching. Cover with towels and let rise for another 30 minutes.

Preheat oven to 450° F.

6. Bake in oven for about 10 minutes, or until golden brown and puffed.

Serve flat breads warm. The bread is used to scoop up sauces and stews

Cold dishes, such as this recipe, are the salads at Muslim feasts. They are eaten with *chirkasia* (recipe page 50) for *Eid al-Fitr* and with spit-roasted lamb or chicken for *Eid al-Adha.*

Marinated Chick-peas

Yield: serves 6 to 8
- 2 (12- to 15-ounce each) cans of **chick-peas**
- 1 **finely chopped** onion
- 3 cloves garlic, minced, or 1 teaspoon garlic granules
- ½ cup finely chopped green onions
- ¼ cup vinegar
- 1 tablespoon sugar
- ¼ cup vegetable oil
- salt and white pepper to taste

Equipment: **Colander**, medium mixing bowl or large plastic baggie, mixing spoon

1. Put chick-peas in colander and rinse under cold water. Drain well.

2. In medium mixing bowl or large baggie, mix chick-peas, onion, garlic, green onions, vinegar, sugar, oil, and salt and pepper to taste. Cover or tightly seal, refrigerate; stir or rotate bag several times before serving.

Serve at room temperature for best flavor.

Lassi is a hot weather drink that is both refreshing and nourishing. After hours in prayer, a glass of *lassi* renews one's strength.

Lassi   Iced Yogurt Drink

Yield: 1 drink
  ½ cup ice water
  ½ cup plain yogurt
  ½ glass ice cubes

Equipment: Electric **blender**

1. Put water and yogurt in a blender and blend until smooth.

2. Pour mixture over ice cubes

Serve as a refreshing and nourishing summer drink.

It is the custom in the Middle East during Muslim holidays to invite guests for tea, coffee, or *lassi* (recipe precedes), and serve them cookies, such as these apricot squares or the next recipe for **chick-pea** flour squares, *bereshtook nokhochi.*

Apricot Squares

Yield: 48 pieces
  2 cups (1 pound) butter or margarine, at room temperature
  1 cup sugar

1 **egg yolk**
1 teaspoon almond extract
2 cups all-purpose flour
1 cup **finely chopped** almonds or walnuts
1 cup or 8-ounce jar apricot jam

Equipment: Large mixing bowl, egg beater or electric mixer, mixing spoon lightly greased or nonstick 13- x 9- x 2-inch baking pan, **spatula**, oven mitts

Preheat oven to 350° F.

1. In large mixing bowl, use egg beater or electric mixer to mix butter or margarine with sugar until light and fluffy, about 3 minutes. Add egg yolk and almond extract, and mix well. Add flour, a little at a time, while mixing constantly. Add nuts, and mix well. Dough should be soft.

2. Spread half the dough evenly over bottom of greased or nonstick baking pan. Cover with layer of apricot jam. Drop remaining dough by spoonfuls over jam, and, using spatula or fingers, spread dough to partially cover jam, leaving some showing through.

3. Bake in oven for about 45 minutes, until top is golden. Cool to room temperature.

To serve cut into 1½-inch squares.

This next cookie recipe, *bereshtook nokhochi*, is very rich and tasty, but it is easy to make.

Bereshtook Nokhochi   Chick-pea
                                Flour Squares

Yield: 50 cookies
  2 cups (1 pound) butter or margarine
  4 cups **chick-pea** flour (available at all Middle East and health food stores)
  2 cups confectioners' sugar
  1 tablespoon ground cardamom
  3 tablespoons ground almonds or pistachio nuts (optional)

Equipment: Large skillet or saucepan, flour **sifter**, mixing spoon or **whisk**, lightly greased or non-stick 10- x 15-inch **jellyroll pan, spatula**, oven mitts

Preheat oven to 325° F.

1. Melt butter or margarine in large skillet or saucepan over medium heat. Reduce heat to warm, and sift in chick-pea flour, a little at a time, stirring constantly until smooth.

2. Remove from heat and add confectioners' sugar and cardamom; mix well.

3. Use spatula to spread mixture ¼ inch thick onto greased or nonstick jellyroll pan. Smooth top, and sprinkle with nuts.

4. Bake in oven for about 40 minutes, or until golden brown.

Serve when cool, cut into 1½ x 3 inch pieces.

Bahrain

Bahrain is series of islands, known as an archipelago, in the Persian Gulf. These islands are home to a large Muslim population, a few Christians, and a small indigenous Jewish community. Islamic laws govern the country, including dietary restrictions prohibiting pork or alcoholic beverages. Shops and businesses close for all Muslim holidays. As in many Islamic nations, the most important celebration is the feast of *Eid al-Fitr* at the end of *Ramadan*, the holy month of fasting.

For affluent Bahrainis, the grandest food at a holiday feast is *ghouzi*, whole roasted lamb stuffed with chicken, rice, and eggs. Others enjoy a lamb stew, such as this recipe.

Lamb with Dates

Yield: serves 6
- 6 tablespoons butter or margarine
- 2 pounds lean lamb, cut into bite-size chunks
- 1 onion, **finely chopped**
- 1 teaspoon ground turmeric
- 1 teaspoon ground cinnamon
- ½ teaspoons salt, more or less to taste
- 1 cup pitted dates, halved
- 3 tablespoons sugar
- 1 cup rice
- 2½ cups water
- 1 teaspoon **grated** lemon rind

Equipment: Dutch oven or large saucepan with cover, mixing spoon, **grater**, fork

1. Melt 4 tablespoons butter or margarine in Dutch oven or large saucepan over medium-high heat. Add lamb and onion, and, stirring constantly, fry until meat lightly browns, about 5 minutes. Add turmeric, cinnamon, ½ teaspoon salt (more or less to taste), dates, sugar, rice, and water. Stir well and bring to a boil.

2. Reduce heat to simmer, cover, and cook for about 25 minutes, until meat and rice are tender.

3. Add grated lemon rind and remaining 2 tablespoons butter or margarine, and fluff with a fork.

To serve, mound stew on a serving platter, and place it in the middle of the table. Everyone helps themselves using the fingers of the right hand.

Candy, such as this recipe for *lowzina b'shakar,* is a favorite midday snack. It is often given to friends and relatives as a gift during the Muslim holidays.

Lowzina B'shakar

White Sugar Candy

Yield: serves 8 to 10

1 cup sugar
½ cup water
½ teaspoon lemon juice
1 teaspoon rose water (optional—available at most pharmacies and all Middle East food stores)
1 cup ground **blanched** almonds
⅛ teaspoon ground cardamon

Equipment: Small saucepan, wooden mixing spoon, 8-inch square cake pan, aluminum foil

1. Mix sugar and water in a small saucepan. Stirring frequently, cook over medium heat until mixture forms threads when dropped from a spoon, about 8 minutes. Add lemon juice and rose water (optional), stir, and bring to a boil. Remove from heat, and, stirring frequently, cool to warm. Add ½ cup almonds, and beat with wooden spoon until mixture turns white.

2. Line bottom and sides of cake pan with foil. Add cardamom to remaining ½ cup almonds, and mix well. Spread half of the almond mixture over bottom of pan. Cover with candy mixture and spread smooth. Sprinkle with remaining almond mixture. Allow candy to cool for about 5 minutes and cut into 1-inch squares.

Serve as a sweet snack. Candy keeps well when refrigerated for several days in an airtight container.

Europe

In Europe, Christianity is the principal religion, although today most countries have sizable Jewish and Muslim communities. Hindus and Buddhists live in Europe in smaller numbers. Even though Christianity is the primary religion, there are differences between the various Christian branches—Protestant, Greek Orthodox, and Catholic. Most of the Protestants live in Scandinavia and northwestern Europe, while most Catholics and Orthodox followers live along the Mediterranean Sea and in Eastern Europe.

In most European countries, the major Christian observances are national holidays. Easter is generally considered the most important holiday for the Catholic and Orthodox churches. For Protestants, Christmas is the biggest celebration. Each country, however, has its own unique customs and rituals that have remained unchanged for centuries.

In fact, many European countries have ancient holiday traditions that have changed little since their primitive beginnings. There are symbolic foods related to the celebrations of the winter solstice (the shortest day of the year in the Northern Hemisphere) that predate Christianity by many years. One example is a mixed pudding of meats, fruits, and spices that was served to honor Dagda, the Druids' god of plenty. This mixture was the forerunner of the English pudding. French yule log cakes are another example. They are a reminder of the burning log in the fireplace that was used in pre-Christian winter solstice festivals to celebrate the return of the sun. The yule log cake is symbolic not only in France (recipe page 102) but also in Italy, where it is called *ceppo di natale;* in Lithuania, where it is known as *berzo saka;* in Norway, where it is called *julestamme;* and in England.

Breads, pastries, cakes, cookies, and candies are the most exciting, creative, and symbolic Christian holiday foods. The task of holiday baking has been a labor of love passed from generation to generation for centuries.

In Eastern Europe, eggs and breads are the heart of every holiday feast. The eggs, symbolic of life, are not only decorated for Easter, but hard-cooked for every holiday feast. Feast breads are works of art made into large rings, braids, or wreaths and decorated with birds and flowers shaped out of the dough.

Greece

Most Greeks are Orthodox Christians, and every holiday, from New Year's celebrations and civic holidays to birthdays, has some religious significance. Every community celebrates with traditional songs, pageants, and rituals, many of which are centuries old. The Orthodox church maintains a number of fast days or meatless days, and it is very strict about what can be eaten during Lent and Holy Week, which is the week before Easter. On Wednesdays and Fridays in Lent, and during Holy Week, meat, eggs, fish, and milk products are forbidden.

On Holy Thursday, Greek families get together and boil eggs and then dye them red to remind people of the blood of Christ. The eggs are then polished with olive oil until they shine. Eggs are supposed to be dyed only on Holy Thursday or Holy Saturday; coloring them on any other day, especially Holy Friday, is considered bad luck. Holy Friday, also called Good Friday, is the day the Easter bread, *lambropsoma* (recipe follows later in this section), is baked.

On some Greek islands, on Holy Saturday (the day before Easter Sunday) processions of people dress in their finest clothes and march through the village and into the sea to bless the waves. This is called Blessing-of-the-Waters Day.

Easter Sunday, however, is the most important holiday. Easter is a solemn but ultimately joyful holiday in Greece. The climax of the celebration begins with Saturday night services. Everyone brings a decorated candle to be lit during the liturgy. The glowing candle is then carried home to protect the family from the evil eye. Although services don't finish until the middle of the night, hungry parishioners hurry home to eat. Red Easter eggs are on the table, and each person cracks his or her egg against another person's egg for luck.

Traditional Easter soup, *mayeritsa*, is made with the head and innards of the lamb that is to be roasted for Easter Sunday dinner. For this recipe, lamb bones and lamb meat are substituted for the head and innards.

Mayeritsa   Easter Soup

Yield: serves 6

- 8 cups water
- 1 pound lamb bones, rinsed
- ½ pound lean lamb meat, cut into bite-size chunks
- 1 cup **trimmed** and coarsely sliced celery
- 1 cup trimmed, **peeled**, and coarsely sliced carrots
- 2 potatoes, peeled and cut into bite-size pieces
- 1 onion, **finely chopped**
- 1 tablespoon fresh, finely chopped dill or 1 teaspoon ground dill
- 4 tablespoons trimmed and finely chopped fresh parsley or 1 tablespoon dried parsley flakes
- ½ cup rice
- 1 tablespoon cornstarch
- 1 cup whole milk
- 3 **egg yolks**
- salt and pepper to taste
- juice of 1 lemon, strained

Equipment: **Dutch oven** or large saucepan with cover, mixing spoon, small mixing bowl, ladle

1. Pour water into Dutch oven or large saucepan, and add lamb bones and meat, celery, carrots, potatoes, onion, dill, and parsley. Stir and bring to a boil over high heat. Reduce heat to medium, and cook, uncovered, for about 30 minutes. Remove and discard froth and fat that forms on the surface during cooking. Add rice, and stir. Cover and **simmer** for 30 minutes.

2. In small mixing bowl, mix cornstarch, milk, and egg yolks. Add milk mixture and salt and pepper (to taste) to soup while stirring constantly. Simmer for 5 minutes. Remove from heat, add lemon juice, and stir well.

To serve, ladle hot soup into individual bowls.

The Greek Easter bread is usually either *tsoureki*, sweet bread, or *lambropsoma* (recipe follows). Holy Friday, or Good Friday, is the only day Easter bread may be baked. On Holy Saturday the freshly baked bread is placed in a napkin-lined basket filled with red Easter eggs and other foods, and then it is taken to the church to be blessed. The Holy Saturday supper includes the Easter bread, cheese, and *mayeritsa*, Easter soup (recipe precedes).

Lambropsoma   Greek Easter Bread

Yield: 1 loaf

> 2 (1-pound each) loaves frozen white bread (thaw according to directions on package); do not allow to rise
> 4 uncooked eggs in shell, tinted red with fast-color Easter egg dye
> **egg glaze**

Equipment: Floured work surface, greased or nonstick baking sheet, kitchen towel, **pastry brush**, oven mitts, wire rack

1. Put thawed loaves on floured work surface. Using clean hands, stretch each loaf into a rope about 24 inches long. Hold both dough ropes together at one end, and twist into one thick rope. On greased or nonstick baking sheet, form coiled rope into an oval-shaped circle. Brush both ends lightly with water, pinch together, and tuck under coil.

2. Evenly space eggs between coils of dough, and tuck them in deep (but still visible) so they will not be pushed out when dough rises. Cover with towel, and set in warm place to double in size, about 1 hour.

Preheat oven to 350° F.

3. Using pastry brush, coat bread with egg glaze. Bake in oven for about 1 hour, or until golden brown. Remove bread from oven and place on wire rack to cool.

Serve as the centerpiece on the dinner table. To eat, slice or break off chunks of bread. The eggs get hard-cooked in the oven, and so they can be **peeled** *and eaten.*

Baklava is a famous pastry that Greek cooks prepare to serve guests during every holiday. It is also very popular throughout the Middle East, where it is called *baglawa*.

Baklava   Nut Pastry

Yield: about 5 dozen pieces

> 2 cups *each* **finely chopped** almonds and walnuts
> ¾ cup sugar
> 3 tablespoons ground cinnamon
> 1 pound (1 box) frozen **phyllo pastry sheets**
> 1½ cups bread crumbs
> 1 cup melted butter or margarine, more or less as needed
> Syrup for *baklava* (recipe follows)

Equipment: Small mixing bowl, mixing spoon, work surface, sharp knife, buttered 10- x 15-inch baking pan, kitchen towel, pastry brush, oven mitts

Preheat oven to 350° F.

1. Mix nuts, sugar, and cinnamon together in small mixing bowl.

2. Remove phyllo from box. Unwrap and un-roll on work surface. Cut stack of phyllo to size of pan, 10 x 15 inches. Cover stack and scraps with damp towel to prevent drying out.

3. Spread one sheet of phyllo in buttered baking pan, generously brush with melted butter or margarine, and sprinkle lightly with crumbs. Repeat layering 7 more sheets of phyllo, brushing each one with melted butter or margarine and sprinkling with bread crumbs. (If sheets tear, simply repair them by overlapping with scrap pieces and brushing them with butter or margarine.) Spread half the nut mixture over phyllo. Layer 5 more sheets; brush each with butter or margarine and sprinkle with crumbs. Spread remaining nut mixture over phyllo, and continue layering remaining 7 or 8 sheets; brush each with melted butter or margarine and sprinkle with crumbs.

4. Brush top generously with melted butter or margarine, melting more if necessary.

5. Using a sharp knife, make 6 equally spaced cuts, lengthwise in pastry. Keep knife straight to slice through all layers. Use your free hand to guide knife and keep it from tearing pastry. To make diamond-shaped slices, begin at one corner of the pan and cut diagonally across to the opposite corner. Repeat making diagonal cuts (parallel with the first), beginning at each end of a lengthwise cut. All diagonal cuts run in the same direction. (See diagram.) Brush top again with melted butter or margarine.

6. Bake in oven for about 45 minutes, or until golden brown.

7. While still warm, spoon syrup evenly over top.

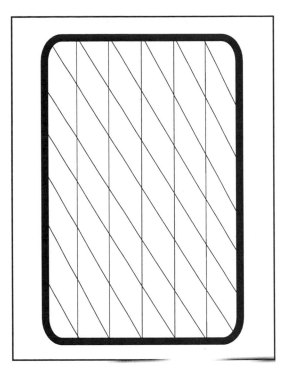

To serve, remove slices from pan along diamond marks. Baklava keeps well for up to a month if covered and refrigerated.

Syrup for Baklava

2 cups water
4 cups sugar
juice of 1 lemon, strained
1 small cinnamon stick

Equipment: Medium saucepan, wooden mixing spoon

In medium saucepan, mix water, sugar, lemon juice, and small cinnamon stick; mix until sugar dissolves. Bring to a boil over high heat. Reduce heat to **simmer**, and cook for about 20 minutes, or until thickened. Remove and discard cinnamon stick.

To continue, spread over baklava *(recipe precedes).*

Every Greek island seems to have its own special Easter dishes. On the island of Sifnos, this honey pie, *melopitta*, is a favorite Easter dessert.

Melopitta   Honey Pie

Yield: serves 8 to 10
  2 cups cottage cheese
  ½ cup cream cheese, at room temperature
  ½ cup sugar
  1 cup honey
  4 eggs, lightly beaten
  1 teaspoon almond extract
  ½ cup **coarsely chopped** almonds
  1 single prepared pie crust, homemade (recipe page 108) or frozen prepared pie crust, thawed
  1 teaspoon ground cinnamon, more or less as needed

Equipment: Large mixing bowl, mixing spoon or **food processor**, **whisk**, rubber **spatula**, 9-inch pie pan, oven mitts

Preheat oven to 350° F.

1. In large mixing bowl, use mixing spoon or food processor to mix cottage cheese, cream cheese, and sugar until well blended. Mixing constantly, add honey, eggs, and almond extract.

2. Using whisk or mixing spoon, **fold in** nuts.

3. Pour mixture into pie crust and bake in oven for about 45 minutes, until crust is golden brown and pie is set. When done, remove from oven and sprinkle with cinnamon.

To serve, cool to room temperature and cut into small wedges.

Albania

The majority of Albanians are Muslim, although there are sizable Roman Catholic and Christian Orthodox populations. For Muslims, the most important celebration is the feast of *Eid al-Fitr* at the end of the holy month of *Ramadan*. Everyone eagerly waits for the sighting of the new moon that signals when *Ramadan* is over. Like neighboring Greece, the most important Christian celebration is Easter. In Albania, the Greek Easter soup and *baklava* are prepared for both the Muslim *Eid al-Fitr* feast and the Christian Easter. In this part of the world, most dishes have crossed borders, including Bulgarian yogurt walnut soup (recipe page 79) and most Middle Eastern dishes.

Yogurt is very popular throughout Eastern Europe, and yogurt dishes accompany many feasts. The first thing many Christians eat at the end of Lent, and many Muslims eat at the end of *Ramadan* to break the fast, is yogurt soup. It nourishes the body, soothes the stomach, and revives the soul. For those who can afford it, the centerpiece of the Muslim feast is a whole roasted lamb, and for Christians it's either lamb or suckling pig.

Yogurt Soup

Yield: serves 6 to 8

4 cups chicken broth, homemade (recipe page 52) or canned

1 cup quick-cooking barley (available at most supermarkets and all health and Middle East food stores)

1 cup **finely chopped** onions

4 cups (2 pints) plain yogurt

1 egg

1 tablespoon all-purpose flour

½ cup finely chopped fresh **coriander**, parsley, or mint or ¼ cup dried coriander, parsley, or mint

salt and pepper to taste

Equipment: Medium saucepan with cover, mixing spoon, medium mixing bowl

1. Pour chicken broth into medium saucepan, and add quick-cooking barley and onion. Bring to a boil over high heat, and stir. Reduce heat to **simmer**, cover, and cook for about 30 minutes, until barley is tender.

2. In medium mixing bowl, mix yogurt, egg, and flour until smooth. Add yogurt mixture to chicken broth, a little at a time, while mixing constantly. Add coriander, parsley or mint, and salt and pepper to taste; mix and heat through, about 5 minutes.

Serve soup hot in individual bowls with plenty of crusty bread for sopping.

Bulgaria

Most Bulgarians belong to the Orthodox Christian Church, and Christian holidays in Bulgaria are observed with solemn processions and religious zeal. Since the country is no longer under communist rule, the people can once again worship freely. The most important celebration is Holy Week, climaxing with Easter.

The traditional Easter feast begins with soup, *tarator*, made with Bulgaria's two most famous products, yogurt and walnuts.

Tarator   Yogurt Walnut Soup

Yield: serves 4 to 6

4 cups plain yogurt

1 (about 6-inch) cucumber, **peeled** and **finely chopped**

½ cup olive oil

1 cup finely chopped or **ground** walnuts

1 clove garlic, finely chopped, or ½ teaspoon garlic granules

salt to taste

3 teaspoons finely chopped fresh parsley or 2 teaspoons dried parsley flakes, for **garnish**

Equipment: Electric **blender**, medium serving bowl or soup tureen, mixing spoon, soup ladle

1. Blend yogurt, cucumber, olive oil, walnuts, and garlic in blender at high speed until smooth. (It may take a couple of batches depending on the blender.)

2. Pour into medium serving bowl or soup tureen. Add salt to taste. Mix well and refrigerate for at least 2 hours before serving.

To serve, ladle cold soup into individual bowls and sprinkle each with parsley, for garnish.

Bread is eaten at almost every meal in Bulgaria, and for Easter dinner bird-of-paradise bread, *khliah raiska ptitsa*, is sure to be on the dinner table. This recipe has been simplified by using prepared frozen bread dough.

Khliah Raiska Ptitsa Bird-of-Paradise Bread

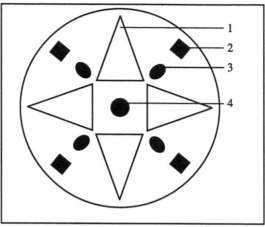

1. cheese, 2. ham, 3. olive, 4. pimento

Cut bread into thick slices, serving slightly warm for best flavor.

Yield: 1 loaf

2 (1-pound each) frozen loaves of white bread (thaw and let rise according to directions on package)

1 egg

1 tablespoon milk

1 (1-inch) piece red pimento, cut round, for decoration

4 slices (each ¼ inch thick) Münster or Swiss cheese, each cut into a 3-inch triangle, for decoration

4 pieces (each ¼ inch thick x 1 inch square) boiled ham, for decoration

4 pitted black olives, for decoration

Equipment: Lightly floured work surface, greased or nonstick baking sheet, cup, spoon, **pastry brush,** oven mitts

1. When the two loaves have risen (according to directions on package), transfer to lightly floured work surface. Using clean hands, **punch down** and **knead** the two loaves into one ball. Place on greased or nonstick baking sheet and shape into 8-inch round loaf.

2. Mix egg and milk in cup. Using pastry brush, brush egg mixture over surface of bread.

3. Decorate top of bread with a symmetrical design: Place pimento in the top center, like a bull's-eye. Place cheese triangles around the bull's-eye, making a 4-pointed star design. Place an olive and a square of ham, one above the other, in the space between the cheese in the star design and gently press in place. Repeat placing remaining 3 olives and 3 squares of ham exactly like the first. (See diagram.) Set loaf in warm place for about 40 minutes to double in bulk.

Preheat oven to 400° F.

4. Bake in oven for 15 minutes, and then reduce heat to 350° and bake for about 35 minutes more, until loaf is golden brown.

Romania

Most Romanians belong to the Romanian Orthodox Christian Church, but every region of the country observes holidays in its own special way. Many religious observances are held in connection with the rhythm of the agrarian calendar. For example, harvest time or the time of the departure of sheep to the mountains in the spring and their return in autumn are observed with religious processions and jubilation.

Easter is the most important national holiday, and it is steeped in ancient traditions. On the Sunday before Easter many people dress in their finest regional costumes, and they carry willow branches to church to be blessed. This is known throughout the Christian world as Palm Sunday, and it celebrates Jesus' entry into Jerusalem when people greeted him by waving palm branches. Today many churches give out and bless palms as part of the service, and in other countries, where palms are not easily available, worshipers bring pussy willows or other branches from home instead.

Mamaliga de Aur, a Romanian bread made of cornmeal mush, is a staple in Romanian homes, and it is eaten at almost every meal, especially holiday feasts. Because of its rich yellow color, it's called "bread of gold."

Mamaliga de Aur Romanian Bread of Gold

Yield: serves 4 to 6

4 cups water
1 cup coarsely ground yellow cornmeal
salt and pepper to taste

Equipment: Medium saucepan, mixing spoon, buttered cookie sheet, piece of string about 12 inches long

Pour water into medium saucepan, and bring to a boil over high heat. Stirring constantly, slowly add cornmeal. Reduce heat to low and cook for 15 minutes, stirring frequently, until mixture comes away from sides of pan. Remove from heat, add salt and pepper to taste, and mix well. Mound mixture into a round loaf in center of buttered cookie sheet, and cool to room temperature.

As the mamaliga *cools it becomes firm. In Romanian homes the corn bread is sliced by pulling a taut string through the round loaf.*

The first thing most Romanians like to eat after Easter Mass is a bowl of thick soup, such as this vegetable lentil soup.

Vegetable Lentil Soup

Yield: serves 6

3 to 6 tablespoons butter or margarine
2 carrots, **peeled** and thinly sliced
2 celery ribs, **trimmed** and thinly sliced
1 onion, **finely chopped**
1 cup lentils (preferably red)
8 cups water
1 cup tomato paste
salt and pepper to taste
½ teaspoon ground coriander
½ teaspoon curry powder
1 cup plain yogurt, more or less as needed, for serving

Equipment: **Dutch oven** or large saucepan with cover, mixing spoon, ladle

1. Melt 3 tablespoons butter or margarine in Dutch oven or large saucepan over medium-high heat. Add carrots, celery, and onion, and, stirring frequently, fry until soft, about 3 minutes.

2. Add lentils, water, tomato paste, salt and pepper to taste, coriander, and curry powder, and stir. Increase heat to high, and bring to a boil. Reduce heat to simmer, and stir. Cover and cook for about 45 minutes, until lentils are soft.

To serve, ladle soup into bowls, and top with a large dollop of yogurt.

The following recipe is a way of making *mamaliga*, the everyday mush, a little fancier for special occasions such as Easter and Christmas dinners.

Mamaliga Umpluta Cornmeal Mushroom Balls

Yield: serves 6 to 8

8 slices lean bacon
1 cup **finely chopped** mushrooms
salt and pepper to taste

4 cups water

2 cups cornmeal

2 eggs, beaten

½ cup melted butter or margarine or butter-flavored vegetable spray

1 cup sour cream, for serving

Equipment: Medium skillet, **slotted spoon**, paper towels, medium mixing bowl, medium saucepan, wooden spoon, greased 13- x 9-inch baking pan, oven mitts

1. In medium skillet, fry bacon over medium-high heat until crisp and **rendered**, about 3 minutes. Remove bacon with slotted spoon and drain on paper towels. Save the drippings.

2. Add mushrooms to skillet with bacon drippings, and, stirring constantly, fry over medium-high heat, until soft, about 3 minutes. Remove mushrooms with slotted spoon, and drain well over skillet; transfer to medium mixing bowl. Crumble bacon, and add to mushrooms. Add salt and pepper to taste, mix, and set aside.

3. Bring water to a boil over high heat in medium saucepan. Stirring constantly, add cornmeal, a little at a time, so boiling doesn't stop; stir until smooth and lump-free. Reduce heat to low, and, stirring frequently, cook for about 10 minutes, or until mixture is very thick. Remove from heat, and beat in eggs and mushroom mixture, using a wooden mixing spoon. Let mixture sit until cool enough to handle.

Preheat oven to 350° F.

4. Using clean hands, form mixture into small egg-size balls. Place balls side by side in greased 13- x 9-inch baking pan. **Drizzle** with melted butter or margarine or butter-flavored vegetable spray.

5. Bake in oven for about 30 minutes, or until golden brown.

Serve while warm with bowl of sour cream to spoon over balls.

Yugoslavia—Bosnia-Herzegovina, Croatia, Macedonia, Montenegro, Serbia, and Slovenia

To appreciate the many different holidays celebrated in the former Yugoslavia, it is necessary to understand the complex nature of that country. Even before the current troubles, it was not just one nation but rather a mixture of six republics: Bosnia-Herzegovina, Croatia, Macedonia, Montenegro, Serbia, and Slovenia. Today these republics have formed independent nations, but not without a lot of bitterness, killing, and fighting, which continues as this book goes to press. Within the six nations, there are five principal nationalities: Croatian, Serbian, Slovene, Macedonian, and Montenegrin; three main languages: Slovene, Serbo-Croatian, and Macedonian; three religions: Christian, Muslim, and Jewish; two alphabets; and a wide variety of customs and traditions.

From national festivals to family holiday feasts, there is a rich diversity of ethnic cooking. This recipe is from the largely Catholic city of Dubrovnik on the Adriatic Sea, now in newly formed Croatia.

Fish are plentiful along the coastline, and fish stews are served at many celebrations, among them *Slava*, an old religious custom honoring a family's patron saint. For many families, the annual event is often the best holiday of the year. Before World War II, *Slava* celebrations were very elaborate and sometimes lasted two or three days. During the years of communism, the celebrations were limited to family dinners. Today families are reviving *Slava* celebrations with feasting and folk music, singing, and dancing.

Dubrovnik Fish Stew

Yield: serves 4 to 6

- 2 tablespoons vegetable oil, more if necessary
- 2 onions, **finely chopped**
- 16-ounce can stewed tomatoes
- 2 tablespoons vinegar
- 1 cup chicken broth, homemade (recipe page 52) or canned
- salt and pepper to taste
- 2½ pounds skinless fish fillets, cut into bite-size pieces
- 2 tablespoons finely chopped fresh parsley or 1 teaspoon dried parsley flakes, for **garnish**
- 4 to 6 cups cooked rice (keep warm, for serving)

Equipment: Large saucepan with cover, mixing spoon, fork

Heat 2 tablespoons oil in large saucepan over medium-high heat. Add onions, and, stirring constantly, fry, until soft, about 3 minutes. Add tomatoes, vinegar, chicken broth, and salt and pepper to taste. Bring to a boil over medium-high heat, stir, and add fish. Reduce heat to **simmer**, cover, and cook for about 15 minutes, or until fish is **opaque** white and flakes easily when poked with a fork. Sprinkle with parsley, for garnish.

Serve fish stew over rice.

Musakas (eggplant stews) are found in homes all around the Mediterranean region, including Greece. They might differ from country to country, but the basic ingredient is eggplant. *Musaka* is usually made in an earthenware casserole, and it is Serbian comfort food.

Familiar dishes such as *musaka* are always prepared for the Easter Sunday feast. *Musaka* is an excellent dish to take for a covered-dish supper at church, school, or the community center.

Serbian Musaka   Eggplant Casserole

Yield: serves 8

- 1 or 2 eggplants (about 2 to 3 pounds total)
- 1 teaspoon salt, more or less as needed
- ½ cup flour, more as needed
- 4 eggs
- ½ cup water
- ½ cup olive oil, or vegetable oil, more if necessary
- 1½ pounds lean ground lamb, ground pork, or combination
- 1 onion, **finely chopped**
- 2 cloves garlic, finely chopped, or ½ teaspoon granulated garlic
- ½ cup bread crumbs
- ½ teaspoon *each* ground nutmeg and ground cinnamon
- 2 cups white sauce, homemade (recipe follows) or prepared mix (available at most supermarkets)

Equipment: Work surface, sharp knife, **colander**, paper towels, 2 pie pans, cup, fork, large skillet, **slotted spoon**, greased 13- x 9-inch baking pan, oven mitts

1. Cut eggplant, with the peel on, lengthwise into ¼-inch-thick slabs. Place in colander, sprinkle with salt, and set in the sink to drain for about 30 minutes. Rinse eggplant under cold running water, and pat dry with paper towels.

2. Put ½ cup flour in one pie pan. Using fork, beat 2 eggs with ½ cup water in cup, and pour into the other pie pan. Dust eggplant slices with flour, and then dip in egg.

3. Heat 2 tablespoons oil in large skillet over high heat. Add eggplant slices, and brown on both sides. Fry in batches, adding more oil, if necessary. Remove eggplant slices with slotted spoon and drain on paper towels. Set aside.

4. In same large skillet, mix meat, onion, and garlic; fry over medium-high heat, stirring frequently, until lightly browned, about 5 minutes, adding more oil if necessary. Remove from heat. Add remaining 2 eggs to meat mixture, and mix well. Add bread crumbs, nutmeg, cinnamon, and salt to taste; mix well.

Preheat oven to 350° F.

5. Cover bottom of greased 13- x 9-inch baking pan with half the eggplant slices, and cover evenly with meat mixture. Top with remaining eggplant slices. Spread white sauce (recipe follows) over mixture, and bake for about 1 hour, or until golden brown and set.

To serve, cool to warm, and cut into serving-size squares.

White Sauce for Eggplant Casserole

Yield: about 2 cups
   ¼ cup butter or margarine
   ¼ cup all-purpose flour
   1½ cups milk
   1 teaspoon ground nutmeg
   salt and white pepper to taste

Equipment: Medium saucepan, mixing spoon

Melt butter or margarine in medium saucepan over low heat. Add flour, and mix until smooth and lump-free. Add milk, and, stirring constantly, increase heat to medium, and cook until thickened, about 5 minutes. Add nutmeg, salt, and white pepper to taste; mix well.

Add sauce to musaka *(recipe above).*

The people of the various republics of the former Yugoslavia believe good food, and plenty of it, is a sign of a good host. For most holiday feasts, such as Easter and Christmas or *Eid al-Fitr*, it is the custom to prepare familiar bean and grain casseroles, one of which is *prebanac*.

Prebanac   Baked Lima Beans

Yield: serves 4 to 6
   2 tablespoons vegetable oil
   3 onions, **finely chopped**
   1 tablespoon paprika
   4 cups canned lima beans, drained (save ½ cup of juice)
   salt and pepper to taste

Equipment: Medium skillet, mixing spoon, medium mixing bowl, greased medium oven-proof casserole, oven mitts

Preheat oven to 350° F.

1. Heat oil in medium skillet over medium-high heat. Add onions and paprika, and, stirring constantly, fry until soft, about 3 minutes.

2. In medium mixing bowl, mix beans, ½ cup reserved juice, fried onions with pan scrapings, and salt and pepper to taste. Transfer to greased oven-proof casserole, and bake in oven for about 1 hour, until top is golden.

Serve as a side dish with meat or fowl or as a main dish during Lent. Baked lima beans are delicious at room temperature and excellent to take on picnics.

Almost every culture has special candies and cookies reserved for holiday celebrations. The following is a Slovenian recipe for almond bars.

Slovenian Almond Bars

Yield: about 32 pieces

  1 cup all-purpose flour
  ¾ cup **ground** almonds
  ¾ cup confectioners' sugar
  ½ cup butter or margarine, at room temperature
  4 **egg whites**
  4 ounces (4 squares) semisweet chocolate,
    finely **grated**
  1 egg, lightly beaten
  32 **blanched** whole almonds

Equipment: Large mixing bowl, mixing spoon or electric mixer, **grater**, rubber **spatula**, buttered 8-inch-square baking pan, **pastry brush**, knife, oven mitts

Preheat oven to 350° F.

1. In large mixing bowl, use mixing spoon or electric mixer to mix flour, ground almonds, confectioners' sugar, butter or margarine, egg whites, and chocolate.

2. Using rubber spatula, spread mixture evenly in buttered 8-inch baking pan. Using pastry brush, brush top with beaten egg. Using a knife, mark surface into serving-size bars, 1- x 2-inches each, and place an almond in the center of each.

3. Bake in oven for about 40 minutes. Cool to room temperature and cut along marked lines.

Serve as a sweet treat or pack in a box or tin and give as a holiday gift.

Hungary

Most Hungarians are Roman Catholic, and, now that communist rule has ended, they are free to observe Christian holidays with processions and religious devotion. The most important holiday season is Holy Week, which begins with Palm Sunday and ends with Easter. With the arrival of Holy Week, people try to buy new clothes or at least a new pair of shoes, sweep the streets, and adorn graves with fresh flowers.

Easter dinner is either roast ham or lamb or chicken and dumplings, which is a national dish of Hungary. Hungarian cooking differs from that of neighboring countries by the generous use of paprika, a ground spice with a dark red color. How the paprika shrub arrived in Hungary is somewhat of a mystery; it is now cultivated in great quantities and shipped all over the world.

Csirke Paprikas Galuskaval

Chicken Paprika with Dumplings

Yield: serves 6 to 8

  1 cup all-purpose flour, more as needed
  salt and pepper to taste
  2½ to 3 pounds chicken cut into serving-size
    pieces
  2 to 4 tablespoons vegetable oil, more if
    necessary
  2 onions, **finely chopped**
  3 cloves garlic, finely chopped, or 1 teaspoon
    garlic granules
  3 tablespoons sweet Hungarian paprika
  3 cups water
  2 cups sour cream
  dumplings, for serving (recipe follows)

Equipment: Paper or plastic grocery bag, mixing spoon, wax paper, work surface, **Dutch oven** or large skillet with cover, 13- x 9-inch baking pan, tongs, oven mitts, small bowl

Preheat oven to 350° F.

1. Put 1 cup flour and salt and pepper to taste in bag, and mix well. Add 2 or 3 pieces of chicken at a time, tightly seal bag, and shake to coat with flour. Shake off excess, and place chicken on wax-paper-covered work surface. Continue coating all the chicken.

2. Heat 2 tablespoons oil in Dutch oven or large skillet over medium-high heat. Carefully add chicken and fry about 10 minutes on each side, until golden brown. Fry in batches, adding more oil, if necessary, to prevent sticking. Drain well, transfer to baking pan, and bake in oven while preparing sauce, about 20 minutes.

3. Prepare Sauce: Add onions and garlic to pan drippings, and, stirring constantly, fry over medium heat until soft, about 3 minutes. Add paprika, 2 cups water, and salt and pepper to taste, and stir. Bring to boil, reduce heat to **simmer**, and cook for 5 minutes.

4. In small bowl, mix sour cream, remaining 1 cup water, and 2 tablespoons flour until smooth and lump-free. Stirring constantly, add sour cream mixture to paprika sauce in Dutch oven or large skillet, and simmer for about 5 minutes or until thickened. Pour mixture over chicken in baking pan, and return to oven for about 30 minutes, or until chicken is tender.

Serve from baking pan, and scatter dumplings on top.

Csipetke   Dumplings

Yield: serves 6 to 8
  ½ cup butter or margarine
  1 cup water
  1 cup all-purpose flour
  4 eggs

Equipment: Medium saucepan, wooden mixing spoon, large saucepan, teaspoon, **slotted spoon**, large baking pan, oven mitts

1. Put butter or margarine and water in medium saucepan, and bring to a boil over high heat. Stir constantly until butter or margarine melts, and then add flour, all at once; beat until well blended using wooden mixing spoon. Reduce hear to medium and continue cooking, stirring constantly until mixture leaves sides of pan and forms a ball. Remove from heat and add eggs, one at a time, beating with wooden mixing spoon after each addition.

2. Prepare to cook dumplings: Fill large saucepan half full with water, and bring to boil over high heat. Reduce heat until water maintains **rolling boil**. Cook dumplings by dropping teaspoonfuls of dough, a few at a time, into boiling water and cooking them for about 4 minutes. Cook dumplings in batches to keep them from sticking together. Remove with slotted spoon, and drain. Transfer to large baking pan and keep warm until ready to serve.

To serve, scatter dumplings over chicken paprika (recipe precedes).

The holiday season is a time to have freshly baked pastries, especially cookies, for visiting relatives and friends. This recipe for Hungarian butter cookies, *pogacsa*, is very tasty.

Pogacsa   Hungarian Butter Cookies

Yield: about 1 dozen
  2¾ cups all-purpose flour
  1 teaspoon baking powder
  $^2/_3$ cup sugar
  ¼ teaspoon salt
  1 cup butter or margarine, at room temperature
  1 egg
  $^1/_3$ cup sour cream

Equipment: Large mixing bowl with cover, mixing spoon, buttered or nonstick cookie sheet, fork, oven mitts

1. Mix flour, baking powder, sugar, and salt in large mixing bowl. Add butter or margarine, and, using clean hands, blend until mixture resembles coarse meal. Add egg and sour cream, and mix until dough holds together. Cover and refrigerate for about 2 hours.

Preheat oven to 350° F.

2. Pinch off small egg-size pieces of dough and form into balls. Place on buttered or nonstick cookie sheet, and use fingers to press to about ½ inch thick. Make a crosshatch design by pressing the back of fork tines on top of each cookie. Cookies should be spaced about 1 inch apart.

3. Bake in oven for about 20 minutes, or until pale golden. Continue baking in batches.

Serve as a sweet snack.

Czech and Slovak Republics

Once a single country composed of Czechs and Slovaks, Czechoslovakia has become two countries, the Czech and Slovak Republics. The Roman Catholic Church is the dominant religion in both countries, and all Christian holidays are observed with processions and pageantry. The seasonal festivals are regional, combining ancient pagan rituals with Christian beliefs.

Dumplings are a specialty in both the Czech and Slovak republics as well as in most Eastern European countries. Most cooks save their fancier recipes for Sundays and holidays. Dumplings in all sizes and shapes are added to soups, eaten as the main dish, or filled with fruit for dessert. Roast goose, served with bread dumplings, *houskové knedliky*, is the highlight of the holiday dinner table.

Houskové Knedliky   Bread Dumplings

Yield: 8 to 10 balls

2 cups coarsely torn white bread
2 tablespoons butter or margarine
1 onion, **finely chopped**
2 eggs, beaten
½ cup cracker crumbs
2 tablespoons finely chopped fresh parsley or 1 tablespoon dried parsley flakes
1 teaspoon ground nutmeg
salt and pepper, more or less to taste
1 cup sour cream, for serving

Equipment: **Colander**, large skillet, mixing spoon, large saucepan, **slotted spoon**

1. Put bread in colander, soak under water, and squeeze dry.

2. Melt butter or margarine in large skillet over medium-high heat. Add onion, and, stirring constantly, fry until soft, about 3 minutes. Add bread, eggs, cracker crumbs, parsley, nutmeg, and salt and pepper to taste. Using mixing spoon, stir well. Cool to room temperature, and refrigerate for 30 minutes.

3. Prepare to cook dumplings: Fill large saucepan half full with water, add 1 teaspoon salt, and bring to a boil over high heat.

4. Using clean hands, form bread mixture into small, egg-size balls. Drop balls into boiling water, and reduce heat to **simmer**. Cook for about 15 minutes, or until cooked through. Remove with slotted spoon. Keep warm.

Serve as a side dish with sour cream.

This black barley dish, *cerna kuba*, is traditionally served on Christmas Eve or after a fast day.

Cerna Kuba — Black Barley Dish

Yield: Serves 4 to 6

1 pound lean pork sausage, cut into ½-inch pieces
1 large onion, **coarsely chopped**
3 cloves garlic, **finely chopped,** or 1 teaspoon garlic granules
1 cup finely chopped celery
2 cups mushrooms, coarsely chopped
2 cups cooked, quick-cooking barley (prepare according to directions on package)
1 cup water, canned chicken broth, or beef broth
salt and pepper to taste

Equipment: **Dutch oven** or large skillet with cover, mixing spoon

1. In Dutch oven or large skillet, fry sausage over medium-high heat to release a little fat, about 3 minutes. Add onion, garlic, celery, and mushrooms, reduce heat to medium, and, stirring frequently, cook until sausage has browned, about 5 minutes.

2. Add cooked barley, water or broth, and salt and pepper to taste, and stir. Cover and cook over medium-low heat for 30 minutes for flavors to blend.

Serve while hot as the main dish or as a side dish with holiday ham or goose.

These Moravian Christmas cookies, *Moravské váno ni kukysé,* can be cut into any shapes you like. (Moravia is a region in the Czech republic, which is made up of the ancient lands of Bohemia and Moravia.)

Moravské Váno ni Kukysé
Moravian Christmas Cookies

Yield: about 24

⅓ cup molasses
3 tablespoons vegetable shortening
2 tablespoons dark brown sugar
½ teaspoon *each* ground cinnamon, **ginger,** cloves, baking soda, and salt
1¼ cup, sifted all-purpose flour, more as needed

Equipment: Large mixing bowl, mixing spoon or electric mixer, aluminum foil, **sifter,** damp kitchen towel, lightly floured work surface, floured **rolling pin, cookie cutters** or glass, greased or nonstick cookie sheet, oven mitts

1. In large mixing bowl, use mixing spoon or electric mixer to mix molasses, shortening, sugar, cinnamon, ginger, cloves, baking soda, and salt. Add flour, a little at a time, and, using clean hands, mix into a firm dough. Cover with foil, and refrigerate for about 4 hours.

Preheat oven to 375° F.

2. Divide dough into 4 balls, and keep covered with damp towel. On lightly floured work surface, use floured rolling pin to roll each ball, one at a time, to about ⅛ inch thick. (Keep other balls covered.) Using cookie cutters or rim of glass, cut into desired shapes, and place on greased or nonstick cookie sheet.

3. Bake in oven for about 6 minutes, until lightly browned. Continue in batches until all cookies are made.

Serve cookies as a sweet snack and store in airtight container.

Austria

Ninety-eight percent of the people in Austria are of Germanic origin, and most are Roman Catholic. As is true throughout Europe, many Christian holidays in Austria are combined with agrarian festivals dating back to pre-Christian times. One such festival is *Tyrol* at the beginning of spring. The name and date varies from region to region, but observances are pretty much all the same. People wearing ancestral costumes and masks march through the streets waving sticks in the air pretending to chase away the "evil spirits" of winter. The *Tyrol* festival ties in with the other springtime celebrations of Carnival and Easter.

For centuries Austrians have had an international reputation as fine cooks and pastry makers. Holiday pastries are legend, and bakers turn out breads, cakes, and cookies that dazzle the senses. This recipe is for hazelnut sandwich cookies, called *haselnuss-küchlein*.

Equipment: Medium mixing bowl, mixing spoon or electric mixer, floured work surface, floured **rolling pin**, 3-inch **cookie cutters** or drinking glass, ½-inch cookie cutter or bottle cap, greased or nonstick cookie sheet, oven mitts

Preheat oven to 350° F.

1. In medium mixing bowl, use mixing spoon or electric mixer to beat butter or margarine and sugar until light and fluffy, about 3 minutes. Add nuts and 1 cup flour, a little at a time, and, using clean hands, mix to a smooth dough. Cover and refrigerate for about 30 minutes.

2. On floured work surface, use floured rolling pin to roll dough ⅛ inch thick. Using 3-inch cookie cutter or glass rim, cut out disks. Place half the disks on cookie sheet; these are the cookie bottoms.

3. Make cookie tops: Using ½-inch cookie cutter or bottle cap, cut a hole in the middle of remaining disks. Place on cookie sheet side by side with cookie bottoms. Bake in oven for about 15 minutes, or until lightly browned around edges. Cool to room temperature.

4. Spread jam on cookie bottoms and cover each with a top, sandwich-fashion. Fill each hole with a little more jam. Continue assembling and sprinkle with confectioners' sugar.

Serve as a sweet snack.

Another favorite Austrian treat is *küpferlin*, crescent cookies.

Haselnuss-Küchlein   Hazelnut Cookies

Yield: about 18 cookies

- ½ cup butter or margarine
- ½ cup sugar
- 1½ cups finely **ground** hazelnuts
- 1 cup all-purpose flour, more as needed
- ½ cup raspberry jam, for **garnish**
- 2 teaspoons confectioners' sugar, more or less as needed, for garnish

Küpferlin   Crescent Cookies

Yield: about 20 to 24

- ½ cup margarine (do not use butter), at room temperature
- ¼ cup sugar
- ½ cup finely **ground** almonds (not **blanched**)
- 1 cup all-purpose flour, more if necessary
- ¼ cup confectioners' sugar, more or less as needed

Equipment: Medium mixing bowl with cover, mixing spoon, greased and floured or nonstick cookie sheet, oven mitts

Preheat oven to 325° F.

1. In medium mixing bowl, mix margarine and sugar until creamy and blended. Add almonds and 1 cup flour, and, using clean hands, mix into a smooth dough, adding more flour if dough is sticky. Cover and refrigerate for about 30 minutes.

2. Pinch off walnut-size pieces of dough, and roll them between the palms of your hands into a rope, about 3 inches long. Place ropes on greased and floured or nonstick cookie sheet, and curve into a C-shape; space about 1 inch apart. Repeat until all dough is used.

3. Bake in oven for about 30 minutes, or until firm to the touch. The baked cookies will still be white, not golden, when fully baked.

4. While still warm, sprinkle with confectioners' sugar.

Serve as a snack or pack in a box or tin and give as a gift.

Apples, spices, and nuts are traditionally used in German and Austrian Christmas baking, such as in this recipe for *apfelkuchen*, Bavarian apple cake.

Apfelkuchen   Bavarian Apple Cake

Yield: serves 8 to 10
  2 cups all-purpose flour
  4 teaspoons baking power
  ½ teaspoon salt
  ½ cup sugar
  ⅓ cup butter or margarine, at room temperature
  1 egg
  ⅓ cup milk
  5 cooking apples, **peeled**, **cored**, and thinly sliced
  ½ cup **cinnamon sugar**

Equipment: Large mixing bowl, mixing spoon, greased or nonstick 9-inch round cake pan, oven mitts

Preheat oven to 350° F.

1. In large mixing bowl, mix flour, baking powder, salt, and sugar. Add butter or margarine and egg, and mix until mixture is crumbly. Add milk and mix until dough holds together. Spread in greased or nonstick 9-inch round cake pan and smooth top.

2. Arrange apple slices, slightly overlapping, on top of the dough, and sprinkle generously with cinnamon sugar.

3. Bake in oven for about 35 minutes, or until apples are tender and edges of cake are golden brown.

Serve warm or at room temperature, cut into wedges.

Switzerland

Swiss agrarian festivals date back to a time when local inhabitants were totally dependent on farming. Because of this relationship, these festivals celebrate the changing seasons, such as the winter solstice and, therefore, the eventual coming of spring. Among the many spring festivals is *Alp Aufzug*. This festival celebrates the movement of cows to higher, summer pastures. (The dates varies with the weather.) One lively (and loud!) part of this holiday is the custom of having children chase winter away by rattling cowbells. Another springtime custom is to throw straw puppets, representing winter, into community bonfires to celebrate the death of winter.

Switzerland is completely landlocked, surrounded by France, Italy, Austria, and Germany. Because of its location, many Swiss combine their national heritage with the lifestyle and language of their nearest neighbor. These mixed influences cause celebrations to differ in each region, and each tries to outdo the other.

The most important religious holiday, *Fastnacht*, the German equivalent of Carnival, dates back to the thirteenth century. As in many Christian countries, *Fastnacht* gives people a chance to have a final blast before the rigors of Lent. Each region has an elaborate celebration, and in some regions the people get up at midnight and dress in grotesque or beautiful costumes and masks. At 4 A.M. all the lights go out, and the costumed people parade past the town lit by huge lanterns.

In the Ticino region bordering Italy, whole villages cook huge pots of *risotto* in the city square and freely feed everyone partaking in the merriment.

1. Heat broth in small saucepan over high heat until bubbles appear around edge of pan. Reduce heat and keep at steady **simmer**.

2. In medium saucepan, melt butter or margarine over medium-high heat. Add onion, and cook until soft, about 3 minutes. Reduce heat to medium, add rice, stir to coat, and cook for about 2 minutes.

3. Add simmering broth, about ½ cup at a time, to the rice, and stir while cooking. Allow the rice to absorb the broth before adding more. Continue adding simmering broth, ½ cup at a time, stirring constantly, until all the broth is used. Cook the rice over medium-low heat for about 25 minutes or until it is creamy. Remove from heat.

4. Add salt and pepper to taste, peas, and ¼ cup grated cheese, more or less to taste. Stir well, and cover for 5 minutes before serving.

Serve with extra cheese.

Carnival, known as *Fastnacht*, goes nonstop for three days, and the Swiss people revive themselves with a nourishing soup, *mehlsuppe*, that dates back to the Middle Ages. Every cook makes it differently, but it is a tradition to eat it in the morning after the first masked, middle-of-the-night parade.

Risotto in Bianco — White Rice

Yield: serves 4 to 6

3 cups canned beef broth,
¹/₃ cup butter or margarine
½ onion, **finely chopped**
1¼ cups rice
salt and pepper to taste
1 cup peas, fresh or frozen, thawed
¼ cup **grated** Swiss or Parmesan cheese, more or less to taste

Equipment: Small saucepan, wooden mixing spoon, medium saucepan with cover, **grater**, ladle

Mehlsuppe — Browned-Flour Soup

Yield: serves 6

7 tablespoons butter or margarine
6 tablespoons all-purpose flour
6 cups hot water, more if necessary
6 whole cloves
1 medium whole onion
2 bay leaves
salt to taste
4 tablespoons **grated** Swiss cheese, more as needed

Equipment: Medium saucepan with cover, **whisk** or mixing spoon, **grater**

1. Melt 6 tablespoons butter or margarine in medium saucepan over medium heat. Add flour and mix until smooth and browned, about 3 minutes. (Do not let the mixture burn.) Reduce heat to low, and, mixing constantly, add 6 cups hot water, a little at a time, until smooth and lump-free.

2. Poke cloves into the onion, and add to soup. Add bay leaves and salt to taste, and mix well. Cover and cook over low heat, mixing frequently, for about 1 hour. Before serving, remove the onion and bay leaves and discard. Add remaining 1 tablespoon butter or margarine and 4 tablespoons grated cheese; mix well.

Serve soup in individual bowls with extra cheese on the side. Some people like to eat the onion instead of discarding it; just be sure to remove the cloves.

Along with *mehlsuppe*, the browned-flour soup, another Carnival specialty is *zwiebelwähe*, an onion tart.

Zwiebelwähe   Onion Tart

Yield: serves 6 or 8
  1½ cups **shredded** Swiss cheese
  10-inch pie crust, homemade (recipe page 108) or frozen prepared crust, thawed
  ½ cup finely **diced** bacon
  3 onions, thinly sliced
  4 eggs, well beaten
  1½ cups light cream
  salt and pepper to taste

Equipment: 9-inch pie pan, large skillet, **slotted spoon**, medium mixing bowl, mixing spoon, oven mitts

Preheat oven to 425° F.

1. Sprinkle 1 cup cheese over bottom of pie crust in pie pan.

2. Fry bacon pieces in large skillet over medium-high heat until soft and rendered, about 3 min-

utes. Add onions, and, stirring frequently, fry until soft, about 3 minutes. Remove with slotted spoon and drain well. Spread over cheese in pie crust.

3. In medium mixing bowl, use mixing spoon to mix eggs, cream, remaining ½ cup cheese, and salt and pepper to taste. Pour into pie crust and bake in oven for 15 minutes. Reduce heat to 325°, and bake for about 30 minutes longer, until top is browned.

Serve warm or at room temperature, cut into wedges.

Rösti is a popular potato dish especially enjoyed during Carnival.

Rösti   Crusty Potato Cake

Yield: serves 4 to 6
  4 or 6 baking-size potatoes, boiled and **peeled**
  salt and pepper to taste
  4 tablespoons vegetable oil, more or less as needed

Equipment: 4-sided **grater**, large mixing bowl, mixing spoon, 8- or 10-inch skillet, metal **spatula**, heat-proof 12-inch platter

1. Using coarse side of grater (the side with larger holes), shred potatoes into large mixing bowl. Add salt and pepper to taste, and lightly toss to mix.

2. Heat 2 tablespoons oil in skillet over medium-high heat. Carefully add shredded potatoes, and, using spatula, press on potatoes to cover bottom of skillet. Reduce heat to medium, and fry potatoes about 15 minutes or until firm and bottom side is golden brown and crusty. Remove skillet from heat, and loosen edges. Invert a platter over skillet. Holding both firmly together, flip over. Potato cake will drop onto platter, bottom side up.

3. Add 2 tablespoons oil to skillet. Carefully slide potato cake, browned side up, back into skillet,

and fry over medium heat for about 10 minutes, until second side is browned and crusty.

Serve at once while warm as a side dish.

Italy

In Italy, many parts of life revolve around the Roman Catholic Church, and almost everyone speaks Italian, but that is where any similarity ends. Italians are extremely territorial, and each region of the country has its own food, lifestyle, customs, and celebrations. (In fact, Italy didn't become a unified country until 1870.)

For most Italians, the traditional Christmas Eve feast is called *cenone*, or "big dinner," and almost all Italians, regardless of region, abstain from meat. Included in the *cenone* are 12 different fish and seafood dishes, among them calamari (squid), clams, fried whiting, shrimp, salmon, tuna, and hake. In Rome, eel cooked in olive oil and vinegar is the centerpiece of the *cenone*. The 12 kinds of fish symbolize the 12 Apostles, and the Christmas Eve feast represents the Last Supper.

At Christmas, gift-giving is a matter of local traditions. In some areas, such as Sicily, gifts are exchanged on St. Lucia's Day, December 13. (St. Lucia was a Sicilian maiden,

and for some unknown reason this day is also celebrated in Sweden; see Sweden, page 123.) Within the last 15 years, the children in larger cities in Italy, among them Naples, Rome, and Milan, have been eagerly awaiting the visit of Santa Claus bearing gifts for children on December 25. Other children wait until New Year's Day when *Babbo Natale*, "Old Man Christmas," arrives. Still others in the Campania and Abruzzi regions and the Isle of Capri wait until January 6, Epiphany, for a visit from *La Befana*. As the legend goes, *Befana* rides around on a broomstick searching for the Christ child to bring him gifts. She doesn't find the *bambino* (the Christ child), and so, instead, she leaves the gifts with all the good little children.

Many Christmas dinners include a side dish of lentils, which according to legend are eaten to ensure prosperity and good fortune for the coming year. In Italy, the best lentils are grown in the Abruzzi region. After the harvest, growers, pickers, and villagers have *Sagra delle Lenticchie*, a Lentil Festival, celebrating a successful crop.

Lenticchie in Umido Stewed Lentils

Yield: serves 4 to 6
- 2 tablespoons olive oil
- 2 pounds sweet Italian sausage, cut into 1-inch slices
- 2 onions, **finely chopped**
- 3 ribs celery, **trimmed**, and finely sliced
- 3 cloves garlic, finely chopped, or 1 teaspoon garlic granules
- 2 cups water
- 1 cup canned tomato sauce
- 1½ cups lentils
- salt and pepper to taste

Equipment: **Dutch oven** or large skillet with cover, mixing spoon

1. Heat oil in Dutch oven or large skillet over medium heat. Add sausage, onions, celery, and garlic, and, stirring frequently, fry until sausage is browned, about 5 minutes.

2. Add water, tomato sauce, and lentils, mix well, and bring to a boil. Reduce heat to **simmer**, cover, and, stirring frequently, cook until lentils are tender, about 30 minutes. Add salt and pepper to taste, and mix well.

Serve hot as a side dish with Christmas turkey or baked ham.

Eggs are a symbol of life and are served for all Christian holidays. The following recipe for tuna-stuffed eggs, *uova tonnate*, is popular in southern Italy.

Uova Tonnate Tuna-Stuffed Eggs

Yield: serves 4

  6 hard-cooked eggs, **shelled**
  1 tablespoon **finely chopped** fresh parsley or 1 teaspoon dried parsley flakes
  1 tablespoon mayonnaise
  4 ounces canned tuna fish, drained
  1 clove garlic, finely chopped, or ½ teaspoon garlic granules
  salt and pepper to taste
  1 tablespoon chopped pimento, for **garnish**

Equipment: Paring knife, work surface, small mixing bowl, fork, teaspoon

1. Cut eggs in half lengthwise and remove yolks. Put yolks in mixing bowl and add parsley, mayonnaise, tuna fish, garlic, and salt and pepper to taste. Mash mixture, using back of fork, into a smooth paste.

2. Fill egg white halves with mixture. For garnish, place 2 or 3 pieces of pimento on top of each egg.

Serve eggs as an appetizer with the holiday feast.

In many regions of Italy, it wouldn't be Christmas if pasta were not on the table. When pasta is served with a meal, it is usually eaten first and by itself. On the Isle of Capri, off the coast of Naples, and in the surrounding regions, *linguine con funghi* is the favorite noodle dish for the Christmas meal. It is lightly sauced with olive oil, making it a healthy way to eat pasta.

Linguine con Funghi Linguini Pasta with Mushrooms

Yield: serves 4 to 6

  ¾ cup olive oil
  2 tablespoons butter or margarine
  3 cloves garlic, sliced, or 1 teaspoon garlic granules
  2 cups sliced fresh mushrooms
  1 pound linguini pasta cooked, drained, and kept warm
  salt and pepper to taste
  grated Parmesan cheese, for serving

Equipment: Large skillet, mixing spoon, 2 forks

1. Heat oil and butter in large skillet over medium-high heat. Add garlic and mushrooms, and, stirring constantly, fry for about 5 minutes until soft.

2. Reduce heat to medium, add cooked linguini and salt and pepper to taste, and mix using 2 forks in an up-and-down motion. Heat through, about 3 minutes.

Serve at once with grated Parmesan cheese sprinkled on pasta.

Panettone has become the symbolic Christmas bread of Italians all over the world. As the legend goes, in the fifteenth century, around Christmas time, a Milanese baker, Antonio (Toni), concocted this bread to impress a girlfriend. He made extra loaves, and before long everyone wanted *pan de Toni,* "Toni's bread."

In the following recipe the cylinder loaves can be baked in clean cans (such as 1-pound coffee cans), about 6 inches high by 4 inches in diameter.

Panettone   Italian Christmas Bread

Yield: 2 loaves
- 2 packages (¼-ounce each) dry yeast
- 1 cup lukewarm water
- 4½ cups all-purpose flour, more as needed
- ½ cup butter or margarine, at room temperature, more as needed
- ½ cup sugar
- 3 eggs
- ½ teaspoon salt
- grated rind of 1 orange
- ½ cup mixed **finely chopped** candied fruit (also called fruitcake mix—available at most supermarkets)
- ½ cup seedless raisins

Equipment: Medium mixing bowl, mixing spoon, kitchen towel, large mixing bowl, egg beater or electric mixer, large mixing bowl (greased), **grater**, 2 (1-pound) greased coffee cans, small saucepan, **pastry brush**, oven mitts, can opener

1. In medium mixing bowl, sprinkle yeast over warm water, and set aside for 5 minutes to dissolve. Add 1 cup flour, and, using mixing spoon, mix well. Cover with towel, and set in warm place to double in bulk, about 1 hour.

2. In large mixing bowl, use egg beater or electric mixer to mix butter or margarine and sugar until light and fluffy. Mixing constantly, add eggs, one at a time, salt, and orange rind.

3. Using mixing spoon, beat down yeast mixture, and add to sugar mixture; mix well. Add candied fruitcake mix and raisins.

4. Add remaining 3½ cups flour, a little at a time, and, using clean hands, **knead** to form soft dough. Transfer to large, greased mixing bowl and turn dough to grease all sides. Cover with towel, and set in warm place to double in bulk, about 1½ hours.

5. **Punch down** dough, and divide it in half. Place a piece in each greased can. Melt 2 tablespoons butter or margarine in small saucepan. Brush tops with melted butter, loosely cover with towel, and set in warm place to rise over tops of cans, about ½ hour.

Preheat oven to 350° F.

6. Bake in oven for about 35 minutes until browned and loaves sound hollow when tapped gently on the top with a spoon handle. Remove from oven, and invert cans to cool. Using a can opener, remove can bottoms and push bread out.

Serve either warm or at room temperature, cut into wedges.

During the *Natale,* the Christmas holiday, friends and relatives drop in to exchange presents and good wishes and have something sweet to eat. Baking great quantities of sweets, including cakes, cookies, and candies for the hungry visitors, is an Italian holiday tradition. Among the favorite recipes are *cassata alla siciliana* (recipe follows) and *torta mandorla.* (See recipe for the Festival of San Gennaro, United States, page 271.)

Cassata Alla Siciliana   Sicilian Cake

Yield: serves 10 to 12
- 2 cups cream cheese, at room temperature
- 2 tablespoons heavy cream
- ¼ cup confectioners' sugar
- 1 teaspoon almond extract
- ½ cup **coarsely chopped** candied fruitcake mix (available at all supermarkets)

½ cup semi-sweet chocolate chips
½ cup sliced or chopped almonds
1 (9- x 5-inch) pound cake, packaged mix, homemade (prepare according to directions on package) or commercially baked
chocolate frosting (recipe follows)

Equipment: Medium mixing bowl, mixing spoon, or electric mixer, rubber **spatula**, work surface, **serrated knife**, serving platter, aluminum foil

1. In medium mixing bowl, use mixing spoon or electric mixer to mix cream cheese and heavy cream until smooth. Add confectioners' sugar and almond extract, and mix well.

2. Using rubber spatula, **fold in** candied fruitcake mix, chocolate chips, and almonds.

3. Put pound cake on work surface, and, using serrated knife, cut cake horizontally into 3 or 4 layers. Place the bottom layer on serving platter and spread generously with cheese mixture. Place a layer of pound cake over the filling, and repeat until layers are filled and assembled, ending with cake on top. Refrigerate for at least 2 hours to set.

4. Using a metal spatula, spread chocolate frosting in a swirling motion over top and sides of cake. Cover loosely with foil and refrigerate for at least 8 hours before serving.

To serve, cut into slices.

Chocolate Frosting

Yield: about 2½ cups
2 cups semi-sweet chocolate chips
1 teaspoon instant coffee granules
¾ cup strong coffee
1 teaspoon almond extract
1 cup cold butter or margarine, cut into small pieces

Equipment: Small saucepan, wooden mixing spoon, medium mixing bowl with cover, rubber **spatula**

1. In small saucepan, melt chocolate over low heat, stirring frequently. Add coffee granules, strong coffee, and almond extract, and stir well.

2. Remove from heat, and, using wooden mixing spoon, beat in butter or margarine, a few pieces at a time until smooth.

3. Transfer to medium mixing bowl, cover, and refrigerate until thickened to spreading consistency, about 30 minutes.

Spread over Sicilian cake (recipe precedes).

Portugal

Portugal is a Roman Catholic country, and many aspects of life revolve around the church. Each region has festivals, some so bizarre and ancient no one has the slightest idea how they came to be. For example, in the city of Tomar there is the unusual *Festa dos Tabuleiros* (feast of the trays), held annually. According to ancient folklore, the rite gives thanks for a good harvest. Gigantic trays of decoratively stacked bread, more than five feet high, are carried on the heads of young girls. Priests bless the stacks of bread as well as all the meat and wine to be consumed during the holiday. On festival day the girls, adorned in their bread headdresses, parade through the town with marching bands, soldiers, bagpipers, and oxen, which are to be slaughtered for the feast held on the church grounds. The day-long festivities end with fireworks. Hundreds of cakes, tortes, cookies, and candies are prepared for the feasting crowd; among desserts served are *bolo de amêndoa* and *bomboms de figo* (recipes follow later in section).

Easter is the most important national holiday in Portugal, and the favorite Easter feast is roast pork.

Porco Assado — Stuffed Roast Pork

Yield: serves 6 to 8

3 to 4 pounds lean pork loin or shoulder (have butcher prepare it for stuffing)
salt and pepper
2 tablespoons olive oil
1 onion, **finely chopped**
1 green pepper, **coarsely chopped**
3 cloves garlic, finely chopped, or 1 teaspoon garlic granules
1 cup stewed whole tomatoes, coarsely chopped
½ teaspoon chili powder, more or less to taste
¼ cup chopped pitted green olives or stuffed green olives
½ cup seedless raisins
2½ cups cooked rice
2 cups water
2 pounds small new potatoes, peeled

Equipment: Work surface, large skillet, mixing spoon, medium mixing bowl, kitchen string, roasting pan, oven mitts, heat-proof surface, **bulb baster**

1. Place meat flat on work surface and sprinkle with salt and pepper.

2. Heat oil in large skillet over medium-high heat. Add onion, green pepper, and garlic, and, stirring frequently, fry until browned, about 5 minutes. Reduce heat to medium, add tomatoes, ½ teaspoon chili powder (more or less to taste), olives,

and raisins. Stir well and cook for 5 minutes. Remove from heat.

Preheat oven to 350° F.

3. Put cooked rice in medium mixing bowl, add half the tomato mixture, and mix well. Spoon mixture onto pork, staying about 2 inches within the edges, and roll closed. Using string, tie in several places to keep closed. Place meat in roasting pan, seam-side down. Roast for 1½ hours.

4. Using oven mitts, remove from oven, and place on heat-proof surface. Using bulb baster or spoon, drain off grease in roasting pan and discard. Add potatoes to roasting pan.

5. Add water to remaining tomato mixture, mix, and pour over potatoes and meat. Return to oven, and bake for about 1 hour longer, or until meat is tender; baste occasionally.

To serve, transfer meat to serving platter, and arrange potatoes around it. Skim off any grease from the remaining sauce. Serve sauce in a separate bowl.

A large variety of vegetables always accompanies the Easter pork. Spinach with pine nuts and raisins is an easy-to-prepare favorite.

Spinach with Pine Nuts and Raisins

Yield: serves 4

1 tablespoon olive oil
1 pound fresh spinach, washed, **trimmed**, and **coarsely chopped** or 1 (16-ounce) package frozen chopped spinach, thawed, and excess moisture squeezed out
½ cup seedless raisins, soaked in warm water for 1 hour and drained well
½ cup pine nuts
salt and pepper to taste

Equipment: Large skillet, mixing spoon

1. Heat olive oil in large skillet over medium-high heat. Add spinach, and, tossing constantly, fry until tender, about 3 minutes.

2. Reduce heat to low, and add raisins, pine nuts, and salt and pepper to taste; toss to mix well, and heat through, about 3 minutes.

Serve warm as a side dish with meat.

A delicious dessert or fresh fruit always comes at the end of the Easter feast. The following cake, *bolo de amêndoa,* is a perfect dessert after an Easter feast.

Bolo de Amêndoa   Almond Cake

Yield: 8 to 10

6 **eggs, separated**
1 cup sugar
½ teaspoon salt
2 tablespoons cocoa
1 teaspoon cinnamon
1 teaspoon almond extract
2 tablespoons bread crumbs
2 cups finely **ground** almonds
4 tablespoons **finely chopped** candied cherries
sliced fresh fruit of choice or ice cream, for
    serving (optional)

Equipment: Medium mixing bowl, egg beater or electric mixer, large mixing bowl, rubber **spatula**, mixing spoon, buttered 9-inch round cake pan, oven mitts

Preheat oven to 350° F.

1. In medium mixing bowl, use egg beater or electric mixer to beat egg whites until soft peaks form. Add ½ cup sugar, a little at a time, and beat constantly until stiff peaks form.

2. Put egg yolks in large mixing bowl, and, mixing constantly with egg beater or electric mixer, add salt, cocoa, remaining ½ cup sugar, cinnamon,

almond extract, bread crumbs, and ground almonds; blend well.

3. **Fold** egg whites into egg yolk mixture, using rubber spatula or mixing spoon. Pour batter into buttered 9-inch cake pan, and sprinkle candied cherries over the top.

4. Bake in oven for 30 minutes, or until toothpick inserted in center of cake comes out clean.

To serve, cut the cake into wedges, and add fresh fruit or ice cream.

Sugarplums and the sugarplum tree written about so wistfully in Christmas songs and poems may well have originated with the figs and plums of Portugal. Today all candied dried fruits, such as figs, dates, and prunes, are called sugarplums.

Bomboms de Figo   Fig Bonbons

Yield: about 14 pieces

½ pound soft dried figs, **stemmed** and **finely
    chopped** or ground
1/3 cup finely chopped **blanched** almonds
½ cup sugar, more if necessary

Equipment: Medium mixing bowl, wax paper, cookie sheet, aluminum foil

In medium mixing bowl, mix chopped or ground figs and chopped almonds. Shape 1 tablespoon of mixture into a ball and roll in sugar to coat. Continue making balls and place side by side on wax-paper-covered cookie sheet. Set aside for about 10 minutes, and roll in sugar again. Place on wax paper, cover with foil, and refrigerate until ready to serve.

Serve as a sweet snack.

Spain

All Christian holidays are important to Spain's large Roman Catholic population, but the month-long Christmas celebration is particularly festive. The Christmas season begins on December 8 with the Feast of the Immaculate Conception. In churches and most homes a *Nacimiento*, manger scene, is set up. Families gather around it each evening during the holiday to sing carols. Groups of carolers go house to house singing and playing hand bells, guitars, tambourines, and mandolins.

For nine days prior to Christmas, before dawn each morning, church bells call worshipers to early-morning mass. On Christmas Eve, Midnight Mass is called *Misa del Gallo,* the "Mass of the Rooster," celebrating the rooster that announced the birth of Jesus on Christmas morning.

On January 6, Epiphany, people exchange gifts, and parades are held in large cities, honoring the three kings who visited the Christ child.

Many Spanish people love snack foods, which they call *tapas.* An assortment of snacks is always offered to hungry carolers, such as this tasty recipe for *queso frito,* fried cheese.

Queso Frito — Fried Cheese

CAUTION: HOT OIL USED

Yield: serves 4 to 6

- 2 eggs, beaten
- 2 tablespoons water
- 1 cup bread crumbs
- salt and pepper to taste
- 12 ounces cheese, Monterey Jack or mozzarella, cut into 2-inch squares or triangles, ¼ to ½ inch thick
- 3 cups vegetable oil, more or less for frying

Equipment: Small mixing bowl, pie pan, plate, baking sheet, paper towels, medium skillet, wooden spoon, **slotted spoon**

1. In small mixing bowl, mix eggs and water.

2. Put bread crumbs in pie pan, and mix with salt and pepper to taste.

3. Coat each piece of cheese twice: Dip first in egg mixture and then in bread crumbs, and then repeat dipping in egg and then bread crumbs. Repeat with remaining cheese pieces and place side by side on plate.

4. Have adult help with frying: Cover baking sheet with several layers of paper towels. Pour about ¼ inch oil into medium skillet, and heat over medium-high. Oil is hot enough for frying when small bubbles appear around a wooden spoon handle when it is dipped in the oil. (It should only take 3 to 5 minutes to get hot enough.)

5. Fry breaded cheese in batches, about 3 or 4 at one time. Fry about 2 minutes on each side, or until browned. Use slotted metal spoon to turn cheese and to remove it from oil. Drain on paper towels. Keep in warm place.

Serve at once as a light snack or appetizer.

The ultimate holiday feast is *paella*, the national dish of Spain. Each region has its own recipe, and even within regions the recipe varies with the season, the cook, and the family budget. This one-dish meal is cooked and served in a large skillet-type pan called a *paellera*. *Paella* is traditionally made with saffron and freshly caught shrimp with heads and shells on. This recipe uses less expensive turmeric and less-messy peeled and deveined shrimp.

Paella   Spain's National One-Dish Meal

Yield: serves 6

12 mussels (optional)

½ cup olive oil, more or less as needed

2 to 3 pounds chicken, cut into small, serving-size pieces

salt and pepper to taste

2 onions, **coarsely chopped**

3 cloves garlic, **finely chopped,** or 1 teaspoon garlic granules

1 green pepper, **cored**, **seeded**, and cut into ¼-inch strips

3 (6-inch) links spicy sausage (such as Chorizo or Italian), cut into 1-inch chunks

4 cups water

2 cups rice, (preferably **basmati)**

1 teaspoon ground turmeric

1 (16-ounce) can stewed tomatoes, coarsely chopped

30 shrimp (about 1 pound) with heads off, **peeled**, **deveined**, rinsed, and drained

1 cup sliced green beans, fresh or frozen, thawed

1 cup finely chopped cooked ham

1 cup frozen green peas, thawed to room temperature

Equipment: **Vegetable brush**, medium mixing bowl, **colander**, **Dutch oven** or large oven-proof saucepan with cover, tongs or **slotted spoon**, large baking pan, oven mitts

Prepare mussels (optional): Using vegetable brush, scrub mussel shells under cold running water. Discard mussels whose shells do not close when tapped. Put mussels in medium mixing bowl, cover with water, and soak for about 10 minutes to remove sand. Transfer to colander to drain in sink.

Preheat oven to 350° F.

1. Heat 2 tablespoons oil in Dutch oven or large oven-proof saucepan over medium-high heat. Carefully add chicken pieces, and fry, in batches, for about 5 minutes on each side, until browned. Season with salt and pepper to taste. Add more oil, as needed. Place cooked chicken pieces in large baking pan, and keep in oven for at least 15 minutes.

2. In same Dutch oven or large saucepan, add 2 more tablespoons oil, onions, garlic, green pepper, and sausage. Stirring frequently, fry until sausage is browned, about 3 minutes. Add water and bring to a boil. Add rice, turmeric, tomatoes, and salt and pepper to taste. Bring to boil again, stir, and remove from heat.

3. Add shrimp, green beans, and ham to rice mixture, and stir well. Layer fried chicken pieces and mussels on top. Cover and bake in oven for 30 minutes, or until rice and chicken are tender and mussels are open. Discard any mussels that did not open. Sprinkle with peas, and cover for about 3 minutes to heat through before serving.

Serve paella from the pan it was cooked in. Spoon some of each major ingredient into individual bowls. A fork, spoon, and clean hands are needed to eat paella. Serve with plenty of crusty bread.

France

In France, Christmas, or, in French, *Noël*, is a joyous time. December 6, the feast day of Saint Nicholas, marks the beginning of the holiday season. Children set out their shoes to be filled with gifts from *Père Noël*, Father Christmas. *Père Noël* is a thin, bearded man, who travels with a donkey. His helper is *Père Fouettard* (in English, Father Whipper), a mean-spirited, mangy-bearded person. He gives out switches to parents of naughty children. For most families, the *crèche*, the manger scene, is more important than a Christmas tree and setting it up is a family project.

After Midnight Mass, many families hurry home to the grandest meal of the year, the Christmas Eve supper, *Réveillon* (in English, wake-up). According to legend, a gaggle of geese welcomed the Wise Men as they approached the stable where Jesus was born, and to symbolize this event, roast goose is prepared for the *Réveillon*.

This potato recipe is a favorite that is often served with the holiday goose.

Gratin Dauphinois   Potato Au Gratin

Yield: serves 8

2 cups heavy cream
2 cups milk
4 **egg yolks**, lightly beaten
2 cloves garlic, **finely chopped**, or ½ teaspoon garlic granules
1 teaspoon ground nutmeg
4 pounds russet potatoes, **peeled**, and thinly sliced
salt and pepper to taste
1 cup **grated** cheddar cheese

Equipment: Medium saucepan, **whisk** or mixing spoon, buttered 13- x 9-inch baking pan, **grater**, oven mitts

Preheat oven to 350° F.

1. In medium saucepan, use whisk or mixing spoon to mix heavy cream, milk, egg yolks, and garlic. Cook over medium heat until small bubbles appear around edge of pan. Remove from heat, and add nutmeg; mix and set aside.

2. Spread potato slices in buttered baking pan, and sprinkle with salt and pepper to taste. Pour cream mixture over potatoes, and sprinkle with grated cheese.

3. Bake in oven for about 1 hour, or until potatoes are tender and top is golden brown.

Serve potatoes hot from the baking pan.

The *Bûche de Noël*, or Yule log cake, is a Christmas tradition for French families everywhere in the world. For hundreds of years, on Christmas Eve, it was the custom for families to gather around as the father blessed and lit the yule log in the fireplace. (See note in introduction to the European section about the pre-Christian origins of the Yule log.) Today the *Bûche de Noël* is a log-shaped cake, usually placed as the centerpiece on the dinner table.

DECORATING NOTE: The log can be decorated in different ways, such as with cookies and candy in the shape of Santa, pine trees, and reindeers. It can also be sprinkled with confectioners' sugar to look like snow. Sometimes people add candles, flowers, or nonedible decorations (available at most bakeries, craft supply, toy, or novelty stores).

The *Bûche de Noël* is about 15 inches long. Prepare a large, flat serving tray or a piece of wood or bottom-side of baking sheet at least 18 inches long, covered with foil, to set the cake roll on. (The cake can be set diagonally on the pan to utilize maximum length.)

Bûche de Noël   Yule Log Cake

Yield: serves 12 to 15

    cooking spray, or 1 tablespoon butter or
      margarine
    3 eggs
    1 cup sugar
    $1/3$ cup water
    1 teaspoon baking powder
    ¼ teaspoon salt
    ¼ cup cocoa, more as needed
    1 teaspoon vanilla extract
    1 cup cake flour
    cream filling (recipe follows)
    chocolate frosting (recipe follows)

Equipment: 15- x 10-inch **jellyroll pan**, aluminum foil, large mixing bowl, egg beater or electric mixer, rubber **spatula**, oven mitts, toothpick, heat-proof work surface

Preheat oven to 375° F.

1. Prepare jellyroll pan: Smoothly line bottom and sides of pan with foil. Grease with cooking spray, butter, or margarine.

2. In large mixing bowl, use egg beater or electric mixer to beat eggs until thick and lemon-colored, about 5 minutes. Mixing constantly, add sugar, a little at a time. Add water, and mix well. Add baking powder, salt, ¼ cup cocoa, vanilla, and flour, a little at a time. Mix until smooth and well blended. Spread batter evenly in foil-lined jellyroll pan.

3. Bake in oven for about 15 minutes, until toothpick inserted in center comes out clean. Using oven mitts, remove from oven and place on heat-proof work surface. Sprinkle top surface of cake with cocoa.

4. Leaving oven mitts on, cover cake with a piece of foil (at least 12- x 18-inches), and wrap foil around pan. Firmly holding foil and cake pan together, invert onto work surface. Remove pan and peel off top foil. Sprinkle bottom surface of cake with cocoa. While cake is warm, roll bottom foil and cake together, jellyroll fashion, from narrow end. (The finished cake roll is 15 inches long.) Cool to room temperature.

The next step in making the Yule log is to fill cake roll with cream filling (recipe follows).

Cream Filling

Yield: about 2¼ cups

    1½ cups heavy cream
    1 teaspoon vanilla extract
    1½ teaspoons white corn syrup
    ¼ cup confectioners' sugar

Equipment: Medium mixing bowl, egg beater or electric mixer, **spatula** or knife

In medium mixing bowl, use egg beater or electric mixer to beat heavy cream until soft peaks form when you lift the egg beaters out of the cream. Beating constantly, add vanilla, corn syrup, and confectioners' sugar, a little at a time, until stiff peaks form.

Refrigerate until ready to use.

Bûche de Nöel—Cake   Yule Log Assembly

1. To assemble cake: Have serving tray, foil-covered board, or inverted baking sheet ready.

2. Unroll cake on work surface. Using spatula or knife, spread filling evenly over cake to within 1-inch of the edges. Reroll cake (without foil), and place seam-side down onto tray or board. Refrigerate 1 hour to set.

3. Frost *Bûche de Noël* (recipe follows): Using spatula or knife, thickly cover cake roll with frosting. Using fork handle or knife, make rough bark-like ridges in frosting. Decorate by adding candles, flowers, or other cake decorations.

To serve, cut into 1- to 1½-inch slices.

SHORTCUT TIP: For frosting: Canned (1-pound-size) prepared chocolate frosting covers one log.

Chocolate Frosting

Yield: about 3 cups
  2½ cups confectioners' sugar
  ½ cup (4 ounces) melted semisweet chocolate chips
  ⅓ cup butter or margarine, at room temperature
  1 teaspoon vanilla extract
  3 tablespoons hot water, more or less as needed

Equipment: Medium mixing bowl, egg beater or electric mixer, **spatula**, knife or fork

In medium mixing bowl, use egg beater or electric mixer to mix confectioners' sugar, melted chocolate, butter or margarine, and vanilla until smooth. Add just enough hot water to make mixture spreadable.

Use chocolate mocha frosting to frost Yule cake (directions precede).

The holiday season is a time for sweets, and *truffles* are a specialty of French candy makers.

Truffles   Chocolate Candy

Yield: about 20 to 25 pieces
  2 squares (1 ounce each) unsweetened chocolate
  1 cup (8 ounces) semisweet chocolate chips
  ½ cup butter or margarine, at room temperature
  1 teaspoon vanilla extract
  1½ cups confectioners' sugar
  1 cup chocolate sprinkles, finely ground nuts, coconut, or cocoa; or ¼ cup *each* for assorted coatings

Equipment: Medium saucepan, wooden mixing spoon, tablespoon, wax paper, work surface, small shallow bowl, cookie sheet

1. Put chocolate squares and chocolate chips in medium saucepan, and, stirring frequently, heat over low heat until melted, about 8 minutes. Chocolate should be smooth and lump-free. Remove from heat.

2. Add butter or margarine and vanilla, and stir well. Add confectioners' sugar, ½ cup at a time. After each addition, beat mixture with a wooden spoon until well blended. Refrigerate for about 1 hour, or until mixture is firm enough to be shaped into balls.

3. Using clean hands, roll a tablespoonful of mixture into each ball. Place on wax-paper-covered work surface. Continue until all mixture is used.

4. Coat truffles: Select one or more coatings of your choice: chocolate sprinkles, finely ground nuts, grated coconut, or cocoa. Put about ¼ cup of each into a its own small, shallow bowl. Using clean hands, completely cover each ball with one of the coatings. Place on wax-paper-covered cookie sheet. Loosely cover with wax paper and refrigerate for about 4 hours before serving.

Serve truffles as a candy treat. Store in airtight container for up to 3 days in refrigerator or several weeks in freezer.

Belgium

Belgium is divided culturally and ethnically into Flemish-speaking Flanders in the north and French-speaking Walloonia in the south. Most Belgians are Roman Catholic, and they cherish festivals of all sorts. Besides Christian holidays, there are festivals for historic battles, trade guilds dating back to the Middle Ages, and even ones for cats.

Carnival, the festival held the last day before Lent, is the most exciting Belgium holiday, and every region celebrates it differently. An oddity unique to Belgium is the "March of the *Gilles*." Men and boys wearing brightly colored suits and huge ostrich-feathered headdresses strut down the street, throwing oranges at onlookers. According to an old legend, the *Gilles* represent Inca Indians, and oranges symbolize their gold.

The one thing most Belgians have in common is their love of food, and food is a part of every celebration.

Fresh fruit is eaten at almost every meal, especially holiday feasts. *Stoofperen* is a Flemish recipe for stewed pears.

Stoofperen — Stewed Pears

Yield: serves 6

- 6 firm, ripe pears, **peeled**, halved, and **cored**
- juice of 2 lemons
- 2 cups water
- ½ cup sugar
- 1 teaspoon cinnamon
- 12 red or green maraschino cherries (available at all supermarkets), for **garnish**

Equipment: Medium saucepan with cover, mixing spoon, dessert bowls

1. Sprinkle pears with juice of half a lemon to prevent discoloration.

2. Pour remaining lemon juice and water into medium saucepan. Add sugar and cinnamon, and bring to a boil over high heat. Add pears, reduce heat to simmer, cover, and cook for about 20 minutes, or until pears are tender but still firm.

Serve two halves in each dessert bowl and garnish with a cherry in the center of each.

In Belgian homes, baking is an important part of all holiday celebrations. This apple tart is a popular Walloonia dessert recipe.

Tarte Tatin — Apple Tart

Yield: serves 8

- 1¼ cups all-purpose flour
- 1 teaspoon baking powder
- 1½ cups sugar
- ½ teaspoon salt
- 1 cup butter or margarine
- 1 egg, beaten
- 3 pounds small apples (such as Granny Smiths), **peeled**, halved, **cored**

Equipment: Large mixing bowl, mixing spoon, large skillet with cover, buttered 9-inch cake pan, toothpick, oven mitts

Preheat oven to 400° F.

1. In large mixing bowl, mix flour, baking powder, ¹/₂ cup sugar, and salt. Using clean hands, blend in ¹/₃ cup butter or margarine. Add egg, and mix as little as possible to make a smooth dough. Set aside.

2. Melt remaining ²/₃ cup butter or margarine in large skillet over medium heat. Add remaining 1 cup sugar, and, stirring constantly, cook until sugar melts and turns golden, about 5 minutes. Add apples, and baste with sugar mixture. Reduce heat to medium-low, cover, and cook, basting frequently, until almost tender, about 10 minutes.

3. Arrange apples in buttered cake pan in rows with cut-side down. Pour sugar mixture from skillet over apples. Spread dough over apples and press evenly in pan.

4. Bake in oven for about 30 minutes, or until browned and fully baked. If a toothpick inserted in the middle comes out clean, tart is done. Cool to warm and invert on serving platter.

Serve warm, cut into squares.

United Kingdom

The United Kingdom, also known as Great Britain, comprises England, Wales, Scotland, and Northern Ireland. English is the official language, but Welsh is widely spoken in Wales, and some Gaelic is spoken in Scotland. At one time, these countries were independent. Wales united with England in 1536, and in 1707 Scotland united with England and Wales to form the United Kingdom of Great Britain. Although these countries are now unified politically, many distinctive cultural traditions, especially cooking traditions, are maintained in each country.

England

Christmas is perhaps the favorite English holiday. In fact, it was the English who began the custom of sending greeting cards on Christmas. The English Christmas is steeped in traditions, and English holiday feasts are legend. In many households preparations begin months in advance, and festivities continue until the Twelfth Night of Christmas, January 6.

In England the grand holiday feast is called Christmas lunch. The dinner table is set with the best linen, china, and silverware. An English tradition is to place a party favor called a **Christmas cracker** (a small colorful noise maker with a limerick or a tiny toy inside) at each place setting. When the guests are seated, they pop the crackers and have fun revealing the prize inside. For many years, the traditional lunch was "roast joint" (roast beef) with Yorkshire pudding. Today beef, somewhat of a luxury, is being replaced by less expensive turkey or pork. For many, however, nothing can ever replace beef for Christmas, regardless of cost. (For a recipe for roast beef and Yorkshire pudding, see Canada, page 260.)

Besides the roast beef, plum pudding has been the highlight of the English Christmas feast for centuries. Made in the traditional way, its preparation is very labor-intensive, but the preparation is part of the celebration.

The Sunday before Advent is "stir-up Sunday." This is the last possible date for puddings to have time to mellow to be ready for Christmas. Cooks dedicated to pudding making the old fashioned way have some "stirred up" almost a year in advance. Part of the tradition is to have every family member stir the pudding for luck, and another tradition is to hide a rich man's six pence, a bachelor's button, a spinster's thimble, or a poor man's bean in the batter so that the finders will know their fate for the coming year.

Today, easy-to-make puddings are preferred by busy English cooks. This recipe is a simplified version of the traditional pudding.

Christmas Pudding

Yield: serves 10

2¼ cups all-purpose flour

1 teaspoon baking soda

¼ teaspoon *each* ground allspice, ground cinnamon, and ground cloves

1½ cups seedless raisins, soaked in warm water for 30 minutes

½ cup butter or margarine, at room temperature

1 cup sugar

4 eggs

½ cup sour cream

good luck token (optional—see discussion of traditional tokens in the introductory text above)

lemon cream cheese hard sauce (recipe follows), for serving

Equipment: Medium mixing bowl, mixing spoon, large mixing bowl, mixing spoon or electric mixer, rubber **spatula**, buttered 1½-quart steamed pudding mold with cover or buttered 2-pound coffee can, aluminum foil, **steamer pan** (see glossary for tips on how to make one), oven mitts, heat-proof work surface, long knife, can opener

1. In medium mixing bowl, use mixing spoon to mix flour, baking soda, allspice, cinnamon, cloves, and raisins.

2. In large mixing bowl, use mixing spoon or electric mixer to mix butter or margarine and sugar until fluffy, about 3 minutes. Add eggs, one at a time, beating after each. Then, alternate adding flour mixture, a little at a time, and sour cream, a little a time, mixing constantly until well blended.

3. Fill pudding mold or coffee can with batter, insert good luck tokens (optional), and tightly cover with foil.

4. Prepare steamer: Place metal rack in steamer pan, and set pudding on rack. Fill pan halfway up sides of pudding container with water. Bring to a boil over high heat, cover, and reduce heat to **simmer**. Let simmer for 3 hours. Maintain water level by adding more hot water to steamer pan when necessary.

5. Using oven mitts, remove pudding from water and place on heat-proof work surface until cool enough to handle. Remove cover, and, using knife, loosen pudding from sides of container and invert onto serving plate. If using coffee can, open bottom with can opener and push out.

Serve warm pudding sliced in wedges. Add a dollop of lemon cream cheese hard sauce to each serving.

Lemon Cream Cheese Hard Sauce

Yield: about 1½ cups

¹/₃ cup cream cheese, at room temperature

1 cup confectioners' sugar

¼ cup heavy cream, more if necessary

juice and **grated** rind of ½ lemon

Equipment: Medium mixing bowl, mixing spoon, **grater**

In medium mixing bowl, use mixing spoon to beat cream cheese and confectioners' sugar until light and fluffy. Mixing constantly, add ¼ cup cream, a little at a time, and lemon juice and rind. If sauce seems too thick, add more cream. (Mixture should be easily spreadable.) Refrigerate until ready to serve.

To serve, spoon a little sauce over each slice of warm pudding.

Roasting chestnuts conjure up memories and images lyricists love to put to music. No English Christmas is complete unless chestnuts are roasted in the fireplace or oven and munched on during the holiday.

Roasted Chestnuts

SAFETY NOTE: It is important to cut a slit in the chestnut shell; otherwise, it will explode when heated.

Yield: serves 8 to 10
   2 to 3 pounds fresh chestnuts with shells on
   3 tablespoons water

Equipment: Sharp knife, baking sheet, spray bottle, oven mitts

Preheat oven to 375° F.

On the flat side of the chestnut shell, cut a small slit with a sharp knife. Spread nuts out on baking sheet and spray with water. Bake in oven for 30 or 40 minutes, until golden brown.

To serve, keep chestnuts warm by wrapping them in a napkin. To eat chestnuts, peel off the hard brown outer shell and the thin brown inner skin to reveal the edible nut.

Boiled Chestnuts

Yield: serves 4 to 6
   2 to 4 pounds fresh chestnuts
   cold water, as needed

Equipment: Sharp knife, large saucepan, heatproof work surface, **slotted spoon**, oven mitts, kitchen towel, medium bowl with cover

1. On the flat side of the chestnut shell, cut a small slit with a sharp knife. Place chestnuts in large saucepan, and cover with cold water. Bring to a boil over high heat. Boil for 3 minutes and remove from heat. Place on heat-proof work surface.

2. Using slotted spoon, remove 2 or 3 chestnuts at a time from the water. Hold them with a kitchen towel, and peel off outer shells; then, using a small sharp knife, peel off brown inner skins. Keep unpeeled chestnuts warm in water until ready to peel, or the inner skin won't come off. (Bring chestnuts to a boil again for a few seconds if inner skins are difficult to remove.) Put peeled nuts into a medium bowl.

Store peeled nuts in covered container and place in refrigerator until ready to use.

Chestnuts can be added to stuffing, mixed with vegetables, or made into desserts or holiday cakes. One pound of chestnuts with the shells on yields about 2 ½ cups shelled nuts. Dried shelled chestnuts are available at some supermarkets and all Asian food stores. They can be rehydrated by soaking overnight in water. Drain and pat dry with paper towels, discard water.

This recipe combines chestnuts with brussels sprouts.

Chestnuts and Brussels Sprouts

Yield: serves 6
   1½ pounds brussels sprouts, fresh, **trimmed** or frozen, thawed
   water, as needed
   salt and pepper to taste
   2½ cups boiled and shelled chestnuts (recipe precedes)
   ½ cup butter or margarine

Equipment: Small sharp knife, medium saucepan, **colander**, mixing spoon, large skillet with cover

1. Using a small, sharp knife, cut a shallow X on the stem end of brussels sprouts (to ensure they will cook evenly), and put in medium saucepan. Cover with cold water, add 1 teaspoon salt, and bring to a boil over high heat. Reduce heat to **simmer**, and cook until tender, about 15 minutes. Drain well in colander.

2. Melt butter or margarine in large skillet over medium heat. Add brussels sprouts and chestnuts, and toss to coat evenly. Cover and cook until heated through, about 10 minutes, stirring occasionally. Add salt and pepper to taste, stir, and keep warm until ready to serve.

Serve as a side dish with main dish of meat or fowl.

Scotland

Hogmanay, the Scottish New Year's Eve is the most popular holiday and is full of superstitions. Traditionally, the house and old, bad trolls are scrubbed away, making room for new trolls and good fairies. The first person to cross the threshold in the new year is a "first-footer." A redhead is considered unlucky, and a female first-footer is thought to be a total disaster. The ideal first-footer is a tall, dark, handsome man, but he must not arrive empty-handed. He brings a piece of coal, for warmth in home and heart; the *black bun*, also called the *hogmanay bun* (recipe follows), which symbolizes plenty of food; and a bottle of spirits for prosperity. He puts the coal in the fireplace, the black bun on the table; then he pours a drink for his host and shouts, "Happy New Year!" He arrives through the front door and must go out the back.

The following recipe for a pie crust can be used to make the black bun but frozen pie crust can be used as well.

Basic Pie Crust

Yield: 2 crusts

2½ cups all-purpose flour, more as needed
1 teaspoon *each* salt and baking powder
2 tablespoons sugar
¾ cup cold butter or margarine, **finely chopped**
½ cup ice water, more if necessary

Equipment: Large mixing bowl, aluminum foil, lightly floured work surface, floured **rolling pin**, 9-inch pie pan, oven mitts

1. In large mixing bowl, use clean hands to mix flour, salt, baking powder and sugar. Add butter or margarine and blend until mixture resembles coarse crumbs. Add 6 tablespoons ice water, mix, and form into ball. If dough is too dry, add more water, and, if too sticky, add more flour. Wrap in foil and refrigerate for 1 hour.

2. Divide dough in half. On lightly floured work surface, use floured rolling pin to roll dough about ⅛ inch thick and large enough to cover bottom and sides of pie pan, allowing ½ inch overhang. Roll out remaining dough for top crust.

Continue to make Hogmanay bun *(directions follow).*

Hogmanay Bun Scottish New Year's Bun (also Black Bun)

Yield: serves 8 to 10

1 cup all-purpose flour

½ teaspoon baking powder

½ cup dark brown sugar

1 teaspoon *each* ground cloves and ground ginger

2 cups seedless raisins, soaked in warm water for 30 minutes and drained

½ cup dried cranberries or currants, soaked in warm water for 30 minutes, and drained

2 cooking apples, **peeled**, **cored**, and **finely chopped** (use apples such as Granny Smith or Greening)

½ cup **coarsely chopped** almonds

2 eggs

½ cup milk

1 teaspoon almond extract

2 (9-inch) pie crusts, homemade (recipe precedes) or frozen prepared crusts, thawed

egg glaze

Equipment: Medium bowl, mixing spoon, 9-inch pie pan, fork, pastry brush, knife, oven mitts

1. Prepare filling: In medium mixing bowl, mix flour, baking powder, brown sugar, cloves, ginger, raisins, cranberries or currants, apples, almonds, eggs, milk, and almond extract until well blended.

Preheat oven to 350° F.

2. To assemble: Poke bottom crust about 6 times with fork tines before filling. Fill crust with raisin mixture, and cover with top crust. Fold edges of both crusts together, and tuck along inside edge of pie pan.

3. Using pastry brush, brush top crust with egg glaze. Using knife, cut about 6 vent slits in top crust.

4. Bake in oven for about 2 hours, or until golden brown. Allow to mellow overnight at room temperature before serving.

To serve, cut into wedges. The Hogmanay bun *keeps for about 2 weeks if well wrapped and refrigerated.*

Hogmanay is a night full of good cheer, dancing, singing, and eating. There is plenty of food since no one comes empty-handed. The first-footer brings the *Hogmanay bun* (black bun), and shortbread, such as the following recipe, is brought by other guests.

Berry Oatmeal Shortbread

Yield: 9 pieces

1½ cups flour

1 cup *each* brown sugar and quick-cooking oatmeal

1 teaspoon cinnamon

½ cup melted butter or margarine

1 teaspoon vanilla extract

1½ teaspoons cornstarch

½ cup water, more or less as needed

2 (10-ounce) packages frozen raspberries, thawed and drained (save juice)

½ cup granulated sugar

Equipment: Large mixing bowl, mixing spoon, cup, medium saucepan, oven mitts, greased or nonstick 9-inch square baking pan

Preheat oven to 325° F.

1. In large mixing bowl, use spoon or clean hands to mix flour, brown sugar, oatmeal, cinnamon, melted butter or margarine, and vanilla until mixture resembles coarse crumbs.

2. In cup, mix cornstarch and 2 tablespoons water. Add reserved raspberry juice to make 1 cup. If not enough juice, add water until mixture measures 1 cup. Pour cornstarch mixture into medium saucepan, and add granulated sugar. Cook over medium heat, stirring frequently, until clear and thickened, about 5 minutes. Add raspberries, stir, and cook for about 3 minutes, or until thickened.

3. In greased or nonstick 9-inch baking pan, press 2 cups of oatmeal mixture evenly in pan. Cover with raspberry mixture, and sprinkle remaining oatmeal crumbs over the top.

4. Bake in oven for about 50 minutes, until top is golden brown. Cool for 15 minutes before cutting into 3-inch squares.

Serve warm or at room temperature.

Wales

On March 1, the Welsh celebrate Saint David's Day, named for the patron saint of Wales, who is said to have eaten a great many leeks as part of his vegetarian diet. (A leek is a vegetable that looks like an extremely large, green onion and that has a pleasant, mild taste.) The leek is the national emblem of Wales, and on Saint David's Day the Welsh celebrate by wearing leeks in their hats or around their necks in honor of both the patron saint and a seventh-century victory over the English. According to the legend, Saint David convinced the Welsh to wear leeks in their hats as a way of identifying their fellow soldiers in battle.

Traditionally, leeks are eaten on Saint David's Day. Leek pies and leek soup are Welsh favorites.

Leek Soup

Yield: serves 6 to 8
   8 cups water
   1 cup instant potato flakes
   2 leeks (about 1 pound)
   2 tablespoons butter or margarine
   1 (14-ounce) can stewed tomatoes
   salt and pepper to taste

Equipment: Medium saucepan with cover, wooden mixing spoon, work surface, sharp knife, **colander**, medium skillet with cover

1. Pour water into medium saucepan, and bring to a boil over high heat. Remove from heat, slowly add potato flakes, and stir until well blended and smooth. Cover and set aside.

2. On work surface, using sharp knife, **trim** leeks, cutting off and discarding the root and coarse green stems. (Only the white and pale green part of the leek, about 6 inches, are tender and edible.) Split leek lengthwise and cut crosswise into ¼-inch pieces. Put leeks in colander, and rinse under running water, tossing constantly with your hand to remove sand; drain well. (There should be about 1½ cups sliced leeks.)

3. Melt 2 tablespoons butter or margarine in medium skillet over medium heat. Add leeks, and cook, stirring occasionally, for about 3 minutes. Reduce heat to low, cover, and cook until soft, about 10 minutes.

4. Add leeks with pan drippings, stewed tomatoes, and salt and pepper to taste to potato mixture in saucepan from step 1; stir with wooden spoon. Return saucepan to medium heat, cover, and cook for about 45 minutes, stirring occasionally.

Serve warm in soup bowls.

Leek and chicken pot pie is a favorite St. David's Day supper. It is quick and easy with no bottom crust to make. Puff pastry is fun to work with, and the rougher it looks before baking the better it looks when golden brown.

Leek and Chicken Pot Pie

Yield: serves 8

3 leeks (about 1½ pounds)

2 tablespoons vegetable oil

3 eggs

½ cup heavy cream

½ cup **shredded** Swiss cheese

2 cups **coarsely chopped**, cooked chicken (this is a good recipe for leftover chicken)

¼ teaspoon salt

4 thin slices smoked ham

8-inch square frozen puff pastry, thawed (available at most supermarkets; 17-ounce box contains 2 unbaked 9½-inch squares of puff pastry)

egg wash

Equipment: Knife, work surface, **colander**, large skillet, mixing spoon, medium mixing bowl, buttered 9-inch pie pan, lightly floured **rolling pin**, **pastry brush**, scissors, baking sheet, oven mitts

Preheat oven to 400° F.

1. On work surface, use sharp knife to trim leeks, cutting off and discarding the root and coarse green stems. (Only the white and pale green part of the leek, about 6 inches, are tender and edible.) Split lengthwise and cut crosswise into ¼-inch pieces. Put in colander, and rinse under running water, tossing constantly with your hand, to remove sand; drain well. (There should be about 2½ cups sliced leeks.)

2. Heat oil in large skillet over medium-high heat. Add leeks, and, stirring constantly, fry until soft, about 6 minutes. Remove from heat.

3. In medium mixing bowl, beat eggs, cream, and Swiss cheese. Add chicken, leeks, and salt, toss to mix well, and pour into buttered pie pan. Arrange slices of ham over the top, overlapping, if necessary. Set aside.

4. Place pastry square on lightly floured work surface, and, using lightly floured rolling pin, roll out to about 10 inches square. Using a knife, cut a 2-inch X in the center of the pastry. Lay pastry over filling, and, using scissors, trim pastry along the outer edge saving the scraps. Using clean hands, crimp pastry around top edge of pan. (If it's rough looking, that's just fine; you can't mess up puff pastry.) Using the scissors, cut the scraps into leaf, star- or confetti-like shapes and scatter them over the top. Using a pastry brush, brush top pastry well with egg wash.

5. Bake in oven for 1 hour, or until top is golden brown.

6. Remove from oven and cool to room temperature.

To serve, cut into wedges and serve at room temperature, or warm in microwave.

Ireland

The Irish are predominately Catholic, and they celebrate all Christian holidays as well as many ancient Celtic agrarian festivals. From the harvest festivals through spring festivals, every celebration of the Celtic druids (ancient Celtic priests) was geared to help the reawakening of spring. The people feared the darkness of winter, and they had no guarantees that spring would come. It became the custom, in early November, for the Celtic druids to make great symbolic fires, built to give power to the declining sun.

Our modern-day Halloween celebration has its roots in the Celtic celebration *Samhain*, an ancient Celtic harvest festival that honored the lord of the dead on the first day of winter. According to legend, the spirits of all the people who had died in the previous year gathered together and were led out of town by people wearing masks and costumes. In the ninth century, the Catholic Church made November 1 the day for remembering all the saints, so it became All Saints' Day or All Hallows' Day. The day before became All Hallows' Eve, or Hallowe'en.

Most outdoor community celebrations include fiddle playing, dancing, courting, and feasting on a potato dish that has been traditionally eaten on all Irish holidays since the potato was introduced to the Irish sometime after the sixteenth century when the Spanish brought it to Europe from South America.

Colcannon is a favorite way of fixing potatoes, and sometimes tokens of good fortune are hidden in the potato casserole. Another Irish custom is to set out a plateful of *colcannon* on Halloween for the fairies and the ghosts to munch on.

Colcannon   Potato Casserole

Yield: serves 4 to 6

6 potatoes, **peeled** and quartered
6 tablespoons butter or margarine, more as needed

½ cup milk, more if necessary
6 green onions, washed, **trimmed**, and **finely chopped**
salt and pepper to taste
4 cups **coarsely chopped** green cabbage

Equipment: Medium saucepan with cover, fork, **colander**, large mixing bowl, potato masher, large skillet with cover, mixing spoon

1. Put peeled and quartered potatoes in medium saucepan, and cover with water. Bring to boil over high heat. Reduce heat to medium, cover, and cook until soft, about 20 minutes. Poke with a fork to test if potatoes are done—they will be soft. Drain in colander, and transfer to large mixing bowl. Add 2 tablespoons butter or margarine and ½ cup milk, and, using potato masher, mash until smooth and fluffy. Add more milk, if necessary. Add green onions and salt and pepper to taste, and, using mixing spoon, stir well. Set aside.

2. Melt 4 tablespoons butter or margarine in large skillet over medium-high heat. Add cabbage and stir. Reduce heat to **simmer**, cover, and cook for about 15 minutes, or until cabbage is tender. Add potato mixture to cabbage in skillet, stir, and dot 4 or 5 teaspoons butter or margarine on top of potato mixture. Cover and heat through over medium-low heat for about 10 minutes.

Serve colcannon *warm, as a side dish.*

Christian and Celtic holidays often come together, joining unusual rituals, such as St. Stephen's Day, December 26, which is called Wren Day in Ireland. The wren was a sacred bird to the druids. According to legend, the wren is king of the birds because it can fly higher than any other. On Wren Day, young Irishmen dress in outlandish costumes and paint their faces. The "Wren boys," as they are called, go from house to house, "hunting the wren." Their singing, dancing, and buffoonery earn them a few coins from onlookers. The St. Stephen's Day feast is made from

Christmas dinner leftovers, steaming hot giblet soup, cold cuts, and fruitcake.

The traditional fruitcake is called spotted dog, curnie cake, sweet cake, or railway cake, depending upon the region of Ireland.

Boiled Fruitcake

Yield: serves 10 to 12
  2 cups butter or margarine
  2 cups dark brown sugar, firmly packed
  3 cups golden seedless raisins
  1 teaspoon ground allspice
  ½ cup water
  2 eggs, beaten
  4 cups whole wheat flour

Equipment: Large saucepan, mixing spoon, scissors, wax paper, buttered or nonstick 9 inch round cake pan, rubber **spatula**, oven mitts

1. Melt butter or margarine in large saucepan over medium-high heat. Add sugar, raisins, allspice, and water. Stir ingredients and bring to a boil. Reduce heat to **simmer**, and cook for 10 minutes, stirring frequently. Remove saucepan from heat and cool to room temperature.

Preheat oven to 250° F.

2. Add eggs to mixture in saucepan, and stir well. Add flour, a little at a time, and, using clean hands, mix until well blended.

3. Cut wax paper to cover bottom of buttered or nonstick 9-inch round cake pan. Fit wax paper into pan and butter it. Spread mixture in cake pan, and smooth top.

4. Bake in oven for about 2 hours, or until golden brown. Cool to room temperature and allow cake to mellow for at least 24 hours before serving.

Serve the cake cut into wedges.

Netherlands

In the Netherlands young and old alike look forward to the arrival of Saint Nicholas by ship, barge, motorcycle, wagon, bicycle, or even helicopter on December 5. He sports a white beard and wears a bishop's hat, white robe, and red cape. His arrival marks the beginning of the holiday season. Once on land, Saint Nicholas, known in the Netherlands as "Sinterklaas," travels by white stallion, and children set their shoes out filled with carrots and hay to feed the horse. In the morning good children find gifts, and naughty children find switches.

Grownups spend the evening of the fifth partying and exchanging gifts. Amidst festivities trays of sweets are set out to snack on. A favorite snack is boiled chestnuts (recipe page 107), dipped in melted butter and sprinkled with salt.

Baking Christmas cookies of all kinds and shapes is a meaningful Dutch tradition. *Speculaas,* Dutch spice cookies in the shapes of windmills or St. Nicholas on horseback, are typical Dutch cookies. *Speculaas* molds and patterned rolling pins make embossed designs on the cookies. These molds and rolling pins are available in the kitchen gadget section of many stores. Cutting the dough into initials or number shapes, *letterbankets,* is also popular with Dutch children.

Speculaas — Dutch Spice Cookies

Yield: about 2 dozen 2- x 3-inch cookies

2 cups all-purpose flour
½ tablespoon baking powder
2 teaspoons ground cinnamon
½ teaspoon ground allspice
½ cup butter or margarine, at room temperature
1½ cups dark brown sugar, firmly packed
1 egg, well beaten
1 teaspoon vanilla extract

Equipment: Small mixing bowl, mixing spoon, large mixing bowl with cover, mixing spoon or electric mixer, rubber **spatula**, floured work surface, floured **rolling pin**, **cookie cutters** or knife, greased or nonstick cookie sheet, metal spatula, oven mitts

1. In small mixing bowl, combine flour, baking powder, cinnamon, and allspice.

2. In large mixing bowl, use mixing spoon or electric mixer to beat butter or margarine and brown sugar until light and fluffy. Add egg and vanilla, and mix well. Mixing constantly, add flour mixture, a little at a time. Using clean hands, form dough into a ball, cover, and refrigerate for about 1 hour, until firm.

Preheat oven to 350° F.

3. On floured work surface, use floured rolling pin to roll out dough ⅛ inch thick. Using cookie cutters or knife, cut into desired shapes. Place 1 inch apart on greased or nonstick cookie sheet.

4. Bake in oven for about 15 minutes until lightly browned. Remove from oven and cool for 2 minutes on cookie sheet before removing with metal spatula. Continue baking in batches.

Serve as a snack. Cookies keep well in airtight container.

Spritz — Dutch Sugar Cookies

Yield: about 4 dozen

1 cup butter or margarine, at room temperature
1 cup sugar
1 egg
2¼ cups all-purpose flour
½ teaspoon baking powder
¼ teaspoon salt
1 teaspoon vanilla extract

Equipment: Large mixing bowl, mixing spoon or electric mixer, mixing spoon, rubber **spatula**, **cookie gun with decorative tip,** cookie sheet, oven mitts, metal spatula, wax paper, work surface

Preheat oven to 375° F.

1. In large mixing bowl, use mixing spoon or electric mixer to beat butter or margarine and sugar until light and fluffy, about 3 minutes. Mixing constantly, add egg, flour, baking powder, salt, and vanilla. Refrigerate dough for about 20 minutes to firm.

2. Assemble cookie gun with decorative tip (according to directions) and fill with dough.

3. Force dough through gun onto cookie sheet and space about 1 inch apart.

4. Bake in oven for about 10 minutes, until edges are golden brown. Remove from cookie sheet with metal spatula, and cool to room temperature on wax-paper-covered work surface. Continue baking in batches.

Serve cookies as a snack and store in an airtight container.

Another sweet treat that is a holiday favorite are *olie bollen,* doughnut-like pastries.

Olie Bollen   Dutch Fried Pastries

CAUTION: HOT OIL USED

Yield: about 3 dozen

¾ cup milk

½ cup sugar

¼ cup vegetable oil

2 eggs, beaten

1 teaspoon vanilla extract

2½ cups all-purpose flour

3 teaspoons baking powder

½ teaspoon salt

½ cup seedless raisins

2 apples, **peeled**, **cored**, and **finely chopped**

vegetable oil for **deep frying**

½ cup confectioners' sugar, more or less as needed, for **garnish**

Equipment: Large mixing bowl, mixing spoon or electric mixer, **deep fryer** (see glossary for tips on making one), wooden spoon, baking sheet, paper towels, **slotted spoon**

1. In large mixing bowl, use mixing spoon or electric mixer to mix milk, sugar, ¼ cup oil, eggs, vanilla, 1 cup flour, baking powder, and salt until smooth and lump-free. Mixing constantly, slowly add remaining 1½ cups flour, and blend well.

2. Using mixing spoon, **fold in** raisins and apples.

3. Prepare deep fryer: Have an adult help you heat oil to 375° F. Oil is hot enough for frying when small bubbles appear around a wooden spoon handle when it is dipped in the oil. Place several layers of paper towels on baking sheet.

4. Very carefully drop heaping tablespoonfuls of batter into hot oil, and fry 3 or 4 at a time for about 3 minutes on each side, or until golden brown. Remove with slotted spoon, and drain on paper towels. Continue frying in batches. While still warm, sprinkle with confectioners' sugar.

Serve at once, while still warm.

Germany

In Germany, many holiday celebrations are regional, and some of them are centuries old. These regional festivals are mostly agrarian, combining ancient pagan customs with Christian beliefs.

Unique to Germany is *Oktoberfest*, a secular harvest festival lasting several weeks. Germans everywhere in the world celebrate their heritage during *Oktoberfest*, with lots of eating, drinking, singing, and camaraderie. (For recipe, see U.S. Octoberfest page 269.)

As in many nations with a Christian majority, Christmas is the favorite German holiday. On Christmas Eve the pine tree is decorated. (The custom of decorating a pine tree for Christmas actually originated in Germany.) Gifts are exchanged, and children hang up their stockings or set out boots to be filled with goodies.

Christmas Day is for feasting on stuffed goose, hare, venison, or, more recently, veal cutlets. Spices, apples, and nuts seem to go into almost everything cooked or baked for the holidays.

German Christmas cookies are wonderful, and baking them is a labor of love. Many cookie recipes, such as this one for *pfeffernüsse*, are centuries old. Similar spicy drop cookies are found throughout northern Europe. In Denmark they are called *pebernodder*, and in Sweden they are known as *pepparnötter*.

Pfeffernüsse — German Pepper Nut Cookies

Yield: about 4 dozen
- ½ cup butter or margarine, at room temperature
- ¼ cup dark brown sugar, firmly packed
- ½ cup molasses
- 1 egg
- 3¼ cups all-purpose flour, more if necessary
- 1 teaspoon baking soda
- ½ teaspoon *each* ground cloves and ground nutmeg
- ¼ teaspoon black pepper
- 1 teaspoon ground cinnamon
- 1 cup confectioners' sugar, more or less as needed, for **garnish**

Equipment: Large mixing bowl, mixing spoon or electric mixer, tablespoon, greased or nonstick cookie sheet, oven mitts, wire rack, small bowl, wax paper, work surface

Preheat oven to 350°.

1. In large mixing bowl, use mixing spoon or electric mixer to mix butter or margarine and brown sugar until creamy. Add molasses and egg, and mix well. Mixing constantly, add 3¼ cups flour, baking soda, cloves, nutmeg, black pepper, and cinnamon, a little at a time, until well blended.

2. Using clean hands, shape dough into walnut-size balls, and place about 1½ inches apart on greased or nonstick cookie sheet.

3. Bake in oven for about 10 minutes or until set. Cool for about 3 minutes on cookie sheet before transferring to rack.

4. Put confectioners' sugar in small bowl. While cookies are warm, roll each in sugar and place side by side on wax-paper-covered work surface to cool to room temperature. Continue making cookies in batches.

To serve cookies first allow them to mellow in an airtight container for about 2 days. Pfeffernüsse *keep well for weeks.*

It was German bakers, several generations ago, who created gingerbread people, animals, tree ornaments, and houses for the Christmas holiday.

Basic Gingerbread Dough

Yield: about 5 to 6 cups
- ¾ cup butter or margarine, at room temperature
- ¾ cup dark brown sugar
- ¾ cup molasses
- ¼ cup water
- 1½ teaspoons ground **ginger**
- ½ teaspoon ground cinnamon
- 1 teaspoon baking soda
- 3¼ cups all-purpose flour

Equipment: Large mixing bowl with cover, mixing spoon or electric mixer, wax paper

In large mixing bowl, use mixing spoon or electric mixer to beat butter or margarine and brown sugar until creamy. Add molasses, water, ginger, cinnamon, and baking soda; mix well. Mixing constantly, add flour and blend well. Cover and refrigerate for about 2 hours.

To make gingerbread people or animals, use cookie cutters in the desired shapes, which are usually available in the kitchen gadget section of many stores, or cut a pattern out of cardboard. To make tree ornaments, poke a hole about the size of a pencil into the top of each cookie before it is baked. After it is baked, thread a thin ribbon through the hole for hanging.

For decorating gingerbread cookies with icing, a pastry bag with writing tip is necessary (available in kitchen section of many stores).

Gingerbread People, Animals, or Tree Ornaments

Yield: about 10 to 20 cookies

4 cups basic gingerbread dough (recipe precedes)

1 cup raisins, more or less as needed, for decoration

6 or 8 candied cherries, more or less, for decoration

1 cup lemon icing, for decorating (recipe follows)

Equipment: Lightly floured work surface, lightly floured **rolling pin, cookie cutter** or cardboard pattern and paring knife, lightly greased or nonstick cookie sheet, metal **spatula**, oven mitts, wax paper, pastry bag with writing tip

Preheat oven to 350° F.

1. On lightly floured work surface, roll out dough ⅛ inch thick, using lightly floured rolling pin. Cut desired shape with cookie cutter or knife. (If using cardboard pattern, grease underside before placing on dough.) Using spatula, transfer cookie to lightly greased or nonstick cookie sheet; place 1 inch apart.

2. Press in raisins to make eyes and shirt buttons. Press in a small piece of cherry for a mouth.

3. Bake in oven for about 12 minutes, or until lightly browned. Cool for 3 minutes before removing from cookie sheet with spatula. Place on wax-paper-covered work surface, and cool to room temperature before decorating. Lightly grease cookie sheet each time, if necessary, and continue baking cookies in batches.

4. Put icing in pastry bag fitted with writing tip. Outline eyebrows, nose, tie, belt, pockets, and cuffs.

Allow icing to dry at room temperature before stacking in airtight container. Cookies keep well for several weeks.

Lemon Icing

Yield: 1 cup

grated rind of ½ lemon

1 tablespoon lemon juice

1 tablespoon hot water, more if needed

1 cup confectioners' sugar

Equipment: **Grater**, small mixing bowl with cover, fork or tablespoon, paper towels

Add lemon rind, lemon juice, and hot water to confectioners' sugar in small mixing bowl. Using fork or tablespoon, beat until smooth and thick. The icing should pass through tip of pastry bag when bag is squeezed; if it is too thick, add a few drops of hot water, and if it is too thin, add a little confectioners' sugar.

SPECIAL NOTE: Icing dries out quickly. Keep covered with damp paper towels or place in a container with a tight-fitting lid.

Lemon icing keeps for several weeks covered and refrigerated.

Lebkuchen, spice bars, were first made in Nürnberg during the Middle Ages. Generations of Swiss, German, and Austrian children have loved this holiday treat.

Lebkuchen   Spice Bars

Yield: about 4 dozen

4 eggs

2¼ cups (1 pound) light brown sugar

2 cups flour

1 teaspoon ground cinnamon

1 cup **finely chopped** nuts: almonds, walnuts, or pecans

½ cup finely chopped **citron**

confectioners' sugar glaze (recipe follows), for **garnish**

Equipment: Large mixing bowl, mixing spoon or electric mixer, medium mixing bowl, greased or nonstick 9-inch square baking pan, oven mitts

Preheat oven to 375° F.

1. In large mixing bowl, use mixing spoon or electric mixer to beat eggs and brown sugar until creamy.

2. In medium mixing bowl, mix flour, cinnamon, nuts, and citron. Add to egg mixture, and mix well. Spread mixture evenly over bottom of greased or nonstick 9-inch square baking pan.

3. Bake in oven for about 25 minutes, or until browned. While still warm, spread with confectioners' sugar glaze.

To serve, cut into 1- x 3-inch strips.

Confectioners' Sugar Glaze

Yield: about 1 cup

    1 cup confectioners' sugar, more if necessary
    2 tablespoons hot water, more if necessary
    ½ teaspoon vanilla extract

Equipment: Small mixing bowl, mixing spoon, metal **spatula**

In small bowl, mix 1 cup confectioners' sugar and 2 tablespoons hot water. Add vanilla, and mix until smooth. The mixture should coat spoon. If mixture is too thick, add a few drops of water. If it is too thin, add a little confectioners' sugar.

When finished, spread on lebkuchen *(recipe precedes) using metal spatula.*

Scandinavia

Scandinavian countries of northern Europe—Denmark, Norway, Sweden, Finland, and Iceland—share many of the same things: food,

cold winds, dark winters, short growing seasons, holidays, and love of crayfish. The love of crayfish is related to an unusual Scandinavian custom—the Crayfish Festival.

It is strange to consider the Crayfish Festival a holiday along with Easter and Christmas, but to Scandinavians the crayfish season is a chance to enjoy the last rays of sunshine before the long, dark winter begins. Every August, when crayfish are plentiful, there are numerous outdoor crayfish festivals. They can be simple picnics, backyard affairs with friends, or gigantic community cookouts drawing tourists and visitors from distant places. During the celebration thousands of pounds of crayfish are cooked and piled high on tables set up in parks or other public recreation areas. All the festival goers have a great time eating their fill of the tiny lobster-like crustaceans. It is not unusual for someone to eat ten or more pounds in one sitting. It takes five pounds of live crayfish to pick out one pound of edible meat.

Holiday baking is a big part of many celebrations, and many of the same recipes are shared by all Scandinavians; only the names change. *Sandkake* is a basic Scandinavian holiday cake of Danish origin. The recipe calls for pearl sugar, a product of this region, but coarsely crushed sugar cubes are a good substitute.

Sandkake   Scandinavian Pound Cake

Yield: serves 10

    ¼ cup coarsely crushed sugar cubes
    ¾ cup butter or margarine, at room temperature
    ¾ cup granulated sugar
    3 eggs, at room temperature
    1 teaspoon vanilla extract
    1½ cups all-purpose flour
    1 teaspoon baking powder
    ¼ teaspoon salt
    2 tablespoons milk

Equipment: Buttered 9- x 5-inch loaf pan, large mixing bowl, mixing spoon or electric mixer, medium mixing bowl, rubber **spatula**, toothpick, oven mitts

Preheat oven to 350° F.

1. Sprinkle crushed sugar over bottom and sides of well-buttered loaf pan.

2. In large mixing bowl, use mixing spoon or electric mixer to mix butter or margarine and granulated sugar until light and fluffy. Add eggs and vanilla, and mix well.

3. In medium mixing bowl, mix flour, baking powder, and salt.

4. Mixing constantly, add flour mixture to egg mixture, a little at a time, alternating with milk. Transfer batter to prepared loaf pan.

5. Bake in oven for about 40 minutes, or until toothpick inserted in the middle comes out clean. Cool for 5 minutes, and invert onto rack to cool to room temperature.

To serve, cut in slices.

Rice puddings are almost always included in Scandinavian Christmas dinners. In Denmark, the pudding, called *grod,* is often served at the beginning of the meal. In Sweden a dish of pudding is always set out for *Julenissen,* the gnome who lives in the attic or barn and guards the family. Another Swedish custom is to have each person at the table recite a poem before eating the pudding, and it is the custom in both Sweden and Finland to hide an almond, bean, or coin in the cooked pudding. People must eat with care so they don't swallow the lucky token. The tradition holds that if the finder of the token is a young woman, she will marry before the year's end.

Scandinavian Christmas Rice Pudding

2 cups cooked rice
3 cups milk or light cream
3 tablespoons butter
½ cup sugar, more or less to taste
1 teaspoon vanilla extract
cinnamon sugar, for serving

Equipment: Medium saucepan, wooden mixing spoon

In medium saucepan, mix cooked rice, milk or light cream, butter, and ½ cup sugar (more or less to taste). Bring to a boil over high heat. Reduce heat to simmer, and cook for about 20 minutes, or until mixture thickens. Remove from heat, add vanilla, and mix well.

To serve, add a lucky token and mix well. Spoon into individual dessert bowls and sprinkle with cinnamon sugar.

Denmark

The people living in Denmark are called Danes. Danes and their ancestors have inhabited the region since prehistoric times. Almost all Danes belong to the Lutheran Church, although people are free to follow their own religions. During the Viking period (ninth to eleventh centuries), Denmark was a great power. Viking raids brought Denmark into contact with Christianity and the rest of Europe.

Danes observe many holidays, most of which are celebrated with a hearty meal. On Liberation Eve, May 4, homes display lighted candles in windows to commemorate Denmark's freedom from German occupation at the end of World War II. Liberation Day, May 5, is a national holiday, as is Constitution Day on June 5. Midsummer's Eve, the festival of light, celebrates the summer solstice, when the day is at its longest. Danish communities light bonfires, have festivals, and watch for the "Midsummer Night" love magic. Getting married on this night is very popular.

The most important Christian holiday is Christmas, and it is a tradition to hang a stalk of corn on the door or to spread grain for the birds. The corn symbolizes a good harvest to come and sharing the grain promotes good will with other creatures on earth. Families have Christmas trees, and children look forward to the Christmas troll (also called a "gnome") who brings them gifts. It is often the custom after dinner for adults and children to join hands around the Christmas tree in the middle of the living room and sing carols. Afterwards, the children drink hot chocolate, and the adults have coffee while sharing holiday cookies.

The Danish Christmas Eve dinner is usually pork or fowl served with fruit, like the chicken with apples recipe below, and red cabbage. (See next recipe for *rodkaal*, braised red cabbage.)

Chicken with Apples

Yield: serves 4

4 (about 6 ounces each) boned, skinless chicken breasts
½ cup all-purpose flour
½ cup butter or margarine, more or less as needed
1 cup canned apple pie filling (available at supermarkets)
1 cup heavy cream
4 tablespoons slivered almonds, for **garnish**
4 cups cooked rice or noodles, for serving

Equipment: Wax paper, work surface, large skillet with cover, metal **spatula**, small bowl, mixing spoon

1. Place chicken breasts on wax-paper-covered work surface. Sprinkle both sides with flour.

2. Melt 2 tablespoons butter or margarine in large skillet over medium heat. Carefully fry chicken on each side for about 6 minutes, or until golden brown. Add more butter or margarine if needed to prevent sticking. Remove from heat.

3. In small bowl, stir apple pie filling and cream, and then spread over chicken in skillet. Return skillet to stove over medium-low heat, cover, and cook for 20 minutes, until sauce thickens and chicken is tender. Before serving, sprinkle with almonds.

Serve hot over rice or noodles.

Rodkaal   Braised Red Cabbage

Yield: serves 6 to 8

4 tablespoons butter or margarine
2 tablespoons brown sugar
2 apples, **peeled** and **grated**
½ cup *each* white vinegar and water
8 cups (about 2 pounds) finely **shredded** red cabbage
½ cup red currant jelly
salt and pepper to taste

Equipment: **Dutch oven** or large skillet with cover, mixing spoon, **grater**

1. Melt butter or margarine in Dutch oven or large skillet over medium heat. Add brown sugar and apples, and, stirring constantly, cook for about

3 minutes. Add vinegar, water, and cabbage, stir, and bring to a boil. Reduce heat to simmer, cover, and cook for about 30 minutes, or until cabbage is tender.

2. Add currant jelly and salt and pepper to taste. Stir, cover, and heat through, about 3 minutes.

Serve cabbage as a hot side dish with Christmas dinner.

The Christmas dessert is usually fruit and cookies. The red berries used in the following recipe are in keeping with the holiday colors.

Rødgrød Med Fløde   Raspberry Pudding with Cream

Yield: serves 4 to 6

4 cups mashed and strained raspberries or strawberries, fresh or frozen, thawed
1 tablespoon sugar, more or less to taste
2 tablespoons arrowroot powder (available in the spice section of supermarkets)
¼ cup cold water
1 cup cream, more or less, for serving

Equipment: Medium saucepan, wooden mixing spoon, cup

1. In medium saucepan, combine berries and 1 tablespoon sugar. Stir and heat over medium heat until sugar is dissolved, about 3 minutes. Stirring constantly, bring to a boil, and then reduce heat to **simmer**. Adjust sweetness by adding sugar, if necessary.

2. In cup, add arrowroot to water, and mix to smooth paste. Stirring constantly, add arrowroot to berry mixture, and cook until thickened, about 3 to 5 minutes.

To serve, pour into individual dessert bowls. Refrigerate until serving time. Serve with a pitcher of cream.

Norway

Most Norwegians are Lutheran, which is the state church, but the people of Norway enjoy complete religious freedom. All Christian holidays are observed as well as a few pre-Christian observances, among them midsummer celebrations. On Midsummer Eve, Norwegian communities celebrate the longest day of the year by lighting bonfires called "earth suns." Families like to picnic or barbecue while enjoying the unusual all-night daylight. The number of hours of sunshine range from 24 hours in the northern part of the country to about 17 hours in the south.

Christmas is the favorite Norwegian holiday, especially for children. Most families decorate their Christmas tree with homemade ornaments, and some light them with candles. The children believe the Christmas elf (also called a "gnome"), *Julenisse*, brings presents from Santa Claus and places them under the tree. In some communities, during the week after Christmas, children dress up in *Julenisse* masks and costumes and go door to door collecting treats from neighbors.

The Norwegian Christmas feast is an impressive assortment of foods served from the buffet, called *koldtbord*. All the dishes are set out at one time, and family members and friends help themselves. The meal begins with soup and ends with fruit, cookies, and cakes. The dishes served for *koldtbord* include *gammelost* (old cheese); several kinds of meats such as reindeer, jellied pigs feet, and grouse; and a variety of fish dishes, among them *surstomming* (sour herring) and *lutefisk*, which is cod soaked in lye for a week until the bones dissolve, rinsed in water for three days, boiled slowly in salt water, and then put on the back porch to cool. Don't worry, the neighborhood dogs won't touch it! Also included in the feast are *fiskeboller*, fish balls (recipe follows).

Fiskeboller   Norwegian Fish Balls

Yield: serves 6

1 pound skinless fish fillets: cod, haddock, trout, or whiting **finely chopped**
½ cup light cream
1 tablespoon cornstarch
1 cup heavy cream
salt and white pepper, to taste
dill shrimp sauce, for serving (recipe follows)

Equipment: Food grinder or electric **food processor**, small bowl, mixing spoon, medium mixing bowl with cover, rubber **spatula**, baking sheet, aluminum foil, medium saucepan, **slotted spoon**

1. Using food grinder or electric food processor, mash fish, and add light cream, a little at a time, to make a smooth paste.

2. In small bowl, mix cornstarch and heavy cream until smooth. Add cream mixture to fish paste. Add salt and white pepper to taste, and, using mixing spoon or electric food processor, mix until light and fluffy, about 3 minutes. Transfer to medium mixing bowl, cover, and refrigerate for 1 hour.

3. Shape fish mixture into ping-pong-size balls, and place balls on baking sheet. Cover with foil, and refrigerate for at least 1 hour.

4. Fill medium saucepan half full with water. Add ½ teaspoon salt, bring to a boil over high heat, and then reduce heat to **simmer**. Drop 5 or 6 fish balls at a time into simmering water, and cook for about 3 to 5 minutes. Remove with slotted spoon, drain, and keep warm until ready to serve. Continue cooking in batches until all the fish balls are finished.

Serve fish balls warm with dill shrimp sauce (recipe follows).

Dill Shrimp Sauce

Yield: about 3 ½ cups

2 tablespoons butter or margarine
2 tablespoons flour
1 cup milk
½ cup heavy cream
2 cups **coarsely chopped**, cooked, **peeled**, and **deveined** shrimp
salt and white pepper to taste
2 tablespoons **finely chopped** fresh dill or 1 teaspoon dried dill

Equipment: Small saucepan, **whisk** or mixing spoon

Melt butter or margarine in small saucepan over medium heat. Remove from heat, add flour, and mix until smooth. Add milk and cream, and return saucepan to low heat, stirring constantly until mixture thickens. Add shrimp, salt and white pepper, and dill. Cook for 3 minutes until shrimp are heated through.

To serve, pour sauce over fish balls (recipe precedes).

Some Norwegians say a dinner without potatoes is no dinner at all. Most assuredly potatoes are served at every holiday feast.

Stuede Poteter   Creamed Potatoes

Yield: serves 6

1 cup milk
2 tablespoons melted butter or margarine

2 tablespoons all-purpose flour
4 cold, cooked potatoes, **peeled**, and cut into
   bite-size pieces (leftovers are good to use)
salt and white pepper, to taste

Equipment: Small saucepan, medium saucepan, mixing spoon

1. Heat milk in small saucepan over medium-high heat until small bubbles appear around edges. Remove from heat.

2. Melt butter or margarine in medium saucepan over low heat. Stirring constantly, add flour until smooth and lump-free. Increase heat to medium, and slowly add hot milk, stirring constantly until mixture thickens, about 5 minutes. Add potatoes and salt and white pepper to taste. Toss to coat potatoes with sauce, and heat through, about 3 minutes.

Serve creamed potatoes as a side dish.

This recipe for Mother Monsen's cake, *Mor Monsen's kaker*, is very popular during the Christmas holidays. The little cakes can be made a week ahead, wrapped in foil, and refrigerated. It is best to use butter instead of margarine in this recipe.

Mor Monsen's Kaker   Mother Monsen's Cake

Yield: about 10 to 24 pieces
2 cups (1 pound) butter, at room temperature
2 cups sugar
4 eggs
2 cups flour
1 teaspoon vanilla
½ cup **finely chopped** almonds or walnuts
½ cup dried currants or seedless raisins, soaked
   in warm water for 10 minutes and drained

Equipment: Large mixing bowl, mixing spoon or electric mixer, buttered 12- x 18-inch **jellyroll pan**, oven mitts, heat-proof work surface, knife

Preheat oven to 375° F.

1. In large mixing bowl, use mixing spoon or electric mixer to mix butter and sugar until light and fluffy. Mixing constantly, add eggs, one at a time, flour, and vanilla.

2. Spread mixture evenly onto buttered jelly roll pan, and sprinkle with nuts and currants or raisins.

3. Bake in oven for about 25 minutes, until golden.

4. Remove from oven, and place on heat-proof work surface to cool to room temperature. Using a knife, cut cake into serving-size triangle, diamond, or square shapes.

Serve cake as a sweet treat with hot chocolate or milk.

Sweden

The Swedish Christmas season begins with the feast of St. Lucia on December 13. St. Lucia was a young Sicilian girl who had done good deeds and was unjustly put to death. For reasons that are lost through time, the Swedish people made her a Christian martyr and call her Queen of Light. Lucia symbolizes hope and an end to the long, dark winter.

The feast of St. Lucia requires a daughter to be Lucia. If there are no girls in the family, one can be borrowed from a relative or friend. The girl chosen to be Lucia wears a white dress or robe and a crown with seven lit candles. Early in the morning Lucia, followed by her sisters and brothers, carries a tray of Lucia buns and coffee to her parents. The singing and aroma wake them up, and everyone happily joins in the merriment.

Lucia buns are made into countless shapes and decorated with raisins, currents, crushed rock candy, glazed fruit, and nuts.

Lussekatter   Lucia Buns

Yield: serves 8 to 10

    1 cup milk
    ½ cup butter or margarine
    ½ teaspoon salt
    2 teaspoons turmeric
    ½ cup warm water
    2 packages (¼-ounce each) regular or rapid rise
        yeast
    ½ cup plus 1 teaspoon sugar, more if needed
    3 large eggs
    1 teaspoon ground cardamom
    1 tablespoon **grated** orange peel
    5½ cups sifted all-purpose flour, more if
        necessary
    ½ cup seedless raisins, soaked in warm water
        for 10 minutes and drained
    egg glaze for **garnish**

Equipment: Medium saucepan, wooden mixing spoon, large mixing bowl, **grater**, floured work surface, greased medium mixing bowl, kitchen towel, lightly greased or nonstick baking sheet, pastry brush, oven mitts

1. Pour milk into medium saucepan, and heat over high heat until small bubbles appear around edges. Remove milk from heat, and add butter or margarine, salt, and turmeric; stir until butter or margarine melts. Set aside to cool until mixture is warm, about 10 minutes.

2. Pour warm water into large mixing bowl. Add yeast and 1 teaspoon sugar, stir, and set aside for 5 minutes. Add warm milk mixture to yeast mix-

ture, and stir well. Stirring constantly, add remaining ½ cup sugar, 2 eggs, cardamom, orange peel, and 3 cups flour, a little at a time; stir until well blended. Add just enough remaining flour for dough to hold together and not be sticky.

3. Transfer dough to floured work surface, and **knead** for about 6 minutes, until smooth and elastic. If necessary, sprinkle with more flour.

4. Transfer dough to greased medium mixing bowl and turn dough to coat evenly with oil. Cover with towel, and set in warm place to double in bulk, about 1 hour.

5. **Punch down** dough and transfer to floured work surface. Knead for about 3 minutes, and divide into about 16 equal-size pieces. Roll one piece of dough between the palms of your hands into ropes about ½ inch thick and about 8 to 10 inches long.

6. Use 1 piece of dough to make letter shapes of O, S, or C and 2 pieces to make an H or X shape. (See diagram.) Tightly coil the ends of the rope. (Like fire fighters coil their hoses after a fire.) Put a raisin in the middle of each coil, and place buns about 2-inches apart on greased or nonstick baking sheet, cover with kitchen towel, and set in warm place to double in bulk, about 1 hour.

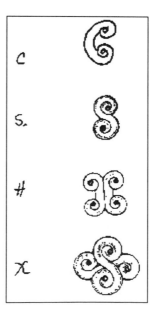

Preheat oven to 375° F.

7. Brush buns with egg glaze. Bake in oven for about 25 minutes, or until golden brown.

Serve the buns while still warm for the best flavor.

The Swedish *smorgasbord,* the table loaded with foods, is famous around the world. The Christmas day *smorgasbord* is an unbeliev-able array of dishes. Guests help themselves and change plates after each course. The cold foods are served first, a variety of herring dishes, patés, and salads. After the cold dishes, come the *småvarmt,* "the small warm dishes."

The Swedes follow the ancient tradition of serving a whole ham for Christmas. *God Yul,* meaning Merry Christmas, is decoratively written on the ham in white frosting or soft-ened cream cheese to wish everyone sharing the feast Merry Christmas.

Julskinka   Mustard-Glazed Ham

Yield: serves 6 to 8
  3 to 4 pound boneless baked ham
  ¼ cup butter or margarine
  ¼ cup Dijon mustard
  ¼ cup corn syrup or honey
  2 egg yolks
  ½ tablespoon cornstarch
  ¾ cup bread crumbs
  1 teaspoon sugar

Equipment: Roasting pan, medium skillet, mix-ing spoon, oven mitts

Preheat oven to 350° F.

1. Place ham in roasting pan.

2. Melt butter or margarine in medium skillet over medium heat. Add mustard, corn syrup or honey, egg yolks, and cornstarch. Stir and heat until warm, about 2 minutes. Remove from heat, add bread crumbs and sugar, and stir well. Spread sauce evenly over ham.

3. Bake ham in oven until heated through and crumbs are browned, about 1 hour. (Allow approxi-mately 15 minutes per pound.)

To serve, cool to warm, decorate, and set whole ham on buffet table to slice.

Red tulips traditionally decorate the *smor-gasbord* table, which includes among "the small warm dishes" Jansson's Temptation. As the legend goes, Mr. Jansson would preach to everyone about the evils of giving in to temp-tations of any kind when, lo and behold, he was caught sneaking a taste of the potato cas-serole that now bears his name.

Janssons Frestelse   Jansson's Temptation

Yield: serves 6
  6 medium potatoes, **peeled** and cut into thick, matchstick-size strips
  1 (2-ounce) can anchovies, drained or 1 (1¾-ounce) tube anchovy paste (optional)
  2 onions, thinly sliced
  1 cup light cream, more as needed
  4 tablespoons bread crumbs
  3 tablespoons butter or margarine, at room temperature, or butter-flavored cooking spray

Equipment: Buttered medium oven-proof casse-role, oven mitts

Preheat oven to 350° F.

1. Spread half the potatoes over the bottom of buttered medium casserole. Cover with anchovies and sliced onions, and top with remaining pota-toes. Pour 1 cup cream over mixture, sprinkle with bread crumbs, and dot with butter or margarine or spray with butter-flavored cooking spray.

2. Bake in oven for about 45 minutes, or until golden brown and potatoes are tender. During baking check mixture; it should be moist, not soupy. If too dry, add cream, as needed.

Serve potatoes warm directly from the casserole.

A pile of *klenäter*, Swedish Christmas bowknot cookies, is a very simple but attractive dessert to complete the smorgasbord.

Klenäter Swedish Christmas Bowknots

CAUTION: HOT OIL USED

Yield: about 2 dozen

4 **egg yolks**

¼ cup confectioners' sugar, more as needed

1 teaspoon vanilla extract

grated rind of 1 lemon

2 tablespoons melted butter or margarine

1¼ cups all-purpose flour

vegetable oil for **deep frying**

Equipment: Medium mixing bowl with cover, mixing spoon, **grater,** floured **rolling pin**, floured work surface, knife, **deep fryer** (see glossary for tips on making one), wooden spoon, paper towels, baking sheet, **slotted spoon**

1. In medium mixing bowl, use mixing spoon to beat egg yolks and ¼ cup confectioners' sugar until thick and light, about 3 minutes. Add vanilla, lemon rind, and melted butter or margarine, and mix well.

2. Add flour, a little at a time, and, using clean hands, form into a smooth dough. Cover and refrigerate for 1 hour.

3. Using floured rolling pin, roll dough out about ¹⁄₈ inch thick on floured work surface.

4. Using knife, cut dough into strips 8 inches long by ¾ inches wide. Use knife to make a 1-inch lengthwise slit on each strip, about 2 inches from one end. Slip the opposite end about halfway through the slit, forming a small loop in the

dough (about the thickness of a finger) and let the ends hang loose. (See diagram.) Cover with a damp towel to keep from drying out. Repeat with remaining dough.

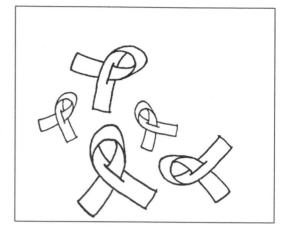

5. Prepare deep fryer: Have an adult help you heat oil to 375° F. Oil is hot enough for frying when small bubbles appear around a wooden spoon handle when it is dipped in the oil. Place several layers of paper towels on baking sheet. Very carefully fry bowknots, a few at a time, until golden, about 3 minutes. Drain on paper towels, and sprinkle with confectioners' sugar while still warm.

To serve, pile on a serving dish and eat as a sweet treat.

Finland

Finland lies on the northernmost edge of Europe, where cold winters create an ongoing struggle with nature. Finnish and Swedish are the official languages in Finland, where most of the people are Lutheran.

Finnish holiday celebrations blend pre-Christian folk traditions with customs from Sweden, Russia, and Germany. Christmas is the most important holiday of the year, coming after the long, dark autumn. At noon on December 24, church bells proclaim the "peace of Christmas," and all businesses and shops close for the three-day celebration. Almost all Finns follow the old custom of placing lighted candles in the windows of their house, in the yard, and in the cemeteries to "lighten the spirit and the way." The Christmas cemetery candles are called "fire of life." In the past, when people sometimes had to drive for hours by sleigh to reach the church or attend a party or family gathering, their way was brightened by the lighted candles along the roadside.

Traces of some pre-Christian harvest festivals are now tied in with Christmas decorations like the straw goat figurines and the *himmeli* (Heaven), a large mobile made of straw, which hangs above the Christmas table. The straw goat symbolizes the harvest processions. The Finnish Santa Claus is called *Joulupukki*, which literally translated means "Christmas goat." How Santa got that name is a mystery.

Christmas Eve usually begins with a trip to the sauna before indulging in the Christmas Eve feast. The sauna is a small room or building, apart from the house, that is heated with extremely hot and dry air. The Finns sit in the sauna for health reasons. Following the sauna, the Finns eat a robust meal with several kinds of fish, ham, and rice pudding.

On May 1 all of Finland celebrates May Day, known as *Vappu*. Once a Roman festival, May Day celebrates the end of winter. Finns, especially students, dress in their most colorful summer clothes to take part in the festivities. Little children go to the parks to enjoy the sunshine, special sweet treats, and the carnival-like atmosphere. Even if it snows, which is possible in this northern country, people dance and sing for joy, for it is May Day, and summer is not far off.

Crullers are a symbol of spring and are traditionally eaten with the May Day tonic, *sima*.

Tippaleipä   May Day Crullers

CAUTION: HOT OIL USED

Yield: serves 8

2 cups all-purpose flour
1 tablespoon baking powder
½ teaspoon salt
½ teaspoon ground mace
2 eggs
⅓ cup sugar
½ cup milk
vegetable oil for **deep frying**
4 tablespoons confectioners' sugar, for **garnish**

Equipment: Flour **sifter**, large mixing bowl, medium mixing bowl, egg beater or electric mixer, wooden mixing spoon, plastic wrap, **deep fryer** (see glossary for tips on making one), wooden spoon, paper towels, baking sheet, tablespoon, **slotted spoon**

1. **Sift** flour, baking powder, salt, and mace into large mixing bowl.

2. In medium mixing bowl, use egg beater or electric mixer to mix eggs and sugar until light and creamy. Add milk and mix well. Add egg and milk mixture to flour mixture in large mixing bowl, and mix with wooden spoon. Cover bowl with plastic wrap, and let it sit at room temperature for 30 minutes.

3. Prepare deep fryer: Have an adult help you heat oil to 375° F. Oil is hot enough for frying when small bubbles appear around a wooden spoon handle when it is dipped in the oil. Place several layers of paper towels on baking sheet.

4. Carefully drop heaping tablespoonfuls of batter into oil. Fry about 3 minutes on each side, and drain on paper towels. Continue frying, in batches of 3 or 4. Sprinkle with confectioners' sugar.

Serve crullers as a sweet snack.

Sima is the traditional May Day tonic. It is popular all summer long.

Sima — Finnish Lemonade

Yield: serves 6 to 8
  2 quarts water
  ½ cup brown sugar
  ½ cup granulated sugar, more if necessary
  2 lemons, washed, **trimmed**, and thinly sliced
  ⅛ teaspoon active dry yeast
  1 tablespoon seedless raisins

Equipment: Medium saucepan, wooden mixing spoon, 4-quart glass or ceramic heatproof pitcher with cover (do not use metal)

1. In medium saucepan, mix water, brown sugar, and ½ cup granulated sugar. Stirring frequently, bring to a boil over high heat.

2. Transfer mixture to the heatproof pitcher, add lemon slices, and stir well. Adjust sweetness by adding more sugar if necessary. Set aside to cool to lukewarm. When lukewarm, add yeast and raisins, and stir well.

3. Set aside in warm place, uncovered, for 8 hours or more. The drink is ready when tiny bubbles appear around the edge of the pitcher and the raisins have risen to the top. Refrigerate until ready to serve.

Serve over ice cubes as a refreshing summer drink.

Candy is another favorite May Day treat, and this is an easy recipe for Finnish chocolate candy, *choklad.*

Choklad — Finnish Chocolate Candy

Yield: about 20 pieces
  6 ounces semisweet chocolate squares or 1 cup chocolate chips
  3 tablespoons butter or margarine
  1 egg, beaten
  2 teaspoons **grated** orange peel

Equipment: Small saucepan, wooden mixing spoon, **grater,** rubber **spatula,** cookie sheet, wax paper

1. Melt chocolate and butter or margarine in small saucepan over low heat, and stir well. Remove from heat, add egg and orange peel, and stir well.

2. Cover cookie sheet with wax paper, shiny-side up. Drop mixture by teaspoonfuls (each about 1 inch wide) onto wax paper. Refrigerate until firm, about 4 hours.

Serve as a sweet treat.

Iceland

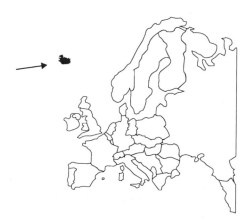

The people of Iceland add the myths and folklore of their Nordic ancestors to Christian holiday celebrations. In Iceland there is not one Santa but 13 very mischievous descendants of *Gryla* the Ogre. Also known as the Christmas Men or Yuletide Lads, they start visiting homes, one per day, and by Christ-

Poland

The Roman Catholic Church has been the all-powerful force in Poland for over a thousand years. The church even maintained some power and influence during the years of communist rule. It is the guardian of Polish nationality and the protector of the language and culture. Cathedrals and rural churches overflow at almost every mass, and religious holidays are national events. The current pope, John Paul II, is Polish.

The *Wigilia*, Christmas Eve, celebrates the vigil kept by shepherds on the night Christ was born. To prepare for the Christmas Eve feast, straw is placed in the corners of the dining room to assure good crops, and hay is laid beneath the white tablecloth as a reminder of the manger. The 12-course meatless meal is in honor of the 12 disciples. The meal and how it is served is steeped in symbolism.

The meal begins with the ritual of sharing the *oplatek*. It is a wafer-like bread baked by nuns from the same dough that is used for Communion wafers, and it has been blessed by the priest. The parents bite off a piece, and each person does likewise as it is passed to them. This ceremony symbolizes family love and unity, "one for all and all for one."

The meatless meal includes 12 dishes to symbolize the 12 Apostles, but one extra place is set at the table, for the Holy Spirit. The meal begins with clear beet soup with mushrooms, and it is followed by carp (see recipe below), a Polish favorite, several other fish dishes, winter vegetable dishes, and noodle and grain puddings.

After eating, everyone regroups around the Christmas tree where simple, often handmade, gifts are exchanged. The family then leaves for *Pasterka*, the Shepherds' Mass, at midnight.

The family and friends gather on Christmas Day for a feast of ham, Polish sausage, or *bigos* (recipe follows in this section), which is also served on New Year's Eve.

In Poland, the favorite fish, carp, is a symbol of strength and courage, but any white, firm-flesh fish can be used in this recipe.

Karp Smazony   Fried Carp

Yield: serves 4

½ cup all-purpose flour
salt and pepper to taste
4 (6 to 8 ounces each) fish fillets: carp, haddock, trout, catfish, whiting, or red snapper
2 tablespoons vegetable oil, more as needed
2 lemons, cut in wedges, for **garnish**

Equipment: Pie pan, wax paper, work surface, large skillet, fork, metal **spatula**

1. In pie pan, combine flour with salt and pepper to taste. Coat each fillet on both sides with flour, and place on wax-paper-covered work surface.

2. Heat 2 tablespoons oil in skillet over medium-high heat. Add fillets, and fry for about 8 minutes on each side or until golden and cooked through. The fish is done when it flakes easily when poked with a fork. Drain well and keep warm until ready to serve.

mas Eve they've all arrived. They've never been seen, but each leaves a gift and does some devilish act. The lads have names; among them are Door Slammer, who wakes people by slamming doors; Candle Beggar makes off with a few candles; and Meat Hooker might dangle a hook down the chimney and make off with the Christmas roast.

The Christmas feast would be incomplete if soup were not served before the traditional roast lamb or beef.

Cheddar Cheese Soup

Yield: serves 4

2 tablespoons flour
2 cups chicken broth, homemade (recipe page 52) or canned
2 tablespoons butter or margarine
1 onion, **finely chopped**
1 rib of celery, **trimmed** and finely chopped
1 cup milk
2 cups **shredded** cheddar cheese
salt and pepper to taste

Equipment: Cup, mixing spoon, medium saucepan with cover

1. In the cup, mix flour with ½ cup chicken broth until smooth.

2. Melt butter or margarine in medium saucepan over medium-high heat. Add onions and celery, and, stirring constantly, fry until soft, about 3 minutes.

3. Add remaining 1½ cups chicken broth, milk, cheese, flour mixture from step 1, and salt and pepper to taste. Continue stirring until cheese melts. Reduce heat to low, cover, and cook until well blended, about 10 minutes. Stir before serving.

Serve warm in individual soup bowls.

Iceland, at one time, had a unique calendar, dividing the year into two seasons, winter and summer, of 26 weeks each. On the "first day of summer" the people hoped to find frost from the evening before, because it was a sign that summer and winter had "frozen together," a good omen. The first day of summer is still a national holiday; it is celebrated with parades and festivals.

Fruit is always eaten on this occasion as a symbol of hope for a warm and fruitful growing season. At this time of year, the only available fruit is dried, canned, or frozen. The growing season has not begun, and the only fresh fruit is imported and very expensive.

Poached Dried Fruit

Yield: serves 6 to 8

2 cups white grape juice
3 tablespoons honey
2 teaspoons ground anise seed
1 teaspoon ground cinnamon
½ lemon rind, **grated**
3 cups dried mixed fruit: apricots, apples, and pears
½ cup dried cherries or dried papaya

Equipment: **Grater**, medium saucepan with cover, mixing spoon

1. In medium saucepan, mix grape juice, honey anise seed, cinnamon, and lemon rind. Bring mixture to a boil over high heat. Add dried mixed fruit cherries or papaya, stir, and bring back to a boil

2. Reduce heat to simmer, cover, and cook for 15 minutes. Remove from heat, and keep covered for 30 minutes. Remove cover, and cool to room temperature.

Serve hot, warm, or cold as a side dish or for dessert.

Serve fish with lemon wedges, for garnish. Traditionally the fish is served with boiled potatoes.

A grain pudding called *kutya* is a symbolic reminder of centuries past and of life's difficulties. Various symbolic ingredients are added to the grain: walnuts for promises of a better life, poppy seeds to ensure a peaceful night's sleep, and honey as a symbol of the sweetness at the day's end. In Poland, honey is believed to be a gift from God, and killing even one bee is considered an evil act.

Kutya   Wheat Berry Pudding

Yield: serves 6 to 8
   2 cups warm, cooked whole or cracked wheat
      berries (cook according to directions on
      package—available at all health food stores
      and Middle East food stores, where it is
      called *gorgod*)
   1 cup **coarsely chopped** walnuts
   ½ cup honey
   2 tablespoons poppy seeds

Equipment: Medium mixing bowl, mixing spoon, serving plate, rubber **spatula**

1. In medium mixing bowl, combine cooked wheat berries, walnuts, and honey. Mix well and transfer to serving plate.

2. Sprinkle poppy seeds over the top.

To serve kutya, *give each person a spoon. The eldest guest or family member eats first from the* kutya *and extends a wish for a good and long life to others. The dish of* kutya *is passed around the table, and, one by one, each person makes a similar wish, while dipping a spoon into the pudding.*

Cranberry pudding, *kisiel zurawinowi*, is a popular dessert served at the end of the Christmas Eve feast for its symbolic red color.

NONCOOKING SHORTCUT FOR CRANBERRY PUDDING: Use canned jellied cranberries. Spoon cranberries into individual serving dishes and add a dollop of whipped topping on each.

Kisiel Zurawinowi   Cranberry Pudding

Yield: serves 6
   1 pound fresh cranberries
   2½ cups water
   ¼ cup cornstarch
   ½ cup sugar
   6 tablespoons frozen whipped topping, thawed,
      for **garnish**

Equipment: Medium saucepan, wooden mixing spoon, **food mill, blender** or **food processor**, strainer (optional), cup

1. Put cranberries in medium saucepan, and add 2 cups water. Bring to a boil over high heat, and, stirring frequently, boil until berries soften, about 5 minutes. Remove from heat and cool to warm.

2. Using food mill, blender, or food processor, mash cranberries with liquid until smooth and lump-free. If necessary, strain mixture to make lump-free. Return to medium saucepan.

3. Add cornstarch to remaining ½ cup water, and mix until smooth. Add cornstarch mixture and sugar to cranberries, and mix well. Stirring constantly, heat over medium heat until mixture thickens, about 5 minutes.

To serve, pour into individual serving dishes, and top with dollop of whipped topping.

Poppy seeds are added to Polish Christmas dishes because they are thought to ensure peaceful sleep. Noodles tossed with sweetened poppy seeds are a favorite.

Kluski z Makiem Poppy Seed Noodles

Yield: serves 4

   3 tablespoons butter or margarine, at room
     temperature
   1 tablespoon poppy seeds
   1 tablespoon sugar
   ½ cup seedless raisins
   ½ pound medium-wide egg noodles, cooked,
     drained, and kept warm

Equipment: Large skillet, 2 mixing spoons or forks

Melt butter or margarine in large skillet over medium heat. Add poppy seeds, sugar, and raisins, mix well, and cook about 3 minutes. Add drained noodles, and, using 2 spoons or forks together in an up-and-down motion, toss to mix well. Heat through, about 3 minutes.

Serve warm noodles as a side dish or for dessert.

In Polish homes great quantities of breads, cakes, and cookies are baked for every holiday. Two favorites are *chrust*, bow ties, the same as Sweden's *klenäter* (recipe page 126), and this recipe for poppy seed cookies.

Poppy Seed Cookies

Yield: about 30

   1 cup poppy seeds
   ½ cup **scalded** milk, cooled to room temperature
   ½ cup butter or margarine
   ½ cup sugar
   1½ cups flour
   ¹/₈ teaspoon salt
   ½ teaspoon cinnamon
   1 cup seedless raisins

Equipment: Large mixing bowl, mixing spoon or electric mixer, greased or nonstick cookie sheet

Preheat oven to 350° F.

1. Add poppy seeds to scalded milk, stir, and soak for about 30 minutes.

2. In large mixing bowl, use mixing spoon or electric mixer to mix butter or margarine and sugar until creamy. Mixing constantly, add flour, salt, cinnamon, raisins, and milk with poppy seeds. Mix until well blended.

3. Drop tablespoonfuls of dough onto cookie sheet, about 1½ inches apart. Bake in oven until lightly browned, about 20 minutes.

Serve cookies as a sweet treat.

In Poland the most important secular celebration is New Year's. Every country seems to have a special good-luck dish to welcome the new year; in Poland it's *bigos*, a traditional hunter's stew. At one time it was eaten only by the Polish aristocracy. It was the tradition to make the stew out of game they hunted on their large estates. It is now the traditional New Year's dish eaten by anyone lucky enough to be able to afford the ingredients.

Bigos Polish Hunter's Stew

Yield: serves 6

   1 cup **finely chopped** bacon
   1 pound boneless, lean pork shoulder, cut into
     1-inch chunks
   3 cloves garlic, finely chopped, or 1 teaspoon
     garlic granules
   3 onions, quartered
   ½ pound fresh mushrooms, sliced
   1 cup canned condensed beef broth
   2 tablespoons sugar
   2 bay leaves
   2 cups canned sauerkraut, rinsed under water
     and drained well
   2 medium apples, **cored** and sliced
   2 cups Italian-style whole tomatoes with juice
   1 cup **diced** cooked ham
   1½ cups coarsely sliced Polish sausage

Equipment: **Dutch oven** or large saucepan with cover, mixing spoon

1. Fry bacon pieces in Dutch oven or large saucepan over high heat for about 3 minutes, to **render.** Add pork, garlic, onions, and mushrooms, and, stirring constantly, fry until meat is browned, about 5 minutes; reduce heat to medium.

2. Add beef broth, sugar, bay leaves, drained sauerkraut, apples, and tomatoes with juice, and bring to a boil over high heat. Reduce heat to **simmer**, cover, and cook for about 1½ hours, stirring occasionally, to prevent sticking.

3. Add cooked ham and sausage, and stir. Cover and cook over medium-low heat for about 30 minutes more to blend flavors. Remove bay leaves and discard before serving.

Serve bigos *in a large bowl with plenty of crusty bread. In Poland the stew is traditionally served with boiled potatoes and a dish of sour cream.*

Baltic Nations—Lithuania, Latvia, Estonia

Although the Baltic republics of Lithuania, Latvia, and Estonia are neighbors and have shared many of the same difficulties over the years, they have very different cultural backgrounds. In northerly Estonia, most people are Lutheran with strong Scandinavian ties. Latvia has large Lutheran and Roman Catholic communities, and Lithuania is mostly populated by Roman Catholics.

Despite these differences, Easter is the most important holiday for all three countries where people grow, raise, and enjoy very similar foods and recipes. The Easter feast is either pork, goose, or duck together with fruit, potatoes, and grains, which are eaten in everything from soup to desserts.

Potato and Apple Pudding

Yield: serves 6 to 8
½ cup butter or margarine
4 apples, **peeled** and **finely chopped**
2 tablespoons sugar
1 teaspoon nutmeg
4 large boiled potatoes, peeled and mashed or 4
    cups prepared instant mashed potatoes
    (prepare according to directions on package)
1½ cups light cream
1 egg, beaten
salt and white pepper to taste
6 tablespoons bread crumbs

Equipment: Large skillet, mixing spoon, large mixing bowl, buttered or nonstick 9-inch baking pan, oven mitts

Preheat oven to 350° F.

1. Melt 2 tablespoons butter or margarine in large skillet over medium heat. Add apples, sugar, and nutmeg. Stirring frequently, fry for about 3 minutes until apples are softened. Remove from heat, and transfer to large mixing bowl. Add potatoes, cream, egg, and salt and white pepper to taste; stir well.

2. Transfer mixture to buttered or nonstick 9-inch baking pan. Smooth top, sprinkle with bread crumbs, and dot with remaining butter or margarine.

3. Bake in oven for about 30 minutes, or until golden brown.

Serve as a side dish for the Easter feast.

The following dessert is popular throughout northern and eastern Europe. The names differ from country to country, but the ingredients remain pretty much the same.

Sweet Apple Bread Pudding

Yield: serves 8 to 10

½ cup butter or margarine

½ cup light brown sugar

2 cups milk

2 eggs

½ cup plain yogurt

1 teaspoon vanilla extract

½ teaspoon ground allspice

¾ cup seedless raisins

8 slices stale white bread, crusts removed and cut into ½-inch cubes

3 cooking apples, **peeled**, **cored**, and thinly sliced

lemon sauce (recipe follows)

Equipment: Small skillet, mixing spoon, large mixing bowl, buttered or nonstick 13- x 9-inch baking pan, oven mitts

Preheat oven to 350° F.

1. Melt butter or margarine in small skillet over medium heat. Add brown sugar, stir, and cook until sugar melts, about 1 minute. Pour into large mixing bowl, add milk, eggs, yogurt, vanilla, allspice, and raisins, and mix well. **Fold in** bread cubes and apple slices, and transfer to baking pan.

2. Bake in oven for about 40 minutes, or until puffy and golden brown.

Serve pudding warm with side dish of warm lemon sauce.

Lemon Sauce

Yield: about 2 cups

1 cup sugar

2 tablespoons cornstarch

1 cup water

3 tablespoons butter or margarine

juice of 1 lemon

Equipment: Small saucepan, mixing spoon

In small saucepan, mix sugar, cornstarch, and water until smooth. Bring to a boil over high heat. Reduce heat to low, add butter or margarine and lemon juice, and, stirring constantly, cook until mixture thickens, about 3 minutes.

Serve warm over Sweet Apple Bread Pudding (recipe precedes).

Russia

Despite years of communist rule, the Russian Orthodox Church remains strong in Russia, and religious holidays are celebrated with much fervor. There is no celebration more sacred to the Russians than Easter. During the latter part of the tenth century, when they first accepted Christianity, the rituals of Easter were combined with an older, agrarian festival celebrating the spring planting.

When it comes to celebrating Easter, the Russian people do it as well as anyone; it is the one holiday that unites Russians everywhere in the world. Preparations often begin near the end of February when everyone is tired of the cold winter and anxious for change. Hope returns with *Maslenitsa*, the Butter Festival, a week-long celebration prior to the 40 days of Lent. Before communism this was an exciting carnival, much like Mardi

Gras. Under communism festivities were limited to small family gatherings. Since the fall of communism, changes are taking place, and most Russians are relieved to have their church triumphant over the state atheism. The political overtones are vanishing, and the church is slowly regaining its place of importance with the people.

On Holy Saturday morning, the day before Easter, Russians pack eggs, sausage, cheese, ham, butter, horseradish, and Easter bread in a napkin-lined basket to be blessed at church and kept for Easter Sunday breakfast.

Easter itself is celebrated with beautifully decorated eggs (recipe page 139) and *kulich* (recipe follows), a tall, golden yeast cake eaten with *paskha* (recipe after *kulich*).

The use of eggs as part of the holiday festivities dates back to pre-Christian times when they were used in pagan fertility rituals. The Easter egg is also a symbol of spring renewal and rebirth. Platters of stuffed eggs are often served at holiday celebrations in Russia.

Yaitsa Po-Russki
Russian-style Stuffed Eggs

Yield: serves 6

6 hard-cooked eggs, shelled and halved lengthwise
2 tablespoons mayonnaise
1 tablespoon Dijon mustard
3 tablespoons sweet pickle relish, drained
salt and pepper to taste
sprinkle of paprika, for **garnish**

Equipment: Small mixing bowl, fork, work surface

1. Carefully remove yolk from egg halves, and put into small bowl. Place whites, cut side up, on work surface.

2. Add mayonnaise and mustard to yolks, and, using the back of a fork, mash until smooth. Add relish and salt and pepper to taste, and mix well.

3. Spoon mixture equally into egg white halves. Sprinkle with paprika, for garnish.

Serve stuffed eggs as an appetizer before the main meal.

After the lean days of Lent, the Russian people look forward to Easter. Following an almost all-night church service, hungry worshipers hurry home to enjoy the holiday feast they have spent weeks preparing. The centerpiece on the table is the *kulich*, the Easter cake with a rounded top resembling the Russian church domes, which are known as cupolas.

The *kulich* is baked in a cylindrical-shaped pan. If you don't have a pan like this, two clean two-pound coffee cans or 46-ounce juice cans can be used. The bread is always served with rich, creamy *paskha* (recipe follows). The tradition of eating *kulich* and *paskha* is an important part of the Easter feast. The top of the *kulich*, called the crown, is sliced off and set aside to be eaten at the end of the meal. Each person is served a piece of *kulich* with a thin slice of *paskha*.

Kulich
Easter Cake

Yield: 2 loaves

3 packages (¼ ounce each) active dry yeast
¼ cup milk, **scalded** and cooled to lukewarm
2 tablespoons granulated sugar
¾ cup butter or margarine, at room temperature
1 cup light brown sugar
1 teaspoon almond extract
3 **eggs, separated**
1 cup heavy cream, warmed slightly
5 cups all-purpose flour, more as needed
½ cup seedless raisins, soaked in warm water for 15 minutes and drained

½ cup **finely chopped** mixed candied fruit (also called fruitcake mix—available at supermarkets)

1 cup **coarsely chopped** almonds

glaze (recipe follows)

Equipment: Cup, mixing spoon, large mixing bowl, mixing spoon or electric mixer, large greased bowl, kitchen towel, medium mixing bowl, small mixing bowl, floured work surface, 2 well greased (2-pound) coffee cans or juice cans (46-ounce), wax paper, oven mitts, skewer, can opener

1. In cup, dissolve yeast in warm milk. Add granulated sugar, stir, and allow to stand until frothy, about 5 to 10 minutes.

2. In large mixing bowl, use mixing spoon or electric mixer to beat butter or margarine and brown sugar until smooth. Add almond extract, egg yolks, and warm cream, and mix well. Add yeast mixture, and mix well.

3. Add 4 cups flour, a little at a time, and, using clean hands, mix or **knead** until smooth and elastic, adding more flour if necessary. Transfer dough to greased large mixing bowl, and turn it to coat all sides. Cover with towel, and set in warm place until dough doubles in bulk.

4. Put egg whites into medium mixing bowl, and, using clean and dry beaters, beat egg whites with electric mixer or mixing spoon until stiff.

5. In small mixing bowl, mix remaining 1 cup flour, raisins, candied fruit, and almonds; mix well to coat ingredients with flour. Add fruit mixture to egg whites, and toss to mix well.

6. **Punch down** dough, transfer to floured work surface, and knead in fruit mixture. If dough is sticky, add a little more flour. It should be smooth and soft.

7. Fit round pieces of greased wax paper into bottoms of greased coffee cans. Divide dough in half, and put each half into a coffee can. Cover with greased wax paper, greased-side down, and set in warm place for dough to rise. The dough should rise to about the top edge of the can, but no

higher. Remove wax paper from top of bread before baking.

8. Place rack near bottom of oven.

Preheat oven to 375° F.

9. Bake cans in oven for 20 minutes. Reduce heat to 325°, and bake for 40 to 50 minutes longer. To check if bread is done, insert skewer in center of bread. If it comes out clean, bread is done. Remove bread from oven, and cool to warm. Using a can opener, remove bottom of can, and push bread out.

10. Glaze and decorate bread: While the bread is still warm, spread glaze over tops, allowing some to drizzle down the sides. Sprinkle glaze with multicolored sprinkles or scratch letters into the glaze.

To serve kulich, *first cut off and set aside the glazed top. Then cut the bread in half vertically and cut each half into thick half-moon slices.*

Glaze for Kulich

1 cup confectioners' sugar

2 tablespoons warm water, more if necessary

1 tablespoon lemon juice

2 or 3 teaspoons multicolored sprinkles

Equipment: Small mixing bowl, mixing spoon

In small mixing bowl, mix confectioners' sugar, 2 tablespoons water, and lemon juice until smooth and creamy. It should spread easily. Add more water if necessary.

*To use glaze, pour over top of kulich (recipe precedes). **Drizzle** with multicolored sprinkles.*

Paskha is a traditional Easter dessert. In Russia, it is made in a special, tall mold which is also called a *paskha*. The mold allows the whey to drain off, which can take several days. The following recipe is quick and delicious. To give the dessert the authentic pyramid shape, use a 24-ounce plastic cottage cheese container with lid.

Paskha Russian Easter Cheese Dessert

Yield: serves 6

2 cups large curd cottage cheese (you can use a 24-ounce package and save it for the mold—see equipment list below; save leftover cottage cheese for another time)

1 cup (8-ounce package) cream cheese, at room temperature

½ cup heavy cream

2 **egg yolks**

¼ cup sugar

¼ teaspoon salt

1 teaspoon vanilla

½ cup **coarsely chopped** mixed candied fruit (also called fruitcake mix), more as needed

⅓ cup **finely chopped** walnuts, more as needed

Equipment: Strainer, wooden mixing spoon, or electric **food processor**; medium bowl; plastic wrap; small saucepan; empty, clean, and dry 24-ounce plastic cottage cheese container with cover

1. Pour cottage cheese into strainer, and rinse under cold running water, leaving chunks of curd; drain well.

2. Make cottage cheese smooth and lump-free either by either pushing through strainer, using the back of a wooden spoon, into medium mixing bowl, or placing it in an electric food processor and processing until smooth, about 3 minutes. Add cream cheese and mix well. (If using food processor, transfer to medium bowl after mixing). Cover bowl with plastic wrap, and refrigerate while preparing the egg sauce.

3. Prepare egg sauce: In small saucepan, mix heavy cream, egg yolks, sugar, and salt. Stirring constantly, cook over medium-low heat until mixture thickens and coats spoon, about 5 minutes. Cool to room temperature, add vanilla, and mix.

4. Remove bowl of cheese from refrigerator and uncover. Add egg sauce, ½ cup candied fruit and ½ nuts. **Fold in** nuts using a wooden spoon

5. Assemble *paskha*: Line cottage cheese container with plastic wrap, leaving about 5 inches hanging over the top. Spoon mixture into plastic-lined container. Tap bottom of container against work surface to remove air bubbles, and pack solid. Cover with overhanging plastic wrap and then the container's lid; refrigerate at least 8 hours to set.

6. Unmold *paskha*: Open top of cheese container and plastic overhang, invert it onto serving plate, and remove container and plastic wrap. Decorate cheese mold with candied fruit and nuts.

To serve paskha, *cut into thin slices, and serve with wedges of* kulich, *the Easter bread.*

Russians have a curious habit of drinking hot tea from a glass. An old Russian custom is to dunk a cube of sugar, a piece of candied citrus peel, or a hard candy in the hot tea, nibble on it, and dunk it again. This practice has been satisfying the Russian sweet tooth for centuries.

Candied fruit peelings are also a favorite holiday candy in the Middle East, Italy, and Spain.

Candied Citrus Peels

Yield: about 50 pieces

1 pink grapefruit

2 thick-skinned oranges

water

3 ½ cups sugar

vegetable oil cooking spray

Equipment: Sharp paring knife, medium saucepan, **colander**, mixing spoon, wax paper, work surface, tongs, medium plastic or paper bag

1. Using sharp paring knife, carefully peel grapefruit and oranges, keeping each peel strip at least ¼ inch wide and 2 inches long. Remove as much **pith** as possible from each strip of peel. (Save fruit for another use.)

2. Put peels in medium saucepan, and cover with water. Bring to boil, and cook over medium-high heat for about 10 minutes; drain in colander. Repeat this step two more times; covering with water, bringing to boil for 10 minutes, and draining in colander. This process is done to remove bitterness of the peel.

3. Pour 1¼ cups water into medium saucepan, add 1½ cups sugar, and stirring constantly to dissolve sugar, bring to boil over high heat. Reduce heat to simmer, and add drained strips of peel. Simmer, stirring frequently, until nearly all syrup is absorbed, about 45 minutes.

4. Place a 10-inch length of sheet wax paper on work surface and lightly spray with vegetable oil spray. Using tongs, separate peels and place on greased wax paper to cool for at least 3 hours.

5. Place a 14-inch length of wax paper on work surface. (Do not spray it with oil spray.) Put remaining ½ cup sugar into bag. Add peels, a few at a time, close bag and gently shake to coat with sugar. Place coated pieces of peel on larger, dry sheet of wax paper for about 8 hours or overnight to set.

Store in airtight container with wax paper between layers. May be stored in cool place as long as 3 months.

Ukraine

The newly independent state of Ukraine has a long and storied past. Like the Russians, most Ukrainians are Orthodox Christians. In fact, when Russia converted to Christianity in the late tenth century, the capital of Russia at that time was the Ukrainian city of Kiev.

As in Russia, the Easter celebration is very important to Ukrainians and is filled with traditions. Ukrainian Easter eggs are famous throughout the world. According to legend, the practice of decorating eggs, *pysanky*, dates back to pre-Christian times when tribes conducted fertility rituals to welcome spring. By the late nineteenth century, the beautiful eggs were considered works of art. The tsar of Russia loved the eggs so much that he ordered Carl Fabergé, the jeweler to the court of St. Petersburg, to copy them in pure gold and to encrust them with precious jewels for the royal family.

Easter Eggs

The eggs used for decorating can be hard-cooked or blown empty. To blow empty, puncture a small hole in each end of an egg with a heavy-duty sewing needle. Also puncture the egg yolk. Using a manicure scissors, carefully enlarge one hole to the size of a pea. Pressing your lips over the smaller hole, blow contents out through the larger bottom hole into a bowl. Carefully rinse and dry the empty shell. The larger hole can be covered with a bow or cut-out design. If you'd like to make the egg less fragile, insert a small funnel in the larger hole and fill the empty shell with melted wax. Use a warm knife to smooth over the wax at the hole opening so that it blends with the shell.

Empty egg shells need no refrigeration, and they can be hand painted with oil paints or acrylics. Ukrainian eggs decorated in this way have become family heirlooms.

Hard-Cooked Eggs

12 eggs
cold water, as needed
1 teaspoon vinegar
¼ teaspoon baking soda

Equipment: Large enameled or heat-proof glass saucepan, slotted spoon

Put eggs in large saucepan and cover with cold water. Add vinegar and baking soda. Bring just to a boil over high heat, and then reduce heat to simmer. Cook small eggs for 10 minutes and large eggs for 15 minutes. Remove from heat and cool under cold, running water.

Once the eggs are hard-cooked, they can be used for dyeing or for stuffing. Stuffed eggs, called jajka, *are eaten at all Ukrainian Christian holidays as a symbol of good luck. They are similar to the Russian stuffed eggs,* yaitsa po-russki. *(See recipe, page 135.)*

Convenient and inexpensive dyeing kits are available at most supermarkets and craft shops around Easter time.

To make different colored eggs, a separate cup is needed for each color.

Coloring Easter Eggs

hot water, as needed
food coloring (available at all supermarkets)
12 hard-cooked eggs (recipe precedes)

Equipment: Cups, tablespoon, paper towels

1. To each ½ cup hot water, add about 1 teaspoon food coloring. Stir and add eggs, one at a time, until desired color intensity is obtained. Pick up the egg with a spoon and transfer to paper towels. Let stand a few minutes to dry.

Refrigerate until ready to use.

Easter Egg Decorating Tips

Traditional Ukrainian Easter Eggs are decorated in bold, geometric designs. To try such a design, first mark the egg in half, lengthwise, and across the center with a pencil. Divide sections into triangles using a wax writer, wax crayon, or melted candle wax applied with a fine brush. When the egg is dipped into cooled dye, the waxed portions do not color. Layered designs can be achieved by adding wax before dipping in the next color. Colors look best when the lighter colors are applied first. To remove the wax when you are done, roll the eggs around on paper towels while heating them with a hair dryer.

The Easter feast always begins with *borshch Ukraïnsky,* a ruby-colored beet soup.

Borshch Ukraïnsky Ukrainian-style Beet Soup

Yield: serves 6 to 8
2 (12 ounces each) cans sliced beets
2 (8 ounces each) cans beef broth
salt and pepper to taste
3 or 4 hard-cooked eggs, shelled and halved
½ cup sour cream or plain yogurt, for **garnish**

Equipment: Medium saucepan, mixing spoon, ladle

In medium saucepan, combine beets, beef broth, and salt and pepper to taste; mix well and cook over low heat for 10 minutes.

Serve either warm or cold. Ladle into individual bowls, place a halved, hard-cooked egg in each bowl, cut side up, and top with dollop of sour cream or yogurt.

For centuries the Ukraine, with its rich, black soil, has been known as the "bread basket of Europe." The pride and joy of the Ukrainian Easter feast are the bread and the noodle dishes, such as the following recipe.

Ukrainian Spinach and Noodles

Yield: serves 4
 ½ cup butter or margarine, more if necessary
 ½ cup **finely chopped** onion
 1½ pounds fresh spinach, rinsed, dried, **stemmed**, and torn into bite-size pieces or 20-ounce package frozen spinach, thawed, squeezed dry, and **coarsely chopped**
 2 cups cooked egg noodles (keep warm)
 ½ cup **grated** Swiss cheese
 salt and pepper to taste

Equipment: Dutch oven or large saucepan, 2 mixing spoons, **grater**

1. Melt butter or margarine in Dutch oven or large saucepan over medium-high heat. Add onion, and, stirring frequently, cook until tender, about 3 minutes.

2. Add spinach, and cook until spinach is limp and moisture has evaporated, about 3 to 5 minutes. Using 2 spoons, toss frequently. Add more butter or margarine if needed to prevent sticking.

3. Add noodles, and toss gently until heated through. Remove from heat, add cheese and salt and pepper to taste, and toss gently to mix through. Transfer to serving bowl and serve.

Serve as a side dish with the Easter feast. Meatless noodle dishes are also eaten as the main dish during Lent.

Fruit and nut breads and cakes are prepared weeks in advance for the Easter celebration. This recipe for *chereshyanyk*, cherry bars, is a typical Easter treat.

Chereshyanyk   Cherry Bars

Yield: about 14 bars
 2 cups flour
 1 teaspoon baking soda
 ½ teaspoon salt
 ¾ cup sugar
 ½ cup butter or margarine, at room temperature
 1 tablespoon lemon juice
 1 teaspoon **grated** lemon rind
 1 cup sour cream
 1½ cups pitted cherries, fresh or frozen, thawed and drained or 21-ounce can pitted cherries, drained
 confectioners' sugar, for **garnish**

Equipment: Flour **sifter**, large mixing bowl, small mixing bowl, **grater**, mixing spoon, nonstick or lightly greased and floured 9-inch square baking pan, oven mitts

Preheat oven to 350° F.

1. **Sift** flour, baking soda, salt, and sugar into large mixing bowl. Add butter or margarine, and, using clean hands, blend until mixture looks like coarse bread crumbs.

2. In small mixing bowl, use mixing spoon to stir lemon juice, lemon rind, and sour cream. Add to flour mixture, and mix well. The dough should be soft. Set aside about 1 cup of dough to use as topping.

3. Press dough evenly over bottom of nonstick or lightly greased and floured 9-inch baking pan. Form a raised edge (about ¼ inch) around the edges of pan to hold in the filling.

4. Spread fruit evenly over the dough, staying within the raised edge.

5. Using 1 cup dough set aside for topping, pinch off marble-size pieces and drop them onto fruit filling, polka-dot fashion. Bake in oven for about 30 minutes, or until lightly browned.

To serve, cool to warm, sprinkle with confectioners' sugar, and cut into serving-size squares or bars.

Ukrainians observe Christmas on January 7, in keeping with the old Julian calendar, which is 13 days behind the Gregorian calendar. (See pages xxxii for a description of Gregorian calendar.) On Christmas Eve, the feast begins soon after the first star appears in the sky. Traditionally, Ukrainians use their finest tablecloths to cover a few strands of hay that have been spread on the table as a reminder of the manger where the Christ child was born. The table is beautifully set, and candles are lit for this meatless meal called the Holy Supper. The meal always begins with *kutia*, a dish of pre-Christian origin. The custom is to throw a spoonful of *kutia* at the ceiling. If it sticks, the bees will swarm, the harvest will be good, and there will be good fortune in the year ahead. It is the same as Polish *kutya* (recipe page 131). (Poland and Ukraine border one another, and at various times Poland has been part of the Ukraine, and vice versa.)

On Christmas Eve it is the tradition to eat *pampushky*, filled doughnuts, for good luck. This is a quick and easy recipe.

Pampushky   Filled Doughnuts

CAUTION: HOT OIL USED

Yield: makes 8

1 loaf (1 pound) frozen white bread dough, thaw (according to directions on package) until dough is pliable (1 to 2 hours)

1 cup marmalade, or jam of your choice, cherry, apricot, or strawberry

vegetable oil, for **deep frying**

cinnamon sugar

Equipment: Lightly floured work surface, knife, teaspoon, fork, kitchen towel, **deep fryer** (see glossary for tips on making one), paper towels, baking sheet, slotted spoon

1. On lightly floured work surface, cut thawed loaf lengthwise and crosswise to make 16 equal-size pieces; shape pieces into balls. Using clean hands, flatten balls into 3-inch disks.

2. Place 1 teaspoon marmalade or jam in the center of a disk. Dampen a finger with water and run it around the edge. Cover with another disk, matching edges. Seal edges by pressing together, using fork tines. Continue making filled doughnuts. Place side by side on lightly floured work surface, cover with towel, and let rise until double in bulk, about 45 minutes.

3. Prepare deep fryer: Have an adult help you heat oil to 375°. Oil is hot enough for frying when small bubbles appear around a wooden spoon handle when it is dipped in the oil. Place several layers of paper towels on baking sheet.

4. Carefully fry 2 or 3 doughnuts at a time for about 3 minutes on each side or until golden brown. Remove with slotted spoon, and drain on paper towels. Sprinkle both sides with cinnamon sugar while still warm. Continue frying in batches.

Serve warm or at room temperature for best flavor.

Caucasus

The countries of the Caucasus region are Georgia, Armenia, and Azerbaijan. Although the republics are neighbors, sharing the same climate and food, there are extreme differences between them. Each has its own strong national identity, language, and religion, all of which have been strengthened since communism have been lifted. Unfortunately the differences between these Caucasian countries have erupted into bloodshed and long-lasting wars, especially the ongoing war between Armenia and Azerbaijan.

Georgia

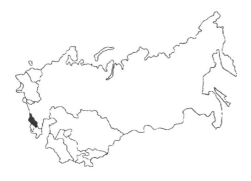

The majority of the people living in the republic of Georgia belong to the Georgian Orthodox Church. They passionately observe all Christian holidays, especially Easter. In many homes the holiday feast includes *shashlik*, which is meat (usually pork) cooked on a skewer.

Shashlik — Pork Shish Kebabs

CAUTION: GRILL OR BROILER USED

Yield: serves 6

½ cup vegetable oil

1 onion, **finely chopped**

1 teaspoon ground oregano

salt and pepper to taste

2½ to 3 pounds boneless lean pork, cut into 1-inch cubes

3 tomatoes, each cut into 6 wedges, for **garnish**

6 green onions, **trimmed**, for garnish

pomegranate syrup (available at Middle East food stores—optional)

Equipment: Large mixing bowl, mixing spoon, 6 wood or metal 10- or 12-inch skewers (if using wooden skewers, first soak in water for at least 30 minutes so they don't burn), charcoal **grill** or broiler pan, metal tongs, oven mitts

1. In large mixing bowl, combine oil, onion, oregano, and salt and pepper to taste. Add pork cubes and toss to coat. Refrigerate for about 4 hours, stirring frequently.

2. Have an adult help prepare charcoal grill or preheat broiler.

3. Thread pork pieces tightly together on skewers. Place side by side on grill or broiler pan. Turn to brown on all sides, and cook through, about 15 to 20 minutes.

To serve, arrange skewers on large platter, and garnish with tomato wedges and green onions. Serve with pomegranate syrup in a separate bowl to use as sauce or dip (optional).

Pilafs in Georgia are made with rice, while most Armenians prefer cracked wheat, called bulgur (also spelled bulghur). Pilafs are traditionally served with spit-roasted lamb or *shashlik* (recipe precedes) for the Easter feast.

Rice Pilaf with Dried Fruits and Almonds

Yield: serves 4 to 6

6 tablespoons butter or margarine

1 cup *each* **coarsely chopped**, dried apricots and pitted prunes, soaked in warm water for 10 minutes and drained

1 cup seedless raisins, soaked in warm water for 10 minutes and drained

½ cups **blanched** whole almonds

1 tablespoon sugar, more or less to taste

½ teaspoon cinnamon

3 cups chicken broth, homemade (recipe page 52) or canned

1½ cups rice

Equipment: Medium skillet, mixing spoon, medium saucepan with cover, fork

1. Melt 4 tablespoons butter or margarine in medium skillet over medium heat. Add apricots, prunes, raisins, almonds, 1 tablespoon sugar, and cinnamon. Stirring constantly, fry for about 3 minutes. To adjust sweetness add more sugar. Stir and keep warm.

2. Pour broth into medium saucepan, and bring to a boil over high heat. Add rice, and stir. Reduce heat to simmer, cover, and cook for about 20 minutes, or until tender. Remove from heat, and add remaining 2 tablespoons butter or margarine. Stir and keep covered for about 5 minutes; fluff with a fork. Add half the fruit mixture, and, using the fork, toss to mix well.

To serve, mound pilaf in serving bowl and drizzle with remaining fruit mixture.

Bread is the staff of life for Georgians. An Easter feast without several kinds of bread on the holiday table is unthinkable. Georgian cheese bread, *khachapuri*, is one of the most popular.

Khachapuri   Georgian Cheese Bread

Yield: 1 loaf
   3 cups (32 ounces) **shredded** cheese, such as Swiss, Mozzarella, or cheddar
   3 tablespoons melted butter
   2 eggs
   ½ teaspoon *each* crushed **coriander** and white pepper
   2 (1 pound each) frozen prepared white bread dough, thawed and risen (according to directions on package)
   2 tablespoons cornmeal, more or less as needed
   egg glaze

Equipment: **Grater**, medium mixing bowl, mixing spoon, floured work surface, floured **rolling pin**, 9-inch pie pan, kitchen towel, **pastry brush**, oven mitts

1. In medium mixing bowl, mix cheese, butter, eggs, coriander, and white pepper. Set aside.

2. Place dough on floured work surface, and **punch down**. **Knead** the 2 loaves into one, and flatten it round. Using floured rolling pin, roll dough out into a disk about 15 inches across. Gently fold in half for easy handling.

3. Sprinkle greased pie pan generously with cornmeal. Place folded dough over half the pie pan, unfold and center on pan with excess dough hanging over the edges. Mound cheese mixture from step 1 in the center of dough.

4. Bring overhanging dough together in folds over the filling, like enclosing in a pouch. (Allow no space between filling and dough.) Pinch the folds of dough together between the thumb and index finger of one hand, and, with the other hand, twist dough closed, making a knob-like top. Cover with towel, and let rise in a warm place for about 30 minutes.

Preheat oven to 350° F.

5. Brush top of cheese bread with egg glaze, and bake in oven for 1 hour, or until golden brown. Let the bread cool in the pan for 10 minutes before cutting.

Cut bread into wedges and serve while still warm.

This candy recipe is made with two popular Georgian ingredients, walnuts and honey.

Walnut Honey Candy

Yield: serves 10 to 12
   1 pound honey
   1 pound walnuts, shelled and **coarsely chopped**
   1 teaspoon ground **ginger**

Equipment: Medium saucepan, wooden mixing spoon, buttered heat-proof plate, knife

1. In medium saucepan, heat honey over low heat. Add walnuts and ginger, and, stirring frequently, cook for 20 minutes.

2. Pour mixture onto buttered, heat-proof plate, and spread to about ½-inch thick. Cool to room temperature and refrigerate.

To serve, cut into serving-size pieces, using a knife dipped in water.

Armenia

Armenia was the first country officially to adopt Christianity as its religion when it converted in the third century A.D. Today, the people of Armenia observe all Christian holidays, with Easter being the most important. Preparing the food for Easter is a labor-intensive ritual that begins weeks ahead. The preparation is as much a part of the holiday as the eating is, even special pots and pans are used.

Armenians eat the first post-Lenten meal immediately following Midnight Mass before Easter. As the people file out of church, the bells ring, and in some communities there are fireworks. The families then hurry home to a feast in the middle of the night. It begins with red-dyed Easter eggs and bread that has been blessed by the priest. There is always soup, which is made from the innards of the lamb to be roasted for Sunday's dinner. The feast is doubly joyous in its celebration of the Resurrection and the end of Lent.

The Easter Sunday feast centers around whole spit-roasted lamb, and a great many very filling side dishes. This feast is a pleasant occasion, and eating takes several hours.

This recipe for potato dumplings, *topik*, is a holiday specialty eaten in many Armenian homes. With modern conveniences, canned foods, ground spices, and electric gadgets, the dish can be prepared in a flash.

Topik   Potato Dumplings

Yield: serves 6

- 4 potatoes, **peeled**, boiled, and mashed or 4 cups prepared instant mashed potatoes
- 2 cups mashed, canned **chick-peas** (including juice)
- salt and white pepper to taste
- 2 tablespoons vegetable oil
- 4 onions, thinly sliced
- ½ cup **finely chopped** walnuts
- ½ cup seedless raisins
- 1 tablespoon ground cumin
- 1 teaspoon ground allspice
- ¾ cup *tahini*, homemade (recipe page 68) or prepared (available at all Middle East food stores)
- juice of 1 lemon, more or less, for serving
- ½ cup olive oil, more or less, for serving
- sprinkle of cinnamon, for serving

Equipment: Large mixing bowl, large skillet, mixing spoon, 6 (dinner-napkin size) cotton squares, work surface, twist ties or kitchen string, large saucepan, slotted spoon, colander, aluminum foil

1. Prepare crust: In large mixing bowl, use wet hands (to prevent sticking) to mix mashed potatoes, mashed chickpeas, and salt and white pepper to taste until well blended and smooth. Set aside.

2. Prepare filling: Heat oil in large skillet. Add onions, and, stirring constantly, fry over medium-

high heat until soft, about 3 minutes. Reduce heat to medium-low, and add nuts, raisins, cumin, allspice, *tahini*, and salt to taste. Stir, and fry for 3 minutes. Set aside to cool.

3. To assemble: Wet squares of cloth, and squeeze as dry as possible. Flatten cloth squares out and stack on work surface. Divide potato mixture into 6 balls and place one in the center of top cloth. Using wet hands, flatten potato ball into a disk about 6 inches across and about ½ inch thick.

4. Divide filling into 6 portions, and mound one portion in middle of potato disk. Enclose filling and potato mixture in cloth (making a tennis-ball-size pouch). Allow no space between filling and cloth, twist and secure with a twist tie or string. Repeat making *topiks*.

5. To cook: Fill large saucepan half full with water, add 1 teaspoon salt, and bring to a boil over high heat. Add *topiks*, two or three at a time (don't crowd pan), and bring back to a boil. Reduce heat until water maintains a **rolling boil**, and cook *topiks* for 20 minutes. Continue cooking in batches.

6. Remove from water with slotted spoon, and drain well over pot. Place colander in sink, and set *topiks* in colander to drain while cooling to room temperature. Do not untie cloth; wrap each dumpling in foil, and refrigerate overnight before serving.

Serve topiks *cold as an appetizer after removing foil and cloth; serve one* topik *to each person. To eat, cut crust open and pour a little lemon juice and olive oil onto the filling. Sprinkle with cinnamon and eat with a fork.*

Armenian feasts always begin with a large assortment of appetizers such as *lahmajoun*, Armenian pizza.

Lahmajoun (also Lahmajoon) Armenian Pizza

Yield: makes 6 to 8

4 pieces of pita bread; separate the top from the bottom, making 8 disks (available at most supermarkets and all Middle East food stores)
6 tablespoons tomato paste
1 (8-ounce) can whole tomatoes, crushed
1 pound finely ground beef, veal, or lamb, or combination
1 onion, **finely chopped**
1 green bell pepper, **cored**, **seeded**, and finely chopped
2 cloves garlic, finely chopped, or ½ teaspoon garlic granules
1 jar (2-ounce size) diced pimentos
salt and pepper to taste

Equipment: Greased or nonstick baking sheet, medium mixing bowl, mixing spoon, oven mitts, pizza wheel or sharp knife

Preheat oven to 450° F.

1. Place pita disks, cut side up, side by side on baking sheet.

2. In medium mixing bowl, use clean hands or mixing spoon to mix tomato paste, crushed tomatoes, ground meat, onion, bell pepper, garlic, pimentos, and salt and pepper to taste. Spread mixture equally over tops of pita breads.

3. Bake in oven for about 20 minutes, or until edges of crust are browned and meat is done.

To serve, cut each pizza into 4 wedges while still warm.

Armenians prepare for Easter and Christmas holidays by baking great quantities of cookies and other sweets. The Armenian people are very hospitable, and they enjoy entertaining. Part of the holiday fun is having plenty of cookies on hand to serve visiting relatives and friends.

Shakarishee — Butter Cookies

Yield: makes about 60

1 cup butter or margarine at room temperature
1½ cups sugar
2½ cups all-purpose flour
about 60 walnut halves

Equipment: Large mixing bowl, mixing spoon or electric mixer, cookie sheet, aluminum foil, oven mitts

Preheat oven to 325° F.

1. In large mixing bowl, use mixing spoon or electric mixer to beat butter or margarine and sugar until light and fluffy, about 3 minutes. Add flour, a little at a time, mixing constantly until smooth.

2. Cover cookie sheet with foil. Using clean hands, shape each cookie into a ping-pong-size ball, and place about 1½ inches apart on foil. Gently press each cookie to slightly flatten, and set a walnut half in center of each.

3. Bake in oven for 15 minutes. (Cookies should not brown.) Remove from oven. Slide foil with cookies intact onto work surface. (Cookies easily crumble when freshly baked but get firmer as they dry out.) Cool before removing from foil. Continue baking on foil, in batches.

Serve cookies as a holiday snack.

Azerbaijan

In Azerbaijan, the majority of people are Muslims. Despite the current conflict with Armenia, the people of Azerbaijan eat basically the same foods as their Christian neighbors, except for pork, which Muslims are forbidden to eat.

For Muslim families a special holiday is the *Lailat al-Qadr*, the "Night of Power," a children's celebration. Muslim children begin studying the Koran, the Islamic holy book, when they are very young, and the first time they read all 114 chapters, the parents take them from house to house where they read verses and receive candy and gifts. The celebration commemorates the first time Muhammad received a revelation from God. These revelations are what formed the Koran. The children receive citrus peel candy (recipe page 137) or the very popular *locum* (recipe page 66). If they're offered cookies, they probably would be *chereshyanyk* (recipe page 140).

The Muslim's *Eid al-Fitr* feast would include roast lamb, *shashlik* made with lamb (shish kebab, recipe page 142), meat stews, **pilafs**, fruit, and one or two fish dishes. Lentil and barley soup (recipe follows) or *borshch* (recipe page 139) might also be served. Unlike the Ukrainians, who add sour cream to their beet soup, the Azerbaijanis prefer yogurt. They also eat fresh fruit by dipping it into a bowl of yogurt before each bite. Some other dishes that have crossed the borders are *bulgur pilavi* (recipe page 65), yogurt cheese (recipe page 55), and fresh fruit, such as melon and walnut compote (recipe follows later).

Lentil and Barley Soup

Yield: serves 6

1 ½ pounds meaty lean lamb bones
8 cups water
2 bay leaves
1 onion, **coarsely chopped**

3 cloves garlic, **finely chopped,** or 1 teaspoon
    garlic granules
½ cup pearl barley (available at most supermar-
    kets and all Middle East and health food
    stores)
1 cup brown lentils
½ cup finely chopped fresh parsley or ¼ cup
    dried parsley flakes
salt and pepper to taste

Equipment: **Dutch oven** or large saucepan with
cover, mixing spoon

1. Put lamb bones in Dutch oven or large saucepan. Add water, bay leaves, onion, garlic, and barley, and bring to a boil over high heat. Reduce heat
to simmer, stir, and then cover and cook for 1 hour.
Occasionally skim froth and fat off surface of soup
during cooking and discard.

2. Add lentils, parsley, and salt and pepper
to taste. Stir well, and cook until soft, about 40
minutes. Remove and discard bay leaves before
serving.

*Serve warm in individual soup bowls with plenty
of crusty bread for sopping.*

Because both fruits and nuts grow well in
the Caucasus, they are included in most holiday feasts, including both Christian and Muslim celebrations.

Kompot iz Dyni i Orekhov

Melon and Walnut Compote

Yield: serves 6 to 8
2 cantaloupe or honeydew melons, halved,
    seeded, peeled, and cut into bite-size chunks
3 cups walnuts, **coarsely chopped**
1 cup honey, at room temperature

Equipment: Medium mixing bowl, mixing spoon

Put melon cubes and walnuts in medium bowl.
Add honey and toss to coat. Refrigerate and mix
before serving.

Serve as a salad or dessert.

Asia, India, and South Pacific Area

The region we refer to as Asia, India, and the South Pacific contains the largest concentration of the earth's population. The people of these lands are very diverse ethnically, culturally, and spiritually and celebrate a wide variety of holidays. Two of the world's major religions have their origins in this area—Hinduism and Buddhism. Both of these religions were practiced for many years prior to the development of Christianity and Islam. In addition to Buddhism and Hinduism, the Islamic religion has spread throughout Asia since its introduction to the region in the eighth century by Arab traders especially in Afghanistan, Pakistan, Bangladesh, and Indonesia. Even India, primarily a Hindu state, is home to 129 million Muslims. Australia and New Zealand are predominantly Christian, due in large part to colonization by European settlers. Other small communities of Christians exist where European missionaries brought their religion to the area.

Hinduism

Hinduism is the primary religion in India, where it has been practiced for thousands of years, well before the Christian era. In one form or another, Hinduism is the mainspring of Indian life. The ultimate goal of Hinduism, like that of most of the Eastern religions, is freedom from a cycle of rebirth and the suffering brought by one's own actions. Hindus recognize that food sustains life, and they believe that every part of a meal, not only what is eaten, but how it is eaten, is an element of the religion. Hindus believe that the more enjoyable the meal, the more nourishing it becomes, and that to say a prayer over the food gives it strength.

Sweets hold a special place in India's social and religious life. Every joyous occasion or holiday, every arrival and departure, new baby or new job, and promotion or award is celebrated with sweets. This is especially true of the most important Hindu holiday, *Diwali*, the Festival of Lights, which many Hindus consider the new year. *Diwali* is in the Hindu month of *Kartika* (October-November). In Banaras (in northeastern India), the site of the sacred Temple of Annapurna, Indian hard-candy sweets are piled 10 to 15 feet high during *Diwali* and then distributed to the poor.

Buddhism

Buddhism originally developed as a branch of Hinduism. Buddha, The Enlightened One, was a Hindu prince whose philosophy grew into a separate religion in the sixth century B.C. Buddhism is more a philosophy of life than a religion, because there is no god or gods in Buddhist beliefs. Because of this philosophy, many Buddhists continue to incorporate rituals from other traditional religions, much in the same way that Christian rituals incorporate elements of pre-Christian celebrations, especially in Latin America. Buddha did not consider himself a holy man but rather a teacher who wanted to enlighten the people about life and afterlife.

In principle, Buddhism concerns itself only with the Path to Enlightenment through meditation, doing good work, and purifying the mind by cultivating love and sympathy for all forms of life. In practice, Buddhist monks have acted as advisers to kings and ministers, and Buddhism has become closely connected with family life. Buddhist priests perform rituals at weddings and funerals, for the benefit of ancestors, to pray for rain, and to exorcise evil powers. One of the most popular Buddhist festivals is that of All Souls' Day, which is held on the fifteenth day of the seventh month of the Buddhist lunar calendar. It is devoted to a ritual in which villagers and monks together rescue all suffering souls. Such honorable action is even extended to animals, especially in the widespread custom of *fang sheng*, which means "to buy animals and set them free." Many Buddhist monasteries have large fishponds to contain the fish people set free.

Thailand, Myanmar (Burma), and Sri Lanka are the most solidly Buddhist countries in the world. In Thailand, Buddhism is the state religion, and in Sri Lanka it is the faith of the majority of the people. Laos and Cambodia also have large Buddhist populations, but the communist governments in those countries officially discourage the practice of Buddhism.

Buddhists have influenced the cooking and choice of food for most of the people of Asia. When the Buddhist monks ventured out from India to teach Buddha's philosophy, they took their cooking pots, bags of rice, and mortars and pestles with them.

For Buddhists, all special events in a person's life are reason to celebrate. When a girl's ears are pierced, a boy is to enter a monastery, or a wedding is to take place, there are celebrations of music, dancing, puppet shows, and tremendous feasting.

China /Taiwan

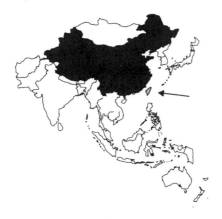

Taiwan, known as the Republic of China, is an island off the coast of China. For many years, it was a Chinese province, until its capture by the Japanese in 1895. Taiwan remained in Japanese hands until 1945, when it returned to Chinese rule. Troubles on mainland China between communists and nationalists ended in 1949 with the communists winning in China, and the nationalists fleeing the mainland and setting up their government in Taiwan. In Taiwan, all traditional holidays are celebrated; some Western celebrations are national holidays as well, such as New Year's Day, January 1.

On the mainland, the communist Chinese government has restricted and discouraged many traditional holiday practices, and just in recent years restrictions have relaxed somewhat, allowing people to celebrate traditional holidays in moderation. May Day, International Labor Day, is a big holiday in China, especially for children. On May Day students of all ages spend the day in the park, playing games and eating a picnic lunch. College students are known to do all sorts of things on May Day, ranging from dressing in outlandish costumes and performing for fellow classmates to parading through the streets in political protest.

The New Year's celebration, also known as the Spring Festival, has been banned since the onset of the Cultural Revolution in 1966, but beginning with the 1980 lunar New Year, some cities in southern China revived the old traditions of fireworks and parades with costumed serpents, lions, and clowns. Today many villages and cities throughout China are once again enjoying the ancient Spring Festival celebrations. Before the holiday, which usually falls in January or February, the house is cleaned, family squabbles are settled, and old debts are paid to begin the new year with a clean slate. All Chinese are one year older during the New Year's celebration, regardless of their actual day of birth. In the countryside, celebrations last as long as a month, and in cities the festivities go on for several days. Gifts are exchanged, and children receive a few coins in red "happiness" envelopes. (Red has symbolized happiness in China for centuries, and it is used in decorations for auspicious occasions.) As the new moon rises, children of all ages honor their elders by formally bowing before them. This most reverential of Chinese acts is known as *kow tow*. Children, facing their elders, kneel on the floor and bow, with arms outstretched, until their foreheads touch the floor.

After the bowing ceremony everyone not playing cards or outside shooting firecrackers pitches in to make *chiao-tzu*. Northern Chinese have a saying, "There is no better rest then lying down, and there is no better food than *chiao-tzu*." Eating *chiao-tzu* is said to bring good fortune for the coming year. It is not unusual for big eaters to consume several dozen of these delicious dumplings.

The wrappers can be homemade (recipe follows), or commercial wonton wrappers can be used.

Chiao-Tzu Wrappers

Dumpling Wrappers

Yield: about 4 dozen

2 cups all-purpose flour, more as needed

¾ cup cold water, more if necessary

Equipment: Flour **sifter**, large mixing bowl, damp kitchen towel, lightly floured work surface, sharp knife, floured **rolling pin**, dry kitchen towel

1. **Sift** flour into large mixing bowl. Slowly add ¾ cup water, and, using clean hands, mix into a stiff dough. Add more water if dough is too stiff. **Knead** in the bowl for about 5 minutes, until smooth. Cover bowl with damp kitchen towel, and let rest for 30 minutes.

2. Transfer dough to lightly floured work surface, and knead, using heel of your hand, for about 3 minutes.

3. Divide dough into 2 pieces, and, on the work surface, roll each piece into a rope shape, at least 1 inch thick and about 12 inches long.

4. Using a knife, cut ropes crosswise into ½-inch-thick slices, and place on lightly floured work surface; sprinkle lightly with flour.

5. Using the heel of your hand or floured rolling pin, flatten each piece into a thin 3-inch disk. Sprinkle lightly with flour and stack.

Cover with dry towel until ready to fill.

Pork Filling for Chiao-Tzu (Dumplings)

Yield: about 4 dozen

2 cups (about ½ pound) trimmed and **finely chopped** bok choy (Chinese cabbage—available at most supermarkets and all Asian food stores)

1 pound lean, boneless pork, finely ground

1 tablespoon **peeled** and finely chopped fresh ginger or 1 teaspoon ground **ginger**

1 tablespoon soy sauce

salt and pepper to taste

dumpling wrappers, homemade (recipe precedes) or 1 package wonton wrappers (available at all supermarkets and Asian food stores)

2 to 3 quarts water, more or less as needed

dipping sauce (recipe follows), for serving

Equipment: Paper towels, medium mixing bowl, mixing spoon, work surface, baking sheet, clean kitchen towel, large saucepan, **slotted spoon**

1. Squeeze chopped bok choy in paper towels to remove any excess water and put into medium mixing bowl. Add pork, ginger, soy sauce, and salt and pepper to taste. Using clean hands or mixing spoon, mix ingredients well.

2. To assemble dumplings: Place a wrapper on the work surface, and spoon 1 teaspoon of filling in the center of wrapper. Dip a finger in water and lightly brush around edge; fold wrapper in half, enclosing filling. Pinch edges tightly together, giving the curve a rippled effect. Repeat assembling dumplings, and place side by side on baking sheet. Cover with dry towel until ready to cook.

3. Boiling directions: Fill large saucepan half full with water and bring to a boil over high heat. Reduce heat until water maintains a **rolling boil**. Carefully put dumplings in boiling water, 6 or 8 at a time. Using slotted spoon to turn dumplings, cook for 15 minutes. Remove, drain, and keep warm. Continue boiling in small batches.

Serve at once while warm with dipping sauce.

Dipping Sauce

Yield: ½ cup

¼ cup rice wine vinegar (available at most supermarkets and all Asian food stores)

¼ cup soy sauce

2 or 3 drops sesame oil (available at all Asian food stores)

Equipment: Cup, teaspoon

In cup, mix vinegar, soy sauce, and sesame oil.

Serve in small, individual sauce dishes. To eat, pick up dumplings with chopsticks or fork, and before each bite, dip into sauce.

There are many legends, folktales, and superstitions about the food served during traditional holidays. A simple dish of plain boiled pork slices was a specialty of the Manchurians who ruled China as the Qing dynasty from 1644 to 1912.

As the legend goes, it was the custom of the king to bestow favors on his subjects who came to wish him happiness during the New Year's celebration. Each person was invited to cut as much as they could eat from a large piece of pork. The more a guest ate, the happier it made the king. Ever since, platters of boiled pork slices with three dipping sauces are served at New Year's, weddings, and other auspicious occasions. Numbers are symbolic to the Chinese, and the sauces must be three, no more, no less. The number three has been a significant Chinese symbol since ancient times, with the number one representing prosperity, number two good health, and number three happiness.

Jo Pien San Wei Boiled Pork Slices with 3 Dipping Sauces

Yield: serves 6 to 8

2 pounds cooked (baked or boiled) lean ham or pork shoulder, sliced paper-thin

prepared sauces: hot mustard sauce, sweet and sour sauce, and oriental chili sauce (available at all supermarkets and Asian food stores), for serving

Equipment: Serving platter

Arrange slices of ham or pork, slightly overlapping, in rows on the serving platter.

Serve meat slices cold with each sauce in a separate small dish. To eat, pick up slices with chopsticks or fork, and, before each bite, gently dab with the sauces.

Celebrating New Year's means spring is not far behind. It's a double happiness when the first day of spring falls within the first month of the lunar year. Spring rolls are eaten all year long, but they have special meaning when eaten in the spring, especially during New Year's.

Spring roll wrappers, traditionally made with rice flour, are much thinner than egg roll wrappers, but either can be used in this recipe.

Chinese Spring Rolls

CAUTION: HOT OIL USED

Yield: makes 12

2 tablespoons light soy sauce

2 teaspoons cornstarch

¼ pound lean pork or chicken, finely ground

2 tablespoons peanut oil, more or less as needed

1 clove garlic, **finely chopped**, or ½ teaspoon garlic granules

1 teaspoon fresh **grated ginger** or 1 teaspoon ground ginger

½ cup finely chopped green onions

1 cup finely **shredded** cabbage

1 cup bean sprouts, fresh or canned, drained (available at supermarkets)

¼ cup finely grated carrot

12 spring or egg roll wrappers (available in the refrigerated section of most supermarkets and all Asian food stores)

1 egg white

vegetable oil for **deep frying**

hot mustard and sweet and sour sauce (available at all super markets), for serving

Equipment: Small bowl, spoon, **grater**, **wok** or medium skillet, mixing spoon, work surface, **deep fryer** (see glossary for tips on making one), paper towels, baking sheet, wooden spoon, metal tongs or **slotted spoon**

1. In small bowl, mix soy sauce and cornstarch. Add pork or chicken, and stir to coat.

2. Heat 1 tablespoon peanut oil in wok or medium skillet over medium-high heat. Add pork or chicken mixture, garlic, and ginger, and, stirring constantly, fry until browned, about 3 minutes. Add onions, cabbage, bean sprouts, and carrot, and, stirring constantly, fry for 3 minutes. Add remaining 1 tablespoon oil, if necessary, to prevent sticking. Set aside to cool for about 10 minutes.

3. To assemble: Place a wrapper on work surface and mound ½ cup filling into a sausage-shape log, about 3½ inches long, along one side of wrapper. Enclose filling in the wrapper: tuck sides over filling, roll into a sausage-shaped package, and seal the last flap by brushing inside edge with egg white and pressing closed. Place seam-side down on work surface. Repeat making spring rolls until filling is gone.

4. Prepare deep fryer: Have an adult help you heat oil to 375° F. Oil is hot enough for frying when small bubbles appear around a wooden spoon handle when it is dipped in the oil. Place several layers of paper towels on baking sheet. Fry spring rolls 2 or 3 at a time, carefully turning with tongs or spoon to brown all sides, about 5 minutes. Transfer to paper towels to drain. Keep warm until ready to serve. Repeat frying in batches.

Serve at once while still warm, with small dishes of dipping sauces. Before each bite, dip spring roll in the sauces.

In some regions of China, it is a New Year's custom to place a bowl full of cooked rice on a home altar dedicated to family ancestors. Rice is an offering of thanks for the good fortune of the passing year and a wish for happiness and prosperity for the new year. This ceremony is called "presenting the new year's rice." In the countryside, one day is set aside during the month-long celebration to honor growing rice and the first planting, over five thousand years ago.

New Year's Rice

Yield: about 3 cups
  1 cup rice
  1¾ cups water

Equipment: Medium saucepan with cover, mixing spoon, fork

1. In medium saucepan, combine rice and water. Bring to a boil over high heat, and stir. Reduce heat to simmer, cover, and cook for 20 minutes.

2. Remove saucepan from heat and keep covered for 10 minutes. Before removing from saucepan, fluff rice with a fork.

Serve rice at once while very hot.

The Chinese love all kinds of eggs: chicken, duck, geese, quail, peacock, and turtle. Since ancient times, eggs have been symbolic of a fruitful life, and they have long been a popular offering to the gods. Tea eggs are served during the New Year celebration to "roll in" good luck for the coming year.

Ch'a Yeh Tan — Tea Eggs

Yield: serves 6
  6 eggs
  4 to 8 cups water, more or less as needed
  2 tablespoons black tea leaves
  1 tablespoon vinegar
  ½ tablespoon salt
  1 teaspoon soy sauce
  2 whole star anise (available at most supermarkets or Asian food stores)

Equipment: Small saucepan with cover, spoon

1. Put eggs in small saucepan, cover with water, and bring to a **rolling boil** over medium-high heat. Reduce heat to simmer, and cook for 10 minutes. Cool under cold water and drain. Using back of spoon, gently tap egg shells, making tiny cracks all over the surface. *Do not peel;* set aside.

2. In small saucepan, combine tea leaves, vinegar, salt, soy sauce, star anise, and 3 cups water. Bring to a boil over high heat. Reduce heat to simmer, cover, and cook for 20 minutes.

3. Add cracked eggs to tea mixture, and simmer for about 15 minutes. Remove pan from heat, and let eggs cool in liquid until cool enough to handle. Remove eggs, carefully peel off shell, and discard liquid.

Serve tea eggs in a bowl or basket. Notice the pretty design on the egg whites. Tea eggs are eaten either at room temperature or chilled.

Afghanistan

Landlocked and mountainous Afghanistan is a Muslim country, and Islamic laws control all aspects of life. Most Afghans engage in some form of agriculture, and people are divided into clans and tribal groups who follow centuries-old customs and religious practices.

Shab-Barat, "the Night of Forgiveness," is an Islamic holiday celebrating Allah's mercy (God's mercy). Muslims ask forgiveness for people who have died, illuminate the outside of mosques, and set off fireworks to honor Allah. *Shab-Barat* is also a time to give bread and sweets, such as *halvah* (recipe page 162), to the poor.

In Afghanistan food prepared for special feasts is colored yellow, red, or orange, making it more festive. The colors also symbolize wealth and good luck.

Pakaura   Golden Potato Coins

CAUTION: HOT OIL USED

Yield: Serves 6 to 8

4 potatoes with skins on (about 1½ pounds), washed, boiled for 10 minutes, drained
1 cup all-purpose flour
½ cup water
½ teaspoon salt
½ teaspoon **turmeric**
1 egg, beaten
2 to 4 cups vegetable oil, more or less as needed
cilantro chutney (recipe follows)

Equipment: Knife, medium mixing bowl with cover, mixing spoon, **Dutch oven** or large skillet, wooden spoon, paper towels, baking sheet, **slotted spoon**

1. Cool potatoes to room temperature, and cut into ¼-inch thick slices.

2. In medium mixing bowl, mix flour, water, salt, turmeric, and egg until smooth. Cover and refrigerate for 30 minutes. Mix before using.

3. Prepare to fry: With an adult present, add 1 inch of oil to Dutch oven or large skillet. Heat over medium-high heat. Oil is hot enough for frying

when small bubbles appear around a wooden spoon handle when it is dipped in the oil. Place several layers of paper towels on baking sheet.

4. Dip potato slices in batter from step 1, and shake off excess. Carefully fry potatoes, a few at a time, for about 2 minutes on each side, until golden brown. Remove with slotted spoon, and drain on paper towels. Sprinkle with salt to taste, and keep warm until ready to serve. Continue frying in batches.

Serve potatoes warm with a bowl of cilantro chutney, chutni gashneetch.

Chutni Gashneetch Cilantro Chutney

Yield: about 1½ cups
- 1 cup **finely chopped** fresh **cilantro**
- 1 onion, finely chopped
- 4 tablespoons lemon juice
- 2 teaspoons dried mint leaves
- 2 tomatoes, **peeled**, **trimmed**, and finely chopped
- 3 drops liquid hot red pepper sauce, more or less to taste (optional)
- salt and pepper to taste

Equipment: Small mixing bowl with cover, mixing spoon

In small mixing bowl, mix cilantro, onion, lemon juice, mint, tomatoes, liquid hot pepper sauce (to taste), and salt and pepper (to taste). Refrigerate until ready to serve.

Serve as a dipping sauce with pakaura, *golden potato coins (recipe precedes).*

The following recipe is for *sheer payra,* a rich Afghan candy made especially for holiday celebrations.

Sheer Payra Cardamom Candy

Yield: about 45 pieces
- 2 cups sugar
- ⅔ cup milk
- ¼ teaspoon salt
- 2 tablespoons corn syrup
- 2 tablespoons butter or margarine
- ½ teaspoon ground cardamom
- ½ cup chopped nuts: walnuts, almonds, or peanuts

Equipment: Medium saucepan, wooden mixing spoon, **candy thermometer** or cup, buttered 8-inch square baking pan

1. In medium saucepan, mix sugar, milk, salt, and corn syrup, and cook over medium heat, stirring constantly, for about 5 minutes, until sugar dissolves. Cook, stirring frequently, until mixture reaches 240° F. on candy thermometer or until a few drops of mixture dropped into a cup of cold water form a soft ball, about 8 to 10 minutes. Remove from heat. Add butter or margarine and cardamom, stir, and set aside to cool to lukewarm.

2. Add nuts, and beat vigorously until thick and no longer glossy, about 5 to 10 minutes. Spread mixture evenly over bottom of buttered 8-inch square baking pan. Refrigerate until firm, about 3 hours.

To serve, cut into 1-inch squares.

Pakistan

In Pakistan most of the people are Muslims, and the most important holiday for Pakistanis is *Eid al-Fitr*, "Breaking the Fast" of *Ramadan*. When the new moon has been sighted at the end of *Ramadan*, cannons shoot off and drums beat to let everyone know that the three-day *Eid al-Fitr* celebration is beginning. People put on new clothes, children receive presents, and every household prepares an elaborate holiday feast.

A bowl of *yakhni* is the first nourishment Pakistanis have at the end of *Ramadan*. *Yakhni* is made with chicken or beef bones, and vegetable scraps, such as potato peelings, carrot or beet tops, celery trimmings, and broccoli stems.

Yakhni   Pakistani Broth

Yield: serves 6 to 8

2 quarts water

1 (12-ounce) can beef broth

1½ pounds chicken or beef bones, or combination

1 large onion, **finely chopped**

2 cups **coarsely chopped** vegetable scraps, potato or carrot peelings, celery leaves, or combination, which have been thoroughly washed

3 cloves garlic, finely chopped, or 1 teaspoon garlic granules

1 tablespoon finely **grated** fresh **ginger** or 1 teaspoon ground ginger

1 teaspoon ground cinnamon

2 bay leaves

½ teaspoon ground cardamom

½ teaspoon finely crushed dried mint, for **garnish**

Equipment: **Dutch oven** or large saucepan with cover, **grater**, mixing spoon, large bowl with cover, strainer, coffee filters, medium saucepan, ladle.

1. Pour water and beef broth into Dutch oven or large saucepan, and add bones, onion, vegetable scraps, garlic, ginger, cinnamon, bay leaves, and cardamom. Bring to a boil over high heat, and stir. Reduce heat to simmer, cover, and cook for about 3 hours. Occasionally remove and discard any froth or scum that rises to the surface. Remove from heat and cool to room temperature. Transfer to large bowl, cover, and refrigerate for about 8 hours.

2. Skim congealed fat from surface of stock and discard. Pour soup back into Dutch oven or large saucepan, and bring to a boil over high heat. Remove from heat, and set aside to cool until soup is warm.

3. Place strainer lined with coffee filters over a medium saucepan. Ladle the stock into the filter. Discard residue in filter. Bring clear broth to a boil over high heat before serving.

To serve, ladle broth into individual soup bowls and garnish with pinch of mint. It is the custom in Pakistan to pick up the bowl and drink the broth. Leftover broth keeps well if covered and frozen.

Pakistanis love meat, and holiday feasts almost always include mutton, beef, or chicken, such as the following recipe for tandoori chicken—*murgh tikha lahori*. (For religious reasons Muslims are forbidden to eat pork.) The holiday meal also includes bread, rice, vegetables, pickles, and fresh fruit.

Murgh Tikha Lahori Tandoori Chicken

CAUTION: GRILL OR BROILER USED

Yield: Serves 6

2½ to 3 pounds skinless chicken, cut into serving-size pieces

1½ cups plain yogurt

juice of 1 lemon

3 cloves garlic, **finely chopped**, or 1 teaspoon garlic granules

½ tablespoon **grated** fresh **ginger** or 1 teaspoon ground ginger

salt and pepper to taste

1 teaspoon ground **coriander** (cilantro)

¼ teaspoon *each* ground cardamom and ground cloves

1 teaspoon paprika

2 tablespoons vegetable oil

½ cup *ghee* (recipe page 160) or melted butter or margarine, more or less as needed

Equipment: Sharp knife, **grater**, large mixing bowl with cover, mixing spoon, rubber gloves or baggies to cover hands, charcoal grill or oven broiler pan, oven mitts, pastry brush, metal tongs

1. Using a sharp knife, slash each piece of chicken in several places.

2. In large mixing bowl, combine yogurt, lemon juice, garlic, ginger, salt and pepper to taste, coriander, cardamom, cloves, paprika, and oil; mix well. Using covered hands, coat chicken pieces with **marinade**. Refrigerate at least 8 hours, turning chicken frequently to coat with marinade.

Prepare charcoal grill or preheat broiler.

3. Brush marinated chicken on both sides with *ghee*, melted butter, or margarine, and place on grill or broiler pan. Cook about 10 minutes on each side, until browned and well done. Brush frequently with marinade while cooking. If chicken seems too dry, brush again with *ghee*, melted butter, or margarine. To test whether chicken is done, pierce the thickest part of chicken with fork tines or knife. If juices that trickle out are clear, instead of pinkish, the chicken is done.

Serve chicken with Pakistan rice, pulao arasta *(recipe follows).*

No holiday feast is complete unless a rice dish known as *pulao* is on the table. From a gala feast celebrating the crowning of an emperor to the simple wedding meal of poor peasants, a rice dish is always included.

Pulao Arasta   Pakistani Rice

Yield: serves 6 to 8

4 tablespoons *ghee* (recipe page 160), butter, or margarine

3 onions, **finely chopped**

1 teaspoon ground cumin

2 cups long-grain rice, preferably **basmati** (available at some supermarkets and all Middle East food stores)

4 cups beef, chicken broth, or *yakhni* (recipe page 157)

½ cup *each* sliced almonds and seedless raisins

Equipment: **Dutch oven** or medium saucepan with cover, mixing spoon, small skillet, fork

1. Heat 3 tablespoons *ghee*, or melt butter or margarine, in Dutch oven or medium saucepan over medium-high heat. Add 1 chopped onion, and fry until soft, about 3 minutes. Add cumin and rice, and stir well. Add broth or *yakhni*, stir, and cover. Reduce heat to simmer, and cook for 20 minutes.

2. Heat 1 tablespoon *ghee*, or melt butter or margarine, in small skillet over medium-high heat. Add remaining 2 onions, and fry until soft and golden, about 3 minutes. Add almonds and raisins, and, stirring constantly, fry for about 2 minutes.

3. Transfer rice to serving bowl, fluff with a fork, and spread onion mixture over the top.

Serve as a side dish with tandoori chicken *(recipe precedes).*

This recipe for Pakistani sweet bread, *shahi tukra*, is reserved for special occasions and is taken as a gift when visiting friends during a holiday.

Shahi Tukra   Pakistani Sweet Bread

Yield: serves 6 to 8

½ cup butter or margarine, at room temperature

8 slices bread, crusts trimmed off

2 cups water

1 cup sugar

5 cups milk

1 teaspoon **turmeric**

¼ cup **finely chopped** pistachio nuts or almonds

edible silver leaf (optional—available at Middle East food stores)

Equipment: Butter knife, wax paper, work surface, large skillet, metal **spatula**, buttered or nonstick 13- x 9-inch baking pan, medium saucepan, mixing spoon, oven mitts

1. Spread butter or margarine on both sides of bread and stack on wax-paper-covered work surface.

2. In large skillet, fry buttered bread, 2 or 3 at a time, over medium-high heat for about 3 to 5 minutes on each side, until golden. Place bread in buttered or nonstick 13- x 9-inch baking pan. Arrange bread slices side by side or slightly overlapping, and keep in warm place.

3. Heat water in medium saucepan over medium heat. Add sugar, and, stirring frequently, cook until thick and syrupy, about 10 minutes. Remove from heat, and, stirring constantly, add milk and turmeric. Pour over bread slices. Refrigerate for about 1 hour.

Preheat oven to 350° F.

4. Bake bread in oven for 30 to 45 minutes, until mixture is thick and pudding-like. Sprinkle with nuts before serving.

To serve, spoon into dessert bowls. In Pakistan, edible silver leaf is sometimes spread over this dessert before serving.

India

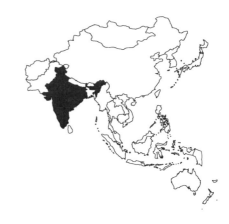

The majority of people living in India are Hindus. *Diwali*, "Festival of Lights," is the most important Hindu holiday. This joyous festival, celebrated in the Hindu month of *Kartika* (October-November), marks the beginning of winter, and many Hindus consider it the beginning of a new year.

On the first night of *Diwali*, houses and yards glow with flickering lights. According to folklore, *Lakshmi*, the Hindu goddess of wealth and prosperity, visits all houses but blesses only those lit up to greet her. The lights are tiny oil lamps called *dipa*. Many families follow the ancient custom of burning *ghee* in their lamps, but today most people use candles. In cities with electricity, strings of white bulbs outline houses and public buildings.

On the morning of *Diwali*, everyone bathes, dresses in new clothes, and eats a festive breakfast. Orange lentils, *massoor dal*, are served at the *Diwali* breakfast and for most religious feasts, because the color orange is symbolic of wealth and good luck. Regardless of color, however, all lentils cook and taste the same.

Massoor Dal   Orange Lentils

Yield: serves 6 to 8

- 2 tablespoons vegetable oil
- 1 onion, **finely chopped**
- 3 cloves garlic, finely chopped, or 1 teaspoon garlic granules
- 1 teaspoon ground cumin
- 1 green pepper, **cored, seeded**, and finely chopped
- 1½ cups lentils (preferably orange)
- 3 cups water
- 2 cups (16 ounces) canned stewed tomatoes
- 1 tablespoon sugar
- salt and pepper to taste
- 4 cups cooked rice, for serving (optional—keep warm)

Equipment: **Dutch oven** or medium saucepan with cover, mixing spoon

1. Heat oil in Dutch oven or medium saucepan over medium-high heat. Add onion, garlic, cumin, and green pepper, and, stirring frequently, fry until onion and pepper are soft, about 3 minutes.

2. Add lentils, water, stewed tomatoes, sugar, and salt and pepper to taste; stir well, and bring to a boil. Reduce heat to low heat, cover, and cook for 1 hour, or until lentils are tender. Mix before serving.

Serve as a main dish over rice or as a side dish with meat or fish.

After the *Diwali* breakfast the day is spent visiting friends and relatives; family and friends exchange gifts, and children are given money.

Almost every community has some sort of a parade or street fair to mark the occasion. If the children aren't busy buying firecrackers, toys, and sweets with their newfound wealth, they are entertained by dancing bears, trained monkeys, snake charmers, and street musicians.

At sunset families return home to pray together at the family altar, which is bedecked with flowers, sweets, and incense around a picture or statue of the goddess *Lakshmi*. When it is dark, the families, along with neighbors, light up their houses and yards, turning the neighborhood into a spectacle of thousands of glowing lights.

For centuries *ghee*, a clarified butter-like substance, has been used not only for cooking but in religious ceremonies. During *Diwali* thousands of tiny *dipa* lamps are fueled with *ghee*.

Most Hindu holiday feasts include *panch armit*, the "five immortal nectars": honey, sugar, milk, yogurt, and *ghee*. One advantage of *ghee* is that it keeps indefinitely, even when left unrefrigerated. The residue can be refrigerated and added to enrich soups, stews, and sauces.

Ghee   Indian Clarified Butter

Yield: about 1 cup

- 1 pound unsalted butter or margarine

Equipment: Small saucepan, large spoon or **bulb baster**, small bowl

1. In small saucepan, melt butter over very low heat, undisturbed, for about 45 minutes, until it separates, with the solids on the bottom and clear oil on top. Do not let it brown.

2. The clear oil on the top is the *ghee*; it can be carefully spooned off or removed with a bulb baster into a small bowl. Save solids and refrigerate (see above). Cool *ghee* to room temperature, cover, and refrigerate.

Serve ghee over vegetables, spread on bread, or use in cooking instead of butter.

Bread is used to scoop food from the plate. *Paratha* is a flat bread made with lovage seeds (available at Middle Eastern food stores). Celery seeds are a good substitute.

Paratha
(also Paratlas)   Flat Bread

Yield: serves 6
- 2 cups whole wheat flour
- 1 teaspoon salt
- 1 teaspoon ground celery seeds or 14 lovage seeds, crushed (available at Middle East food stores)
- ½ cup milk
- ½ cup water
- ¼ to 1 cup *ghee* (recipe precedes) or melted butter, more as needed

Equipment: Flour sifter, large mixing bowl, mixing spoon, damp kitchen towel, lightly floured work surface, lightly floured rolling pin, pastry brush, large skillet or griddle, metal **spatula**

1. Sift flour and salt into large mixing bowl. Make a well in the center of flour, add seeds, milk, and water, and mix to form a very soft, smooth dough. Cover with damp towel, and set aside to rest at room temperature for about 2 hours.

2. Divide dough into 6 balls. Using clean hands, flatten each ball into a 7-inch disk and then smooth out with floured rolling pin on floured work surface. Brush top side of disks with *ghee* or melted butter, and stack on work surface. Continue making disks.

3. Heat 2 tablespoons *ghee* or melted butter in large skillet or griddle over medium heat. Add one disk, and fry for about 3 to 5 minutes on each side until golden and speckled with brown spots. Continue frying disks in batches. Keep warm until ready to serve.

Serve paratha *warm.*

Hindus believe sweets nourish the body, the spirit, and the soul, and this recipe is a favorite.

Roshmalay   Sweet Cheese Balls

Yield: serves 6 to 8
- 16 ounces cream cheese, at room temperature
- ¾ cup corn syrup
- ¼ cup water
- 2 cups heavy cream
- ½ cup slivered almonds
- ½ cup sugar
- ½ teaspoon vanilla extract
- 2 teaspoons ground nutmeg, more or less as needed
- ½ teaspoon ground cardamom

Equipment: Medium mixing bowl, wax paper, baking sheet, small bowl, mixing spoon, small saucepan, small bowl with cover

1. Put cream cheese in medium mixing bowl, and, using clean hands, form into ping-pong-size balls. Place balls side by side on wax-paper-covered baking sheet.

2. In small bowl, mix corn syrup and water. Spoon about 1 teaspoon of corn syrup mixture over each cheese ball. Cover balls loosely with wax paper and refrigerate.

3. In small saucepan, mix heavy cream, almonds, sugar, vanilla, 1 teaspoon nutmeg, and cardamom. Heat over medium-high heat. When bubbles appear around the edges, reduce heat to simmer and let cook for about 30 minutes. Remove from heat, and cool to room temperature. Transfer to small bowl, cover, and refrigerate. When ready to use, mix well.

4. To assemble and serve: Place 3 or 4 cheese balls on each dessert plate, and spoon about 2 tablespoons almond cream mixture over each serving. Sprinkle with remaining 1 teaspoon nutmeg (dividing among each serving).

In India, sweets are made with such things as rice, grains, beans, cornmeal, cheese, and vegetables; a thick syrup is added for sweetness. *Savia* is an Indian noodle, akin to Italian vermicelli noodles. During *Diwali*, it is customary to send friends a platter of sweet *savia* garnished with edible gold or silver leaf. (Gold and silver leaf are available at Middle East food stores.)

Savia   Sweet Noodle Dessert

Yield: serves 4 to 6

4 tablespoons *ghee* (recipe page 160), butter, or margarine

½ cup seedless raisins

½ cup **coarsely chopped** pistachio nuts or almonds

¾ cup sweetened shredded coconut

½ pound vermicelli noodles (broken into 1- to 2-inch lengths, cooked, and drained)

edible gold or silver leaf (optional—see above)

1 cup plain yogurt, more or less, for serving (optional)

Equipment: Large skillet with cover, mixing spoon

Heat *ghee*, or melt butter or margarine in large skillet over medium heat. Add raisins, nuts, and ½ cup coconut, and, stirring constantly, fry for about 3 minutes. Add noodles, toss to mix, and heat through, about 3 minutes.

To serve, pile savia *on a serving platter, and sprinkle with remaining ¼ cup coconut. (If adding gold or silver leaf, it is spread over the mixture at this time.) Spoon into individual dessert bowls, and add a **dollop** of yogurt.*

Halvah is a favorite dessert enjoyed by young and old alike.

Halvah   Dessert

Yield: serves 8 or 10

4 teaspoons butter, margarine or *ghee* (recipe page 160)

1 cup farina (Cream of Wheat)

2 cups warm water

1 cup sugar

½ cup chopped nuts: almonds, peanuts, or walnuts

Equipment: Medium saucepan, wooden mixing spoon, 8-inch pan

1. In medium saucepan, melt butter or margarine or heat *ghee* over medium heat. Stirring constantly, add Cream of Wheat, and cook for about 3 minutes. Continue stirring, and add water and sugar. Continue cooking for about 10 minutes, stirring frequently to prevent sticking. Mixture will become very thick.

2. Pour mixture into pan, and sprinkle the top with nuts.

To serve, cool to room temperature, and spoon into individual dessert bowls.

Sri Lanka

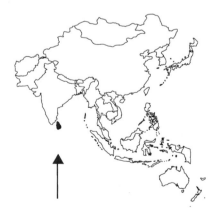

Sri Lanka is a small island in the Indian Ocean. After the introduction of Buddhism from India in the third century B.C., Sri Lanka became one of the world centers of that religion. Many Sri Lankans are devout Buddhists, and every aspect of Buddha's life is sacred to them. Many traditions have grown out of this devotion. On *Sangamitta Day*, for instance, Buddhists make a pilgrimage to pray at a tree that grew from a sapling of the tree that, according to legend, Buddha sat under to attain Enlightenment. The spectacular *Esala Perahera* festival is another example. For over 2,000 years, the temple at Kandy has treasured a tooth of Buddha. For nine nights during the festival, a small gold casket containing the sacred tooth is carried out of the temple on the back of a richly decorated elephant. Each night more elephants, actors, dancers, and drummers join the parade. On the final night over 130 elephants march in the long torch-light procession.

In Sri Lanka, Hindus, Muslims, and Christians live side by side with the Buddhists, although sometimes this coexistence is marred by violence. All Sri Lankans eat the same food for their different holiday feasts, except when religious taboos against certain foods prevent it. Buddhists and Hindus do not eat beef, and many are vegetarians. Muslims do not eat pork or animals not slaughtered the Islamic way.

As in Hindu and Muslim countries, Sri Lankans eat sitting on the floor, using only the right hand to eat. It is considered bad manners to get food on the fingers above the first knuckle and to let the left hand touch food. (The left hand is used only for personal grooming.)

A flatbread, such as *rotis* (recipe follows), is served with every meal. The bread is torn into pieces, which are used as scoops, carrying the food from the plate to one's mouth. Flatbread is eaten by all Sri Lankans regardless of religious beliefs.

Rotis — Sri Lankan Coconut Flatbread

Yield: about 12 pieces

 1 cup **grated** or finely shredded coconut, homemade (recipe page 193) or canned
 2¼ cups **self-rising flour**, more as needed
 1 cup cold water, more if necessary
 vegetable oil cooking spray

Equipment: **Grater**, medium mixing bowl, mixing spoon, kitchen towel, floured work surface, large skillet or griddle, wide metal **spatula**

1. In medium mixing bowl, mix coconut and 2¼ cups flour.

Add 1 cup water, a little at a time, and, using clean hands, mix until the soft dough holds together. Add a little more water, if necessary. Cover with towel, and let rest for 30 minutes.

2. Divide dough into 12 pieces. Place 1 piece of dough on floured work surface, and, using floured hands, flatten into a thin disk about 5 inches across. Repeat making disks with remaining dough.

3. Have an adult spray cooking oil spray over bottom of large skillet or on griddle. Heat over medium-high heat, and fry breads, 1 or 2 at a time, for about 2 minutes on each side or until bread is golden brown. Add more cooking spray, if necessary, to prevent sticking.

Serve rotis *while still warm, and have guests use it to scoop up food from the plate.*

Ghee is used by Hindus for religious rituals and cooking. Buddhists, Hindus, Muslims, and Christians in Sri Lanka use it in their cooking. *Ghee* can be homemade (recipe page 160), or it is available at Middle East food stores.

Rice is eaten at almost every meal, including holiday feasts, and the following recipe is a popular way to eat it. The *ghee* rice is eaten with *dal* (lentils, recipe page 160), vegetables, and *rotis* (recipe precedes).

Ghee Rice

Yield: serves 6 to 8

1 cup *ghee* (recipe page 160), butter, or
   margarine, more or less as needed
2 onions, thinly sliced
1 teaspoon ground turmeric, more as needed
1 teaspoon ground curry powder
½ teaspoon ground cinnamon
4 cups long-grain rice
6 cups chicken broth, homemade (recipe page
   52) or canned
1 cup seedless white raisins
5 hard-cooked eggs, shelled, for garnish
salt to taste
1 ½ cups frozen peas, thawed
½ cup sliced almonds, for **garnish**

Equipment: **Dutch oven** or large saucepan with
cover, mixing spoon, toothpick, medium skillet,
slotted spoon, paper towels, fork

1. Heat ½ cup *ghee* or melt butter or margarine
in Dutch oven or large saucepan over medium-
high heat. Add onions, stir, and fry until golden,
about 3 minutes. Reduce heat to medium; add 1
teaspoon turmeric, curry powder, and cinnamon;
stir well. Add rice, and, stirring constantly, cook
for 5 minutes.

2. Add chicken broth and raisins, increase heat
to boil, and stir. Reduce heat to simmer, cover, and
cook for 20 minutes, until rice is tender.

Prepare shelled, hard-cooked eggs for garnish:

3. Rub eggs with turmeric and salt to taste. Prick
each egg 4 or 5 times with a toothpick.

4. Heat 2 tablespoons *ghee*, butter, or margarine
in medium skillet over medium-high heat. Add
eggs and fry until golden brown on all sides, about
5 minutes. Add more *ghee*, butter, or margarine, if
necessary. Using slotted spoon, transfer eggs to

paper towels and drain. Cool to room temperature,
cut in half, and set aside.

5. Before transferring rice to serving platter, add
salt to taste and peas, and fluff with fork. For garnish, sprinkle almonds over rice and place halved
eggs around the rice.

*To serve, place platter of rice in center of table,
and have guests help themselves using the fingers
of the right hand.*

Gingered bananas (recipe follows) are a
popular, easy-to-fix recipe. The bananas have
a candy-like taste, which both Hindus and
Buddhists favor as part of their holiday feasts.
The Muslims always end a meal with fresh
fruit. Gingered bananas are a festive fruit for
the feast of *Eid al-Fitr.*

Gingered Bananas

Yield: serves 6 to 8

½ cup sugar
½ cup water
¼ cup lemon juice
8 bananas, **peeled** and cut lengthwise in half
1 tablespoon ground **ginger**

Equipment: Small saucepan, mixing spoon

1. In small saucepan, mix sugar, water, and
lemon juice. Stirring constantly, bring to a boil over
medium heat. Continue stirring until sugar dissolves. Reduce heat to low, and cook for about 8
minutes until thickened.

2. Arrange bananas on serving platter, cut-side
up, and sprinkle with ginger. Spoon hot sugar mixture over bananas. Refrigerate before serving.

Serve chilled bananas with syrup as dessert.

Bangladesh

Most people living in Bangladesh are Muslims, and Islam is the official religion of the country. All Islamic observances are national holidays. Only about 15 percent of the people in Bangladesh are Hindus, but strong cultural, historic, and commercial ties with neighboring India reinforce Hindu traditions. A handful of Christians live in large cities, and there are small Buddhist communities.

Rice is eaten at every meal, and a holiday feast is unlikely without it. In Bangladesh, to properly welcome in the Muslim or Hindu New Year it is important to eat sweetened yellow lentils for sweet happiness, fertility, and health as well as countless spiritual rewards. The following recipe, *shakkar pongal*, includes rice and yellow lentils.

Shakkar Pongal — Rice and Lentil Pudding

Yield: serves 6

- 1 cup lentils (preferably yellow)
- 2 cups water
- 1 cup rice
- 3 cups milk
- 1 cup light brown sugar
- 1 teaspoon ground cardamom
- ¼ cup seedless raisins
- ¼ cup roasted cashews or almonds, **coarsely chopped**
- 2 tablespoons *ghee* (recipe page 160), butter, or margarine

Equipment: **Dutch oven** or medium saucepan with cover, mixing spoon

1. Put lentils and water in Dutch oven or medium saucepan, and bring to a boil over high heat. Reduce heat to simmer, and stir. Cover and cook for 10 minutes.

2. Add rice and milk, stir, and bring to a boil over high heat. Reduce heat to low, cover, and cook for about 20 minutes until rice and lentils are almost tender. Add brown sugar, cardamom, raisins, nuts, and *ghee*, butter, or margarine. Stir, cover, and cook for about 10 minutes, until rice and lentils are tender, not mushy. Set aside, covered, for 10 minutes before serving.

Serve pudding warm, at room temperature, or cold, either as a side dish or dessert.

Foogaths are savory dishes made with different kinds of cooked vegetables and coconut. All castes and classes of Hindus eat *foogaths*. *Foogaths* are tasty, nourishing, and are often the only thing most Bengalis, the most prominent ethnic group in Bangladesh, have to eat at any time, let alone holiday feasts. The following recipe is for an okra *foogath*, *behndi foogath*. Hindus call okra *behndi*, which means lady's fingers.

Behndi Foogath — Stewed Okra

Yield: serves 6

- 2 tablespoons *ghee* (recipe page 160), butter, or margarine
- 1 onion, **finely chopped**
- 3 cloves garlic, finely chopped, or 1 teaspoon garlic granules

1 tablespoon **grated** fresh **ginger** or 2 teaspoons ground ginger
½ teaspoon chili powder, more or less to taste
2 cups canned stewed tomatoes
2 tablespoons **shredded** unsweetened coconut (available at all supermarkets)
1 pound fresh whole okras, **stemmed**, washed, and **blanched** or frozen, thawed
salt to taste

Equipment: Large skillet, mixing spoon, **grater**

1. Heat *ghee* or melt butter or margarine in large skillet over medium-high heat. Add onion, garlic, ginger, and chili powder, stir, and fry over medium-high heat until onions are soft, about 3 minutes.

2. Add tomatoes, coconut, okra, and salt to taste. Stir and simmer for about 15 minutes.

Serve as the main dish for a vegetarian meal or as a side dish with meat.

The Muslim New Year's, *Moharram*, is a double celebration for the Muslims of Bangladesh and Pakistan. In addition to the New Year's celebration, they also honor Saint Hussain who fell in battle against Yazid, ruler of Arabia, 1,400 years ago. On the day of the saint's martyrdom, two special dishes are prepared: one is rice with saffron, called *zarda* (recipe follows), and a milk-rice pudding. Although *zarda* is traditionally prepared with saffron, it is expensive, and so ground turmeric is used instead.

Zarda   Sweet Rice

Yield: serves 4 to 6
6 tablespoons *ghee* (recipe page 160), butter, or margarine
1 cup **finely chopped** onion
½ teaspoon ground **turmeric**
½ teaspoon *each* ground cinnamon and ground cloves

2 cups rice (preferably **basmati**, available at some supermarkets and all Middle East food stores)
4 cups boiling water
1 tablespoon dark brown sugar
1 tablespoon dark molasses
salt to taste
¼ teaspoon ground cardamom

Equipment: **Dutch oven** or medium saucepan with cover, wooden mixing spoon, fork

1. Heat *ghee* or melt butter or margarine in Dutch oven or medium saucepan over medium-high heat. Add chopped onion, and, stirring constantly, fry until soft, about 3 minutes. Add turmeric, cinnamon, cloves, and stir well. Add rice and stir to coat.

2. Stirring rice mixture constantly, slowly add boiling water, brown sugar, molasses, salt to taste, and cardamom. Bring to boil over high heat, and then reduce heat to low. Stir, cover, and cook for about 25 minutes, or until rice is tender and has absorbed all the liquid. Remove from heat, and keep covered for 5 minutes. Fluff the rice with a fork before serving.

Serve at once, mounded in a bowl.

Myanmar (Burma)

Most people living in Myanmar are Buddhists. During their New Year's festival in April, the people of Myanmar hold the Water Festival, known as *Thingyan*, where citizens merrily hurl water at one another, even strangers. The free-for-all dousing is supposed to wash away old misdeeds. Artificial monsoons are created with buckets, fire hoses, water balloons, and squirt guns. People also welcome the New Year by setting pet fish and birds free to show compassion for all living things. Many households prepare special food for the monks in the monasteries.

There are many national and regional festivals that are connected with the hundreds of pagodas (temples) in Myanmar. Two examples are the *Tazaungdaing* festival, an all-night weaving contest at the Shwedagon Pagoda, and *Thadingyut*, which marks the end of the Buddhist Lent—a time of much feasting, dancing, and merriment.

The Harvest Festival in the fall, called *Hta-Mu Ne,* is a favorite. *Hta-Ma-Ne,* a rice dish named after the festival, is cooked in a huge pot over an open fire in the monastery courtyard as an offering to the monks and anyone else who wants to eat it. It takes a couple of very strong people, using large, hard wood paddles, to stir the thick and sticky mixture.

Hta-Ma-Ne Sticky Rice with Coconut

Yield: serves 6

  6 cups cooked **glutinous** rice, kept warm
    (available at Asian food stores)
  ½ cup peanut butter
  2 tablespoons finely **grated** fresh **ginger** or 1
    teaspoon ground ginger
  1 tablespoon vegetable oil
  3 tablespoons fresh garlic, **finely chopped**, or 1
    teaspoon garlic granules
  4 tablespoons **sesame seeds, toasted**
  ½ cup **shredded**, sweetened coconut (available
    at supermarkets)

Equipment: Medium saucepan with cover, mixing spoon, **grater**

In medium saucepan, stir cooked rice, peanut butter, ginger, oil, garlic, sesame seeds, and shredded coconut. Cover and cook over low heat for about 10 minutes to heat through.

Serve in individual bowls.

In Myanmar, several different curries are often served at the same meal. Curry sauce can be mixed with any combination of **blanched** or cooked vegetables and meat. The following curried vegetable dish is eaten during *Thingyan*. During *Thingyan*, each family has its own celebration feast.

Curried Vegetables

Yield: serves 6

  2 tablespoons butter or margarine
  2 tablespoons all-purpose flour
  1 tablespoon curry powder
  2 cups chicken broth or water
  2 onions, **coarsely chopped**
  4 tomatoes, **stemmed**, coarsely chopped
  ½ cup raisins
  4 cold, cooked potatoes, **peeled** and cut into
    bite-size pieces
  2 cups fresh cauliflower **florets**, **blanched** or
    frozen, thawed
  salt and pepper to taste
  4 to 6 cups cooked rice, for serving

Equipment: Medium saucepan, mixing spoon

1. Melt butter or margarine in saucepan over medium heat. Add flour and curry powder, and, stirring constantly, cook until mixture thickens and is smooth and lump-free, about 1 minute.

2. Slowly add broth or water, stirring constantly until blended. Add onions, tomatoes, and raisins, and, stirring frequently, cook about 5 minutes. Add potatoes, cauliflower, and salt and pepper to taste. Stir, and heat through, about 5 minutes.

Serve warm with a separate dish of rice.

Thailand

Most festival-loving Thais are Buddhists, and every celebration is a major production, even the "Plowing Day Festival" that marks the beginning of rice-planting season. The Thais' favorite celebration is *Songkran*, the Buddhist New Year, also called the Water Festival, which falls in April. As in Myanmar, people dump buckets of water on each other to wash away misdeeds, giving each person a clean slate for the upcoming year. During *Songkran* young people show respect to elders by sprinkling perfumed water into the older people's hands. Pet fish and birds are set free as a symbolic show of kindness to all living creatures.

Hta-Ma-Ne (recipe page 167) is the only ceremonial dish reserved for Buddhist feasts. Other foods have symbolic meanings, such as the golden threads that are often served on special holidays. Once only eaten by the elite of Thailand, golden threads are simply a wrapping of thin, lace-like egg omelets or noodles around bite-size pieces of food. The egg or noodles (used in this recipe) symbolize threads of gold for prosperity and good fortune. The noodles can be wrapped any way you like.

Foi T'on Rum Golden Threads around Meat Bundles

CAUTION: HOT OIL USED

Yield: about 24

- 48 to 72 (10-inch lengths) linguine noodles, more or less as needed
- 6 to 8 cups hot water, more or less as needed
- 1 pound lean, finely ground beef, pork, or combination
- 1 clove garlic, **finely chopped**, or ½ teaspoon garlic granules
- 1 egg
- 1 tablespoon cornstarch
- ½ onion, finely chopped
- salt and pepper to taste
- vegetable oil, for **deep frying**
- peanut sauce (recipe follows), for serving

Equipment: Large mixing bowl, medium mixing bowl, wooden mixing spoon or electric food processor, wax paper, 2 baking sheets, **deep fryer** (see glossary for tips on making one), paper towels, slotted spoon

1. In large mixing bowl, soak noodles in hot water until softened, about 1 hour. Keep in water until ready to use.

2. In medium mixing bowl, use wooden mixing spoon or electric food processor to beat meat, garlic, egg, cornstarch, and onion until paste-like.

3. Using clean hands, pinch off heaping tablespoonful of meat mixture, and form into an oval-shaped meatball. Place meatballs on wax-paper-covered baking sheet. Continue until all the meat is used. Refrigerate for 1 hour.

4. Wrap 2 or 3 noodle strands around each meatball. (You do not completely cover the meat. The noodles can be wrapped anyway you like.) Set on wax paper with noodle ends underneath. Repeat wrapping meatballs. Refrigerate at least 1 hour, or until ready to fry.

5. Prepare deep fryer: Have an adult help you heat oil to 375° F. Oil is hot enough for frying when small bubbles appear around a wooden spoon handle when it is dipped in the oil. Place several layers of paper towels on baking sheet. Carefully fry 3 or 4 bundles at a time, until meat is browned on all sides and cooked through, about 2 minutes. The noodles will be golden. Remove with slotted spoon, and drain on paper towels. Keep warm until ready to serve. Continue frying in batches.

Serve warm with peanut sauce for dipping.

Peanut Sauce

Yield: about 1 cup
  ½ cup smooth or chunky peanut butter
  ¼ cup water
  ½ teaspoon curry powder, more or less to taste
  1 clove garlic, **finely chopped**, or ½ teaspoon garlic granules

Equipment: Small bowl, mixing spoon

In small bowl, mix peanut butter, water, ½ teaspoon curry powder (more or less to taste), and garlic. Refrigerate until ready to serve.

Serve as a dipping sauce with meat, fish, or vegetables.

Although the Thais eat large quantities of rice, they take small portions of all other good foods. All dishes are served at once and eaten in no special order. Most Thais eat with a fork and spoon, using chopsticks only for eating noodles.

Meat is never eaten in large quantities. The following pork recipe is one of the many dishes on the Thai banquet table. Two of the sauces served with the meat are similar to Mexican green and red salsas. The third is Peanut Sauce (recipe precedes).

Moo Thod Katiem Prik

Cold Sliced Pork with Hot Sauces

Yield: serves 4 to 6
  1 pound lean pork tenderloin fillet (in one piece)
  salt and pepper to taste
  3 tablespoons vegetable oil
  1 tablespoon butter or margarine
  3 cloves garlic, **finely chopped,** or 1 teaspoon garlic granules
  2 teaspoons finely chopped fresh **ginger** or 1 teaspoon ground ginger
  juice of 1 lemon
  2 limes, cut into wedges, for **garnish**
  green and red salsas (available at all supermarkets), and peanut sauce (recipe precedes), for serving

Equipment: Large skillet with cover, metal tongs or meat fork, mixing spoon, cutting board, sharp meat knife

1. Rub pork with salt and pepper. Heat oil and butter or margarine in large skillet over medium-high heat. Add pork and brown on all sides, about 8 minutes. Remove skillet from heat, and remove meat from skillet. Set aside.

2. Add garlic, ginger, and lemon juice to pan drippings, and stir well. Return pork to skillet, and roll it around to coat it well. Cover and cook over medium heat until tender and cooked through, about 25 minutes.

3. Remove from pan, and allow meat to cool to room temperature before slicing.

To serve, thinly slice pork and arrange slices, slightly overlapping, on a serving platter. Garnish with lime wedges, and serve with sauces. To eat, spoon a little of each sauce on the meat, and sprinkle with lime juice, according to individual taste.

Chicken, either grilled, baked, or fried, is prepared for family feasts, banquets, and holidays, like *Songkran*. According to Thai tradition, dishes such as *kai yang* are prepared with bite-size portions, even for important holidays. Meat of any kind is scarce and expensive, and so even a little goes a long way toward making a holiday special.

Kai Yang   Thai Grilled Chicken

CAUTION: GRILL OR BROILER USED
Yield: serves 6

- 2 cloves fresh garlic, **finely chopped,** or ½ teaspoon garlic granules
- 1 tablespoon finely **grated** fresh **ginger** or 1 teaspoon ground ginger
- ½ teaspoon black pepper, more or less to taste
- ½ cup finely chopped fresh **cilantro** or 1 teaspoon dried, crushed **coriander**
- 2 tablespoons sugar
- 2 tablespoons soy sauce
- ½ cup vegetable oil
- 6 (4 to 6 ounces each) boneless chicken breasts or thighs, cut into 1-inch-wide strips
- 6 cups cooked rice (keep warm, for serving)

Equipment: Medium mixing bowl with cover, mixing spoon, **grater,** charcoal grill or broiler pan, metal tongs, oven mitts

1. In medium mixing bowl, combine garlic, ginger, ½ teaspoon black pepper (more or less to taste), cilantro or coriander, sugar, soy sauce, and oil; mix well. Add chicken, and toss pieces to coat with mixture. Cover and refrigerate for at least 2 hours, mixing frequently.

Have an adult help prepare charcoal grill or preheat broiler

2. Place chicken pieces side by side on grill or broiler pan. Cook chicken pieces for about 10 minutes on each side, until browned. Using metal tongs, turn once, and cook through. To test whether chicken is done, pierce the thickest part of chicken with fork tines or knife. If juices that trickle out are clear, instead of pinkish, the chicken is done.

Serve chicken while warm, with a bowl of rice.

Loi Krathong, in November, is one of Thailand's loveliest festivals. Also known as the Festival of Lights, it originated as a thanksgiving to *Mae Khongtkna,* goddess of all rivers and waterways. People set thousands of little lighted (with candles) toy boats adrift in rivers and canals to pay homage to the water spirits. In some areas of Thailand, *Loi Krathong* is only one day long, and in others it is three days long, as in the Chiang Mai region. This happy celebration includes gala parades, beauty contests, feasting, and throngs of people partaking in the festivities.

During the *Loi Krathong* festival there are no special ritual foods or time to eat. The joyous festival brings family and friends together to share the holiday table, which always includes rice, sometimes noodles, and a greater variety of small dishes of food, among them *tam taeng* (recipe follows). This light salad would also be eaten with *kai yang* and other meat or chicken dishes for the *Songkran* feast.

The expression "cool as a cucumber" certainly applies to some of the foods of Thailand: Cucumbers and other vegetables are served as a cool contrast to the hot Thai dishes.

Tam Taeng — Cucumber Salad

Yield: serves 4 to 6

- ½ cup white vinegar
- 2 tablespoons sugar
- 1 onion, **finely chopped**
- 1 teaspoon crushed **coriander**
- 1 large cucumber, **peeled** and thinly sliced

Equipment: Small bowl with cover, mixing spoon

In small bowl, combine vinegar, sugar, onion, and coriander, and mix well. Add cucumber slices and toss to coat with mixture. Cover and refrigerate for at least 1 hour, tossing once or twice.

Serve cucumbers in a small bowl along with other side dishes.

Thais love to have fun, and they look for any reason to have either a family or community celebration. The following recipe for *sangkaya* is a favorite Thai dessert. It is often included in the Thai New Year's feast *Songkran* as well as the feast for the Western New Year's on January 1, which Thais also celebrate.

Sangkaya — Thai Custard

Yield: serves 8 to 10

- 6 eggs
- 1 cup coconut cream (also called cream of coconut, available in a 15-ounce can at most supermarkets and all Asian food stores)
- ½ teaspoon almond extract

Equipment: **Steamer** (see glossary for hints on making one); 9-inch cake pan; medium mixing bowl; fork, **whisk**, or electric mixer; oven mitts

1. Prepare a steamer large enough to hold the 9-inch cake pan. Fill bottom pan of steamer half full with water, and place empty 9-inch cake pan in upper container. Make sure there is about 1-inch of space between the water and upper container. Cover and bring to boil over high heat; reduce heat to medium to keep empty cake pan hot.

2. In medium mixing bowl, using fork, whisk, or electric mixer, beat eggs, coconut cream, and almond flavor, for about 2 minutes until frothy.

3. Pour egg mixture into hot cake pan, cover the steamer, and steam for about 30 minutes, until custard is set and pulls away from sides of pan. Remove from heat.

Allow custard to cool to room temperature before cutting into small, serving-size wedges.

Laos/Cambodia

When the communists took over Laos (in black) in 1975, they allowed some Buddhist monasteries to remain open, though under many restrictions. Today, Laos is a communist nation, and religious beliefs are not discouraged or banned, but they are not encouraged either. Buddhism and spirit worship coexist naturally throughout the country. In rural regions, holidays follow the rice-growing cycle.

As in most countries in Southeast Asia, the new year begins with the rainy season in April, at rice planting time. Also called the Water Festival, the entire country practically comes to a halt for the three-day New Year's celebration. On the first day of this holiday, which Laotians call *Pli Mai*, families light candles in honor of Buddha. On the second day, people throw water on each other to wash away past misdeeds. On the third day, pet birds and fish are set free as a show of kindness. There is dancing and the ritual called *Baci*. During this joyous ritual, families gather around their home shrine, which they have decorated with food, to pray. The food used on the shrine symbolizes freedom from hunger.

Cambodia (in grey) has some of the world's most magnificent ancient temples, called *wats*, which were built by the Hindu state of Funan and the Kingdom of Angkor between A.D. 900 and 1200. Around that time, the people changed their Hindu beliefs to Buddhism, and they altered the temples for Buddhist worship. The temples, known as the "Splendors of Angkor," remained hidden by thick forests until the nineteenth century, when the French and Cambodian governments began restoring these marvelous temples.

Today, although the government does not sanction Buddhism, it does protect the temples, which are major Buddhist shrines.

About 95 percent of all Cambodians are Buddhists, and 90 percent of them belong to the Khmer ethnic group. If they could freely worship, their most important holiday would be *Visak Bauchea*, which is the celebration of Buddha's birth, enlightenment, and death. According to legend, all three events happened on the full-moon day of the same month, which now falls in April on the Western calendar. In Thailand this holiday is called *Vishaka Bucha*; in Singapore it is called *Vesak;* and in Laos it is called *Visakha Puja*.

Before communism, every village and temple would construct colorful rockets, some 30 feet long, decorated with flowers and streamers, to help celebrate this day and honor Buddha. The people took pride in making the best rocket that could shoot further than any other. The rocket festival, *Boun Ban Fai,* was originally a pre-Buddhist rain-making cer-emony that is celebrated between the harvest and rainy season in Thailand and Laos. In Cambodia the rocket festival activities have become part of *Visak Bauchea*. The most famous rocket festival, however, is in the Thai city of Yasothorn, northeast of Bangkok.

Chicken is favored for Buddhist feasts because it is scarce, and therefore valued, in Laos and Cambodia. Eggs are rarely eaten, and a simple boiled egg is served only to the most honored guests. Cambodians prefer to let eggs hatch into chickens, providing food for more people. *Phaneng Kai*, chicken stuffed with peanuts, is reserved for special occasions, among them *Visakha Puja* (Laos) and *Visak Bauchea* (Cambodia).

Phaneng Kai   Chicken Stuffed with Peanuts

Yield: serves 6 to 8

  2 tablespoons vegetable oil
  1 onion, **finely chopped**
  1 cup **ground** lean pork
  1 cup finely **ground** roasted peanuts
  1 cup fresh white bread crumbs
  ½ teaspoon ground red pepper, more or less to taste
  1 teaspoon crushed fennel seeds
  ½ teaspoon cinnamon
  1 tablespoon finely chopped fresh mint leaves or 1 teaspoon dried mint leaves
  salt and white pepper to taste
  3½ to 4-pound whole chicken, rinsed and drained
  3 cups coconut milk, homemade (recipe page 194) or canned
  1 cup water

Equipment: Large skillet, mixing spoon, work surface, large embroidery needle, heavy duty thread, **Dutch oven** or large saucepan with cover

SAFETY TIP: The peanut and pork mixture must be thoroughly chilled before stuffing the chicken, and once stuffed, the bird must be cooked immediately.

1. Prepare stuffing: Heat oil in large skillet over medium-high heat. Add onion, and, stirring constantly, fry until soft, about 3 minutes. Add meat, peanuts, bread crumbs, ¼ teaspoon red pepper (more or less to taste), fennel, cinnamon, mint, and salt and white pepper to taste. Stirring frequently, fry until browned and cooked through, about 5 minutes. Cool to room temperature and refrigerate at least 1 hour.

2. To stuff the chicken: Place chicken on work surface, and stuff with chilled pork and peanut mixture. Using a large embroidery needle and heavy duty thread, sew opening closed.

3. Pour coconut milk and water into Dutch oven or large saucepan, and stir. Place chicken in same pan, and then bring to a boil over high heat. Reduce heat to simmer, and, basting frequently, cover, and cook for 1 hour, or until tender. Transfer chicken to heat-proof bowl and keep warm.

4. Simmer pan drippings, uncovered, over medium heat for about 15 minutes until thickened. Add salt and white pepper to taste, and stir well.

*To serve, remove stuffing from chicken cavity to serving bowl. Cut chicken into serving-size pieces, place around stuffing, and **drizzle** with the coconut-milk pan drippings.*

No Laotian meal is complete without soup, which is served in the middle or at the end of a meal, never at the beginning. Meat is added to the soup only for special feasts and ceremonial banquets, such as for *Visakha Puja*. To add even meat bones or chicken feet is considered a great luxury in Laos. A vegetable soup such as *keng kalampi*, Laotian cabbage soup, is more typical of the type of meal most Laotians can afford.

Keng Kalampi   Laotian Cabbage Soup

Yield: serves 6

  2 tablespoons vegetable oil
  1 onion, **finely chopped**
  3 cloves garlic, finely chopped, or 1 teaspoon
    garlic granules
  1 tablespoon finely **grated** fresh **ginger** or 1
    teaspoon ground ginger
  2 teaspoons ground **coriander**
  4 cups trimmed, finely chopped cabbage
  6 cups canned beef broth
  salt and pepper to taste

Equipment: **Dutch oven** or medium saucepan with cover, **grater**, mixing spoon, ladle

Heat oil in Dutch oven or medium saucepan over medium-high heat. Add onion, garlic, ginger, and coriander, and, stirring constantly, fry for about 3 minutes, until soft. Add cabbage and beef broth, and bring to a boil. Reduce heat to simmer, cover, and cook for about 25 minutes, until cabbage is tender. Add salt and pepper to taste, and stir well.

To serve, ladle into individual soup bowls.

Vietnam

There are three main religions in Vietnam, Confucianism, Buddhism, and Taoism. Most Vietnamese group the three together as the religion of the country, calling it *Tam Giao*, the Triple Religion. *Tam Giao* is sometimes referred to as Vietnamese Buddhism. As in many Asian countries, the Vietnamese combine elements of ancestor worship with the traditions of the other religions.

Confucianism deals with the ethics of life and how to interact with all living things, with no reference to god or any other supreme beings. Buddhist religion centers on the search for enlightenment. Taoism (pronouned "towism") means the "way." Taoists believe the simple life is best, and possessions, such as money and other material wealth, are unimportant. Happiness is gained through harmony and tranquility, by bending with nature rather then fighting with it.

Vietnam has a sizable Catholic population; Catholicism was brought to Vietnam by Portuguese missionaries in the late sixteenth century.

Most Vietnamese live in one village throughout their lifetime, and it is the center of their social, religious, and political life. A Vietnamese could no more move to another village than give up his or her family. There is a strong bond among villagers, and all activity, from the planting and harvesting of the rice fields to religious celebrations, is communal, with everyone expected to participate.

In Vietnam the main religious holidays are Buddhist, among them Buddha's Birthday in the fourth lunar month. Buddhists present offerings at pagodas, and lantern processions parade through the streets and around temples. Wandering Souls' Day in August is devoted to the dead ancestors who have no descendants to pray for them. The Vietnamese clean graves and decorate their home altars with flowers.

There are many political holidays in Vietnam also, such as the Founding of the Communist Party of Vietnam on February 3; and Liberation Day on April 30; and Ho Chi Minh's Birthday, May 19.

A few holidays are associated with legends; the *Lac Long Quan Festival* celebrates the dragon lord who came from his home in the sea to plant the seed of the Vietnamese people by marrying the Chinese immortal Au Co. He is credited with having brought rice culture to Vietnam. According to legend, the union produced 100 eggs from which 100 sons were hatched. The couple divided them equally and went their separate ways, she to the mountains and he to the lowlands. His oldest son, regarded as the true founder of the Hung dynasty and of the nation, is celebrated on *Hung Vuong*, which falls on the tenth day of the third month.

The most important Vietnamese holiday is *Tet*. It is not a religious holiday, but, rather, a combination of an old agricultural planting festival, a celebration of renewal, and and a time to give thanks to the many reasons for living. *Tet* is also a New Year's celebration since it is held on the first three days of the new lunar year. It is a time to pay homage to ancestors, to pay off debts, and to turn over a new leaf, forgiving oneself and others for past mistakes. Each day of the *Tet* celebration has a purpose. On the first day, each family gathers to greet the coming of spring on the eve of the new year, and a favorite friend is invited to be the first visitor in the morning. The second day celebrates friendship, and the third day is traditionally devoted to village business, when the plans for the next crop are discussed.

Besides the traditional firecrackers and holiday sweets, each village celebrates in its own way. Some might have cockfights, some have musical contests, and some plant trees to replenish the earth. There are also sword fights, boat races, puppet shows, tugs-of-war, singing and dancing, martial arts demonstrations, and folk dances. Today, the Vietnamese decorate their houses with boughs of peach and plum blossoms to celebrate *Tet*. These decorations play the same role as the decorated tree at Christmas.

In some ways *Tet* is similar to the Chinese New Year's. For example, on the first day of *Tet* everyone becomes one year older, regardless of the actual birthday.

The highlight of holiday feasts and banquets in Vietnam is beef prepared seven different ways, called "Seven Styles of Beef." The beef is sliced, cubed, and made into meatballs that are barbecued, grilled, fried, simmered, or added to soup. Each preparation is beautifully arranged on a platter and brought to the table separately. The meal often takes several hours to eat. Vegetable salads accompany the meat, and they too are decoratively presented. How the food looks is as important as how it tastes. In addition to these foods, rice or noodles are served at every meal as well as French-style rolls and coffee, a carryover from the French colonial era.

The Vietnamese like smooth, lump-free meatballs, called *bo nuong*. All ingredients are pounded to a paste-like texture. *Bo nuong* can be eaten plain or in a salad known as *goi* (recipe follows), and each can be served as one of the "Seven Styles of Beef."

salt and pepper to taste
water for boiling, as needed

Equipment: Medium mixing bowl, **grater**, electric **blender** or **food processor**, wax paper, baking sheet, medium saucepan, **slotted spoon**

1. In medium mixing bowl, mix beef, onions, garlic, ginger, egg whites, water, oil, and salt and pepper to taste. Using electric blender or food processor, mix until mixture is lump-free and paste-like.

2. Using clean wet hands, form meat mixture into ping-pong-size balls. Place balls on wax-paper-covered baking sheet. Cover baking sheet, and refrigerate for 1 hour.

3. Fill medium saucepan half full with water, and bring to a boil over high heat. Reduce heat so that water maintains a **rolling boil,** and add meatballs, a few at a time. Cook for 2 minutes or until they rise to the surface; remove balls with slotted spoon. Drain and keep warm. Continue cooking in batches.

Serve with dipping sauce (recipe page 176) or in salad (recipe follows).

Most Vietnamese meals seem light and decorative, and are usually prettily arranged. How food is placed on a plate is very important, such as the placement of the meatballs in the following recipe, *goi*.

Bo Nuong   Beef Meatballs

Yield: serves 6 to 8

1 pound finely ground lean beef
3 green onions, finely chopped
1 clove fresh garlic, **finely chopped**, or ½ teaspoon garlic granules
1 tablespoon finely **grated** fresh **ginger** or 1 teaspoon ground ginger
2 **egg whites**, beaten to froth
½ cup water
1 tablespoon vegetable oil

Goi   Salad

Yield: serves 6 to 8

6 to 12 edible rice paper wrappers, about 8 inches square or round (available at all Asian food stores)
5 ounces rice vermicelli noodles, cut into 1-inch lengths, prepared according to directions on package, and drained (available at all Asian food stores)

2 cups fresh bean sprouts or **finely chopped** mixed fresh herbs: mint, basil, **cilantro**, and bean or alfalfa sprouts

1 cucumber, peeled and cut into matchstick-size pieces

6 to 12 leaf lettuce leaves, separated, **trimmed**, washed, and drained well

beef meatballs (recipe precedes)

Equipment: Paper towels, work surface, spray bottle filled with cold water, large platter or tray (a foil-covered cookie sheet can be used)

1. Stack rice paper on paper-towel-covered work surface. Using cold water in spray bottle, lightly spray top sheet of rice paper to rehydrate. Let rice paper rest until it becomes pliable (a few minutes); remove and place on piece of paper towel. Continue spraying rice paper, one sheet at a time, and place each separately on a piece of paper towel. If papers are too moist, they stick together. Let each sheet dry (about 20 minutes) until it can be folded in half without sticking together.

2. Gently fold each sheet in half (do not crease), and place them so they slightly overlap on one side of large platter or tray.

3. On the same tray, add separate mounds of noodles, bean sprouts or assorted herbs, cucumber, carrot, lettuce leaves, and meatballs.

To serve, place platter or tray in center of dinner table, and have guests helps themselves. To eat, open a rice paper, place a lettuce leaf on top, and add a small amount of noodles, assorted vegetables, bean sprouts or herbs, and 3 or 4 meatballs. Roll up into a package and pick it up and eat it. Before each bite, dip in dipping sauce (recipe follows).

Nuoc Cham   Vietnamese Dipping Sauce

Yield: about 2 cups

½ cup creamy peanut butter

½ cup hoisin sauce (available at all Asian food stores)

½ cup chicken broth, homemade (recipe page 52) or canned

1 tablespoon sugar

2 tablespoons cornstarch

¼ cup cold water

Equipment: Small saucepan, mixing spoon, cup

1. In small saucepan, combine peanut butter, hoisin sauce, chicken broth, and sugar. Cook mixture over medium heat until sugar dissolves, about 2 minutes.

2. Dissolve cornstarch in cup of water while peanut mixture is cooking. Stir, and add to peanut butter mixture, stirring constantly until thickened, about 3 minutes. Cool to room temperature.

To serve, spoon about 2 tablespoons sauce into small individual dishes and place at each place setting. The sauce keeps well for several weeks if refrigerated.

Korea—North and South

Since 1948, Korea has been divided into two countries—the Democratic People's Republic of Korea (North Korea) and the Republic of Korea (South Korea). Most North Koreans have Buddhist backgrounds, but religious beliefs are not encouraged by the communist government. South Koreans worship as they please, and most are Buddhists or follow the teachings of Confucius.

Christian missionaries tried for many years to missionize Korea, but it wasn't until after World War II in 1945 that there was a real wave of conversions among Korean intellectuals. The center of Christianization lay in that part of the country that is now North Korea, causing a mass exodus of Christians to the south at the end of the terrible Korean War. Today there are about 10 million Christians in South Korea.

The Koreans use two kinds of calendars: the ancient one, adopted from the Chinese, based on the cycle of the moon, and the newer calendar of the Western world. Because they use two calendars, Koreans enjoy many holiday celebrations. South Koreans living in the cities celebrate both the Western and the lunar new year, which is known as *Sol*. The people living in rural areas observe only *Sol*, which lasts three days . There are no special ritual feasts during *Sol*, and each family and community arranges its own celebrations. One part of the *Sol* holiday tradition that is celebrated throughout Korea, however, is the firecrackers that are shot off to scare away evil spirits.

The next big lunar holiday falls on the fifth day of the fifth month, when Koreans celebrate *Tano*, or "Swing Day." It is celebrated when the first harvest is ready. During *Tano*, villages have carnivals, dances, wrestling matches for the men, and puppet shows for the children. In some communities a swing is erected for women and girls, which is often over 20 feet high, thus the name "Swing Day."

The last big lunar holiday of the year is *Ch'usok*, the "Harvest Moon," which is like Thanksgiving. It falls on the day of the full moon in the eighth month, and it is an autumn celebration that signals the end of the harvest. Koreans celebrate by giving thanks for their good fortune, and they pay respect to their ancestors. In some homes, the men gather at midnight to recite aloud the names of the ancestors who they feel are especially close to them at this time of year.

All Korean holidays center around family, friends, and food. For *Ch'usok* there is a feast with relatives which includes large bowls of rice and noodles. The more important the relatives, guests, or the occasion, the more dishes of food are prepared. Included are several kinds of beans, vegetables, dumplings, *bulgogi* (recipe follows), and other meat and chicken dishes, and everything is served at once. *Kimchi* is always on the table, and a little dab of it is eaten with almost every bit of food.

The way food is served is as important as what is served. Koreans eat with chopsticks and a spoon while they sit on soft cushions around low tables. Special feasts often take hours since there are as many as 30 different dishes, usually made from no more than two or three food items prepared in a variety of ways.

This recipe for *bulgogi*, Korean barbecued beef, is the national dish of Korea, and it would be served at any of the major holidays such as *Sol* or *Ch'usok*. Traditionally, the meat is grilled quickly at the dinner table on a cone-shaped hot plate. To make things simpler, this recipe has been adapted for stove-top use.

Bulgogi   Korean Barbecued Beef

CAUTION: HOT OIL USED

Yield: serves 6 to 8

1½ pounds lean boneless beef, such as sirloin tip or fillet (freeze slightly for easier slicing)

1 onion, **finely chopped**

3 cloves garlic, finely chopped, or 1 teaspoon garlic granules

2 tablespoons **peeled** and finely chopped fresh **ginger root** or 1 teaspoon ground ginger

½ cup soy sauce

1 tablespoon sesame oil

2 tablespoons sugar

2 tablespoons vegetable oil, for skillet or wok frying

4 teaspoons sesame seeds, for **garnish**

10 to 12 romaine lettuce leaves, washed, **trimmed**, patted dry, for serving

6 cups cooked rice (keep warm for serving)

Equipment: Work surface, sharp knife, gallon-size plastic baggie or medium bowl with cover, mixing spoon, large skillet or wok

1. Place slightly frozen beef on work surface, and, using a sharp knife, cut into narrow strips about ¼ inch thick.

2. In plastic baggie or medium bowl, mix onion, garlic, ginger, soy sauce, sesame oil, and sugar. Tightly seal baggie and shake, or mix in bowl until well blended. Add beef, and, using clean hands, coat with mixture. Seal tightly and refrigerate for at least 4 hours, turning or mixing frequently.

3. Have an adult help you heat 2 vegetable tablespoons oil in large skillet or wok over medium-high heat. Add meat and fry on both sides until brown and cooked through, about 3 to 5 minutes on each side.

To serve, mound cooked rice on serving platter, and cover with meat. Sprinkle with sesame seeds, for garnish. Put lettuce leaves on separate plate. To eat bulgogi, *place a little meat and rice on a lettuce leaf, roll it up, and pick it up to eat.*

Kimchi, the Korean national dish, is made with vegetables that are fermented. No Korean meal is complete without *kimchi.* Different vegetables can be used to make *kimchi,* and for holiday feasts like *Sol* or the Western New Year's as many as four or five different types of *kimchi* might be eaten at the same meal. Eaten as a relish, *kimchi* can be made fiery hot or mild.

Kimchi
(also Kim Chee)

Pickled Cabbage

NOTE: Kimchi needs to sit for at least two days to ferment and develop flavor.

Yield: about 4 cups

1 cup **coarsely chopped** cabbage

1 cup finely sliced carrots

1 cup cauliflower **florets**, separated

2 tablespoons salt

2 green onions, finely sliced

3 cloves garlic, **finely chopped**, or 1 teaspoon garlic granules

¼ tablespoon crushed red pepper

1 teaspoon finely **grated** fresh **ginger** or ½ teaspoon ground ginger

Equipment: **Colander**, medium glass or plastic bowl with cover, mixing spoon, **grater**

1. Put cabbage, carrots, and cauliflower in colander, and sprinkle with salt. Toss vegetables and set in sink to drain for about 1 hour. Rinse with cold running water, and drain well.

2. Put drained cabbage, carrots, and cauliflower in medium glass or plastic bowl. Add onions, garlic, red pepper, and ginger, and toss to mix well. Cover and refrigerate for at least 2 days, stirring frequently.

Serve as a side dish with bulgogi *or other meat dishes.*

Most holidays, such as *Sol,* the Korean New Year's, are a time for children to dress up and visit with grandparents. Upon arrival the children follow the ancient tradition of bowing politely to their elders. After receiving little red happiness envelopes with money from their grandparents, they fill their pockets with roasted chestnuts (recipe page 107) and go outside to eat them with friends and to play.

Koreans eat cold or hot soup throughout the meal when celebrating *Sol*. Some families like to pack a picnic for the *Tano* celebration and eat together at the park. *Naing kuk* is very good soup to take along.

Naing Kuk — Cold Cucumber Soup

Yield: serves 4 to 6

- 2 tablespoons light soy sauce
- 1½ tablespoons white vinegar
- 1 green onion, **trimmed** and **finely chopped**
- ½ teaspoon sugar
- ¼ teaspoon ground chili powder, more or less to taste
- 1 teaspoon sesame oil (optional)
- 2 cucumbers, each about 6 inches long, peeled and thinly sliced
- 5 cups chicken broth homemade (recipe page 52) or canned
- 2 teaspoons sesame seeds, for **garnish**

Equipment: Medium mixing bowl, mixing spoon

1. In medium mixing bowl, combine soy sauce, vinegar, green onions, sugar, ¼ teaspoon chili powder (more or less to taste), and sesame oil. Add cucumber slices, and, using mixing spoon, toss to coat. Set aside for 1 hour, tossing frequently to coat with soy sauce mixture.

2. Add cold chicken broth to cucumbers and soy sauce mixture, stir, and refrigerate for one hour before serving.

To serve, stir and ladle into individual soup bowls. Sprinkle each serving with sesame seeds.

Japan

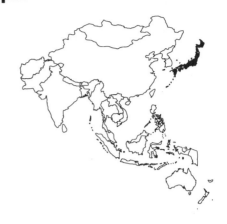

Most Japanese observe all Buddhist and Shinto holidays. Shinto is an ancient Japanese cult and religion, which was the state religion of Japan earlier in this century. There are few Christians in Japan, but, regardless of their beliefs, many Japanese seem to like Christmas. In the mid-fifties, the Christmas holiday spirit was brought to Japan by foreign residents. The Japanese liked Santa Claus, colored lights, and holiday parties, to which they were invited by the Western foreigners. Today, Christmas is regarded as a winter festival by the Japanese, and it is part of the New Year's celebration.

Preparations for *Oshogatsu*, the Japanese New Year, begin early in December with office parties, called *Bonenkai* (year-forgetting parties). New Year's celebrations are the "festival of festivals" for the Japanese, and keeping ancestral traditions alive is important. Pine branches, straw, bamboo stalks, and plum branches are displayed as symbols of prosperity, good health, vigor, and longevity. The decorations mean the good gods are in the house, and evil spirits are not welcome.

Since ancient times *o-mochi*, rice cakes, have been used in all religious and agricultural rituals. For *Oshogatsu*, stacked rice cakes signify abundant good fortune. Most Japanese homes have a small altar where the family prays and the cakes are offered to the gods. Other snacks and something to drink are also set on the altar, just in case the gods are hungry and thirsty when they come to visit. If the rice cakes are still on the altar at the end of the festivities, they are broken into small pieces and eaten in soup, bringing harmony and health to the family for the coming year.

It is the tradition to eat extra long (for long life) buckwheat noodles called *soba* on New Year's Eve. The noodles are eaten in a soup called *toshi koshi*, "cross over year."

Toshi Koshi Soba
Buckwheat Noodles in Broth

Yield: serves 6

   4 cups prepared chicken broth, homemade (recipe page 52) or canned
   ⅓ cup Japanese soy sauce, called *shoya* (available at some supermarkets and all Asian food stores)
   ½ teaspoon sugar
   ½ cup finely **diced** cooked chicken breast or **tofu**
   1 pound *soba* noodles, cooked according to directions on package, drained, and kept warm (available at some supermarkets and all Asian food stores)
   ¼ cup finely sliced green onions, for **garnish**

Equipment: Medium saucepan, mixing spoon, ladle

1. Pour chicken broth in medium saucepan. Add soy sauce, sugar, and chicken or tofu. Stir, and bring to a boil over high heat for 1 minute; remove from heat.

2. Divide noodles between 6 soup bowls, and ladle hot broth with pieces of chicken or tofu over each bowl. Sprinkle green onions over soup for garnish.

Guests eat noodles with chopsticks, and noisy noodle slurping is in perfectly good taste. Instead of using a spoon to drink the broth, the bowl is picked up.

The first day of the new year is spent visiting relatives and shrines. During the holiday many women wear traditional kimonos. It is a day for both joyous and solemn observances.

A dish traditionally eaten on New Year's Day is *ozoni*. There are many ways of making it, and each family has its own recipe. The following is made with either chicken broth or *dashi*.

Ozoni   New Year's Soup with Rice Cake

Yield: serves 6

   6 cups chicken broth, homemade (recipe page 52) or canned, or **dashi**, packaged mix (prepared according to directions on package—available at some supermarkets and all Asian food stores)
   2 teaspoons light-colored Japanese soy sauce
   6 medium fresh mushroom caps, sliced
   1 cup cooked, boneless, skinless chicken breast or thigh, cut into matchstick-size pieces (leftover chicken can be used)
   6 toasted rice cakes (available at Asian food stores)
   rind of ½ lemon sliced into needle-thin pieces, about an inch long, for **garnish**

Equipment: medium saucepan, mixing spoon, ladle

1. In medium saucepan, heat chicken broth or prepared *dashi* over medium-high heat. Add soy sauce and mushrooms, stir, and cook for 3 minutes; reduce heat to low.

2. Divide cooked chicken pieces between soup bowls, and add a toasted rice cake and broth with mushrooms. Sprinkle with a few slivers of lemon rind.

Serve ozoni *in a soup bowl. Chopsticks are used to pick out the rice cake, chicken, and mushrooms. Instead of using spoons, the Japanese lift the bowl and sip the broth.*

Osechi-Ryori   New Year's Food

The Japanese believe food must first please the eyes and then the taste buds, before filling the stomach. For centuries, artistically arranged food was prepared only for the gods; it was presented to them in special little stacking boxes. Today, everyone in Japan enjoys *Osechi-Ryori*, which means New Year's food.

Traditionally, the New Year's food is arranged in boxes; careful thought is given to color and flavors: sweet, sour, hot, and cold. The top box contains ready-to-eat cold tidbits. Another box contains cut, ready-to-cook fish, meat or chicken, vegetables, and seasonings that are to be cooked on the dinner table. A box of pickled vegetables is used for the sour flavor, and one box is always filled with sweets as a symbol of good fortune.

The following recipes for easy-to-prepare cold tidbits can be used for the top box of *Osechi-Ryori*.

NOTE: If you don't have boxes, the food can be arranged on serving plates.

Plum Blossom Eggs

Yield: serves 6
 1 cup water
 2 or 3 drops red food coloring
 3 shelled hard-cooked eggs

Equipment: Small bowl, spoon, paper towels, knife

Pour water into a small bowl, and add just enough red food coloring to make water pink. Put each whole egg in colored water for about 20 minutes. Drain on paper towel, and slice crosswise.

The pink border and yellow center resemble plum flowers. Arrange slightly overlapping slices in cold box or on serving plate.

Sliced Carrots

 2 large carrots, **trimmed** and **peeled**
 2 cups ice water

Equipment: Vegetable peeler, small bowl, toothpicks

Slice raw carrots lengthwise with vegetable peeler. Place in small bowl of ice water for about 1 hour to curl; secure curled carrots with toothpicks.

Keep carrots in ice water until ready to serve. Arrange in the cold box or on plate.

Cucumber Slices

 1 cucumber, **trimmed** and washed (leave the skin on)

Slice cucumber crosswise into silver-dollar-size pieces. Arrange slices, slightly overlapping, in cold box or on serving plate.

The box containing pickled vegetables is the Japanese version of salad; it is usually eaten with the hot food. The vegetables can be cut into any shape you like. Carrots can be cut into small sticks, diamond shapes, or crosswise into copper pennies. Any combination of vegetables can be pickled—cauliflower broken into bite-size pieces, 1-inch chunks of red and green bell peppers, whole green beans, and small white onions.

Tsukemono — Pickled Vegetables

Yield: serves 6

  2 cups vinegar

  1 cup sugar

  1 tablespoon **grated** fresh **ginger** or 1 teaspoon ground ginger

  2 cups of any vegetables listed above, washed, **trimmed**, and cut into desired shapes

Equipment: **Grater**, small saucepan, mixing spoon, small bowl with cover

1. Combine vinegar, sugar, and ginger in small saucepan, and bring to a boil over high heat. Add vegetables, bring to a boil, and cook for 3 minutes. Remove from heat, and cool to room temperature.

2. Transfer vegetables and liquid to small bowl, cover, and refrigerate for about 8 hours before serving. Shake bowl or stir occasionally.

Serve pickled vegetables cold. Drain and arrange by color in a box or on serving plate.

The hot food for *Osechi-Ryori* is cooked at the table in broth.

Each kind of food is kept separate. The pan of broth is set over a tabletop burner or hot plate placed in the middle of the dinner table. An electric wok or large electric skillet also works very well.

SAFETY NOTE: Place a heat-proof pad on the table where the tabletop cooking equipment is going to sit. To prevent tripping over the extension cord, if one is needed, either tape it down or cover it with a throw rug.

If stacking boxes are not available for *Osechi-Ryori*, the food can be placed in bowls.

Mizutaki — Tabletop Cooking in Broth

Yield: serves 6

  1½ pounds Japanese noodles, such as *kishimen* (cooked according to directions on package and drained well—available at all Asian food stores)

  1 to 1½ pounds boneless sirloin or tenderloin steak, sliced paper thin (partially freeze meat and use a sharp knife to make slicing easier)

  12 small mushroom caps, wiped clean

  6 green onions, **trimmed** and **bias sliced** into 1-inch lengths

  ½ pound spinach leaves, trimmed, washed, and dried

  18 (1-inch) cubes soft **tofu**

  6 cups chicken broth, homemade (recipe page 52) or canned

  salt to taste

  ½ cup dipping sauce (recipe follows)

Equipment: Serving bowl with cover, 3 or 4 *Osechi-Ryori* boxes or serving plates, plastic wrap, heat-proof table pad, tabletop burner or hot plate with medium saucepan or electric **wok** or deep skillet, medium saucepan, oven mitts, metal tongs, ladle

1. Put cooked and drained noodles in a serving bowl. Cover and refrigerate until serving time.

2. In 1 or 2 boxes or on serving plates, neatly arrange beef slices, mushrooms, green onions, spinach, and tofu in separate rows. Cover with plastic wrap and refrigerate until serving time.

3. At serving time prepare the table: Place tabletop cooking equipment, including pad, in the middle of the table.

4. Place a small plate, a small sauce dish of dipping sauce, and chopsticks or fork at each place setting.

5. Place the boxes or plates of food to be cooked near the host or hostess. Have the bowl of noodles, 6 soup bowls, and ladle on a nearby table.

6. Heat broth on kitchen stove first: Pour broth into medium saucepan, and add salt to taste. Stir and bring to a boil over high heat on the kitchen stove. Have an adult carefully pour hot broth into the cooking container on the dinner table. The broth should simmer throughout the meal.

When everyone is seated, the host or hostess puts the beef into the hot broth and cooks it 1 or 2 minutes until it reaches the desired doneness. Each person takes some beef onto their plate, and, before each bite, dips it into the sauce. Next the vegetables are added to the broth and cooked for about 5 minutes, and the guests help themselves to the vegetables. Finally, the noodles are added to the broth to heat through, about 5 minutes. The noodle soup is ladled into individual bowls by the host or hostess. The noodles are slurped out of the bowl with the help of chopsticks, and the bowl is picked up so that the broth may be drunk.

Dipping Sauce

Yield: about 1 cup
  ½ cup Japanese soy sauce
  1 tablespoon sugar
  1 teaspoon sesame oil

Equipment: Small bowl, mixing spoon

In small bowl, mix soy sauce, sugar, and sesame oil until well blended.

To serve, pour about 2 tablespoons into individual sauce dishes, and set at each place setting. Pour remaining sauce into a small pitcher, and place on the table.

Philippines

The majority of the Philippine people are descendants of Indonesians and Malays who migrated to the islands long before the Christian era. The Chinese, Spanish, and later the Americans settled in the Philippines, as well as many Muslims from assorted countries around the world.

Most Filipinos are of mixed race, and about 90 percent of the population are Roman Catholic Christians. There are about 87 native languages and dialects spoken throughout the islands, although English is used as a second language by about half the population.

The Philippines has long been a meeting place between Eastern and Western cultures, and holiday traditions reflect both the European influence, especially from Spain, and the Asian traditions. The Philippines is the only Asian country that is predominantly Christian. In fact, the Filipino people proudly claim to have one of the world's merriest and longest Christmas celebrations. For three weeks, beginning on December 16, every home and public building is decorated with Christmas lights and the Nativity scene, called *Belén*, which means "Bethlehem." Some communities display giant stars representing the Star of Bethlehem. On Christmas Eve, churches have several masses called *Simbang Gabi*, or in Spanish, *Misas del Gallo*, "Masses of the Rooster." Following the masses, Filipino families gather for a feast of delicious foods, such as *lumpuang uboi* (recipe page 185).

Christmas Day, *Pasko Ng Bata*, is a family day. Children dress in their best clothes to visit godparents and play in the park. Most families save their holiday feast for Epiphany.

The holiday season ends with the Feast of the Epiphany on the first Sunday in January. It is also known as Elders' Christmas, *Pasko Ng Matanda*, because Filipinos take that day to honor the maturity and wisdom of older people. The Epiphany celebrates the visit of the Three Wise Men: Melchior, Gaspar, and Balthasar. All the relatives gather to feast on their favorite meat, spit-roasted pig called *lechón*. Served with the pork are *sinangag* (recipe follows later in this section) and other rice dishes, *lumpiang uboi* (recipe follows later in this section), vegetable and bean dishes, and assorted fruits, including pineapples, bananas, persimmons, and papayas. A table covered with desserts, cookies, cakes, nuts, candies, and *carabao* cheese (made from the milk of the water buffalo) top off the feast. The eating goes on for several hours and is followed by a long *siesta* (afternoon nap).

In addition to all the feasting on Epiphany, every community has a pageant reenacting the journey of the Wise Men to see baby Jesus. As in Spain, children receive gifts on this evening, the most solemn and final night of the Christmas season.

During the holiday season, street vendors sell rice cakes and hot ginger tea to throngs of hungry, early morning worshippers. Ginger tea, called *salabat,* is a Filipino favorite.

Salabat   Ginger Tea

Yield: about 6 to 8

- 6 ounces fresh **ginger root, peeled** and cut into 1-inch pieces
- 8 cups boiling water, or more as needed
- 1 cup brown sugar or honey, more or less to taste, for serving

Equipment: Work surface, kitchen mallet or **rolling pin**, medium saucepan, coffee filters

1. Place ginger on work surface, and crush with a kitchen mallet or rolling pin.

2. In medium saucepan, combine crushed ginger, 8 cups boiling water, and 1 cup brown sugar or honey (more or less to taste). Stir and bring to a boil over high heat. Reduce heat to simmer, and let cook for 30 minutes. Add more boiling water when necessary to maintain the 6-cup level. Cool to room temperature, and strain through coffee filter. Refrigerate in covered jar or pitcher until ready to serve.

To serve, pour desired amount of ginger mixture (about ¼ cup) into a mug and fill with hot water. Stir, add sugar or honey to taste, and drink.

COOKING SHORT CUT: To make ginger tea in an electric coffee maker, diagonally cut fresh ginger in ⅛-inch thick slices. (Leave the skin on the ginger.) Put about 6 or 8 slices in a coffee filter, and run the water through the coffee maker three or four times to make tea of desired strength. Sweeten to taste.

Homemade ginger ale is made by adding ginger concentrate and honey to carbonated water instead of hot water. Chill with ice cubes.

After midnight mass, the Christmas Eve feast is an elaborate family reunion. The meal traditionally begins with *lumpiang uboi*, Filipino spring rolls.

Lumpiang Uboi   Filipino Spring Rolls

CAUTION: HOT OIL USED

Yield: 12 spring rolls

2 tablespoons peanut or vegetable oil, more or less as needed

1 onion, **finely chopped**

3 cloves garlic, finely chopped, or 1 teaspoon garlic granules

½ cup finely chopped cooked ham

1 carrot, **trimmed** and cut into matchstick-size strips

1 cup finely sliced green beans, fresh or frozen, thawed

1 cup finely **shredded** cabbage

½ cup finely chopped peanuts

12 egg roll or spring roll wrappers (available in the refrigerated section of some supermarkets and all Asian food stores), for assembling

vegetable oil cooking spray

12 leaf lettuce leaves, trimmed, rinsed, and drained, for assembling

brown sauce (recipe follows), for serving

Equipment: Large skillet or **wok**, mixing spoon, paper towels, baking sheet, large skillet or griddle, metal tongs, work surface

1. Prepare filling: Have an adult help you heat 2 tablespoons oil in large skillet or wok over high heat. Carefully add onion and garlic, and, stirring constantly, cook for about 3 minutes. Add ham, carrots, green beans, cabbage, and peanuts, and stirring constantly, cook about 3 minutes, until cabbage is crisp and tender (not limp); remove from heat.

2. Prepare egg or spring roll wrappers: Unwrap wrappers and cover with dampened paper towel to prevent drying. Spread several layers of paper towels on baking sheet.

3. Lightly spray large skillet or griddle with cooking spray. Heat skillet over medium heat, and lightly brown each wrapper, on one side only, for about 30 seconds. Use metal tongs to transfer browned wrappers to baking sheet. Repeat browning wrappers, adding more spray to skillet or griddle if needed.

4. Assemble *lumpiang uboi*: Place a wrapper, browned-side down, on work surface. Cover with lettuce leaf, leaving the frilly edge at the top, and place about ⅓ cup of filling in the middle. Fold the bottom edge up over the filling, and roll wrapper around filling, leaving frilly top edge of lettuce open. (Like wrapping a baby in a blanket or making a burrito.)

Serve lumpiang uboi *immediately with dish of brown sauce. To eat, dip or spoon rolls into sauce before each bite.*

Brown Sauce

Yield: 1 cup

1 tablespoon cornstarch

1 cup water

¼ cup sugar

2 tablespoons soy sauce, more or less to taste

1 clove garlic, **finely chopped,** or ½ teaspoon garlic granules

Equipment: Small saucepan, mixing spoon

In small saucepan, mix cornstarch, water, sugar, soy sauce, and garlic. Cook over medium heat until thickened. Cool to room temperature.

Serve as dipping sauce for lumpiang uboi *(recipe precedes).*

A favorite Filipino Christmas dish is *kari-kari*, **oxtail** stew. This recipe varies with each culture that has settled in the Philippines. The traditional stew has a red color from annatto seed, but red food coloring (optional) can be used to achieve the same effect.

Kari-Kari — Oxtail Stew

Yield: serves 6 to 8

- 2 pounds lean bone-in beef, rinsed and with meat **coarsely chopped** (save bone)
- 3 cloves garlic, **finely chopped**, or 1 teaspoon garlic granules
- 1 large onion, coarsely chopped
- 6 cups water
- ¼ cup smooth peanut butter
- 3 or 4 drops red food coloring (optional)
- 1 small (about ¾ pound) eggplant, **trimmed**, **cored**, and coarsely chopped
- 1 small head (about 1 pound) cabbage, trimmed, cored, and cut into 6 wedges
- ¼ pound green beans, trimmed and cut into 1-inch lengths or 1 cup thawed, frozen cut green beans
- salt and pepper to taste

Equipment: **Dutch oven** or large saucepan with cover, mixing spoon

1. Put meat and bones, garlic, and onion in Dutch oven or large saucepan, add water, and stir. Bring to a boil over high heat, and then reduce heat to simmer. Cover and cook for 1 hour. Occasionally, skim froth from surface and discard.

2. Stir in peanut butter and food coloring. Add eggplant and cabbage, and, using back of spoon, push eggplant and cabbage down into liquid. Cover and simmer for about 1 hour until meat is very tender.

3. Add green beans and salt and pepper to taste, and stir; heat through, about 5 minutes, and serve.

To serve, ladle hot stew into individual soup bowls.

Rice is served at almost every meal during the Christmas season. The following recipe for *sinangag,* garlic rice, is a favorite.

Sinangag — Garlic Rice

Yield: serves 6

- 2 tablespoons vegetable oil, more if needed
- 3 cloves garlic, **finely chopped**, or 1 teaspoon garlic granules
- 4 cups cooked rice
- 6 green onions, **trimmed** and finely sliced
- salt and pepper to taste

Equipment: **Dutch oven** or large skillet, mixing spoon

1. Heat 2 tablespoons of oil in Dutch oven or large skillet over medium heat. Add garlic and fry for about 3 minutes.

2. Add cooked rice, green onions, and salt and pepper to taste, stir, and heat through, about 5 minutes.

Serve warm as a side dish for the Christmas feast.

Malaysia/Singapore

Malaysia and Singapore are small nations bordering each other in Southeast Asia. Both countries have ethnically diverse populations including Malays, Chinese, and Indians. About half the population of Malaysia are Muslims, with large Buddhist and Hindu minorities. In Singapore, a small nation dominated by the port city of the same name, Buddhists, Hindus, Muslims, and Christians all co-exist.

Because of this ethnic and religious diversity, when you ask Malaysians and Singaporeans how they spend New Year's, they'll probably ask, which one? The Chinese, Muslims, and Hindus all celebrate the New Year on different dates with great pageantry. There are few Christians in either country, and so the Western New Year's is insignificant.

The Chinese have the noisiest New Year's celebrations because everyone, regardless of faith, takes part in the festivities. The favorite activity is shooting off firecrackers to keep away evil spirits. The fireworks continue until the people and supply are exhausted. On New Year's Eve rockets and flares are shot skyward to complete the job.

Another exciting part of the Chinese New Year's celebration is the elaborate parades that are held. Huge dragons, symbols of good luck, lead Chinese New Year processions. Sometimes fifty or more people make up the long cloth dragon that weaves through the streets. Dancers, acrobats, clowns, stilt walkers, and actors wearing majestic lion headdresses accompany the dragon to ward off evil spirits.

Family feasts combine elements of Chinese, Indian, and Muslim cooking. Mutton or shrimp, instead of pork, fill New Year's dumplings. Malays of all faiths eat Hindu golden rice for prosperity, and Chinese tea eggs (recipe page 154) are eaten to "roll in" good luck for the coming year.

Sothi (recipe follows) is a popular soup for family holiday feasts because it is made with two easily available ingredients, shrimp and coconut milk. It is a soothing soup favored by Muslims for the feast of *Eid al-Fitr*, following the month of fasting for *Ramadan*.

Sothi   Coconut Shrimp Soup

Yield: serves 6 to 8

2 tablespoons butter or margarine

1 onion, finely **grated**

2 tablespoons all-purpose flour

4 cups chicken broth, homemade (recipe page 52) or canned

1¼ cups unsweetened coconut milk, homemade (recipe page 194) or canned

½ pound (about 30-40 to the pound) shrimp, **peeled**, **deveined**, and **coarsely chopped**

salt to taste

Equipment: **Dutch oven** or medium saucepan, **grater**, mixing spoon

1. Melt butter or margarine in Dutch oven or medium saucepan over medium heat. Add onion, and fry until soft, about 3 minutes. Add flour, stir until smooth, and cook about 3 minutes.

2. Stirring constantly, slowly add chicken broth. Stir until smooth, and then simmer for 15 minutes. Add coconut milk, shrimp, and salt to taste, stir, and continue simmering until shrimp are **opaque** white and fully cooked, about 5 minutes. Do not boil.

Serve warm in individual bowls.

Diwali, the "Festival of Lights," is celebrated by all Hindus to symbolize the triumph of good over evil (see section on India), and for Malay Hindus it traditionally marks the end of the business year. People give their houses a good cleaning and pay off old debts. As in India during this "Festival of Lights," houses and gardens are lit up with candles and twinkling oil lamps filled with *ghee* (recipe page 160).

Gold or yellow colored rice is prepared as a festival dish by Hindus and Muslims all over the world. The actual recipe varies from country to country and kitchen to kitchen, but the color, which symbolizes good fortune and prosperity, is universal.

Nasi Mlinyak   Malaysian Golden Rice

Yield: serves 6 to 8

- 2 tablespoons *ghee* (recipe page 160), butter, or margarine, more if necessary
- 2 onions, finely sliced
- 3 cloves garlic, **finely chopped**, or 1 teaspoon garlic granules
- 1 teaspoon ground cinnamon
- 1 teaspoon ground **turmeric**
- 1½ teaspoons curry powder
- 2 cups rice
- 3½ cups water
- salt and pepper to taste

Equipment: **Dutch oven** or medium saucepan with cover, mixing spoon, fork

1. Heat *ghee* or melt butter or margarine in Dutch oven or medium saucepan over medium-high heat. Add onions, garlic, cinnamon, turmeric, curry powder, and rice. Stirring constantly, fry for about 3 minutes until onions are soft.

2. Add water, stir, and bring to a boil. Reduce heat to simmer, cover, and cook for 20 minutes, or until rice is tender. Set aside, covered, for 5 minutes. Add salt and pepper to taste and fluff with a fork before serving.

Serve yellow rice while warm.

Sweets, revered by Hindus as food for the gods, are offered during prayer as a symbol of happiness and an act of good will. In Malaysia, this Hindu recipe for *sevian* is made with rice noodles, not wheat noodles, as it is in India (recipe page 162).

Rice noodles require no precooking like wheat noodles do.

Sevian   Rice Vermicelli Dessert Pudding

Yield: serves 6 to 8

- 12 ounces rice vermicelli, broken into about 1-inch lengths (available at all Asian food stores)
- 6 cups water, more or less as needed
- 4 tablespoons *ghee* (recipe page 160), butter, or margarine, more if necessary
- ½ cup slivered almonds
- ½ cup seedless raisins, soaked in warm water for 15 minutes and drained
- 2 cups milk
- ½ cup sugar, more if necessary
- ½ teaspoon ground cardamom
- 1 cup heavy cream, for serving

Equipment: Large mixing bowl, **colander**, **Dutch oven** or medium saucepan, **slotted spoon**, small bowl

1. **Rehydrate** rice vermicelli noodles by putting noodle pieces in large mixing bowl filled with about 6 cups water and soaking noodles for 8 minutes, or until softened. Drain in colander.

2. Heat 2 tablespoons *ghee*, or melt butter or margarine, in Dutch oven or medium saucepan over medium heat. Add nuts and raisins, stir, and fry until nuts are golden, about 3 minutes. Remove with slotted spoon and set aside in small bowl.

3. Add remaining 2 tablespoons *ghee* or butter or margarine to pan drippings in Dutch oven or medium saucepan, and heat over medium-high heat. Add drained rice noodles, and toss to coat. (Add more *ghee*, butter, or margarine, if needed, to coat noodles.) Add milk, ½ cup sugar, and cardamom, bring to a boil, and stir. Reduce heat to simmer and cook until mixture thickens, about 5 minutes. Add more sugar to adjust sweetness (if needed, adjust to taste), stir, and remove from heat.

To serve, transfer to serving bowl, and sprinkle with nut mixture. To eat, spoon into individual dessert bowls, and add cream. The pudding is eaten with a spoon.

In tropical Singapore, cooling drinks are very popular during any major celebration. The following drink, *ayer batu bandong*, is enjoyed by people of all faiths in Singapore.

Ayer Batu Bandong   Rose Cooler

Yield: serves 1

¼ cup rose syrup (available at Middle East food stores)

¼ cup water

2 tablespoons evaporated milk

2 tablespoons coconut milk, homemade (recipe page 194) or canned

1 cup crushed ice

Equipment: Tall glass, mixing spoon

1. In tall glass, mix rose syrup, water, evaporated milk, and coconut milk until well blended.

Add ice and serve at once.

Indonesia

Indonesia, one of the world's most populous nations, has a long and storied history involving many different countries and religions.

Today, the majority of Indonesians are Muslims, but many Indonesians keep ancestral Buddhist and Hindu beliefs alive by blending them into Muslim rituals. Pork is banned in most of Indonesia, except for the island of Bali, where most of the people are Hindus.

Food plays an important part in religious observances, and even the poorest family cooks a lavish meal for the *Selamatan* (also *Slametan*), a ritual feast that is a combination of ancient pagan religion mixed with Hinduism, brought to Indonesia about A.D. 400, and some elements of Islam, which was brought to the area about a thousand years later. The ritual feast and prayer session range from a family gathering to a community affair of an elaborate offering to the gods at the Hindu and Buddhist temples

The *rijsttafel*, literally meaning "rice table," is the Indonesian way of serving food. A table is set with hot and cold dishes of different flavors and textures, which surround the rice. Each guest takes a large serving of rice and a little food from each dish.

Centuries ago, the people of Java (now Indonesia) worshipped many gods, who, according to legend, lived in a sacred mountain. A tradition developed of offering foods to the gods to appease the evil spirits and honor the good ones. These ancient beliefs and customs have survived Buddhist, Hindu, and Muslim rulers, and today most Indonesians, regardless of their religious beliefs, honor the gods by including a food offering, the *tumpeng,* in their holiday feasts. The *tumpeng* is a cone-shaped mountain of steamed rice, often more than a foot high. The mound of rice is symmetrically decorated with symbolic foods, such as green beans for long life, hard-cooked eggs and hot red peppers for fertility, and flavored foods for the basic tastes of salty, sweet, sour, and hot. In Indonesia, women prepare the *tumpeng,* but according to strict religious beliefs only the men are allowed to eat it.

Rice is the mainstay of the Indonesians' diet, and it is valued greatly. Indonesian Hindus believe the rice goddess, *Dewi Sri,* watches over the growing rice, and she is honored with an elaborate ceremony at harvest time. It is common to serve several different rice recipes at the same meal. Because of its sunny color, the following rice recipe, *nasi kuning,* is prepared for happy occasions, such as childbirth, weddings, anniversaries, and birthdays.

Nasi Kuning   Indonesian Golden Rice

Yield: serves 4

1 cup rice
2 cups coconut milk, homemade (recipe page 194) or canned
½ teaspoon salt
½ teaspoon ground turmeric
1 stick (about 2 inches long) **lemon grass**, or juice of 1 lemon

Equipment: Medium saucepan with cover, mixing spoon, fork

1. In medium saucepan, combine rice, coconut milk, and salt, and bring to a boil over high heat. Reduce heat to simmer, add turmeric and lemon grass or lemon juice, and stir.

2. Cover and cook for 20 minutes. Remove from heat, and let stand covered for 5 minutes. Before serving, remove lemon grass and discard (if one was added), and fluff rice with a fork.

Serve warm or at room temperature and mound on serving platter.

This recipe for *goda goda,* a vegetable salad, is prepared for auspicious occasions, such as childbirth, *Selamatan,* and wedding ceremonies. It is the custom to cook green beans whole, signifying long life.

Goda Goda   Vegetable Salad

Yield: serves 6

1 cup coconut milk, homemade (recipe page 194) or canned
⅔ cup creamy peanut butter
1 tablespoon sugar, more or less to taste
¼ teaspoon ground red pepper
1 clove garlic, **finely chopped**, or 1 teaspoon garlic granules
½ teaspoon fresh, **grated ginger** or ¼ teaspoon ground ginger
½ cup water, more or less, if necessary
½ pound spinach, fresh, **blanched** or frozen, thawed, and drained
2 cups bean sprouts, fresh, blanched or canned, drained
18 whole string beans, fresh, **trimmed**, and blanched or frozen, thawed
1 cup **peeled** and sliced cooked potatoes
2 hard-cooked eggs, shelled and sliced
1 cup sliced fresh carrots, trimmed and blanched
salt and pepper to taste

Equipment: **Grater**, medium mixing bowl, egg beater or electric mixer, large serving platter, plastic wrap

1. Prepare sauce: In medium mixing bowl, use egg beater or electric mixer to mix coconut milk, peanut butter, 1 teaspoon sugar, red pepper, garlic, and ginger until blended, about 1 minute. Add just enough water to make sauce pourable if needed. To adjust flavor, add more sugar. Refrigerate.

2. Decoratively arrange spinach, bean sprouts, string beans, potatoes, sliced eggs, and carrots on large serving platter. Cover with plastic wrap and refrigerate until ready to serve.

*To serve, stir sauce and **drizzle** over platter of vegetables.*

In Indonesia sweet potatoes and coconuts are plentiful and cheap. This recipe is easy to make and can be served as a side dish with meat or as dessert. It is taken as a sweet offering to the Buddhist temples when a personal favor is requested from the gods, or it is eaten with other dishes for the *Selamatan* feast.

Getuk   Sweet Potato Balls with Coconut

Yield: serves 6

    4 cups cooked, **peeled**, and mashed sweet
        potatoes, homemade or canned, drained
    ½ teaspoon salt
    2 teaspoons sugar, more or less to taste
    1 teaspoon vanilla extract
    1 cup **shredded** sweetened coconut

Equipment: Medium mixing bowl, mixing spoon

1. In medium bowl, combine mashed sweet potatoes, salt, 2 teaspoons sugar (more or less to taste), vanilla, and ½ cup coconut. Mix well.

2. Using clean, wet hands, form potato mixture into ping-pong-size balls, and place on a serving platter. Sprinkle with remaining ½ cup coconut.

Serve at room temperature or refrigerate and serve chilled.

Most of the dishes on the *rijsttafel* are vegetables and fruit. It is not unusual to combine them in the same dish, as in this fruit salad called *rudjak*.

Rudjak   Fruit Salad

Yield: serves 6

    1 fresh pineapple, **peeled, cored,** and cut into
        bite-size chunks or 16-ounce can pineapple
        chunks, drained (save juice)

    1 large cucumber, peeled and cut into bite-size
        chunks
    2 carrots, **trimmed** and coarsely **shredded**
    2 apples, cored and thinly sliced
    3 oranges, peeled and cut into bite-size chunks
    2 cups finely shredded lettuce
    ½ cup shredded sweetened coconut
    ginger dressing (recipe follows), for serving

Equipment: Large salad bowl, salad serving tools

1. In large salad bowl, use salad serving tools to gently toss pineapple, cucumber, carrots, apples, oranges, shredded lettuce, and coconut together.

2. Just before serving, add dressing and toss.

Serve at room temperature as one of the cold dishes on the rijsttafel.

Ginger Dressing for Fruit Salad

Yield: about 1 cup

    2 tablespoons vegetable oil
    1 tablespoon brown sugar, more if necessary
    ½ teaspoon ground **ginger**
    juice of 1 lime
    2 tablespoons white vinegar
    ½ cup pineapple juice
    salt to taste

Equipment: Small mixing bowl, **whisk** or egg beater

In small mixing bowl, use whisk or egg beater to mix oil, 1 tablespoon brown sugar, ginger, lime juice, vinegar, and pineapple juice until smooth. Add salt to taste. To adjust sweetness, add more brown sugar, if necessary, and mix well. Just before serving, pour over salad and toss gently.

Serve at room temperature for best flavor.

A large assortment of sweet dishes, such as the following recipe for Indonesian bread pudding, known as *kueh prol nanas*, is always included on the *rijsttafel*.

Kueh Prol Nanas   Indonesian Bread Pudding

Yield: serves 8

3 **eggs, separated**
½ cup dark brown sugar
1 teaspoon ground cinnamon
grated rind of ½ lemon
1 (15-ounce) can crushed pineapple and syrup
2 cups coconut milk, homemade (recipe page 194) or canned
3 cups of ½-inch chunks crustless white egg bread
¼ teaspoon cream of tartar
¼ cup granulated sugar

Equipment: Medium mixing bowl, **grater**, mixing spoon, greased or nonstick 8-inch square baking pan, toothpick, oven mitts, small mixing bowl, egg beater or electric mixer, rubber **spatula**

Preheat oven to 350° F.

1. In medium mixing bowl, combine egg yolks, brown sugar, cinnamon, lemon rind, and crushed pineapple with syrup. Stirring constantly, add coconut milk, a little at a time, and blend well.

2. Spread bread cubes over the bottom of greased or nonstick 8-inch baking pan, and pour egg mixture over the bread cubes.

3. Bake in oven for about 40 minutes, or until toothpick inserted about 2 inches from the edge of the pan comes out clean. If it is done, remove from oven. (Leave the oven on.)

4. Pour egg whites into small mixing bowl, and use egg beater or electric mixer to beat them until soft peaks form. Continue beating while adding cream of tartar and granulated sugar, a little at a time, until stiff peaks form.

5. Spread egg-white mixture over pudding, using spatula, and bake in oven until peaks are golden brown, about 8 minutes. Remove from oven, and let sit 10 minutes before cutting.

To serve, cut into 2- x 4-inch squares.

Fiji

The indigenous Fijians are descendants of Polynesians and Melanesians who migrated to Fiji centuries ago. Over the years, many people converted to Christianity, which was brought by European explorers and missionaries. Fiji also has a large Indian population, mostly descendants of indentured laborers. Most Indians are Hindus and still celebrate the Hindu festivals. Today, all Christian and Hindu observances are national holidays in Fiji.

The missionaries were able to win Fijians over to Christianity through their love of music. There are no more ardent hymn singers than Fijians, and Christmas is the happiest time of the year. On Christmas Eve the churches quickly fill up with parishioners anxious to help Christmas along through song. After church there are all-night outdoor festivities with more singing, dancing, and eating. The Christmas feast centers around the pit barbecue, and pig is the favorite choice for roasting.

Fiji's Indian population celebrates the Hindu New Year, *Diwali*, also known as the "Festival of Lights." Houses and yards come alive with twinkling candles and lanterns. Hindus who retain the ancient rituals of their homeland burn *ghee* (recipe page 160) in their *dipa* lamps.

It is the custom for Hindus to begin the most important day of *Diwali* by taking a ceremonial bath and dressing in their best clothes. The rest of the day is spent visiting friends and relatives.

Sweets are an important part of the *Diwali* Festival. They are given as an offering to the goddess *Lakshmi*, as a promise of sweeter things to come. Sweets are not eaten to just satisfy the sweet tooth; they are considered nourishment. *Savia* (recipe page 162) are sweets that are given to friends during certain festivals, such as *Diwali*. This recipe for another popular Indian candy, *badam pistaz barfi*, is quick and easy to make.

Badam Pistaz Barfi Hindu Nut Candy

Yield: about 20 pieces
    1 (3-ounce) box vanilla pudding mix (not instant)
    1 cup sugar
    ½ cup evaporated milk
    1 teaspoon ground cardamom
    1 teaspoon almond extract
    2 cups finely **ground** almonds

Equipment: Medium saucepan, mixing spoon, buttered 8-inch square pan, knife

1. In medium saucepan, combine vanilla pudding mix, sugar, and evaporated milk. Stirring constantly, bring to a boil over medium-high heat for 2 minutes. Remove from heat, add cardamom, almond extract, and almonds, and stir. Return to medium-high heat, and cook for 2 minutes until thickened, stirring frequently. Mixture turns tan color as it cooks.

2. Transfer to buttered 8-inch pan and smooth top. Cool to room temperature, and refrigerate to set, about 4 hours.

Serve candy as a sweet treat.

Coconuts provide a source of food for over half the world's population. The coconut tree provides food and drink, vessels, and clothing.

Coconut oils are used not only for cooking but also as lubricants and in shampoos and hand creams. An interesting fact about the coconut is that it played a major role in the Allied forces winning World War I. Nitroglycerine, which is used in explosives, is made from the dried coconut meat, called *copra*.

The nourishment and eating pleasure coconuts provide make them one of the world's great goods; they are the primary ingredient in Fijian cooking.

Fresh Coconut, Grated

When buying a fresh coconut, make sure that it has no cracks and that it contains liquid. Shake it, and if you do not hear swishing liquid, select another.

Yield: 4 cups
    1 ripe coconut (at least 2 pounds)

Equipment: Ice pick or metal skewer, oven mitts, hard surface, hammer, knife, vegetable peeler, hand **grater** or electric **food processor**

1. Have an adult help you pierce the "eyes" of coconut with an ice pick or metal skewer. Drain the liquid and save for another use.

Preheat oven to 400° F.

2. Bake the coconut in oven for 15 minutes. Wearing oven mitts, remove from oven, and let sit until cool enough to handle. On a hard surface, crack coconut with a hammer and remove flesh

from shell, levering it out carefully with the point of a strong knife. Peel off thin, brown inner skin with vegetable peeler. Either hand-grate coconut on fine side of grater or coarsely chop and grind coconut in food processor.

To use, make into coconut milk (recipe follows) or add to recipes calling for unsweetened grated coconut.

When making coconut milk, it is not necessary to remove brown inner skin.

Coconut Milk

Yield: about 1½ cups
   2 cups grated fresh coconut (recipe precedes)
   1¼ cups hot water, more if necessary

Equipment: Electric **blender** or **food processor**, **grater**, coffee filter, small bowl, mixing spoon

In blender or food processor, mix coconut and 1½ cups hot water for about 2 minutes; let cool for 5 minutes. Strain through coffee filter into small bowl, pressing hard on the solid to extract all of the coconut milk. This process makes thick coconut milk. For thin coconut milk, add a little water.

Use in recipes calling for coconut milk.

Papua New Guinea

The indigenous population of Papua New Guinea is made up of several thousand small, separate communities, each with its own language, customs, and traditions. Missionaries converted about two-thirds of the people to Christianity, but most combine it with tribal worship, especially ancestor and spirit worship.

Christian celebrations are similar to neighboring Australia since most foreign residents are Australians. Brightly clad parishioners spend Christmas Eve in church singing songs brought to the islands by missionaries centuries ago. On Christmas Day, Father Christmas, usually a bearded sailor wrapped in a flowered sheet, arrives by catamaran. Unlike Australia, the Christmas dinner is whole pit-roasted pig, instead of beef or lamb, and the meal is eaten with the fingers. The following pork roast recipe can be used in place of a whole pit-roasted pig.

Roast Pork with Plantains and Sweet Potatoes

Yield: serves 6 to 8
   4- or 5-pound boned, lean pork roast
   ½ cup packed brown sugar
   ½ cup soy sauce
   2 tablespoons dark molasses
   3 cloves garlic, **finely chopped**, or 1 teaspoon garlic granules
   1 cup water
   salt and pepper to taste
   4 to 6 tablespoons butter or margarine, more or less as needed
   6 ripe **plantains** or bananas, **peeled** and cut into 2-inch chunks, for serving
   4 sweet potatoes, boiled, peeled, and cut into 2-inch chunks, for serving

Equipment: Roasting pan or 13- x 9-inch baking pan, small mixing bowl, mixing spoon, **bulb baster**, oven mitts, large skillet

1. Place pork roast in roasting pan or baking pan, and set aside.

2. Prepare **marinade**: In small mixing bowl, mix brown sugar, soy sauce, molasses, garlic, water, and salt and pepper to taste. Spread mixture over meat and refrigerate. **Marinate** meat for 4 hours, turning occasionally.

Preheat oven to 450° F, very hot.

3. Bake in oven for 15 minutes, reduce heat to 325°, and, basting frequently, bake for 2½ to 3 hours, or until well done.

4. Just before serving, melt 4 tablespoons butter or margarine in large skillet over medium heat. Add plantains or bananas, and fry, turning frequently, until well coated and heated through, about 5 minutes. (Add more butter or margarine, if necessary.) Add sweet potatoes, toss carefully to coat, and heat through, about 5 minutes.

To serve, place roasted pork on large serving platter and surround with plantains and sweet potatoes. Pour pan drippings over roast.

Australia/New Zealand

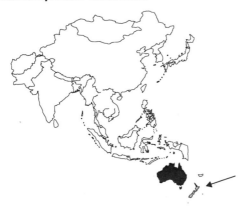

The majority of Australians and New Zealanders are descendants of British and Irish settlers, some of whom were convicts sent to Australia when it was a penal colony in the seventeenth and eighteenth centuries. Both countries have small numbers of indigenous people, the aborigines in Australia and the Maori in New Zealand.

Holiday celebrations combine the best of old English traditions with new practices that developed in Australia and New Zealand. Because Australia and New Zealand are in the Southern Hemisphere, Christmas falls in the middle of summer.

In Australia (in black), schools are closed, and almost everyone is either vacationing at the beach, camping, or partying in the backyard around the "barby" (barbecue). On Christmas Day, people roast lamb or beef on the barby, pop **Christmas crackers**, wear funny hats, watch the Queen's satellite-relayed speech on television, and eat Christmas pudding, usually made with fruit. There are no yule logs burning in the fireplace, nor is there a need (or desire) for hot toddies.

Father Christmas makes his rounds traveling not by sleigh pulled by reindeer but by open car, boat, or water skis.

Christmas dinner includes fresh fruit, possibly grown in one's own backyard orchard or garden.

Pineapple and Cabbage Salad

Yield: serves 4 to 6

  1 large ripe pineapple, **peeled, cored,** and cut into ½-inch cubes or 1 (16-ounce) can pineapple chunks, drained (reserve juice to use at another time)
  1 grapefruit, peeled and **segmented**
  2 cups finely **shredded** cabbage
  1 cucumber, **trimmed**, cut in half, and finely sliced
  1 green or red bell pepper, cored, **seeded**, and sliced into matchstick-size strips
  1 cup **finely chopped** cooked ham

2 tablespoons vegetable oil
4 tablespoons mayonnaise
2 tablespoons white vinegar
2 to 4 tablespoons light cream
sugar to taste
salt and pepper to taste

Equipment: Large salad bowl, small mixing bowl, salad mixing tools

1. In large salad bowl, combine pineapple, grapefruit, cabbage, cucumber, bell pepper, and ham.

2. In small mixing bowl, mix oil, mayonnaise, and vinegar. Add 2 tablespoons cream. If mixture is too thick to pour, add a little more cream to slightly thin it. Add sugar and salt and pepper to taste, and stir. Pour over salad, and, using salad mixing tools, toss to mix. Refrigerate until ready to serve. Toss before serving.

Serve salad with the meat course.

As in England, holiday baking begins in June with traditional fruitcakes and puddings. (See section on England under the United Kingdom.) These puddings take time to "ripen" because brandy and other liquors are added to enhance the flavor. Cookie baking begins in early December with cookies like these *quick bickies*.

Quick Bickies   Quick Cookies

Yield: 2 to 3 dozen
1 cup butter or margarine
1 cup sugar
2 eggs
1 cup all-purpose flour
1 cup **self-rising flour**
pinch of salt

Equipment: Large mixing bowl, mixing spoon or electric mixer, flour **sifter**, aluminum foil, lightly

greased or nonstick baking sheet, oven mitts, metal **spatula**

1. In large mixing bowl, use mixing spoon or electric mixer to beat butter and sugar until light and fluffy. Add eggs, one at a time, and mix well.

2. **Sift** flours and salt into egg mixture, and mix into a firm dough. Form dough into a log about 1 inch thick. Wrap dough in foil, and refrigerate for at least 1 hour.

Preheat oven to 325° F.

3. Cut log crosswise into ½-inch slices, and place cookies side by side, about 1 inch apart, on baking sheet. Bake in oven for about 15 minutes until lightly browned.

Serve cookies after they have cooled.

Australian Caramel Squares

Yield: serves 10 to 12
½ cup melted butter or margarine
1 cup brown sugar
1 egg
1 cup **finely chopped** dates
½ cup **coarsely chopped** fruitcake mix
    (available at all supermarkets)
1½ cups **self-rising flour**

Equipment: Medium mixing bowl, mixing spoon, lightly greased or nonstick 9-inch square baking pan, oven mitts, knife, metal **spatula**

Preheat oven to 400° F.

1. In medium mixing bowl, mix melted butter or margarine and brown sugar. Add egg, dates, fruitcake mix, and flour, and mix well.

2. Using clean hands, press mixture into lightly greased or nonstick 9-inch baking pan.

3. Bake in oven for about 15 minutes, until golden brown.

To serve, cut into squares while still warm.

Fruit is included in almost all holiday baking, including this recipe for upside down cake.

Upside Down Cake

Yield: serves 8 to 10

½ cup light brown sugar
½ cup butter or margarine, at room temperature
1 (12-ounce) can sliced pineapple, drained well
6 or 8 candied red cherries
1 (16-ounce) box vanilla or plain butter cake mix

Equipment: Medium mixing bowl, mixing spoon, **spatula**, 8-inch round cake pan, large mixing bowl, oven mitts, toothpick

Preheat oven to 350° F.

1. In medium mixing bowl, mix brown sugar and butter or margarine until creamy, about 3 minutes. Using spatula, spread brown sugar mixture over bottom of cake pan. Arrange pineapple rings in an attractive pattern, covering bottom of pan, and place a cherry in center of each. Set aside.

2. In large mixing bowl, prepare cake mix (according to directions on package), and spread finished mix over pineapple rings.

3. Bake in oven for about 45 minutes, until toothpick inserted in center comes out clean.

To serve, invert cake onto a serving platter. The decorative pineapple rings will be on the top. Cut into wedges and serve warm or at room temperature.

The pride of New Zealand is a soup made with *toheroa*, a rare shellfish found in the black sands of the North Island and South Island beaches. (The country of New Zealand is actually made up of two separate islands.) The Christmas cookout for lucky clam diggers usually includes *toheroa* or mussel chowder. Fresh or canned minced clams are a good substitute.

Toheroa Soup   Clam Chowder

Yield: serves 4

1 tablespoon butter or margarine
1 tablespoon flour
1 cup clam juice (available at all supermarkets)
1 cup fresh, **finely chopped** and shucked mussels or clams or canned minced clams (available at all supermarkets)
2 cups milk
½ teaspoon ground nutmeg
juice of 1 lemon
salt and white pepper to taste
½ cup light cream, more or less as needed
1 teaspoon paprika, for **garnish**

Equipment: Medium saucepan, mixing spoon

1. Melt butter or margarine in saucepan over medium heat. Add flour, and stir constantly until smooth and lump-free. Continue stirring, and slowly add clam juice and mussels or clams. Increase heat to high, and bring to a boil.

2. Reduce heat to simmer, and, stirring constantly, add milk, nutmeg, lemon juice, and salt and white pepper to taste. Heat through, and, before serving, add light cream and mix well.

Serve warm in individual bowls and sprinkle soup with paprika.

When New Zealand was first settled by the English, the land had almost no native mammals or predators, and so the animals that the settlers brought thrived without any competition. Today, New Zealand is famous for the millions of sheep that graze there. Therefore, it is not surprising that the traditional New Zealand Christmas feast is always lamb. Some people, jokingly, refer to lamb as the Christmas goose.

The following recipe is an easy and inexpensive, yet delicious way many New Zealanders prepare their Christmas dinner lamb

Canterbury Lamb with Honey

Yield: serves 6 to 8

    2 pounds boned, lean leg of lamb, cut into 2-inch cubes
    3 cloves garlic, **finely chopped**, or 1 teaspoon garlic granules
    2 tablespoons all-purpose flour
    salt and pepper to taste
    2 to 4 tablespoons butter or margarine
    2½ cups water
    4 tablespoons honey
    2 teaspoons **grated** fresh **ginger** or 1 teaspoon ground ginger
    2 cups stewed tomatoes
    3 carrots, thinly sliced
    1 onion, finely chopped

Equipment: Medium mixing bowl, mixing spoon, **Dutch oven** or large oven-proof saucepan with cover, **grater**, oven mitts

Preheat oven to 350° F.

1. In medium mixing bowl, toss lamb with garlic, flour, and salt and pepper to taste.

2. Melt butter or margarine in Dutch oven or large oven-proof saucepan over medium-high heat.

Add lamb, and brown on all sides for about 8 minutes, tossing frequently.

3. Add water, honey, ginger, tomatoes, carrots, and onion, and stir well. Bring to a boil, and then remove from heat. Stir, cover, and, using oven mitts, place pan in oven and cook for about 45 minutes, or until lamb is tender.

Serve as the main dish for the Christmas dinner.

Vegetables are served at almost every meal in New Zealand, and several different kinds are included in the Christmas feast.

Many Asians have settled in New Zealand. Their interesting sauces and cooking style have influenced the cooking of New Zealanders. The peanut sauce in the following recipe reflects some of that Asian influence.

Cauliflower with Peanut Sauce

Yield: serves 4

    ½ cup crunchy peanut butter
    ½ cup mayonnaise
    1 tablespoon all-purpose flour
    1 teaspoon honey
    juice from half a lemon
    1 teaspoon soy sauce
    1 fresh cauliflower, washed, broken into **florets**, and **blanched** or frozen 24-ounce package cauliflower florets, thawed
    ½ cup **grated** cheddar cheese

Equipment: Small mixing bowl; mixing spoon; buttered, medium baking dish; **grater**; oven mitts

Preheat oven to 350° F.

1. In small mixing bowl, mix peanut butter, mayonnaise, flour, honey, lemon juice, and soy sauce until well blended.

2. Place cauliflower in buttered medium baking dish, and cover with peanut mixture. Sprinkle with grated cheese, and bake in oven for about 20 minutes until cheese is melted and browned.

Serve immediately from the oven.

Eating the hearty Christmas dishes served in cold, rainy England is not to the liking of New Zealanders. In place of the flaming English plum pudding, ice cream is the preferred dessert. At Christmas, ice cream is made into a plum-pudding-like cake. No baking is necessary in the following easy-to-make recipe.

Plum Pudding Ice Cream Cake

Yield: serves 12

¾ cup butter or margarine, at room temperature, more or less as needed

4 cups (about 1 pound) cookie crumbs, such as Oreos or chocolate wafers

4 cups (32-ounces) thawed, frozen whipped topping, more as needed

1½ cups canned mincemeat (available at most supermarkets)

4 cups (2 pints) strawberry (or other colored) ice cream or frozen yogurt

1 cup **coarsely chopped** candied fruit mix (available at supermarkets)

1 cup sliced almonds

Equipment: Medium (about 9 inches across x 3½ inches deep), rounded-bottom metal mixing bowl or dome mold, small skillet, large mixing bowl, mixing spoon, aluminum foil, sprig of holly for decoration

1. Coat inside of metal bowl or dome mold with butter or margarine.

2. Melt ½ cup butter or margarine in small skillet over medium heat. Put crumbs in bowl or mold, add melted butter or margarine, and mix well to coat crumbs. Make sure all the crumbs are coated, adding a little more melted butter or margarine if needed. Cover inside of bowl or mold with about a ¼-inch layer of crumbs; press crumbs firmly in place. Freeze for about 1 hour, or until firm.

3. In large mixing bowl, mix 4 cups whipped topping and mincemeat. Spoon mixture into crumb-lined bowl or mold, and spread evenly over crumbs, leaving a bowl-shaped hole about 7 inches across the center of the whipped topping mixture. Freeze until firm, about 3 hours.

4. In large mixing bowl, soften ice cream or yogurt just enough to mix. Add candied fruit mix and nuts, and gently mix. Fill hole in lined bowl or mold with ice cream or yogurt mixture. Cover with foil, and freeze for at least 8 hours before serving.

5. Fill sink with about 3 inches hot water. To unmold cake, set bowl or mold in hot water for about 1 minute. Remove bowl from the water, remove foil, and invert a serving platter over top. Hold the bowl and serving platter tightly together, and then flip them over so that cake will drop onto platter. Remove bowl or mold and return cake to freezer. Transfer to refrigerator 30 minutes before serving.

*To serve, **garnish** with **dollops** of whipped topping and decorate top with holly sprig. To serve, cut cake into wedges.*

Caribbean

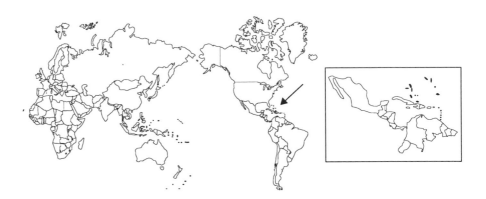

The original inhabitants of the Caribbean islands all died after contact with the Europeans. (They were either killed by the Europeans or died from the diseases the Europeans spread.) Today, people from all over the world make their home in the Caribbean and most of them have brought their holiday customs with them. Over time the mixing of cultures has altered many celebrations, thus creating new traditions. For example, on some islands, new celebrations mix the religious practices that the slaves brought from Africa centuries ago with Christian traditions the Europeans brought to the islands. The ancient rituals have survived and evolved along with Christian spirituality, in some cases forming new religions.

Christmas is an important holiday, but the tropical weather and poverty of the Caribbean people have changed the traditions brought by the European colonizers. A pine tree to decorate for Christmas is a prized treasure few Caribbeans get to enjoy. There is a Santa who travels by donkey, and the island children look forward to his arrival. The ideal holiday feast for many islanders is a goat, pig, or lamb roasted over an open fire. Unfortunately for many, it is only a dream; meat is scarce and expensive. Most natives consider themselves lucky if they are able to share a chicken or rabbit with their family.

Trinidad & Tobago

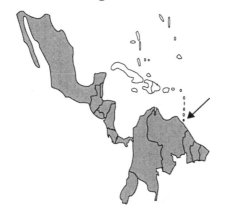

Trinidad and Tobago have two major cultures: the Creoles, descendants of African slaves and the Spanish, French, and English colonists; and the East Indians, who were brought to the islands as indentured laborers.

A large portion of people on both islands are Roman Catholic. As in other places in the Caribbean and Latin America, Carnival is the favorite holiday. Although Carnival is predominantly celebrated by Creoles, many East Indians also participate. Dressed in outlandish costumes, Carnival revelers parade nonstop, night and day, singing and dancing to the calypso beat of steel drums.

Unique to Trinidad and Tobago's Carnival celebration are the children's Carnival and the "jump-up" style of dancing that originated with the people of Trinidad. For the children's Carnival, the boys and girls paint their faces or wear masks, outlandish costumes, hats, and wigs. They then parade down the street, banging on anything that will make a loud noise. Most children are too poor to buy a costume, and so they make their own out of anything they can beg, borrow, or find in the scrap heaps. After the noisy parade, everyone gathers for refreshments provided by the churches and merchants in the town.

Other than the spit-roasted goat, pig, or lamb, there are no special dishes reserved for the holidays. Bananas and plantains, however, are included at almost every meal and for special occasion feasts.

Mariquitas — Fried Banana Chips

CAUTION: HOT OIL USED

Yield: *serves 4 to 6*

3 green bananas or **plantains**, **peeled**
vegetable oil for **deep frying**
salt to taste

Equipment: Vegetable peeler or sharp knife, **deep fryer** (see glossary for tips on making one), wooden spoon, paper towels, baking sheet, **slotted spoon**

1. Using a vegetable peeler or knife, slice peeled bananas or plantains, either crosswise or lengthwise, into paper-thin slices.

2. Prepare deep fryer: Have an adult help you heat oil to 375° F. Oil is hot enough for frying when small bubbles appear around a wooden spoon handle when it is dipped in the oil. Place several layers of paper towels on baking sheet.

3. Carefully drop slices, a few at a time, into hot oil, and fry for about 2 minutes, or until crisp and golden brown. Remove with slotted spoon, and drain on paper towels. Sprinkle with salt to taste. Keep warm and continue frying in batches.

Serve warm, as you would French fried potatoes.

Baked plantains are eaten plain, as a side dish, or they are sweetened to be served as dessert.

Baked Plantains

Yield: *serves 4*

4 black, ripe **plantains** or ripe bananas, rinsed and patted dry
4 teaspoons butter or margarine, at room temperature
4 teaspoons **cinnamon sugar**

Equipment: Knife, 8-inch square baking pan, oven mitts

Preheat oven to 350° F.

1. Cut 1 inch off each end of plantains or bananas, and cut a lengthwise slit through the skin on one side. Place cut-side up in baking pan. Open slit and spread 1 tablespoon butter or margarine in opening of each plantain or banana; sprinkle openings with cinnamon sugar.

2. Bake in oven for about 30 minutes, or until plantains or bananas are tender when pierced with a fork.

Serve plantains or bananas warm in the skin. Eat the edible fruit with a fork or spoon and discard the skin.

Pumpkins, sweet potatoes, or yams are very popular in Trinidad and Tobago and are served at every holiday feast.

Double-Stuffed Sweet Potatoes

Yield: *serves 6 to 8*
  4 large sweet potatoes, baked until tender (let cool to handle)
  2 tablespoons sweetened, **grated** coconut
  ¼ cup light cream
  2 tablespoons melted butter or margarine
  salt and pepper to taste
  ½ teaspoon ground cinnamon, for **garnish**

Equipment: Knife, mixing spoon, medium mixing bowl, lightly greased or nonstick baking sheet, potato masher, oven mitts

Preheat oven to 350° F.

1. Cut each baked sweet potato in half lengthwise, and carefully scoop out pulp, leaving the shell halves intact. Put pulp in medium mixing bowl, and place potato shells on lightly greased or nonstick baking sheet.

2. Using potato masher, mash pulp until smooth and lump-free. Add coconut, cream, melted butter, and salt and pepper to taste. Mix until fluffy and mound in potato shells. Sprinkle each potato with cinnamon, and bake in oven to heat through, about 15 minutes.

Serve each person a stuffed potato with the holiday dinner.

People of East Indian descent comprise 25 percent of the population of Trinidad and Tobago. The majority of them are Hindus, and they observe all Hindu festivals, one of the most important being *Holi* (also called *Hola*). *Holi* is a springtime festival commemorating the burning of *Holika*, a witch who once tormented all of India. In India, fried breads are a staple, and no meal is complete unless some is on the table. On the islands fried breads, called *bammies,* are made with locally grown **cassava**, sweet potatoes, or yams.

Bammies   Sweet Potato Fried Bread

CAUTION: HOT OIL USED
Yield: *serves 4*
  ½ cup yellow cornmeal
  1 cup boiling water
  ½ cup mashed sweet potato (boil 1 small potato until tender, about 20 minutes, and then peel—this recipe is good way to use leftover sweet potatoes.)
  ½ cup warm milk
  1 cup all-purpose flour
  2 teaspoons baking powder
  1 teaspoon *each* ground allspice and salt
  1 egg, beaten
  2 to 4 tablespoons vegetable oil or ghee (recipe page 160), more or less as needed, for frying

Equipment: Medium mixing bowl, mixing spoon or electric mixer, flour **sifter**, large skillet or griddle, metal **spatula**

1. Put cornmeal in medium mixing bowl, add boiling water, and use mixing spoon or electric mixer to mix; let stand for 5 minutes. Add mashed sweet potatoes and warm milk, and mix until smooth.

2. Put flour, baking powder, allspice, and salt into sifter. Stirring cornmeal mixture constantly, **sift** in flour mixture and blend well. Add egg, and stir until smooth and lump-free.

3. Have an adult help you heat 2 tablespoons oil or *ghee* in skillet or on griddle over medium-high heat. Carefully spoon potato mixture into 4- or 5-inch pancakes, about ⅛ inch thick, and fry for about 3 minutes, until bottom is brown. Turn pancakes over, and fry the other side until brown and crisp, about 3 minutes. Keep warm, and continue frying the rest of potato mixture in batches.

Serve bammies *while still warm. To reheat* bammies, *fry in oil or heat in a microwave for about 1 minute.*

Everyone wants holiday cookies to give to friends and family, and this recipe uses sweet potatoes, which are a staple on the islands.

Sweet Potato Cookies

Yield: *about 4 dozen*
- ½ cup butter or margarine, at room temperature
- 1½ cups light brown sugar
- 2 eggs
- 1 cup mashed sweet potatoes (boil 1 small potato until tender and peel after it cools— this recipe is a good way to use leftover sweet potatoes)
- 1 teaspoon vanilla extract
- 2 cups all-purpose flour
- 4 teaspoons baking powder
- 1 teaspoon ground cinnamon
- 1 cup **shredded** coconut
- honey and butter or margarine, for serving (optional)

Equipment: Large mixing bowl, mixing spoon or electric mixer, rubber **spatula**, tablespoon, lightly greased or nonstick cookie sheet, oven mitts

Preheat oven to 375° F.

1. In large mixing bowl, use mixing spoon or electric mixer to mix butter or margarine and brown sugar until smooth. Add eggs, mashed sweet potatoes, and vanilla; mix well.

2. Add flour, baking powder, and cinnamon, a little at a time, while mixing. Continue mixing until well blended, about 3 minutes. Add coconut and mix well.

3. Spoon tablespoonfuls of batter onto lightly greased or nonstick cookie sheet, about 1½ inches apart, and bake in oven for about 10 minutes, or until browned. Continue baking in batches.

Serve cookies as a sweet snack with honey and butter or margarine to spread on cookies.

Grenada

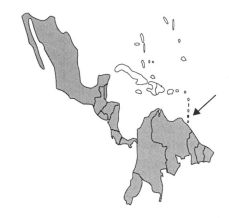

Most people who call Grenada home are descendants of African slaves brought to work on sugar plantations. The French were the first Europeans to settle Grenada, but later it became a British colony. The official language of Grenada is English, and the majority of the population are Christians. The strength of the Roman Catholic Church, to which about 60 percent of Grenadians belong, is a significant reminder of Grenada's historical connection to the French. Most Protestants belong to the Church of England. It is the custom for the Christians to combine traditional Christian celebrations with the ancestral and spirit worship brought by African slaves.

Among the Catholics, the principal family celebration is a feast after Christmas Eve Mass. The meal consists of fish with a variety of vegetables, such as coconut spinach (recipe follows). The custom stems from the fast-day regulations of the church, which, for many centuries, forbade the eating of meat on Christmas Eve. The traditions are still observed by devout Catholics, regardless of the less rigorous religious dietary regulations officially observed by the Catholic Church.

Callaloo is a tropical green much like spinach and is a favorite throughout the Caribbean. Because *callaloo* is not readily available, spinach is used in the following recipe.

Coconut Spinach

Yield: *serves 6*
    2 (10 ounces each) packages frozen chopped
        spinach, thawed
    1 cup coconut milk, homemade (recipe page
        194), or 1 (12-ounce) can, or frozen, thawed
    salt and pepper

Equipment: **Colander**, medium saucepan, mixing spoon

1. Drain spinach in colander, and squeeze out all moisture.

2. Put coconut milk in medium saucepan, and add spinach and salt and pepper to taste. Cook over medium-low heat until heated through, about 5 minutes, mixing frequently.

Serve warm as a side dish with a meat dish.

Exotic spices have long been a part of Caribbean cooking. The following spice cake is a popular holiday dessert to serve to visiting relatives and friends.

Caribbean Spice Cake

Yield: *serves 8 to 10*
    2 cups all-purpose flour
    ½ teaspoon baking powder
    ⅛ teaspoon salt
    1½ cups sugar
    1 cup butter or margarine, at room temperature
    grated peel of half a lime
    1 teaspoon grated nutmeg
    ½ teaspoon *each* cinnamon and allspice
    3 eggs
    ½ cup milk
    sliced fresh fruit: mango, bananas, or strawberries, for serving

Equipment: Flour **sifter**, **grater**, medium mixing bowl, large mixing bowl, mixing spoon or electric mixer, greased and floured 9- x 5-inch loaf pan, oven mitts, toothpick, wire rack, knife

Preheat oven to 350° F.

1. **Sift** flour, baking powder, and salt into medium mixing bowl. Set aside.

2. In large mixing bowl, use mixing spoon or electric mixer to mix sugar and butter or margarine, until light and fluffy. Mixing constantly, add lime peel, nutmeg, cinnamon, allspice, and eggs, one at a time. Mixing constantly again, add flour mixture alternately with milk. Transfer mixture to greased and floured loaf pan.

3. Bake in oven for about 1 hour, or until toothpick inserted in center comes out clean.

4. Place cake pan on wire rack to cool for 10 minutes. Loosen edges with a knife, and invert on serving platter to cool to room temperature before cutting.

To serve, cut cake into 1-inch slices and top with fresh fruit.

All Caribbean and Latin American countries are famous for cooling drinks, such as a tropical smoothie, made with fruit native to the region.

Tropical Smoothie

Yield: *serves 2 to 4*

- ½ cup **coarsely chopped** papaya, fresh, **peeled**, and **seeded** or canned, drained
- ½ cup pineapple juice
- ½ cup orange juice
- ½ cup canned cream of coconut (available in 15-ounce-size can at supermarkets)
- 1 tablespoon honey, more or less to taste
- 1 cup crushed ice or ice cubes, more or less, for serving

Equipment: electric **blender** or **food processor**, rubber **spatula**

Put papaya, pineapple juice, orange juice, coconut cream, and 1 tablespoon honey in blender or food processor, and blend for about 2 minutes or until well blended. Add more honey, if necessary, to adjust sweetness.

Serve in a tall glass over ice.

Dominican Republic

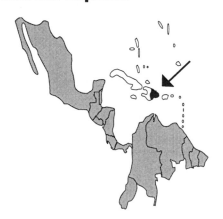

Roman Catholicism is the state religion in the Spanish-speaking Dominican Republic, and the major Christian holidays are special events, especially Christmas. Christmas festivities begin early in December with carolers singing from house to house, continuing throughout the night. At dawn, the carolers are served ginger tea (recipe page 184) and breakfast.

Every church in the Dominican Republic has Christmas Eve Mass, but none is more lavish than the one held at the Cathedral of Santa Maria La Menor, where it is said Christopher Columbus is buried.

On Christmas Eve the sounds of music and bells from the cathedral fill the night, and fireworks light up the sky. Everyone attends the *Misa del Gallo,* the Mass of the Rooster, at midnight, and afterwards they go home to supper.

Roast suckling pig with yucca is the traditional Dominican Christmas feast, but for most people it is too expensive, and a meat stew, such as the following recipe, is more common.

Sancocho   Meat Stew

Yield: *serves 6 to 8*

- 2 **plantains**, washed (keep peels on)
- 4 slices bacon, **finely chopped**
- 2 pounds lean, boneless pork or beef, cut into 1-inch chunks
- 3 onions, finely chopped
- 8 cups water
- 1 cup dried yellow split peas
- ½ pound cooked lean corned beef, cut into 1-inch chunks (available canned or at deli section of supermarkets)
- ½ teaspoon ground red pepper, more or less to taste
- 1 cup coconut milk, homemade (recipe page 194) or canned
- 1 cup heavy cream

salt and pepper to taste
6 new red potatoes, **peeled** and quartered
1 large sweet potato, peeled and coarsely sliced

Equipment: Small saucepan, fork, colander, knife, work surface, **Dutch oven** or large saucepan with cover, mixing spoon, ladle

1. Place plantains in small saucepan, and cover with water. Bring water to a boil over high heat. Reduce heat to low, and simmer for 30 minutes, or until plantains are tender when pierced with a fork. Drain in colander, and discard water. When cool enough to handle, peel and cut plantains crosswise into 1-inch-thick slices.

2. Fry bacon in Dutch oven or large saucepan over high heat, until soft and **rendered,** about 3 minutes. Add beef and onions, and, stirring constantly, brown on all sides, about 5 minutes. Add water, split peas, corned beef, and ½ teaspoon ground red pepper (more or less to taste), and stir. Bring to a boil, reduce heat to simmer, cover, and cook for 40 minutes.

3. Add coconut milk, cream, salt and pepper to taste, new potatoes, and sweet potato, and stir. Cover and simmer for 20 minutes, or until potatoes are tender. Add plantains, cover, and simmer for 5 minutes more, until heated through.

To serve, ladle stew into individual bowls.

This banana pudding recipe is a typical Caribbean Christmas dessert; it is also a wonderful way to use overripe bananas.

Banana Pudding

Yield: *serves 6*
6 overripe bananas, **peeled** and mashed
3 tablespoons melted butter or margarine
1 cup orange juice
1 cup sugar
3 **egg whites**, beaten to stiff peaks
2 tablespoons sweetened **shredded** coconut, for **garnish**

Equipment: Medium mixing bowl, mixing spoon, or electric mixer, **whisk** or rubber **spatula**, buttered or nonstick 1½-quart casserole or 8-inch baking pan, oven mitts

Preheat oven to 325° F.

1. In medium mixing bowl, use mixing spoon or electric mixer to mix bananas, melted butter or margarine, orange juice, and sugar.

2. Using whisk or rubber spatula, carefully **fold in** stiffly beaten egg whites. Transfer mixture to buttered or nonstick casserole or baking pan.

3. Bake in oven for about 40 minutes, or until puffy and golden brown.

4. Remove from oven and sprinkle top with shredded coconut.

Serve immediately right from the casserole or baking pan.

Cooling drinks made with tropical fruits are popular in the hot Caribbean climate.

Refresco de Coco y Piña
Chilled Coconut Milk and Pineapple

Yield: *serves 4*
2 cups coconut milk, homemade (recipe page 194) or canned
2 cups pineapple juice
½ teaspoon almond extract
1 teaspoon sugar, more if necessary
ice cubes, for serving

Equipment: Medium pitcher, mixing spoon

Pour coconut milk in pitcher, add pineapple juice, almond extract, and 1 teaspoon sugar, and stir. Add more sugar, if necessary, to adjust sweetness. Refrigerate.

To serve, stir and pour into tall glasses over ice cubes.

Haiti

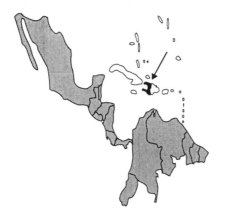

Most Haitians are Roman Catholic, which is the official religion of the country. Carnival, held the last day before Lent, is the biggest celebration of the year in Haiti. During Carnival everyone sets aside poverty, hardships, and responsibilities to live in a fun world of fantasy, if only for a few days.

In many parts of Haiti, Christian holiday traditions are peppered with voodoo. Voodoo beliefs, which Africans brought to Haiti on the slave ships, are widespread among the country's very poor majority. Centuries ago slaves combined African voodoo beliefs with the Catholicism of their French masters, and descendants continue the practices. Voodoo is essentially a cult of the spirits. Its Creole name, *vodou*, derives from *vodun*, which means "spirit" in the language of the Fon people of Benin and Nigeria in West Africa. African-Haitian voodoo belief acknowledges God as *Gran Mèt*, creator of heaven and earth. But according to voodoo beliefs, the master of the universe is too remote to be involved with the daily problems of mankind, and so he has appointed spirits to serve as the go-betweens.

The *Loa* (spirits) are associated with vital forces, such as water and fire, and love and death. Voodooists "serve" these forces to keep in harmony with them and thereby avert disaster. Haitians consult with the spirits to seek their approval or counsel before engaging in almost any activity.

Voodooists do not regard this blending of the two faiths as profaning Christianity, but rather as enriching their voodoo cult. This belief is not held by the Catholic Church. In 1941, the church, backed by Haiti's government, began a brutal, short-lived "antisuperstition" campaign to stamp out voodoo, but it was in vain. During Carnival some believers publicly display their sorcery and witchcraft. It is also not unusual for Haitians to celebrate the saint days of Catholic saints along with the voodoo spirits, the *Loa*. The favorite is the spirit of love, *Ezili Freda*.

Haitians take their celebrating very seriously, exerting a great deal of energy. A bowl of soup, such as this one made with **plantains,** is a soothing way for them to revive themselves during the Carnival celebration.

Plantain Soup

Yield: *serves 4 to 6*

  1 green **plantain** (about 1-pound size), **peeled and finely chopped**
  5 cups chicken broth, homemade (recipe page 52) or canned
  salt and pepper to taste
  3 cups cooked rice (keep warm for serving)

Equipment: **Blender** or **food processor**, medium saucepan, mixing spoon, ladle

1. Use blender or food processor to mash plantains.

2. In medium saucepan, combine chicken broth and mashed plantains. Cook over medium heat, stirring frequently, until soup thickens, about 45 minutes. Add salt and pepper to taste, and stir well.

Serve soup while hot, ladling it into individual bowls over a scoop of rice.

A famous Caribbean dish included in all holiday feasts is *callaloo*. The main ingredient is *callaloo*, the leafy green tops of the taro plant. The taro plant is native to the Caribbean and is not easily available; spinach can be used in this recipe instead.

Callaloo

(Also Calalou or Callilu)   Spinach Stew

Yield: *serves 6*

¼ pound salt pork, **finely chopped**
½ pound boneless lean pork, cut into bite-size pieces
2 onions, thinly sliced
4 cups chicken broth, homemade (recipe page 52) or canned
1 tablespoon ground thyme
1½ pounds fresh spinach, stems removed, washed, drained, and **coarsely chopped**, or 24-ounces frozen spinach, thawed
salt and pepper to taste
liquid hot pepper sauce to taste (optional)
3 cups cooked rice (keep warm for serving)

Equipment: **Dutch oven** or large saucepan with cover, mixing spoon

1. Have an adult help you fry salt pork in Dutch oven or large saucepan over high heat, until browned and **rendered**, about 5 minutes.

2. Reduce heat to medium, and carefully drain off all but about 2 tablespoons fat. Add pork pieces and onions, and fry until browned, about 5 minutes. Add chicken broth, thyme, spinach, and salt and pepper to taste, and stir well.

3. Cover, reduce heat to medium-low, and cook for 1 hour. Add pepper sauce to taste. (A little goes a long way.)

To serve, spoon a half cup of rice into each individual bowl and ladle hot callaloo *over it.*

In the Caribbean, fish are plentiful, and most families serve fish for Christmas Eve supper, even though the Catholic Church no longer officially restricts the eating of meat on Christmas Eve.

Run Down Mackerel

Yield: *serves 6*

6 (6 to 8 ounces each) skin-on fish fillets, such as mackerel, red snapper, trout, cod, or haddock
juice of 2 limes
3 cups coconut milk, homemade (recipe page 194) or canned
1 onion, **finely chopped**
3 cloves garlic, finely chopped, or 1 teaspoon garlic granules
liquid hot pepper sauce to taste (optional)
1 (16-ounce) can stewed tomatoes
2 teaspoons ground thyme
1 tablespoon white vinegar
salt and pepper to taste

Equipment: Buttered 13- x 9-inch baking pan, medium saucepan, mixing spoon, fork

1. Place fish fillets side-by-side, flesh-side up, in buttered baking pan and sprinkle with lime juice. Refrigerate while preparing sauce.

Preheat oven to 350° F.

2. In medium saucepan, combine coconut milk, onion, garlic, pepper sauce to taste, tomatoes, thyme, and vinegar. Stirring frequently, cook over medium heat for about 10 minutes, or until thickened. Add salt and pepper to taste, stir, and then spread mixture over fish fillets.

3. Bake fish in oven for about 20 minutes, or until fish is fully cooked and easily flakes when poked with a fork.

Serve hot as the main dish of the Christmas Eve feast.

All Saints' Day on November 1 is a Catholic observance. In Haiti it is called the Day of the Dead. Numerous Haitians, combining Catholic beliefs with Voodoo, flock to the country's cemeteries to repair graves and visit deceased family and friends. Voodoo ceremonies honor both the dead and *Baron Samedi*, the spirit lord of the graveyard. The day is celebrated with music, food, drink, and prayer begging the dead to help the living.

Most Haitians love very sweet pastries and desserts, usually made with coconuts, which grow throughout the Caribbean. Sweets are brought along in the picnic basket to share with the spirits of the dead at the cemetery on the Day of the Dead.

Coconut Almond Tart

Yield: *serves 8 to 10*

½ cup butter or margarine, at room temperature
1½ cups firmly packed light brown sugar
1 cup plus 2 teaspoons all-purpose flour, more as needed
½ teaspoon baking powder
4 eggs
1 teaspoon almond extract
¼ teaspoon salt
1½ cups sweetened flaked coconut
1½ cups **finely chopped** almonds

Equipment: Large mixing bowl, mixing spoon, lightly greased or nonstick 9-inch **springform pan**, oven mitts

Preheat oven to 425° F.

1. Prepare crust: In large mixing bowl, use mixing spoon to mix butter or margarine and ½ cup brown sugar until creamy. Add 1 cup flour, a little at a time, and form into a smooth dough.

2. Using clean hands, press dough over bottom of greased or nonstick 9-inch springform pan. Prick dough 6 or 7 times with fork tines.

3. Bake in oven for about 10 minutes, or until lightly browned. Remove from oven. Set aside.

Reduce oven to 350° F.

4. Prepare filling: In large mixing bowl, use mixing spoon, stir remaining 1 cup brown sugar, 2 teaspoons flour, baking powder, eggs, almond extract, salt, coconut, and almonds. Pour over baked crust, and bake for another 20 minutes, or until lightly browned and set.

To serve, cool to room temperature, and cut into wedges.

Jamaica

As is the case in many Caribbean nations, most Jamaicans are descendants of slaves brought from Africa. To this day, many Jamaican traditions blend African ancestral rituals with Christian observances and British holiday practices.

These new traditions developed as the African slaves adapted to their new surroundings and religion. During the Christmas season, for instance, groups of masqueraders traveled around entertaining slave settlements. The Black entertainers were known as the *Jonkonnu,* or John Canoe. The *Jonkonnu* originated in West Africa, and the name means "deadly sorcerer" or "sorcerer man." The belief was that they were possessed with witchcraft and evil supernatural powers. For a few hours, the slaves left the harsh realities of everyday life for a fantasy world of mystics, clowns, and acrobats. The entertainers wore bright costumes and massive masks shaped like horses and the devil; two of the *Jonkonnu* actors were always dressed as a king and queen. Musicians played as the actors performed. It was customary to feed the *Jonkonnu* troops, and the community feast traditionally included what has become the national dish of Jamaica, curried goat or lamb. Since goat is not readily available at most supermarkets, this recipe can be made with any kind of meat.

Curried Meat

Yield: *serves 4*

2 tablespoons vegetable oil

2 pounds boneless lamb, beef, or pork (or goat, if available), cut into bite-size pieces

2 onions, **coarsely chopped**

1 clove garlic, **finely chopped,** or ½ teaspoon garlic granules

2 tablespoons curry powder, more or less to taste

1 (12-ounce) can whole stewed tomatoes with juice

2 cups water

salt and pepper to taste

4 cups cooked rice (keep warm for serving)

Equipment: **Dutch oven** or large skillet with cover, mixing spoon

1. Heat oil in Dutch oven or large skillet over medium-high heat. Add meat, onions, garlic, and 2 tablespoons curry powder (more or less to taste). Stirring constantly, fry for about 5 minutes until meat is browned.

2. Add stewed tomatoes with juice, water, and salt and pepper to taste, and stir. Reduce heat to simmer, cover, and cook for 1 hour or until meat is tender.

Serve warm, over rice.

Caribbean Banana Bread

Yield: *1 loaf*

½ cup butter or margarine, at room temperature

½ cup sugar

1 egg

2 cups all-purpose flour

1 tablespoon baking powder

½ teaspoon salt

½ teaspoon ground nutmeg

2 large (about ½ pound each), ripe bananas, **peeled** and mashed

1 teaspoon vanilla extract

1 cup seedless raisins

½ cup **coarsely chopped** nuts; pecans, peanuts, or walnuts

Equipment: Large mixing bowl, mixing spoon or electric mixer, medium mixing bowl, greased or nonstick 9- x 5-inch loaf pan, oven mitts, toothpick

Preheat oven to 350° F.

1. In large mixing bowl, use mixing spoon or electric mixer to mix butter or margarine and sugar until light and fluffy, about 3 minutes. Add the egg and mix well.

2. Mix flour, baking powder, salt, and nutmeg in medium mixing bowl.

3. Mixing constantly, add flour mixture, a little at a time, and mashed bananas to sugar mixture in large bowl. Add vanilla, raisins, and nuts, and mix well. Transfer to greased or nonstick loaf pan.

4. Bake in oven for about 1 hour, or until toothpick inserted into middle of bread comes out clean.

To serve, cool to room temperature, remove from pan, and cut into ½-inch slices.

Jerk chicken and pork is what most Jamaicans eat for the Christmas feast; roasting the traditional whole goat, pig, or lamb is just too extravagant for the average family.

Jerk Pork and Chicken

Yield: *serves 6*

4 tablespoons ground allspice

2 onions, **finely chopped**

2 jalapeño peppers, **stemmed**, **seeded**, and finely chopped (Always wear kitchen gloves or plastic baggies when handling hot peppers, and do not rub hands near eyes while working with peppers.)

4 bay leaves, finely crumbled

salt and pepper to taste

1 cup vegetable oil

2 pounds lean pork loin or pork shoulder, cut into strips about 4 inches long and 1 inch thick

2 to 3 pounds chicken, cut into serving-size pieces

2 onions, thinly sliced, for **garnish**

Equipment: Small mixing bowl, mixing spoon, rubber gloves or plastic baggies to cover hands, bowl with cover, charcoal grill with cover or roasting pan with cover, metal tongs, oven mitts

1. Prepare **marinade**: In small mixing bowl, mix allspice, onions, peppers, bay leaves, salt and pepper to taste, and oil.

2. Wearing rubber gloves or plastic baggies to protect your hands, rub pork and chicken with marinade mixture. Put pork and chicken pieces in large bowl, and cover with remaining marinade. Cover bowl, and refrigerate for at least 2 hours; mix pieces around frequently while in refrigerator.

3. To use grill: Have an adult fire the charcoal to medium hot. Place pork and chicken pieces on grill as far from direct heat as possible. Cover grill and cook to desired doneness, about 2 hours. Using metal tongs, turn meat pieces at least once during cooking.

4. To roast in oven: Preheat oven to 350° F. Put pork and chicken pieces in roasting pan, cover, and cook for about 1½ hours, or to desired doneness.

To serve as they do in the Caribbean, transfer to serving platter and garnish with onions.

No Jamaican holiday feast is complete unless the national dish, the "Jamaica Coat of Arms," is on the table.

Jamaica Coat of Arms   Rice and Peas

Yield: *serves 4 to 6*

2 (16-ounce each) cans coconut milk

2 cups rice

1 onion, **finely chopped**

1 clove garlic, finely chopped, or ½ teaspoon garlic granules

2 (16-ounce each) cans black-eyed peas, drained

liquid hot red pepper sauce, to taste

salt and pepper to taste

Equipment: Medium saucepan with cover, mixing spoon

1. In medium saucepan, combine coconut milk, rice, onion, and garlic. Bring to a boil over high heat, and stir. Reduce heat to low, cover, and cook for 30 minutes, until liquid is absorbed.

2. Add peas, hot pepper sauce (to taste), and salt and pepper to the rice mixture, and stir. Cover and cook over low heat to heat through, about 5 minutes.

Coat of arms is served warm, either as a side dish or the main dish on Christmas Eve.

Bahamas

The most colorful holiday events in the Bahamas are the *Jonkonnu* parades held on Boxing Day, December 26, and New Year's Day. As in Jamaica, *Jonkonnu* was brought to the Bahamas centuries ago by African slaves. The parades begin at four in the morning as revelers prance about in brightly colored crepe-paper costumes. *Jonkonnu* dancers paint their faces or wear scary-looking masks, topped with garish headdresses, some several feet high and covered with all sorts of trinkets, spangles, bells, and feathers. The merrymakers greet the dawn and usher in the year ahead by honking horns, pounding drums, tooting whistles, or simply banging big spoons or sticks on pots and pans.

Fritters, of all kinds, are popular snack food during these holiday festivities.

vegetable oil cooking spray
Salsa, sour cream, syrup, or jam, for serving

Equipment: Medium mixing bowl, mixing spoon, small mixing bowl, egg beater or electric mixer, griddle or large skillet, baking sheet, paper towels, metal **spatula**

1. In a medium mixing bowl, use mixing spoon to lightly beat egg yolks. Add corn, milk, and flour, and stir well.

2. In small mixing bowl, use egg beater or electric mixer to beat egg whites until stiff. **Fold** egg whites and salt and pepper to taste into corn mixture.

3. Prepare for frying: Cover baking sheet with several layers of paper towels. Have an adult help you spray surface of griddle or large skillet with cooking spray, and heat over medium-high heat. Carefully drop tablespoonfuls of corn mixture onto pan, and flatten into patties about 3 inches across, using back of metal spatula. Fry for about 3 minutes on each side until browned. Remove with spatula and drain on paper towels. Keep warm until ready to serve. Fry in batches, carefully adding more cooking spray when necessary.

Serve warm as a snack or part of a meal. Salsa, sour cream, syrup, or jam are served with fritters.

As with many island countries, fish is an important part of the Bahamian diet and is eaten during the holiday season.

Corn Fritters

Yield: *serves 6*
- 2 **eggs, separated**
- 2 cups corn kernels, fresh or frozen, thawed or canned, drained
- 3 tablespoons milk
- 2 tablespoons all-purpose flour
- salt and pepper to taste

Bahamas Fish Pie

Yield: *serves 6*
- 2 tablespoons vegetable oil
- 3 onions, thinly sliced
- ½ pound fresh mushrooms, thinly sliced or 1 cup canned, drained
- 1 (16-ounce) can stewed tomatoes with juice
- 1 tablespoon chopped fresh thyme or 1 teaspoon ground thyme

½ teaspoon liquid hot pepper sauce (optional)
salt and pepper to taste
6 (6- to 8-ounce each) skinless fish fillets, each
    cut into 3 pieces
3 cups prepared mashed potatoes, homemade
    or instant
6 tablespoons butter or margarine, more or less
    as needed, or butter-flavored cooking spray

Equipment: Large skillet, mixing spoon, lightly greased or nonstick 13- x 9- x 2-inch baking pan, oven mitts, fork

Preheat oven to 350° F.

1. Heat oil in large skillet over medium heat. Add onions and mushrooms, and, stirring frequently, fry until soft and lightly browned, about 5 minutes. Add tomatoes with juice, thyme, hot pepper sauce (optional), and salt and pepper to taste. Stir and cook until mixture begins to thicken, about 8 minutes; remove from heat.

2. Place fish fillets side-by-side (slightly overlapping, if necessary) in greased or nonstick 13- x 9-inch baking pan. Cover fish with tomato mixture. Spoon mounds of mashed potatoes over top, and dot with butter or margarine or spray with butter-flavored cooking spray. Bake in oven for about 20 minutes. To check if fish is done, poke with a fork; it should flake easily.

3. Preheat broiler: Place baking pan under broiler to lightly brown potatoes, about 5 minutes.

Serve immediately.

Sweets are an important part of every holiday season. The following recipe for coconut loaf cake is made throughout the Caribbean, where coconuts grow in abundance.

Coconut Loaf Cake

½ cup butter or margarine
1¼ cups sugar
2 eggs, beaten

¾ cup milk
2⅔ cups all-purpose flour
4 teaspoons baking powder
1 cup **grated** sweetened coconut
1 teaspoon coconut or vanilla extract
sliced fresh fruit of choice, for serving

Equipment: Large mixing bowl, mixing spoon or electric mixer, rubber **spatula**, buttered or nonstick 9- x 5-inch loaf pan, oven mitts, toothpick

Preheat oven to 350° F.

1. In large mixing bowl, use mixing spoon or electric mixer to mix butter or margarine and sugar until light and fluffy, about 3 minutes. Add eggs and milk, and, stirring constantly, add flour, a little at a time, baking powder, and grated coconut or vanilla extract; blend well. Transfer cake dough to buttered or nonstick loaf pan.

2. Bake in oven for about 1 hour until toothpick inserted in center comes out clean. Cool on rack.

To serve, cut into 1-inch slices, and top with fresh fruit of choice.

The English who have settled in the Bahamas like to keep traditional Christmas customs alive whenever possible. Baking cookies is an easy and important part of that tradition.

Bullas   Caribbean Christmas Cookies

Yield: *2 to 3 dozen*
3 cups all-purpose flour, more as needed
1 teaspoon baking powder
½ teaspoon baking soda
1 teaspoon ground nutmeg
½ teaspoon ground **ginger**
1 cup firmly packed brown sugar
¼ cup water
2 tablespoons butter or margarine

Equipment: Flour **sifter**, large mixing bowl, small saucepan, mixing spoon, floured work surface, floured **rolling pin**, **cookie cutter** or plastic drinking glass, greased or nonstick cookie sheet

Preheat oven to 375° F.

1. Sift 3 cups flour, baking powder, baking soda, nutmeg, and ginger into large mixing bowl; set aside.

2. In small saucepan, combine brown sugar and water, and, stirring constantly, cook over medium-high heat until mixture thickens, about 5 minutes. Reduce heat to low, add butter or margarine, and stir until melted. Cool to warm and pour into flour mixture. Use mixing spoon to form mixture into a firm dough. If mixture is sticky, add a little more flour.

3. Transfer dough to floured work surface, and, using floured rolling pin, roll it about ¼ inch thick. Use cookie cutter or glass rim to cut dough into shapes or disks. Place side by side on cookie sheet.

4. Bake cookies in oven for about 10 minutes, or until golden. Continue baking in batches.

Serve bullas *to friends when they come to visit on Christmas or New Year's Day.*

Cuba

Cuba's population mainly consists of people of Spanish and African origin. Most Cubans are Roman Catholic, but officially Cuba has been an atheist state for most of the era of Fidel Castro, which began in 1959. However, a constitutional amendment passed in 1992 changed Cuba from an atheist to a secular state, thus enabling religious believers to belong to the Cuban Communist Party. Nevertheless, the only official national holidays are civic.

Christian holidays are celebrated in a very solemn manner, with less pageantry than in the other predominantly Catholic countries in Latin America. This situation is a reflection of the stressful conditions in the country. The most important observance is Holy Week, climaxing with Easter.

Most Cubans eat beans and rice extensively. The national dish of Cuba is *Moros y Cristianos,* which means "Moors and Christians," referring to the Moorish conquest of Spain, which finally ended in 1492. A meal, especially a holiday meal, would be incomplete if black beans and rice were not on the table.

Moros y Cristianos — Black Beans and Rice

Yield: *serves 4*
   2 tablespoons vegetable oil
   2 onions, **finely chopped**
   ½ cup finely chopped cooked ham
   1 green bell pepper, **stemmed**, **seeded**, and finely chopped
   3 cloves garlic, finely chopped, or 1 teaspoon garlic granules
   ½ teaspoon dried oregano, crumbled
   ½ teaspoon ground cumin
   1¹/₃ cups rice
   2 cups water
   1 (16-ounce) can black beans or 2 cups cooked dried black beans (cook according to directions on package)
salt and pepper to taste

Equipment: **Dutch oven** or large skillet with cover, mixing spoon, **colander**, fork

1. Heat oil in Dutch oven or large skillet over medium-high heat. Add onions, ham, bell pepper, garlic, oregano, and cumin, and, stirring constantly, fry until soft, about 5 minutes. Add rice and water, stir, and bring to a boil. Reduce heat to simmer, cover, and cook for 20 minutes, until rice is tender.

2. Put black beans in colander, and rinse under running water; drain well. Add beans and salt and pepper to rice. Stir, cover, and cook on low heat for 5 minutes to heat through. Fluff with a fork before serving.

Serve at once while still hot.

Adding meat to rice or black beans is a luxury reserved for holidays, auspicious occasions, or special family gatherings.

Picadillo Habanera Meat Sauce with Rice

Yield: *serves 4*
  2 tablespoons vegetable oil
  ½ pound lean ground beef
  ½ pound lean ground pork
  1 onion, **finely chopped**
  3 cloves garlic, finely chopped, or 1 teaspoon garlic granules
  1 green bell pepper, **cored, seeded,** and finely chopped
  2 cups (16 ounces) canned stewed tomatoes
  salt, more or less to taste
  10 stuffed green olives
  ½ cup seedless raisins
  4 cups cooked rice (keep warm for serving)

Equipment: **Dutch oven** or large saucepan, mixing spoon

1. Heat 2 tablespoons oil in Dutch oven or large saucepan over medium-high heat. Add ground beef, pork, onion, garlic, and green pepper. Stirring constantly, cook until meat browns, about 5 minutes.

2. Add tomatoes, salt to taste, olives, and raisins, and stir. Reduce heat to medium, and cook until mixture thickens, about 25 minutes. Stir frequently to prevent sticking. Reduce heat to low, if necessary.

To serve, divide rice equally among 4 dinner plates, and spoon picadillo habanera *over each serving.*

Cuban oranges are some of the finest in the world. A holiday dinner usually includes oranges in some form.

Orange and Onion Salad

Yield: *serves 4*
  juice of 1 orange
  2 teaspoons sugar
  1 tablespoon mayonnaise
  ½ head iceberg lettuce, finely **shredded**
  1 onion, **finely chopped**
  2 oranges, **peeled, pith** removed, and cut into bite-size chunks

Equipment: Small mixing bowl, mixing spoon, medium salad bowl

1. Mix orange juice, sugar, and mayonnaise in small mixing bowl.

2. Put lettuce, onion, and oranges in medium salad bowl, add orange juice mixture, and toss to mix well. Refrigerate until ready to serve.

Serve chilled as a side dish with meat dishes.

Preparing pastries and cakes for the holiday season is an important Spanish tradition that is still followed by Cubans, who pass recipes from one generation to the next.

Orange Cake

Yield: *serves 8 to 10*
  2 cups flour
  ½ cup baking soda

¼ teaspoon salt

1 cup butter or margarine, at room temperature

¾ cup sugar

2 eggs

1 cup orange juice

¼ cup **grated** orange rind

3 or 4 **peeled** and sliced fresh oranges, for serving

Equipment: Flour **sifter**, small mixing bowl, large mixing bowl, mixing spoon or electric mixer, mixing spoon, rubber **spatula**, **grater**, greased or nonstick 9-inch square cake pan, oven mitts, toothpick

Preheat oven to 350° F.

1. **Sift** flour, baking soda, and salt into small mixing bowl.

2. In large mixing bowl, use mixing spoon or electric mixer to mix butter or margarine and sugar until light and fluffy. Add eggs, one at a time, mixing after each. Stirring constantly, alternate adding flour mixture and orange juice, a little at a time for both. Add orange rind and mix well. Transfer to greased or nonstick 9-inch cake pan.

3. Bake in oven for about 45 minutes, or until toothpick inserted into center of cake comes out clean.

Serve cake cut into squares, and top each serving with sliced oranges.

Latin America

The Roman Catholic Church is a powerful force in Latin America. Most Latin Americans are influenced by it to one degree or another. The church plays such a large role in Latin American life that even government and military celebrations have religious overtones. Elaborate processions and colorful pageantry dominate most celebrations, letting people set aside poverty and hardships, if only for a few hours, to enjoy singing, dancing, feasting, and drinking.

In Central American countries, except for Panama and Belize, the most important national holiday celebrated is probably Independence Day, September 15. This date honors the founding of *Provincias Unidas del Centro de America* in 1823, with five constituent states—Guatemala, Honduras, El Salvador, Nicaragua, and Costa Rica. Each country in South America has a different Independence Day: Chileans celebrate for two days, September 18 and 19; Argentina, July 9; Uruguay, August 25; Bolivia, August 6; Brazil, September 7; Paraguay, May 15; Peru, July 28; Ecuador, August 10; Colombia, July 20; Venezuela, July 5; and in Guyana, Republic Day (*Mashramani*) is a two-week celebration at the end of February.

Other important holidays in most Latin American countries include *Semana Santa* (Holy Week, the week before Easter) and Saints' Days. Every city, town, and village has its own patron saint, and the annual festival or fair on that Saint's day is the foremost local celebration. Schools and businesses close, and there are church services, processions through the streets, dramas, dances, and fiestas. *Semana Santa* is the time when most people get a week-long holiday from work. People often take a trip somewhere, going to the beach or a resort, or to visit faraway family. Often Holy Week is the only time of the year they can do it, so it's a special holiday for secular as well as religious reasons.

The foods prepared for holidays are steeped in superstitions and folklore. Because meat is a rarity for many people, the supreme holiday feast must include meat: In some countries it's beef, in others, llama, pork, or *cabrito* (roasted goat). For most, adding even a little meat to soup or stew makes a meal special and festive.

Chile

Most Chileans are Roman Catholic, and nearly every aspect of life in Chile centers around the church. Festivals, and there are many, combine the Indian folklore of the native inhabitants with Catholic rituals brought by the Spanish. For instance, the Festival of *la Tirana,* the festival of the tyrant, celebrates an Indian princess who converted to Catholicism. Unfortunately, she went crazy in her zeal to convert her tribe, and so others in the tribe murdered her. Although this sounds like a morbid celebration, it is actually a very joyous occasion. There is music, dancing, feasting, and pageantry, with actors reenacting the story of the tyrant. At the end of the reenactment, everyone cheers and joins in the merriment to celebrate the triumph of good over evil. During the festival, *porotos granados* (vegetable stew, recipe follows later in this section) is cooked in large kettles to be served with tortillas (recipe page 249).

Even secular holidays and events have religious overtones. The cadets in military parades carry statues or pictures of the patron saint of the armed forces. In fishing villages, an image of the patron saint of fishers blesses the first catch of the day.

The religious beliefs are so strong that every Latin American country has a patron saint, and that saint's feast day is celebrated as a national holiday. In Chile, the patron saint is Saint James, and his feast day is celebrated on July 25. The government and churches put together a wonderful celebration, including grand parades, festivals, fireworks, contests, and exhibitions.

Much of Chile borders the Pacific Ocean, and so naturally seafood, especially eel, is eaten at most holiday feasts. The following fish stew, *sopa de pescado,* is often served for Christmas Eve dinner.

Sopa de Pescado   Fish Stew

Yield: serves 4 to 6

  2 tablespoons butter or margarine
  1 onion, **finely chopped**
  1 (12-ounce) can stewed tomatoes
  3 potatoes, **peeled** and **coarsely chopped**
  2 carrots, **trimmed** and coarsely chopped
  4 cups water
  2 bay leaves
  salt and pepper to taste
  1 to 1½ pounds fish fillets or scallops, coarsely chopped

Equipment: **Dutch oven** or large saucepan with cover, mixing spoon

1. Melt butter or margarine in Dutch oven or large saucepan over medium-high heat. Add onion, and, stirring constantly, fry about 3 minutes, until soft. Add tomatoes, potatoes, carrots, water, bay leaves, and salt and pepper to taste. Stir and bring to a boil over high heat. Reduce heat to simmer, cover, and cook for 20 minutes.

2. Add fish or scallops, stir, and cook for 10 minutes more, or until fish and scallops are done. Remove and discard bay leaves before serving.

Serve warm as the main dish for the Christmas Eve supper.

The Indians of Chile believe all food to be sacred. A typical Indian ritual meal, such as the following vegetable stew, combines beans, corn, and squash—some of the food staples native to the Americas.

Porotos Granados   Vegetable Stew

Yield: serves 6 to 8

- 2 tablespoons olive oil
- 1½ cups **coarsely chopped onions**
- 3 cloves garlic, **finely chopped**, or 1 teaspoon garlic granules
- 2 cups coarsely chopped canned Italian tomatoes with juice
- 1 teaspoon ground basil
- 1 teaspoon ground oregano
- 2 cups squash, **coarsely chopped** (½-inch cubes), **peeled**, and **seeded**
- 4 cups cooked navy beans, dried, homemade (cook according to directions on package) or canned navy beans
- 1 cup frozen corn kernels, thawed
- salt and pepper to taste

Equipment: **Dutch oven** or large saucepan with cover, mixing spoon

1. Heat oil in Dutch oven or large saucepan over medium-high heat. Add onions and garlic, and, stirring constantly, fry for about 3 minutes until soft. Add tomatoes with juice, basil, oregano, and squash, and stir. Reduce heat to simmer, cover, and cook for 20 minutes.

2. Add cooked beans with juice, corn, and salt and pepper to taste, and stir well. Cover and cook over low heat for 15 minutes to heat through and blend flavors.

Serve as a vegetarian meal-in-a-bowl or as a side dish with meat.

Throughout Latin America, the traditional Christmas Eve dessert is milk pudding (recipe page 223). The recipe is basically the same in all Latin American countries; only the names change. In Chile it's called *manjar blanco.*

Argentina

Because Argentina is in the Southern Hemisphere, some of the Catholic holiday traditions brought by the Spanish have evolved into new Argentine traditions. Christmas, for example, falls in the middle of Argentina's hot, dry summer. The Christmas season begins on Christmas Eve or with morning mass, and the rest of the day is usually very quiet. Dinner is generally served outside under a shade tree or on the veranda, and the table is decorated with freshly cut red flowers. The Christmas dinner for most Argentines is beef stew, except for the affluent, who feast on roasted suckling pig.

As in Spain and other European countries, all the merriment of Christmas is delayed until Three Kings' Day on January 6, also known as Epiphany. Children place their shoes by the side of the bed to have them filled with toys and candy by the Three Wise Men, who travel by horse or camel. The children set water and hay outside in the yard for the animals.

For the Christmas feast and other special occasions, the beef stew is served in a pumpkin shell, making it much more festive. (It might be hard to find pumpkins at Christmas, so you might try this method around Halloween.)

Pumpkin Shell Bowl

1 pumpkin (about 8 to 10 pounds)

Equipment: Sharp knife, baking sheet, oven mitts

Preheat oven to 250° F.

1. Cut off the top of the pumpkin, about ¼ of the way down. Scoop out seeds and stringy fibers. Place pumpkin shell and top on baking sheet.

2. Bake in oven for about 1 hour.

3. Using oven mitts, remove pumpkin from oven, and set aside to cool to room temperature.

To serve pumpkin shell, place pumpkin on heat-proof serving platter, fill with stew (see next recipe), and cover with the top. Place filled pumpkin on the dinner table and serve guests by ladling stew into individual bowls.

Carbonada Criolla   Meat Stew with Vegetables and Fruit

Yield: serves 6

2 tablespoons vegetable oil

2 onions, **finely chopped**

1 green pepper, **cored, seeded,** and **finely chopped**

2 pounds lean beef steak, cut into ½-inch cubes

1 (12-ounce) can whole stewed tomatoes

2 cups water

2 cups corn kernels, fresh or frozen, thawed or canned, drained

1 pound potatoes, cooked, **peeled,** and sliced

4 fresh peaches, peeled, pitted, and sliced or 2 cups frozen sliced peaches, thawed

1½ pounds cooked sweet potatoes, peeled and cut into ½-inch cubes

2 cups cooked pumpkin or squash, peeled and cut into ½-inch cubes

salt and pepper, to taste

1 tablespoon sugar, more if necessary

Equipment: **Dutch oven** or large saucepan with cover, mixing spoon, prepared pumpkin shell (directions precede) or large heat-proof serving casserole, ladle

1. Heat oil in Dutch oven or large saucepan over medium-high heat. Add onions and green peppers, and fry until soft, about 3 minutes. Add steak cubes, and, stirring constantly, fry until browned, about 5 minutes.

2. Add tomatoes and water, stir, and bring to a boil. Reduce heat to simmer, cover, and cook for 30 minutes until meat is tender.

3. Add corn, potatoes, peaches, sweet potatoes, and pumpkin or squash. Add salt and pepper to taste and 1 tablespoon sugar. (Add more sugar if mixture isn't sweet enough for your taste.) Gently toss so that mixture doesn't get mushy, and cook to heat through, about 10 minutes.

To serve, either transfer stew to prepared pumpkin shell (recipe precedes) or to a large, heat-proof serving casserole.

Milk puddings are a soothing and pleasant end to the Christmas feast. Every Spanish-speaking country has a pudding; the names might be different, but the recipes are basically the same.

Dulce de Leche   Milk Pudding

Yield: serves 6 to 8

1 (15-ounce) can evaporated milk

3 cups whole milk

½ teaspoon baking soda

1 cup dark brown sugar

¼ cup water

Equipment: Medium saucepan, wooden mixing spoon, small saucepan

1. In medium saucepan, combine evaporated milk, whole milk, and baking soda, and, stirring constantly, bring just to a boil over high heat. Remove from heat at once.

2. In small saucepan, combine brown sugar and water. Cook over low heat until sugar dissolves, about 3 minutes. Stirring constantly, add brown sugar mixture to milk mixture in the medium saucepan. Stirring frequently, cook over very low heat for about 1½ hours, until thickened and amber-colored. Cool to room temperature, cover, and refrigerate.

Serve at room temperature or cold in individual dessert cups.

Uruguay

Most people of Uruguay are of Spanish or Italian origin. There are very few *mestizos* (people of mixed Spanish and Indian origin), since no sizable Indian civilization ever existed in Uruguay. Most Uruguayans are Roman Catholic, but unlike many other Latin American countries, the church and state are separate.

Uruguay's most important holiday season begins with Carnival and climaxes with Easter. During Holy Week, the people of Uruguay also celebrate *la Semana Criolla,* a week-long rodeo with horse breaking, stunt riding, dancing, and singing.

Because Uruguay is a cattle-producing nation, Uruguayans love beef. It is often prepared for important occasions. The amount of meat served depends upon the wealth of the family. The most affluent have their cooks prepare an elaborate *asado,* a side of beef roasted on the open fire. Many Uruguayans prepare their own beef on a backyard grill. The less fortunate have a vegetable stew with chunks of beef in it. The following recipe for asado, roasted beef, is baked in the oven instead of using a grill.

Asado   Roasted Beef

Yield: serves 8 to 10

    4 to 5 pounds lean bottom round of beef, in one piece

    ¼ cup vinegar

    1 onion, **finely chopped**

    3 cloves garlic, finely chopped, or 1 teaspoon garlic granules

    2 tablespoons dark brown sugar

    salt and pepper to taste

    ¼ cup olive oil

    3 cups hot water

Equipment: Roasting pan with cover or 13- x 9-inch baking pan and aluminum foil, small mixing bowl, mixing spoon, **bulb baster**, oven mitts

1. Put beef in roasting pan or 13- x 9-inch baking pan.

2. In small mixing bowl, mix vinegar, onion, garlic, brown sugar, salt and pepper, and olive oil. Rub mixture over meat, cover with lid or foil, and refrigerate for 4 hours, turning meat frequently to **marinate.**

Preheat oven to 450° F.

3. Bake meat, uncovered, in oven for 20 minutes; reduce heat to 325°, add hot water, and bake for another 2 hours, or until meat reaches desired doneness; baste frequently using mixing spoon or bulb baster. Allow meat to sit and cool for 30 minutes before slicing.

To serve, cut into ½-inch-thick slices. The pan drippings can be degreased and served as a sauce with the meat.

Throughout Latin American countries, Roman Catholic nuns are credited with creating many wonderful pastries and candies. One popular holiday dessert they created is *chajá,* a delicious cream-filled sponge cake.

Chajá Cream Filled Sponge Cake

Yield: serves 8 to 10
  4 **eggs, separated**
  1 cup sugar
  juice and **grated rind of 1 lemon**
  1 cup all-purpose flour
  ¼ teaspoon salt
  cream filling (recipe follows)
  2 tablespoons confectioners' sugar, for **garnish**

Equipment: Medium mixing bowl, egg beater or electric mixer, **grater**, large mixing bowl, whisk or rubber **spatula**, flour **sifter**, ungreased 9-inch **tube pan,** toothpick, oven mitts

Preheat oven to 325° F

1. In medium mixing bowl, use egg beater or electric mixer to beat egg whites until stiff. Set aside.

2. In large mixing bowl, use egg beater or electric mixer to beat egg yolks until light and thick, about 3 minutes. Mixing constantly, add sugar, a little at a time, lemon juice, and grated rind. Mix until thickened, about 3 minutes. Using whisk or rubber spatula, **fold in** egg white.

3. Put flour and salt in sifter and **sift** over egg mixture. Using whisk or rubber spatula, gently fold in salt and flour, and blend well. Transfer mixture to ungreased tube pan, and bake in oven for 1 hour, or until toothpick inserted in cake comes out clean. Invert cake onto rack, cool to room temperature, and remove from pan.

4. Using serrated knife, cut cake into 3 layers. Place bottom layer of cake on serving plate, spread each layer generously with cream filling (recipe follows), and set top layers in place. Refrigerate for at least 4 hours. Before serving, sprinkle cake with confectioners' sugar.

To serve, cut cake into wedges.

Cream Filling for Chajá

Yield: about 1½ cups
  1 cup thawed, frozen whipped topping
  ½ cup orange, lemon, or pineapple marmalade

Equipment: Small mixing bowl, rubber **spatula** or mixing spoon

In small mixing bowl, use rubber spatula or mixing spoon to **fold** marmalade into whipped topping.

Use as filling for chajá (recipe precedes).

Bolivia

Sixty percent of Bolivia's population are descendants of Inca and other pre-Columbian Indians, and most are Roman Catholic. The Indians interweave Indian and Christian symbolism in their frequent and fascinating regional festivals, which are among the most spectacular in South America.

One example of this blending of traditions is the devil dances at the annual Carnival of Oruro. One of the great folkloric events of South America, it is held annually in the city of Oruro in central Bolivia. The Carnival of Oruro, as well as other festivals, honor Jesus Christ and the local Maya god, as well as celebrating the seasonal planting and harvesting.

The ritual dances performed at these festivals are a form of narrative drama in which events from history are re-enacted. For both dancers and spectators, these dramatizations are powerful, with the actors putting a lot of emotion into their roles. Each performer takes part in telling the age-old story of good over evil.

Another example is the *Pujilay* festival ("Dance of the Conquest"), held in early March in the south central city of Tarabuco, which honors the 1816 victory by local Indians over the Spanish who had come to the region to pillage the silver mines. For the "Dance of the Conquest," performers wear large animal masks, and others dress in black and wear grotesque masks to represent evil.

There are always plenty of food vendors at these festivals selling such things as tortillas, *empanadas* (recipe follows later in this section), and bean and vegetable stews.

The favorite Christian celebration in Bolivia is Carnival. Everyone dons costumes and masks to take part in the merriment. Many people throw water-filled balloons, called *bombast,* and this fun goes on for three days.

Holiday feasts throughout Latin American countries include avocados, which are nutritious, delicious, and plentiful.

The Spanish word for avocado is *aguacate,* but in some South American countries it is called *palta,* a word of Aztecan Indian origin.

Paltas Rellenas   Stuffed Avocados

Yield: serves 4

2 ripe avocados
½ cup **finely chopped** cooked chicken, turkey, or shrimp
½ cup salad dressing or mayonnaise
salt and pepper to taste
4 leaf lettuce leaves, washed and dried, for serving
2 hard-cooked eggs, **peeled** and **sliced,** for **garnish**

Equipment: Knife, teaspoon, medium bowl, mixing spoon

1. Cut avocados in half lengthwise, and remove and discard pit. Using a spoon, scoop out pulp in bite-sized pieces, keeping skin shells intact to refill. Put pulp in medium mixing bowl, and add cooked chicken, turkey, or shrimp; salad dressing or mayonnaise; and salt and pepper to taste. Using mixing spoon, toss gently to coat.

2. Mound mixture into skin shells and serve at once.

To serve, place lettuce leaves on salad plates. Set a filled avocado in the center of each leaf, and garnish with hard-cooked eggs.

During the holiday season street vendors do a brisk business from busy parishioners who pick up *empanadas* to snack on on the way to and from church. They are popular throughout Latin America.

Empanadas de Queso

Cheese Turnovers

CAUTION: HOT OIL USED

Yield: about 30

½ pound **shredded** cheddar cheese

4 green onions, **trimmed** and **finely chopped**

3 eggs, beaten

½ teaspoon chili powder, more or less to taste

½ teaspoon ground cumin

salt and pepper to taste

pie crust dough, homemade (recipe page 108), or commercial pie crust dough for casing

vegetable oil for **deep frying**

Equipment: Medium mixing bowl, mixing spoon, lightly floured work surface, floured rolling pin, 4-inch **cookie cutter** or water glass, tablespoon, cup of water, fork, **deep fryer** (see glossary for tips on making one), wooden spoon, paper towels, baking sheet, tongs or **slotted spoon**.

1. Prepare filling: In medium mixing bowl, combine cheese, onions, eggs, ½ teaspoon chili powder (more or less to taste), cumin, and salt and pepper to taste. Refrigerate for 1 hour before using.

2. Prepare and assemble turnovers: Divide pie crust dough into two balls. Roll out one ball about ⅛ inch thick on lightly floured work surface using floured rolling pin. Using 4-inch cookie cutter or rim of glass, cut dough into circles. Place 1 tablespoon of cheese mixture on each circle and fold over. Dip your clean finger into cup of water, and use it to moisten the edges of pastry; press the edges together with fork tines to firmly seal. Continue making turnovers until dough or filling is used up.

3. Prepare deep fryer: Have an adult help you heat oil to 375° F. Oil is hot enough for frying when small bubbles appear around a wooden spoon handle when it is dipped in the oil. Place several layers of paper towels on baking sheet. Carefully fry turnovers in small batches for about 3 minutes or until golden on both sides. Remove with metal tongs or slotted spoon, and drain on paper towels.

Serve while warm.

It's always nice to have a container of cookies on hand to serve visitors during the holidays. *Pastelitos* (recipe follows) are popular Christmas cookies throughout the Mediterranean region of Europe. The Spanish settlers brought the recipe to Bolivia.

Pastelitos de Almendra

Almond Cookies

Yield: about 28 pieces

2 cups almonds, finely **ground**

1 ⅓ cups sugar

3 **egg whites**

1 teaspoon almond extract

Equipment: Medium mixing bowl, mixing spoon, tablespoon, 2 lightly greased or nonstick cookie sheets, oven mitts

Preheat oven to 325° F.

1. In medium mixing bowl, mix almonds, sugar, egg whites, and almond extract until well blended.

2. Drop heaping tablespoonfuls of dough onto lightly greased or nonstick cookie sheet, about 1 inch apart.

4. Bake in oven for about 25 minutes, or until crisp on the outside, soft on the inside.

Serve as a sweet snack.

Brazil

Most Brazilians are Roman Catholic descendants of Portuguese and Spanish settlers, African slaves brought to work on the plantations, and indigenous Indians. This mix of ancestors has created what people in Brazil like to think of as a "new" race of Brazilians. Brazilians speak Portuguese. The most exciting holiday in Brazil is the famous pre-Lent Carnival. Brazilians, especially in Rio de Janeiro, go all out. Revelers pour buckets of water and flour on anyone unlucky enough to get in the way, and sometimes even paint-filled balloon bombs are used during the wild festivities.

During the three-day Carnival, thousands of people parade around in outlandish costumes or are clad in almost nothing at all. Nonstop singing, dancing, and partying goes on at many high-spirited masquerade balls. All festivities come to a screeching halt with the Cremation of Sadness and the beginning of Lent. The Cremation of Sadness was brought to Brazil by Africans. Combining African ancestral and spirit worship with Catholic rituals, it is a time to remember the dead, attend to graves, and decorate them with flowers.

During Carnival, Brazil's national dish, *feijoada*, is the favorite meal. Eating *feijoada* takes several hours, followed by a much-needed *siesta* (midday nap), and so Brazilians reserve it for special occasions. The side dishes, such as *laranjas*, are as important as the stew.

Laranjas — Orange Salad

Yield: serves 8

    5 oranges, peeled
    1 teaspoon sugar
    salt and pepper to taste

Equipment: Serrated-edge paring knife, serving plate, plastic wrap

1. Remove **pith** from oranges, and, using serrated paring knife, cut oranges into ⅛-inch slices. Arrange them, overlapping, on serving plate and sprinkle with sugar and salt and pepper to taste. Cover with plastic wrap and refrigerate until ready to serve.

Serve as a side dish with feijoada *(recipe follows).*

Feijoada — Brazilian Meat Stew

Yield: serves 8

    4 cups canned black beans with liquid
    3 slices bacon, **coarsely chopped**
    2 onions, **finely chopped**
    3 cloves garlic, finely chopped, or 1 teaspoon
        garlic granules
    1 pound *each* boneless lean beef and pork cut
        into bite-size pieces (any cuts of meat)
    1 pound smoked sausage (such as Mexican
        chorizo), cut into 1-inch pieces
    2 cups stewed tomatoes, with juice
    1 cup hot water, more or less if necessary
    1 tablespoon prepared yellow mustard
    salt and pepper to taste
    ¼ cup bread crumbs, for **garnish**
    4 cups cooked rice (keep warm for serving)

orange salad, for serving (recipe precedes)
shredded greens, for serving (recipe follows)
salsa, for serving, (available at all supermarkets)

Equipment: Small bowl, potato masher or fork, **Dutch oven** or large saucepan with cover, mixing spoon

1. Put 1 cup black beans in small bowl, and, using a potato masher or back of fork, coarsely mash, and set aside.

2. Fry bacon pieces in Dutch oven or large saucepan over medium-high heat, stirring frequently until soft and **rendered,** about 3 minutes. Reduce heat to medium. Add onions and garlic, stir, and fry until soft, about 3 minutes.

3. Add beef, pork, and sausage, and, stirring constantly, fry until browned on all sides, about 5 minutes. Add tomatoes with juice, 1 cup hot water, mustard, mashed beans, and salt and pepper to taste, and stir. Reduce heat to simmer, cover, and cook for 45 minutes, stirring frequently. If stew is getting too thick, add just enough hot water to prevent it from sticking to pan. Stir in remaining 3 cups beans, cover, and cook for 10 minutes to heat through.

To serve, transfer to serving bowl, and sprinkle with bread crumbs for garnish. Serve with side dishes of cooked rice, orange salad (recipe precedes), shredded greens (recipe follows), and a small bowl of salsa.

Couve a Mineira   Shredded Greens

Yield: serves 8

2 slices bacon, **finely chopped**
3 pounds fresh spinach, collard greens, or kale, **stemmed**, washed, and **blanched** or frozen, thawed, and **coarsely chopped**, drained well
salt and pepper to taste

Equipment: Large skillet, mixing spoon or metal tongs

1. Fry bacon in large skillet over high heat, stirring constantly, until soft and **rendered,** about 3 minutes.

2. Reduce heat to medium, add spinach, collard greens or kale, and, tossing constantly, fry for about 3 minutes until soft. Add salt and pepper to taste, toss to mix, and transfer to serving bowl.

Serve warm as a side dish with feijoada *(recipe precedes).*

During Carnival, *acarajé* are the favorite street snack. They originated in the Bahia region of Brazil, made by descendants of West African slaves. The women of the region dress in the brightly colored traditional costumes and work over heavy black pots of boiling palm oil in which they fry *acarajé*.

Acarajé   Black-Eyed Pea Fritters

CAUTION: HOT OIL USED
Yield: serves 6

4 cups cooked black-eyed peas, either frozen (cooked according to directions on package) and drained; or canned, drained
1 onion, **finely chopped**
2 eggs, beaten
2 tablespoons all-purpose flour
salt and pepper to taste
vegetable cooking oil spray
3 to 6 drops liquid red pepper sauce, for serving (optional)

Equipment: Medium mixing bowl and potato masher or electric **food processor**, baking sheet, paper towels, large skillet, metal **spatula**

1. If you are using a potato masher, put black-eyed peas in medium mixing bowl and mash until smooth. If you are using an electric food processor, put black-eyed peas in processor and mix until smooth. Add onion, eggs, flour, and salt and pepper to taste; mix well.

2. Cover baking sheet with several layers of paper towels. Have an adult help you spray cooking oil spray over surface of large skillet; heat over medium-high heat.

3. Make patties out of black-eyed pea mixture. The patties should be about ¼ inch thick and 2 inches across. Carefully fry patties for about 3 minutes on each side, until browned. Remove patties from skillet, and drain on paper towels. Keep in warm place, and continue frying in batches, adding more cooking oil spray each time.

Serve acarajé *as snack food or as a side dish. If you like them hot, sprinkle with liquid red pepper sauce.*

Brazilians love sweets, and no home would be ready to celebrate Easter, Christmas, Carnival, or any other holiday unless batches of very sweet cookies and candies were ready for munching.

Brasileiras   Brazilian Coconut Cookies

Yield: about 3 dozen
  1 cup sugar
  ½ cup water
  4 **egg yolks**, beaten
  ¼ cup all-purpose flour
  2 cups sweetened coconut flakes
  1 teaspoon vanilla extract

Equipment: Medium saucepan, wooden mixing spoon, cup, **candy thermometer**, medium mixing bowl, greased or nonstick cookie sheet, oven mitts

1. Stir sugar and water together in medium saucepan over medium heat until sugar dissolves, about 3 minutes. Cook, without stirring, until mixture reaches 230°F. on candy thermometer. (If you don't have a candy thermometer, watch carefully and test frequently; to test, drop a little syrup off a spoon into a cup of cold water. If the syrup forms a thin flexible thread as it drips into the water it is ready.) Remove from heat.

2. In medium mixing bowl, combine egg yolks and flour. Add 4 tablespoons hot sugar mixture, and mix well.

3. Stirring constantly, add egg yolk mixture, coconut, and vanilla to pan of hot syrup; stir well. Cook over low heat, stirring frequently, until thick and stiff. Do not boil. Cool to room temperature.

Preheat oven to 375° F.

4. Using wet, clean hands, form mixture into ping-pong-size balls. Place balls about 1 inch apart on greased or nonstick cookie sheets.

5. Bake cookies in oven for about 15 minutes, or until golden brown.

Serve as a sweet snack when cool.

Paraguay

Most Paraguayans are Roman Catholic *mestizos*—people of mixed Spanish and Indian origins. Celebrations combine Catholicism with ancient tribal rituals. Every village has a patron saint, and annual festivals are held to honor each village's saint. On the saint's feast days, a statue of the saint, colorfully decorated with streamers and flowers, is carried in a procession around the town. The people of Paraguay love music, and it is the custom for musicians to play guitars, accordions, and the famous Paraguayan harp, *arpa Paraguya*, to accompany the parading worshippers.

As in many countries in Latin America, the most important holiday season begins with Carnival and climaxes with Easter. The holiday feasts are usually *asados* (recipe page 224), roasted beef prepared over an open fire. In many villages a communal feast is prepared on a saint's name day or important holiday so no one will go hungry. The meal begins with meat soup made from bones and innards of the beef. The soup is served with the national dish of Paraguay, *sopa paraguaya*. Although *sopa* means soup, the following recipe is not a soup but rather a soft corn bread eaten with soup.

Sopa Paraguaya — Paraguayan Corn Bread

Yield: serves 8 to 10

- 2 cups canned cream-style corn
- 1 cup yellow cornmeal
- 1 cup melted butter or margarine
- ¾ cup buttermilk
- 1 onion, **finely chopped**
- 2 eggs, beaten
- ½ teaspoon baking soda
- 2 cups **shredded** sharp Cheddar cheese

Equipment: Large mixing bowl, mixing spoon or electric mixer, greased or nonstick 9-inch square baking pan, rubber **spatula**, oven mitts

Preheat oven to 350° F

1. In large mixing bowl, use mixing spoon or electric mixer to mix creamed corn, cornmeal, melted butter or margarine, buttermilk, onion, eggs, and baking soda until well blended. Spread half the mixture in greased or nonstick baking pan. Sprinkle with 1 cup shredded cheese, and cover with remaining mixture. Sprinkle remaining 1 cup cheese over the top.

2. Bake in oven for 1 hour, or until golden and cake pulls away from sides of pan. Cool for 15 minutes before serving.

To serve, cut into squares.

Peru

Much like the other countries along the Andes mountain chain on the west coast of South America, Peru is a country of mixed cultural heritage, the product of the clash between the Incan and Spanish empires. Today, the people of Peru combine Indian beliefs of the Incas with Spanish Catholicism in elaborate and gaudy religious celebrations. During Carnival, the celebration on the last day before Lent, the cultures merge as people parade down the streets wearing outlandish costumes, face paints, and grotesque Indian masks. Some Carnival revelers go wild throwing balloon bombs full of flour, paint, and oil on anyone unlucky enough to get in the line of fire.

One of the highlights of the year is the spectacular Good Friday night procession that ends Holy Week. The image of Christ is carried in a coffin through the streets as onlookers kneel and pray. Peru is plagued with earthquakes, and many villages, hoping for miracles, include *El Señor de los Temblores*, the Lord of Earthquakes, in the procession.

According to Indian legend, eating potatoes ensures a good harvest, and, if the potatoes are yellow, good fortune is added. An herb native to Peru gives the yellow color, but for our purposes turmeric is a good substitute. A holiday feast, such as the ones for Christmas, Easter, or Carnival, would be incomplete if *papas a la huancaína* weren't on the table.

Papas a la Huancaína
Yellow Potatoes

Yield: serves 6

¼ cup lemon juice

⅛ teaspoon ground red pepper, more or less to taste

salt to taste

1 onion, thinly sliced

2 tablespoons vegetable oil

3 cups shredded Monterey Jack, Swiss, or Münster cheese

½ teaspoon ground **turmeric**

1½ cups heavy cream

6 boiled potatoes, drained, **peeled**, and quartered

4 hard-cooked eggs, shelled and halved, for **garnish**

3 ears of corn, cooked (cut each ear crosswise into 3 pieces), for garnish

6 to 8 black olives, for garnish

Equipment: Small mixing bowl, mixing spoon, large skillet, medium serving bowl

1. In small mixing bowl, combine lemon juice, ⅛ teaspoon red pepper more or less to taste, and salt to taste. Add onion slices, coat them with mixture, and set aside.

2. Heat oil in large skillet over low heat. Add cheese, turmeric, and heavy cream. Stirring constantly, continue cooking over low heat, until cheese melts and mixture is smooth. Add potatoes, and gently stir to heat through, about 5 minutes. Do not allow mixture to boil, or it will curdle. Transfer to serving bowl and garnish with eggs,

corn, and olives. Sprinkle onions from step 1 over the potatoes.

Serve at once while hot.

All Saint's Day and All Soul's Day, November 1 and 2, are events in the Catholic religious calendar. Small villages come alive with a procession to the cemetery to remember their dead, clean the graves, and decorate them with flowers. While the purpose is somber, the event is turned into a picnic, full of merrymaking and laughter. Families go to the cemetery and takes lots of food for themselves and their friends. At night, everyone goes visiting from one family plot to another within the cemetery, leaving flowers and lighting candles on the graves of relatives and friends, chatting with one another, and eating.

Included in the picnic basket to eat at the cemetery on All Souls' Day and All Saints' Day are *papas rellenas*.

Papas Rellenas
Potatoes Stuffed with Meat

Yield: serves 6

6 tablespoons butter or margarine, more or less as needed

1 onion, **finely chopped**

1 clove garlic or ½ teaspoon garlic granules

1 pound lean ground pork, beef, or combination

3 hard-cooked eggs, finely chopped

salt and pepper to taste

5 cups mashed potatoes, homemade, or prepared instant potatoes

2 eggs, beaten

¼ cup water

½ cup all-purpose flour, more as needed

Equipment: Large skillet, mixing spoon, wax paper, work surface, small shallow bowl, fork, pie pan, metal **spatula**

1. Melt 2 tablespoons butter or margarine in large skillet over medium heat. Add onion, garlic, and ground meat, and, stirring constantly, fry until onions are soft and meat is browned, about 5 minutes. Remove from heat, add hard-cooked eggs and salt and pepper to taste, and stir well. Set aside until cool enough to handle.

3. Divide meat mixture into 6 balls, and place on wax-paper-covered work surface. Divide mashed potatoes into 6 portions. Using clean hands, cover meat with mashed potatoes, and form into balls. Set on wax paper.

4. In small, shallow bowl, beat eggs and water with a fork. Put ½ cup flour in pie pan. Roll each potato ball in egg mixture and then in flour, coating all sides.

5. Melt 4 tablespoons butter or margarine in large skillet over medium heat. Add potato balls, and fry until browned on all sides, about 10 minutes. Add more butter or margarine, if necessary.

Serve warm or at room temperature.

Most Latin American holiday feasts end with milk pudding (recipe page 223). The recipes are basically the same, but the names are different. In Peru it is called *natillas piutanas*.

Ecuador

Most Spanish-speaking Ecuadorians are Roman Catholic *mestizos* (people of mixed Spanish and Indian heritage). The people of Ecuador combine Catholicism with ancient Inca beliefs. As in many other countries in Latin America, even secular holidays are celebrated with elaborate religious processions. These secular holidays include the birthdays of famous men like Simón Bolívar, the liberator of South America; the discovery of America; Independence Day; Labor Day; and *Carnaval Minero*, a festival honoring miners.

The most important religious observances coincide with spring, and there are festivals in every region of the country beginning with Carnival and coming to a climax at Easter, which is the most important holiday in Ecuador. As part of the Easter celebration, churches stage elaborate processions through towns and villages. The processions generally consist of a statue of Christ being carried through the streets, and it is considered a great honor to be selected to carry the statue. As onlookers rush up to touch the flowers draped over the statue and the stretcher carrying it, other worshippers kneel and pray as it passes.

Most Easter feasts are held on Holy Saturday before mass. The feast usually consists of *sopa de crema de coco* (recipe follows), *llapingachos* with *salsa de mali* (recipes follow later in this section), and *capritoda* (recipe follows later in this section).

Sopa de Crema de Coco

Cream of Coconut Soup

Yield: serves 6 to 8

2 tablespoons butter or margarine

1 onion, **finely chopped**

2 tablespoons all-purpose flour

6 cups chicken broth, homemade (recipe page 52) or canned

1¼ cups coconut milk, homemade (recipe page 194) or canned

Equipment: Medium saucepan with cover, mixing spoon, small bowl, cup

1. Melt butter or margarine in medium saucepan over medium-high heat. Add onion, and fry until soft, about 3 minutes. Reduce heat to medium.

2. In a small bowl, add flour to ¼ cup chicken broth, and stir until smooth. Add flour and broth mixture to onion, stir, and cook for 1 minute until thickened. Stirring constantly, slowly add remaining 5¾ cups broth. Cover and cook for 15 minutes.

3. Stirring constantly, add coconut milk, a little at a time. Continue stirring until heated through, about 3 minutes. Do not boil.

Serve soup warm in individual bowls or cups.

Potatoes, which originally were cultivated in the Andes and brought to Europe, are a mainstay of the Ecuadorian diet and are served at every meal. This recipe for potato cakes, *llapingacho*s, is a favorite for the Easter feast.

Llapingachos   Ecuadorian Potato Cakes

Yield: serves 8
  8 tablespoons butter or margarine, more or less as needed
  2 onions, **finely chopped**
  4 cups mashed potatoes, homemade, or prepared instant potatoes
  2 eggs, beaten
  2 cups **shredded** cheese: Münster, Monterey Jack, mozzarella, or Cheddar
  salt and pepper to taste

Equipment: Medium skillet, mixing spoon, medium mixing bowl, baking sheet, wax paper, metal **spatula**

1. Melt 2 tablespoons butter or margarine in medium skillet over medium-high heat. Add onions, and, stirring constantly, fry until soft, about 3 minutes. Transfer fried onions to medium mixing bowl. Add 4 tablespoons butter or margarine, mashed potatoes, eggs, cheese, and salt and pepper to taste, and stir well. Using wet, clean hands, divide potato mixture into 12 balls.

2. Cover baking sheet with wax paper. Flatten potato balls into patties about ½ inch thick, and place on wax paper. Refrigerate for about 2 hours, or until ready to fry.

3. Melt 2 tablespoons butter or margarine in medium skillet over medium heat. Add patties, in batches, and fry for about 5 minutes on each side, until browned. Add more butter or margarine as needed. Keep patties warm until ready to serve.

Serve patties with peanut sauce, salsa de mali (recipe follows).

Salsa de Mali   Ecuadorian Peanut Sauce

Yield: about 1 cup
  1 tablespoon vegetable oil
  1 onion, **finely chopped**
  1 clove garlic, finely chopped, or ½ teaspoon garlic granules
  ½ cup chunky peanut butter
  ½ cup mild or hot salsa (available at all supermarkets)
  4 tablespoons water, more or less, if necessary

Equipment: Small skillet, mixing spoon

1. Heat oil in small skillet over medium heat. Add onion and garlic, and, stirring constantly, fry for 3 minutes, until soft. Add peanut butter and salsa, and stir until well blended. If mixture is not spreadable, add just enough water to make it so.

Serve warm or cold as a sauce over llapingachos, *potato cakes (recipe precedes).*

In Latin American countries bread pudding is reserved for holiday celebrations and important dinners. In Ecuador and neighboring Colombia and Peru, it is called *capritoda*.

South American Capritoda

South American Bread Pudding

Yield: serves 6

2 cups brown sugar, firmly packed

4 cups water

2 teaspoons ground cinnamon

½ teaspoon ground cloves

8 slices toasted white bread, crusts removed and cubed

2 apples, **peeled**, **cored**, and finely sliced

½ cup seedless raisins

½ cup shelled peanuts

½ pound **shredded** Monterey Jack or mozzarella cheese

Equipment: Medium saucepan, mixing spoon, buttered oven-proof 1½-quart casserole, oven mitts

Preheat oven to 350° F.

1. In medium saucepan, combine brown sugar, water, cinnamon, and cloves, and bring to a boil over medium-high heat. Reduce heat to simmer, and, stirring frequently, cook for 10 minutes, until mixture thickens to a light syrup consistency. Set aside.

2. Spread half the bread cubes over bottom of buttered, oven-proof casserole. Spread apples over bread cubes, and sprinkle raisins and peanuts over apples. Cover with remaining bread cubes, and sprinkle cheese on top. Pour syrup over bread mixture, and bake in oven for about 40 minutes, or until cheese gets bubbly.

Serve warm in individual dessert dishes.

Colombia

Most Colombians are Roman Catholic descendants of a colorful mixture of indigenous Indians, Spanish colonists, and African slaves. Religious holidays are observed according to the strictest doctrine of the Catholic Church. Services are often long and arduous, but Colombians don't seem to mind. They enjoy celebrating so much that they often take off from work the day before and after a holiday, as well as on the big day itself.

Colombia has 18 national holidays, and all of them have religious overtones, including the Labor Day and Independence Day. The Catholic Church has such a strong hold on the people of Colombia that it even has the right to give religious instruction in all public schools.

In Colombia, Easter is the most important holiday, and the rituals leading up to it during Holy Week are long and involved; everyone pitches in to give a spring cleaning to their church. Statues are washed and decorated with fresh flowers, and the church yard is spruced up. From Palm Sunday until Easter, everyone is expected to attend daily mass, and in many villages the priest goes from house to house and leaves a blessing on each.

For Palm Sunday, Colombians weave palm fronds into elaborate designs and bring them to church to wave as a remembrance of Christ's triumphal entry into Jerusalem. After mass, the priest blesses the palms. The faithful take home the palms and hang them above their doors and windows to ward off evil spirits.

Religious processions are held after dark on Holy Monday and Holy Thursday before Easter. Men and older boys take turns pulling or carrying the huge life-size wooden statues through the streets. As the procession passes, onlookers kneel in prayer. On Good Friday penitents dressed in brown robes and crowns of leaves walk barefoot through the streets, dragging heavy wooden crosses on their backs. The processions draw large crowds.

Holy Saturday, the day before Easter, ends with a late night feast after mass. The meal usually consists of *sopa de maíz* (recipe follows) and *tamales* (recipe page 251) followed by either *arroz con leche* (recipe page 242) or *flan almendra* (recipe page 241).

1 cup **shredded** Monterey Jack, Münster, or mozzarella cheese

tortillas, keep warm, for serving (available at most supermarkets)

liquid hot red pepper sauce, for serving (optional)

Equipment: Medium saucepan, mixing spoon

1. Pour broth into medium saucepan. Add corn, milk, garlic, oregano, stewed tomatoes, and salt and pepper to taste. Stir the ingredients, and bring to a boil over medium-high heat. Reduce heat to simmer, and cook for 10 minutes, stirring frequently.

2. Remove soup from heat, add cheese, and stir until cheese is melted.

To serve, ladle soup into bowls, and serve with warm tortillas and bottle of hot pepper sauce.

In most Colombian homes, there is very little difference between an everyday meal and a holiday feast; it is usually stew made with vegetables such as okra, squash, corn, and beans. For Easter, Christmas, or one of the many patron saint day feasts, however, a little meat or chicken would be added to make it a special treat.

Sopa de Maíz   Corn Soup

Yield: serves 4 to 6

2 cups chicken broth, homemade (recipe page 52) or canned

2 cups corn kernels, fresh; frozen, thawed; or canned

2 cups milk

1 clove garlic, **finely chopped,** or ½ teaspoon garlic granules

1 teaspoon ground oregano

1 cup stewed tomatoes

salt and pepper to taste

Cocido Bogotano

Colombian Beef Stew

Yield: serves 4 to 6

2 tablespoons vegetable oil

1 onion, **coarsely chopped**

3 cloves garlic, **finely chopped,** or 1 teaspoon garlic granules

2 pounds boneless lean stewing beef, coarsely chopped

3 cups water

1 cup canned Italian plum tomatoes, coarsely chopped

1 teaspoon ground cumin
3 potatoes, **peeled** and coarsely chopped
4 carrots, **trimmed**, peeled, and coarsely sliced
4 ears corn, shucked and cut into 2-inch lengths
1 cup green peas, fresh or frozen, thawed
salt and pepper to taste

Equipment: **Dutch oven** or large saucepan with cover, mixing spoon

1. Heat oil in Dutch oven or large saucepan over medium-high heat. Add onion and garlic, and, stirring constantly, fry until soft, about 3 minutes. Add beef, and, stirring constantly, brown on all sides, about 5 minutes.

2. Add water, tomatoes, cumin, potatoes, and carrots, and stir. Cover and cook for 30 minutes.

3. Add corn, peas, and salt and pepper to taste, and stir. Cover and cook for 10 minutes, or until meat is tender.

Serve stew while hot, directly from the pot.

Venezuela

As with most countries of Latin America, the majority of Venezuelans are Roman Catholic, but Venezuelans have their own way of celebrating religious holidays. The processions that are so popular in other Latin American countries are not the tradition in Venezuela. The *pesebres*, nativity scenes at Christmas, are important, and, in most homes, they are very elaborate. Today, one is likely to see electric train sets and cartoon figures placed alongside of the traditional shepherds, Wise Men, manger, and Holy Family.

For nine days prior to Christmas Eve, church bells and firecrackers go off in the middle of the night to awaken Venezuelans, calling them to the pre-dawn Christmas services. On Christmas Eve, most families attend *Misa del Gallo*, Midnight Mass, and afterwards the hungry parishioners hurry home to a huge, fancy feast.

Hallacas, a national dish of Venezuela, is always served at Christmas time. In Venezuela, banana leaves are used as the wrappers, but for this recipe aluminum foil is used.

Hallacas Centrales   Filled Cornmeal Patties

Yield: serves 6 or 8
2 cups water
1 cup yellow cornmeal
1 tablespoon butter or margarine, at room temperature
½ cup sugar
1 egg
1 tablespoon baking soda
4 tablespoons vegetable oil
½ pound boneless, skinless chicken, cut into ½-inch cubes
½ pound lean, boneless loin of pork, cut into ½-inch cubes
2 onions, **finely chopped**
3 cloves garlic, finely chopped, or 1 teaspoon garlic granules
1 green bell pepper, **cored, seeded,** and finely chopped
1 teaspoon ground cumin

½ cup drained canned Italian plum tomatoes or
   ½ cup drained chunky salsa (available at
   most supermarkets)
½ cup seedless raisins, soaked in warm water
   for 30 minutes and drained
salt and pepper to taste
8 pimento-stuffed olives

Equipment: Medium saucepan, mixing spoon, wax paper, work surface, large skillet, **slotted spoon**, large mixing bowl, 8 (10-inch) squares aluminum foil, **steamer pan** (see glossary for tips on making a steamer), tongs

1. Prepare dough: In medium saucepan, bring water to a boil over high heat. Stirring constantly, add cornmeal. Reduce heat to simmer, and cook for about 15 minutes, or until very thick; remove saucepan from heat. Using mixing spoon, beat in butter or margarine, sugar, and egg. Cool mixture to room temperature, add baking soda, and mix well. Divide dough into 16 portions and set on wax-paper-covered work surface.

2. Prepare filling: Heat 2 tablespoons oil in large skillet over medium heat. Add chicken and pork, and, stirring constantly, fry until browned and cooked through, about 8 minutes.

3. Add remaining 2 tablespoons oil to meat, if needed to prevent sticking. Add onions, garlic, bell pepper, cumin, tomatoes or salsa, raisins, and salt and pepper to taste to meat in saucepan. Stir and fry until onion is soft, about 3 minutes. Remove from heat and cool to warm.

4. Assemble: Place one 10-inch piece of foil on work surface. Using clean hands, place one portion of dough in center of foil. Press dough into a circle or square about 4 inches wide and about ¼ inch thick.

5. Divide meat mixture into 8 balls, and mound one in the center of dough; slice an olive over the meat.

6. Flatten another portion of dough to fit over meat filling (like making a sandwich), and press edges together to enclose filling. Wrap foil around dough and meat to make a watertight package. Fold ends over seam and press closed. The finished package should be about 4 inches square. Repeat until all packages are made.

7. Steam *hallacas*: Pour water into bottom of steamer, and set upper rack in place. Pile *hallacas* in the upper rack. Bring water to a boil over high heat, reduce heat to simmer, cover, and steam for 1 hour, or until cornmeal holds together and is fully cooked.

SAFETY NOTE: Check water level frequently during steaming to be sure there is at least 1 inch of water in bottom pan; add more hot water, if necessary.

Serve each person a package while warm. Guests should open the hallacas *and eat them right out of the foil.*

The holiday seasons are a time to make all kinds of sweets and cakes. In Venezuela, sweets made with gooey coconut sauce are a favorite.

Bien Me Sabe de Coco

Cake with Cream of Coconut

Yield: serves 10 to 12

5 eggs, separated
½ cup sugar
1 teaspoon vanilla extract
²/₃ cup all-purpose flour
1 teaspoon ground cinnamon
1 (15-ounce) can cream of coconut (available at
   all supermarkets)

Equipment: Large mixing bowl, egg beater or electric mixer, small mixing bowl, rubber **spatula** or whisk, flour **sifter**, buttered or nonstick 8- x 12-inch cake pan, toothpick, oven mitts

Preheat oven to 350° F.

1. In large mixing bowl, use egg beater or electric mixer to beat egg whites until soft peaks form. Add sugar, a little at a time, and continue mixing until stiff and glossy.

2. In small bowl, beat egg yolks and vanilla until thick, about 3 minutes. Using rubber spatula or whisk, **fold** yolks into egg whites, and blend well. **Sift** flour into egg mixture, a little at a time, and fold in, using rubber spatula or whisk.

3. Transfer batter to buttered or nonstick baking pan, smooth top, and bake in oven for 30 minutes or until toothpick inserted in the center comes out clean. Remove from oven, and cool to room temperature.

4. Assemble cake: Leave cake in pan. Cut into 2-inch squares, sprinkle with cinnamon, and **drizzle** with cream of coconut. Refrigerate for at least 2 hours before serving.

To serve, transfer slices to individual dessert plates, and eat with either a fork or spoon.

Guyana

Guyana is unlike other South American countries. English is the official language, and the Catholic Church is not a dominant force in people's lives. The population is a diverse mixture of East Indians, Africans, American Indians, Chinese, and Portuguese. More than 50 percent of the population are Christians; about 33 percent are Hindus, descendants of indentured laborers, brought from India to work the sugar cane fields.

The most important Hindu holiday is *Diwali*, the "Festival of Lights," and the beginning of the Hindu New Year (see India). *Diwali* is in the Hindu month of *Kartika* (October-November). On the most important day of *Diwali*, Hindus follow traditional rituals, have a family breakfast, and later they dress in their finest clothes and join relatives and friends in a holiday feast.

The majority of Christians belong to various independent Protestant churches. Year round, the church is the center of their social life, and everyone within the congregation knows each other. They often share covered-dish suppers at the church community hall. Christmas is the most important holiday, and the children go to Sunday school, where they learn Christmas carols and partake in the holiday pageant. The youngsters believe in Santa Claus, who brings them presents on Christmas morning.

Curry dishes are a favorite of both the Hindus and Christians in Guyana. The Christians eat the curried zucchini soup before the Christmas ham, goat, or goose, but the Hindus eat it along with the other dishes.

Curried Zucchini Soup

Yield: serves 6
   3 medium zucchini, washed, ends **trimmed**, and **coarsely chopped**
   4 cups chicken broth, homemade (recipe page 52) or canned
   2 onions, coarsely chopped
   1 tablespoon curry powder, more or less to taste

1½ cups milk
salt and pepper to taste

Equipment: Medium saucepan, mixing spoon, electric **blender** or **food processor**, ladle

1. In medium saucepan, mix zucchini, chicken broth, onions, and 1 tablespoon curry powder, more or less to taste. Bring mixture to a boil over high heat. Reduce heat to simmer, cover, and cook until zucchini is very tender, about 20 minutes; stir frequently. Set aside to cool to warm.

2. Ladle mixture, in batches if necessary, into jar of blender or food processor, and blend until smooth and lump-free. Transfer back to medium saucepan. Add milk and salt and pepper to taste, stir well, and cook over medium heat until heated through, about 5 minutes. Do not boil.

Serve warm in individual soup bowls.

Panama

Panama is a bridge between two continents, and it is not surprising that Panamanian customs and foods reflect the influences of the countries to the north and the south. The majority of Panamanians are Roman Catholic *mestizos,* people of mixed Spanish and Indian origins. Christmas is the favorite holiday, and it is a very joyous time in Panama. Christmas

comes at the end of the rainy season, and flowers are in full bloom. People spend weeks setting up the *nacimientos,* the nativity scenes.

Panamanians love music, and, during the Christmas Eve mass, children entertain parishioners with old Spanish Christmas carols. After church, the families return home for the Christmas feast. Among the dishes likely to be served are turkey stuffed with pork, hardcooked eggs, onions, olives, and raisins if the budget allows; otherwise, most Panamanians feast on less expensive *sancocho* (recipe follows).

Sancocho   Beef and Vegetable Stew

Yield: serves 6 to 8

    2 pounds lean beef short ribs, cut into serving-size pieces
    8 cups beef or chicken broth
    2 onions, **coarsely chopped**
    2 tomatoes, **cored** and coarsely chopped
    1 green bell pepper, **stemmed**, **seeded,** and coarsely chopped
    ¼ cup **finely chopped** fresh cilantro or 2 tablespoons dried coriander flakes
    1 teaspoon dried oregano leaves
    3 green **plantains** (to peel, score skin lengthwise and pull off; cut into ¼ inch pieces—optional)
    4 potatoes, **peeled** and cut into 2-inch chunks
    2 ears corn, silk and husks removed; cut each into 4 equal pieces
    salt and pepper to taste

Equipment: **Dutch oven** or large saucepan with cover, mixing spoon

1. Rinse meat and put into Dutch oven or large saucepan. Add broth, onions, tomatoes, bell pepper, chopped cilantro or coriander, and oregano, and stir. Bring to boil over high heat. Reduce heat to simmer, cover, and, stirring occasionally, cook for 2 hours.

2. Add plantains, potatoes, corn, and salt and pepper to taste to meat mixture, and gently stir. Increase heat and boil for 5 minutes. Reduce heat to simmer, cover, and cook for about 35 minutes more, or until meat and vegetables are tender when pierced with a fork.

Serve warm in individual bowls. Leftover stew can be frozen in a covered container for up to two months.

Throughout Latin America puddings are a favorite holiday dessert.

Flan Almendra   Almond Pudding

Yield: serves 8 to 10
   1 cup sugar
   1 cup sliced or **coarsely chopped** almonds
   2 (14 ounces each) cans of **sweetened condensed milk**
   1 cup milk
   4 eggs
   4 **egg yolks**
   1 teaspoon vanilla extract

Equipment: Small saucepan, wooden mixing spoon, 9-inch pie pan, medium mixing bowl, rubber **spatula**, aluminum foil, 12-inch baking pan, oven mitts

Preheat oven to 350° F.

1. Melt sugar in small saucepan over medium heat until it becomes syrup, about 10 minutes. Carefully pour melted sugar into pie pan and swirl to cover pan bottom. Sprinkle with almonds and set aside.

2. In medium mixing bowl, mix sweetened condensed milk, milk, whole eggs, egg yolks, and vanilla. Set aside for 10 minutes, and then pour over almond mixture in pie pan. Cover tightly with foil.

3. Place pie pan in baking pan, and add just enough water to go halfway up the side of pie pan. Bake in oven for 1 hour, or until set.

4. Using oven mitts, remove from water. Cool to room temperature and refrigerate until ready to serve.

To serve, loosen edge with knife and invert a plate over the pie pan. Hold plate and pan tightly together and quickly turn over. The flan *will drop onto plate. The nut sauce is now on top. Cut into wedges.*

Costa Rica

The majority of Roman Catholic Costa Ricans are descendants of European settlers, particularly those of Spanish origin.

Christmas is one of the most important holidays in Costa Rica. It is the custom in many Latin American homes to set up a small manger at Christmas time. Many Costa Ricans, however, fill a whole room with the Nativity scene, instead of just reserving a corner. An enjoyable part of the Christmas festivities is going from house to house admiring the different scenes.

For centuries the Christ-child has been the giver of gifts to Costa Rican children. In recent years, however, Santa Claus has made his influence felt. Today, it is not unusual to see jolly old Santa in full regalia greeting children in department stores.

Puddings, of all kinds, are traditionally served in Costa Rica at the end of the Christmas feast and other festive occasions. Chocolate is particularly appropriate because it is made from the bean of the cocoa trees, which are native to Central and South America. The Mayans and Aztecs used the bean as currency and used cocoa in religious rituals. The Aztecs were probably the first to make a drink of the cocoa bean, which they introduced to the conquering Spaniards in the early sixteenth century. It was taken to Europe by the Spaniards, who jealously guarded their discovery for almost a hundred years before other Europeans heard of it. Before long it became a popular beverage, and chocolate houses sprang up all over Europe.

Capirotada   Chocolate Bread Pudding

Yield: serves 6 to 8
  2 cups milk or light cream
  1 cup semisweet chocolate chips or squares, **coarsely chopped**
  1 teaspoon ground cinnamon
  ½ cup seedless raisins
  2 eggs
  ½ cup sugar
  6 cups cubed and toasted egg bread with the crusts removed

Equipment: Medium saucepan, mixing spoon, large mixing bowl, egg beater or electric mixer, buttered medium oven-proof casserole with cover, 13- x 9-inch baking pan (large enough to hold casserole), oven mitts

Preheat oven to 350° F.

1. In medium saucepan, heat milk or cream over medium heat until bubbles form around the edges, about 5 minutes. Reduce heat to low, and add chocolate, cinnamon, and raisins. Stirring constantly, heat until chocolate melts, about 5 minutes. Cool to warm.

2. In large mixing bowl, use egg beater or electric mixer to beat eggs and sugar until creamy and light, about 3 minutes. Add chocolate mixture, and mix well. Add bread cubes, and, using mixing spoon, stir frequently; let mixture stand until bread absorbs all the liquid, about 30 minutes. Transfer mixture to buttered casserole and cover.

4. Set covered casserole in large baking pan. Pour at least 1 inch of hot water into baking pan. Place in oven, and bake for 15 minutes. Uncover and bake until pudding feels slightly firm to the touch, about another 20 minutes.

Serve capirotada *warm in individual dessert bowls.*

Ending the Christmas feast with rice pudding is a family tradition in many Latin American homes.

Arroz con Leche   Spanish Rice Pudding

Yield: serves 4 to 6
  2 cups milk
  1 egg
  1 teaspoon vanilla
  ⅓ cup sugar
  1 cup rice
  ½ cup **finely chopped** mixed candied fruit (fruitcake mix—available at supermarkets)
  ½ cup seedless raisins

Equipment: Medium saucepan with cover, mixing spoon

1. Pour milk into medium saucepan. Add egg, and, stirring constantly, heat over medium-high heat until small bubbles appear around edge of pan.

2. Add vanilla, sugar, and rice, and stir. Reduce heat to low, cover, and cook for about 20 minutes, until rice is tender.

3. Remove from heat, add candied fruit and raisins, and stir. Cover for 10 minutes before serving.

Serve pudding in individual dessert dishes while still warm or refrigerate and serve cold.

Costa Rica has a relatively high standard of living with a history of social justice and respect for human rights. In search of a better life, many people, especially Asians, have immigrated to this tiny country. Finding a job was no problem; many Asians went to work on the large banana plantations. The Asian influence is evident in this popular banana recipe. Sweets like these banana fritters are an important addition to Easter and Christmas celebrations.

Buñuelos de Plátano Banana Fritters

CAUTION: HOT OIL USED

Yield: serves 4 to 6

16 spring roll wrappers (available at some supermarkets and all Asian food stores, thin Thai- or Vietnamese-style ones are best)

4 large bananas, **peeled** and cut in half crosswise and then in half lengthwise

3 tablespoons dark brown sugar

2 **egg whites**, lightly beaten until foamy

vegetable oil for **deep frying**

1 tablespoon confectioners' sugar, for **garnish**

Equipment: Work surface, teaspoon, **pastry brush**, **deep fryer** (see glossary for tips on making a deep fryer), wooden spoon, paper towels, baking sheet, **slotted spoon, sifter**

1. Place a spring roll wrapper on the work surface. Set a piece of banana on top of wrapper, between the center and one corner. Sprinkle with brown sugar. Bring the ends of spring roll wrapper over the banana and roll up. (See diagram.) Using the pastry brush, brush end flap with egg white and press closed. Place on work surface seam-side down. Repeat assembling wrappers.

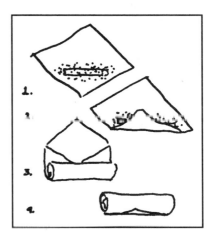

2. Prepare deep fryer: Have an adult help you heat oil to 375° F. Oil is hot enough for frying when small bubbles appear around a wooden spoon handle when it is dipped in the oil. Place several layers of paper towels on baking sheet. Very carefully fry fritters, 3 or 4 at a time, until golden and crisp, about 2 minutes on each side. Remove with slotted spoon, and drain on paper towels.

3. Put confectioners' sugar in sifter and sprinkle over fritters.

Serve warm as dessert or as a sweet snack.

Cooling drinks are especially popular during Christmas when Costa Rica's tropical weather is at its hottest.

Pineapple-Coconut Smoothie

Yield: serves 2 to 4

½ cup pineapple juice
¼ cup canned cream of coconut (available at most supermarkets)
½ cup crushed, canned, or **finely chopped** fresh pineapple
½ cup plain yogurt
1 cup ice cubes or crushed ice, more as needed
1 tablespoon honey, more or less to taste

Equipment: Electric **blender** or **food processor**, mixing spoon

Put pineapple juice, cream of coconut, pineapple, yogurt, 1 cup ice, and ½ tablespoon honey in blender or food processor, and blend for about 2 minutes, until smooth. Add more honey to adjust sweetness; mix well.

Serve at once, over ice.

Nicaragua

Most Nicaraguans are Roman Catholic *mestizos* (people of mixed Spanish and Indian origins). Many Nicaraguans combine ancestral beliefs and rituals with Catholicism.

In Nicaragua, Christmas is a children's holiday, and well before the end of November the children start caroling in the streets. Festivities go almost nonstop until Christmas Eve, concluding with the Midnight Mass. On Christmas Eve every home is decorated with green sawdust, tinsel, and colored lights. Inside the houses an empty crib awaits the infant Jesus at midnight. After church, people feast on turkey, stuffed hen, or *tamales* (recipe page 251).

Sweet desserts, such as the following recipe, are a luxury for most Nicaraguans, and they are reserved for special religious feasts or family celebrations.

Calabaza Enmielada — Honeyed Squash

Yield: serves 6

3 (about 1 pound each) acorn squashes, cut in half, **seeded**, and stringy fibers removed
1½ cups water
2½ cups dark brown sugar
1 cup prepared frozen whipped topping, thawed (optional)

Equipment: 13- x 9-inch baking pan, small saucepan, mixing spoon, aluminum foil, oven mitts

Preheat oven to 350° F.

1. Place squash side by side, cut side up, in baking pan.

2. In small saucepan, mix water and brown sugar and bring to a boil over medium-high heat. Reduce heat to simmer for 3 minutes, or until sugar dissolves and mixture thickens. Carefully pour syrup over cut sides of squash and into pan. Tightly cover baking pan with foil, and bake in oven for 1 hour, or until very tender.

To serve, arrange warm squash on serving platter or in individual dessert bowls and spoon pan dripping over each. Top each squash with dollop of whipped topping (optional).

At Christmas time, *sopapillas* are the most popular sweets. *Sopapillas* are eaten throughout Latin America and the American Southwest.

Sopapillas Fried Pillows

CAUTION: HOT OIL USED

Yield: about 20 squares

   2 cups all-purpose flour
   1 teaspoon baking powder
   ½ teaspoon salt
   1 tablespoon shortening, at room temperature
   ¾ cup hot water, more or less as needed
   oil for **deep frying**
   cinnamon sugar, for **garnish**

Equipment: Large mixing bowl, mixing spoon, kitchen towel, floured work surface, floured **rolling pin**, knife, **deep fryer** (see glossary for tips on making one), wooden spoon, baking sheet, paper towels, **slotted spoon**

1. In large mixing bowl, mix flour, baking powder, and salt. Using clean hands, **blend** in shortening until mixture resembles fine crumbs. Add just enough hot water to make a soft dough that holds together, leaving sides of bowl clean. Divide dough into 2 balls, and cover with towel to prevent drying out.

2. On floured work surface, use floured rolling pin to roll one ball about ¹/₈ inch thick. Using a knife, cut dough into 3-inch squares. Cover squares with towel, and repeat with second ball.

3. Prepare deep fryer: Have an adult help you heat oil to 375°. Oil is hot enough for frying when small bubbles appear around a wooden spoon handle when it is dipped in the oil. Place several layers of paper towels on baking sheet. Carefully fry a few squares at a time in deep fryer, about 2 minutes on each side, until puffy and golden brown. Remove with slotted spoon and drain on paper towels. Sprinkle with cinnamon sugar and keep warm. Continue frying in batches.

Serve sopapillas *while warm.*

Honduras

Most Hondurans are *mestizos* (people of mixed Indian and Spanish origins), and the majority are Roman Catholics. Christmas is the most important holiday in Honduras. Because of its tropical location, Christmas there is greeted with summer weather, bright flowers, and fruit trees, ripe for picking. In churches and homes, the manger, the *nacimiento*, is the center of the Christmas decorations. In every city and village the beautifully decorated mangers are paraded through the streets, surrounded by gaily costumed children singing Christmas songs.

As in Spain, Christmas gifts are exchanged on the twelfth-night, January 6. According to legend, this is the night that the Three Wise

Men brought gifts to baby Jesus. In Honduras and many other Latin American countries, children put their shoes in the window to be filled with toys and candies by Santa Claus, whom the children call *Santa Clausa*.

The Christmas feast is held either after Christmas Eve mass or on the next day. Families who can afford it gather for roast suckling pig, hot foamy chocolate, and cakes. Christmas dinner always begins with soup, and cold soup, such as this recipe for chilled avocado soup, is a favorite.

Sopa de Aguacate   Chilled Avocado Soup

Yield: serves 4

- 3 ripe avocados, **peeled**, pitted, and mashed
- 1 cup sour cream or plain yogurt, or more as needed
- 3 cups chicken broth, homemade (recipe page 52) or canned
- 2 tablespoons lime juice
- salt and pepper to taste
- ½ cup yogurt, for serving
- 1 teaspoon red pepper flakes, for **garnish**

Equipment: Medium mixing bowl, mixing spoon or **whisk**

In medium mixing bowl, blend mashed avocado and 1 cup sour cream or yogurt until smooth and lump-free. Add chicken broth, lime juice, and salt and pepper to taste; mix well. Cover and refrigerate for at least 1 hour.

Serve chilled in individual soup bowls. Add a dollop of yogurt to each bowl, and sprinkle with red pepper flakes.

A favorite Christmas dessert is *torrijas*, a fried cake. It is popular throughout Latin America, Spain, and Portugal.

Torrijas   Fried Cake Dessert

CAUTION: HOT OIL USED

Yield: 8 to 10 servings

- 6 **eggs, separated**
- oil for **deep frying**
- 1 pound stale sponge cake, cut into ½-inch-thick slices
- ½ cup water
- 2 cups corn syrup
- 1 teaspoon ground cinnamon
- 1 cup **coarsely chopped** almonds, walnuts, or pecans

Equipment: Large mixing bowl, fork, medium mixing bowl, egg beater or electric mixer, rubber **spatula**, **deep fryer** (see glossary for tips on making one), wooden spoon, baking sheet, paper towels, **slotted spoon**, oven-proof rimmed platter, oven mitts, small saucepan

1. In large mixing bowl, use fork to beat egg yolks until foamy.

2. In medium mixing bowl, use egg beater or electric mixer to beat whites until stiff. Using rubber spatula, **fold** whites into yolks.

3. Prepare deep fryer: Have an adult help you heat oil to 375° F. Oil is hot enough for frying when small bubbles appear around a wooden spoon handle when it is dipped in the oil. Place several layers of paper towels on baking sheet.

Preheat oven to 200° F.

4. Dip a cake slice into egg mixture and coat well. Shake off excess, and carefully **deep fry** cake piece for about 2 minutes on each side or until golden brown. Remove cake with slotted spoon, and drain on paper towels. Arrange slices, slightly overlapping, on oven-proof rimmed platter, and keep in warm oven.

5. Pour water into small saucepan, and add corn syrup, cinnamon, and nuts. Stir and cook over medium-high heat for about 3 minutes to heat through. Drizzle syrup over fried cake slices.

Serve as a warm dessert at Christmas.

Fresh fruit is plentiful in Honduras, and cool fruit drinks are a welcome treat in the hot Honduran climate, especially after hours spent in prayer.

Refresco de Lechosa

Milk and Papaya Drink

Yield: serves 4

1 ripe papaya, **peeled**, halved, seeded, and **coarsely chopped** or 2 cups canned papaya in juice or syrup, coarsely chopped (available at most supermarkets)

1 cup milk

3 tablespoons lime juice

$^1/_8$ cup sugar, more or less to taste

1 teaspoon vanilla extract or coconut flavoring

4 cups crushed or cubed ice, more or less as needed, for serving

4 thin lime slices, for **garnish**

Equipment: Electric blender or **food processor**, spoon, 4 tall water glasses

In blender or food processor, mix papaya, milk, lime juice, ¼ cup sugar, and vanilla or coconut flavoring. Blend at high speed until mixture is smooth and lump-free. To adjust sweetness, add more sugar, and mix well.

To serve, pour mixture into drinking glasses. Add enough ice to fill each glass, and garnish with lime slices.

El Salvador

El Salvador is a Roman Catholic nation, and most official holidays are religious in nature. There are two important national holidays in El Salvador: Independence Day, September

15, when the country won independence from Spain in 1821, and the Festival of *El Salvador del Mundo*, August 3 to 6, honoring *Salvador del Mundo* (which means the savior of the world), the patron saint of both the country and the capital city of San Salvador. Schools and businesses close throughout the country on Independence Day, and every city, town and village has a celebration with a carnival, parade, and fireworks. The parades are made up of trucks, donkeys pulling carts, and bicycles bedecked with colorful ribbons and crepe paper flowers.

During the celebration of *Salvador del Mundo*, thousands of people flock to the capital city for the festivities. There are elaborate processions, the *feria* (fair), music, dancing, fireworks, and soccer games. Part of the holiday fun is munching on *tamales* (recipe page 251) and sugary candies while drinking *refrescos* (recipe precedes) purchased from street vendors.

This recipe for *crema de aguacate*, avocado whip, is an easy and attractive dessert served in its own shell.

Crema de Aguacate   Avocado Whip

Yield: serves 4

2 large, ripe avocados
½ cup confectioners' sugar
2 tablespoons lime juice
4 maraschino cherries, for **garnish** (optional)

Equipment: Knife, small bowl, fork, mixing spoon

1. Cut avocados in half lengthwise, and remove and discard pit. Scoop out pulp, and put it in small bowl. Keep skin shell intact to refill.

2. Using a fork, mash avocado pulp until smooth. Add confectioners' sugar, a little at a time, and lime juice. Using mixing spoon, beat until fluffy and blended, about 3 minutes.

3. Spoon mixture back into skin shells, and refrigerate until ready to serve. Place a red cherry on the top of each, for garnish.

Serve crema de aguacate *as a dessert or snack.*

Anise seeds (used in this recipe for *biscochitos*) have a licorice flavor, which is popular throughout Latin American countries.

Biscochitos   Latin American Anise Cookies

Yield: about 30 cookies

1 cup butter or margarine, at room temperature
1 cup sugar
1 egg, beaten
1 tablespoon crushed anise seeds
2 cups all-purpose flour
1 teaspoon baking powder
½ teaspoon salt
2 teaspoons **cinnamon sugar**, for **garnish**

Equipment: Large mixing bowl, mixing spoon or electric mixer, medium mixing bowl, lightly greased or nonstick cookie sheet, floured **rolling pin**, oven mitts, knife, metal **spatula**

Preheat oven to 375° F.

1. In large mixing bowl, use mixing spoon or electric mixer to mix butter or margarine and sugar until light and fluffy, about 3 minutes. Add egg and anise seeds, and mix well.

2. In medium mixing bowl, mix flour, baking powder, and salt. Add to egg mixture, a little at a time, mixing constantly, until well blended.

3. Spread dough out on cookie sheet. Using floured rolling pin, flatten to about ⅛ inch thick, covering pan.

4. Bake in oven for about 15 minutes, until golden brown. Remove from oven, and immediately cut into serving-size squares. Sprinkle squares with cinnamon sugar. Using a metal spatula, transfer to serving plate.

Serve biscochitos *as a sweet snack.*

Pralines, or *nogada,* as they are called in Latin America, are a favorite holiday treat throughout all Latin American countries. This is an easy, quick-to-make recipe.

Nogada   Pralines

Yield: about 16 pieces

1 cup sugar
1 (3½-ounce) box of cook-and-serve butterscotch pudding and pie filling mix
½ cup dark brown sugar
½ cup evaporated milk
1 teaspoon vanilla
2 cups **coarsely chopped** pecans

Equipment: Medium saucepan, wooden mixing spoon, tablespoon, teaspoon, wax paper, work surface, plastic wrap

1. In medium saucepan, combine sugar, butterscotch pudding mix, brown sugar, and evaporated milk. Stirring constantly, bring to boil over medium heat for 2 minutes. Add vanilla and pecans, stir, and cook about 2 minutes, or until thickened. Remove from heat.

2. Scoop up a heaping tablespoonful of mixture, and use teaspoon to push it in a mound onto wax-paper-covered work surface. Using back of spoon, flatten slightly. Repeat until all the mixture is used up, placing patties about an inch apart. Cool to room temperature to set.

Serve as a sweet snack. Wrap each piece in plastic wrap.

Guatemala

The area Guatemala encompasses was once part of the ancient Mayan Empire. Even today about half the population are descendants of Mayan Indians. Most Guatemalans are Roman Catholic, and some combine Mayan beliefs with Catholicism. Numerous ancient Mayan agrarian festivals coincide with Catholic holidays. Almost every day, somewhere in the country, a *fiesta* (festival) is held for a patron saint, Mayan god, or historical event.

The Catholic Church dominates the lives of most Guatemalans. As in many other Latin American countries, the most important holiday season begins with Carnival and climaxes at Easter. Every village celebrates Holy Week with elaborate processions. In large cities, thousands jam the streets to watch immense hand-carried floats and marchers dressed as Indian warriors and Roman soldiers walking to the beat of slow, solemn drums.

One of the most beautiful and unique aspects of the parades are the streets, which are covered with colored sawdust and flower petal carpets. Some of the painstakingly hand-crafted carpet creations are four blocks long. Once the procession starts, however, the wonderful carpets simply vanish beneath the marchers' feet.

Tortillas are an important part of the Guatemalan diet, and no meal is complete without them.

Tortillas — Cornmeal Flatbreads

Yield: makes 12

  2 cups masa harina flour (available at most supermarkets and all Latin American food stores)
  1¼ cups cold water, more as needed
  ½ teaspoon salt

Equipment: Large mixing bowl, mixing spoon, lightly floured work surface, lightly floured **rolling pin**, 12 (8-inch) squares of wax paper, ungreased or nonstick griddle or large skillet, metal **spatula**

1. Put masa harina, 1¼ cups water and salt in large mixing bowl, and mix until well blended. Allow dough to sit for 20 minutes; do not refrigerate.

2. On lightly floured work surface, knead dough until smooth, about 2 minutes. Add a little more water if dough doesn't hold together.

3. Divide dough into 12 balls. Using lightly floured rolling pin on lightly floured work surface, flatten each ball into 4-inch disk, $1/8$ inch thick. Stack disks, separating each one with wax paper. Continue making disks until dough is used up.

4. Fry tortillas on ungreased or nonstick griddle or large skillet over medium-high heat for about 2 minutes on each side until lightly browned. Keep warm until ready to serve.

Serve tortillas *warm for best flavor.*

Most Guatemalans are poor and live on a daily diet of tortillas and beans. For many people, meat is a special treat reserved for holiday feasts and the like. The following recipe for *carne en jocón* would be served with side dishes like *arroz Guatemalteco* (recipe follows later in this section) for Christmas Eve supper or the Epiphany feast on January 6.

Carne en Jocón   Beef Casserole

Yield: serves 6

   2 tablespoons vegetable oil
   1 onion, **finely chopped**
   3 cloves garlic, finely chopped, or 1 teaspoon garlic granules
   2 green bell peppers, **cored**, seeded, and **coarsely chopped**
   1 teaspoon chili powder, more or less to taste
   2 pounds boneless, lean stewing beef, cut into 1-inch chunks
   16-ounce can whole tomatoes, coarsely chopped
   2 cups water
   2 bay leaves
   1 teaspoon *each* ground cloves and ground oregano
   salt and pepper to taste
   2 stale corn tortillas, homemade (recipe precedes) or commercial (available at most supermarkets and all Latin American food stores)

Equipment: **Dutch oven** or large saucepan with cover, mixing spoon,

1. Heat oil in Dutch oven or large saucepan over medium-high heat. Add onion, garlic, green peppers, 1 teaspoon chili powder (more or less to taste), and beef. Stirring constantly, cook until browned on all sides, about 5 minutes.

2. Add tomatoes, water, bay leaves, cloves, oregano, and salt and pepper to taste. Stir and bring to a boil. Reduce heat to simmer, cover, and cook for about 1 hour, or until meat is tender. Remove bay leaves and discard.

3. Soak stale tortillas under cold running water, squeeze out the water, and crumble. Add crumbs to beef mixture, stir, and cook uncovered until sauce thickens, about 10 minutes. Stir frequently to prevent sticking.

Serve over beans or arroz Guatemalteco *(recipe follows).*

Arroz Guatemalteco

Guatemala-style Rice

Yield: serves 6

   2 tablespoons vegetable oil, butter, or margarine
   1 cup rice
   1 cup **finely chopped** mixed vegetables, such as onions, carrots, celery, and green and red bell peppers
   2 cups water
   ½ cup green peas, fresh, **blanched**, or frozen, thawed
   salt and pepper to taste

Equipment: **Dutch oven** or large skillet with cover, mixing spoon, fork

1. Heat oil or melt butter or margarine in Dutch oven or large skillet over medium heat. Add rice and mixed vegetables, and, stirring constantly, cook for 1 minute. Add water and stir. Increase heat to high, and bring to a boil. Reduce heat to

simmer, cover, and cook for about 20 minutes, or until rice is tender and water is absorbed. Remove from heat.

2. Add peas and salt and pepper to taste, stir, and cover for 5 minutes to heat through. Fluff with a fork before serving.

Serve rice warm as a side dish or with beef (recipe precedes).

Mexico

More than half of the people living in Mexico are *mestizos* (people of mixed Spanish and Indian heritage). Nearly 90 percent of the population are Roman Catholics, and many are devout followers. All the Christian holidays are a time for family and community gatherings.

Christmas is one of the most important holidays in Mexico. The Mexican Christmas season begins December 16 with *Las Posadas*, a centuries-old Roman Catholic celebration of Mary and Joseph's search for lodging in Bethlehem.

Las Posadas, which means "the shelter," originated with missionary priests who found it necessary to spark an interest in their teachings by blending the indigenous peoples' love

of drama and pageantry with Bible stories. The festivities begin with singing candlelight processions led by a girl and boy dressed as Mary and Joseph. The children go from house to house requesting shelter, and each time they are refused, until finally they are allowed to enter and the merriment begins. The festivities include singing, dancing, breaking of *piñatas*, and feasting on *tamales* (recipe follows), *empanadas* (recipe page 227), and *sopapillas* (recipe page 245).

Children love breaking the *piñata*, which is usually an animal made of colorful papier-mâché. The candy-filled piñata hangs on a string from the ceiling. The trick is to break it open by hitting it with a stick while blindfolded, so that the candy falls out. Originally piñatas were symbols of evil, and breaking one meant conquering evil. The candy symbolizes God's goodness showering down once evil is broken.

Throughout most of Latin America peasants eat *tamales* chiefly on festive days, but today city dwellers eat them at any time. *Tamales* are made with nonedible corn husks or banana leaves. The filling can be made a variety of ways—sweet or savory, hot or mild, with or without meat.

Tamales   Meat-Filled Corn Husks

Yield: about 24 to 30

- 1 (7-ounce) package of dried corn husks (available at some supermarkets and all Latin American stores) or fresh corn husks
- 2½ cups water
- 1 pound (about 2 cups) lean ground pork or beef, or combination
- 1 (6-inch) spicy sausage, such as Mexican chorizo
- 1 teaspoon ground cumin
- ½ cup solid vegetable shortening

2 cups *masa harina* (cornmeal) (available at most supermarkets and all Latin American food stores)
2 teaspoons baking powder
½ teaspoon salt

Equipment: Medium saucepan with cover, mixing spoon, strainer, medium bowl, small bowl with cover, large mixing bowl, electric **food processor**, work surface, about 48 (4½-inch long) twist ties or kitchen string, **steamer pan** (see glossary for tips on making one), metal tongs

1. To buy corn husks: Dried corn husks are available at some supermarkets and all Latin American food stores. There are about 50 usable (some will be torn and broken) husks in a 7-ounce package.

2. To prepare dried husks for filling: Soak dried husks for about 2 hours in warm water to make them soft and pliable. Wipe with paper towels before filling. If the husks are too narrow, use 2 or more overlapping husks for each *tamale.*

3. To prepare fresh husks: Remove the silk, separate the leaves (try not to tear them), and spread them out in a single layer on baking sheets to dry in a preheated 200° F. oven for about 3 hours.

4. Prepare meat filling: Pour water into medium saucepan. Add meat, sausage, and cumin, and bring to boil over high heat. Reduce heat to **simmer**, cover, and cook about 20 minutes until well done. (It's okay if sausage opens.) Cool to warm.

5. Place strainer over medium bowl. Drain meat in strainer, and save juice. Remove and discard sausage casing. Transfer meat to small bowl, cover, and refrigerate until ready to use. Refrigerate meat juice and **degrease**; discard grease. Set meat juice aside to use in dough.

6. Prepare dough: Put shortening in large mixing bowl, and, mixing constantly with a mixing spoon or food processor, alternate adding *masa*, a little at a time, with about 1½ cups reserved meat juice to make a soft, spreadable dough. Add baking powder and salt, and mix well.

7. Assemble *tamales*: Open husk, smooth-side up, on work surface. Spread about 1 heaping tablespoon of dough lengthwise, about 3 inches by 1½ inches, in center of husk, staying well within edges. (If necessary, use 2 overlapping husks.)

8. Spoon about 1 tablespoon meat mixture down center of dough. Enclose filling in dough and husk, and fold end flaps over seam. Wrap a twist tie or string around each end to keep package closed. The finished package is about 4½ inches long and 1½ inches wide. Repeat making *tamales.*

9. To steam *tamales*: Pour water into bottom pan of steamer, set top pan or rack in place, and fill with *tamales*. Bring water to a boil over high heat. Reduce heat to simmer, cover, and steam for about 1½ hours. To test for doneness, unwrap a *tamale*. The dough should be spongy and hold together.

SAFETY NOTE: Check water level carefully during steaming to be sure there is at least 1 inch of water at all times in bottom pan. Add more hot water, if necessary.

Serve warm tamales *in the husk. Each person unwraps the* tamale, *eating only the filling and discarding husk.*

Buñuelos are the traditional Christmas sweets. Eating them is supposed to bring good luck.

Buñuelos   Fried Pastry

CAUTION: HOT OIL USED
Yield: about 5 to 6 dozen
4 eggs
½ cup milk
¼ cup melted butter or margarine
3 cups flour, more as needed
½ teaspoon baking powder
½ teaspoon salt
1 tablespoon sugar
vegetable oil for **deep fryer**
cinnamon sugar, for **garnish**

Equipment: Large mixing bowl, mixing spoon, floured work surface, floured rolling pin, kitchen towel, **deep fryer** (see glossary for tips on making one), wooden spoon, paper towels, baking sheet, **slotted spoon**

1. In large mixing bowl, mix eggs, milk, and melted butter or margarine. Mixing constantly, add 3 cups flour, baking powder, salt, and sugar, a little at a time, until dough is easy to handle without sticking; add more flour if needed to prevent sticking. Using clean hands, divide dough into ping-pong-size balls.

2. On floured work surface, use floured rolling pin to flatten each ball into a disk, about ¹/₈ inch thick. Stack on work surface, and cover with kitchen towel until ready to fry.

3. Prepare **deep fryer:** Have an adult help you heat oil to 350° F. Oil is hot enough for frying when small bubbles appear around a wooden spoon handle when it is dipped in the oil. Place several layers of paper towels on baking sheet. Carefully fry *buñuelos* in small batches for 3 to 5 minutes or until golden on both sides. Remove with slotted spoon, and drain on paper towels. Sprinkle with cinnamon sugar.

Serve buñuelos *as a sweet treat during the holiday season.*

This colorful salad is served on Christmas Eve.

Ensalada de Noche Buena

Christmas Salad

Yield: serves 6 to 8
¾ cup vegetable oil
2 tablespoons orange juice
2 tablespoons white vinegar
1 tablespoon chopped fresh **cilantro (coriander)** or 1 teaspoon dried coriander flakes
salt to taste

3 cups sliced canned beets, drained
3 oranges, **peeled, pith** and seeds removed and **coarsely chopped**
2 cups peeled and coarsely chopped jicama (available in the produce section of most supermarkets and all Latin American stores) or **trimmed** and coarsely chopped celery
2 cups canned pineapple chunks, drained, or fresh pineapple, peeled, cored, and cubed
2 cups finely **shredded** cabbage
3 bananas

Equipment: Large salad bowl, salad mixing tools

1. In large salad bowl, mix oil, orange juice, vinegar, cilantro or coriander, and salt to taste.

2. Add beets, oranges, jicama or celery, pineapple, and cabbage. Using salad mixing tools, toss to coat; refrigerate. Before serving, peel and slice bananas, add to salad, and toss to mix

Serve chilled on individual salad plates.

Mole poblano, the national dish of Mexico, can be made with turkey, chicken, pork, or beef. When it is made with turkey, called *mole poblano de guajolote,* it is Mexico's greatest festival dish. The history of this dish is ancient, dating back many centuries to the Mayan empire. There are countless legends connected to this unusual dish made with chocolate.

Chocolate is made from the beans of the cocoa tree, which is native to Central and South America. The Mayans and Aztecs used the cocoa beans as a form of currency, and cocoa was used in religious rites long before the arrival of Spanish settlers. In 1502, at the time of Columbus's last voyage to the New World, the Spaniards considered chocolate to be a source of great strength. It was forbidden to women, and only royalty and the highest-ranking clergy were allowed to eat it.

Making the *mole poblano* sauce "from scratch" takes many ingredients and is very labor-intensive. Fortunately, prepared *mole poblano* sauce is available in powdered form or concentrate.

Mole Poblano de Guajolote
Fowl in Chocolate Chili Sauce

Yield: serves 4 to 6
  ½ cup *mole pablano* concentrate (available at some supermarkets and all Latin American food stores)
  1½ cups chicken broth, homemade (recipe page 52) or canned
  1 to 2 teaspoons sugar, more or less to taste
  2½ to 3½ pounds turkey or chicken, cut into serving-size pieces
  4 cups cooked rice (keep warm for serving)
  2 or 3 tablespoons sesame seeds, for **garnish**

Equipment: Small saucepan, mixing spoon, baking or roasting pan with cover, oven mitts, metal tongs

1. Put *mole poblano* concentrate in small saucepan. Add chicken broth, stir, and heat over medium heat until blended, about 3 minutes. Taste mixture, add 1 teaspoon sugar more or less to taste, and stir well.

2. Put turkey or chicken pieces in baking or roasting pan, and coat well with *mole* sauce. Cover and refrigerate for at least 2 hours, rotating to coat with sauce 2 or 3 times.

Preheat oven to 325° F.

3. Put baking or roasting pan in oven, and bake fowl, basting frequently, until tender and browned, about 1 hour.

Serve over rice and spoon pan drippings over fowl. Sprinkle with sesame seeds, for garnish.

In ancient times, chocolate was used as an offering to the gods, and it remains a favorite Mexican flavoring. Mexican chocolate is made in a bar marked off in 1-ounce squares (available at all Latin American food stores). This recipe is a good substitute.

Mexican Chocolate

Yield: 1 ounce
  1 ounce bittersweet chocolate, finely **grated** or **finely chopped**
  2 tablespoons sugar
  ¼ teaspoon ground cinnamon

Equipment: Small bowl, **grater**, mixing spoon

In small bowl, mix grated or chopped chocolate, sugar, and cinnamon until well blended.

Use in recipes calling for Mexican chocolate.

Chocolate Mexicano is a special holiday beverage, and there are unique tools for making it. The *molinillo* is a long, wooden stick with a grooved bulbous end. The bulbous end is set in the liquid, and, by quickly rolling the stick handle back and forth between the palms of your hands, the beverage becomes frothy.

The *mancerina* is the cup parishioners bring to church, filled with hot chocolate. Sipping a warm drink in a drafty church can make a lengthy sermon seem quite pleasant.

Chocolate Mexicano   Mexican Hot Chocolate

Yield: 1 cup
  1 cup milk
  1 square (1 ounce) Mexican chocolate (available at Latin American food stores) or substitute (recipe precedes)
  sugar to taste
  ground cinnamon

Equipment: Small saucepan, molinillo or egg beater or electric mixer

In small saucepan, heat milk and chocolate over low heat, stirring constantly until chocolate melts and mixture is foamy. If using semi-sweet chocolate, add sugar to taste and sprinkle with cinnamon; mix well.

To serve, pour into a cup and drink while still warm.

One of the most interesting Mexican holiday traditions is *El Día de los Muertos,* the Day of the Dead. On November 2nd, the people of Mexico visit and tend their family graves. It is not a day of mourning, but rather a joyful *fiesta* (celebration). They decorate the graves with orange marigolds, the flowers of the dead. Families come to picnic, eat candy skulls and skeletons, and a sweet yeast bread called *pan de muerto,* bread of the dead. The bread is decorated with dough shaped into symbols of the dead.

Pan de Muerto   Bread of the Dead

1 package (¼ ounce) dry active yeast
½ cup lukewarm water
4 cups all-purpose flour, more as needed
1 teaspoon *each* salt and ground aniseed
½ cup sugar
½ cup melted butter or margarine
6 eggs, beaten
1 tablespoon orange extract (available at all
    supermarkets)
grated rind of 1 orange
confectioners' sugar icing (recipe follows)
colored sugar sprinkles (available at all
    supermarkets), for **garnish**

Equipment: Small bowl, damp kitchen towel, flour **sifter**, large mixing bowl, floured work surface, greased or nonstick baking sheet, oven mitts

1. In small mixing bowl, sprinkle yeast over lukewarm water, and set aside for 5 minutes. Add 1 cup flour, mix, and form into a soft ball. Cover with damp towel and set in warm place to double in bulk, about 1 hour.

2. **Sift** remaining 3 cups flour into large mixing bowl. Add salt, ground aniseed, sugar, melted butter or margarine, eggs, orange extract, rind, and yeast mixture from step 1; mix well. Using clean hands, **knead** mixture into a smooth dough. Transfer dough to floured work surface, and knead until smooth and elastic, about 5 minutes. Sprinkle with flour, to prevent sticking. Put dough in lightly greased, large mixing bowl, cover with damp towel, and set in warm place to double in bulk, about 1½ hours.

3. Pinch off a piece of dough about the size of a lemon, and set aside. Shape remaining dough into 2 round loaves, and place side by side on baking sheet.

4. To decorate loaves with crossbones, roll the lemon-sized piece of dough between the palms of your hands to form a rope about 12 to 16 inches long. Cut dough rope into 4 equal-size pieces, and use 2 pieces to make an X on each loaf to resemble crossbones. Cover with damp towel, and set in warm place for about 30 minutes, or until almost doubled in bulk.

Preheat oven to 375° F.

5. Bake in oven for about 30 minutes or until bread sounds hollow when tapped on the bottom.

6. When cooled to room temperature, brush tops with icing (recipe follows). Sprinkle with colored sugar sprinkles, for garnish.

To serve, cut breads in wedges.

Confectioners' Sugar Icing

Yield: about 1 cup
1 cup confectioners' sugar
3 tablespoons hot water, more if necessary

Equipment: Small mixing bowl, mixing spoon, **pastry brush** or **spatula**

1. Put confectioners' sugar in small bowl. Add 3 tablespoons hot water, and mix into a smooth, lump-free paste. If paste is too sticky to spread, add more water, a little at a time.

2. Using pastry brush or spatula, spread icing over tops of bread.

Continue icing pan de muerto *(recipe precedes).*

North America

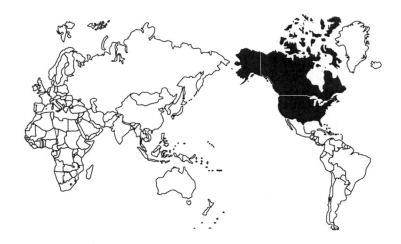

Canada and the United States

People from all over the world have come to Canada and the United States to start a new life. Although some families still cling to the holiday traditions of their ancestral homeland, most cultures have blended together forming new regional celebrations, with new traditions, superstitions, folklore, and legends.

Canada

Canada has a rich ethnic diversity that is reflected in many holiday celebrations, the most important being Christmas. In urban areas, Christmas traditions are similar to those in the United States. Large English and French communities, however, follow the traditions of their ancestral homelands. In fact, even today Canada has two distinct cultures, the French in Quebec and the English influence in the rest of Canada. Canada's official languages are French and English.

Although Canada has not been French since the Peace of Paris ceded the colony of New France to England in 1763, the most enduring Canadian dishes are those that originated with the first French settlers. It is their tastes and traditions that prevail in the distinctive food known as French Canadian.

The *Métis*, people of mixed French-Canadian and Indian heritage, keep alive the memories of their pioneering ancestors by eating pork *tourtière* on Christmas Eve. The early settlers made the pie with large birds, called *tourtes*, which they hunted into extinction. Today, Canadians make the *tourtière* with any kind of meat, and it has become a symbolic national holiday dish.

Réveillon is the feast after Midnight Mass for the Catholic French-Canadians. Families enjoy *tourtière*, stuffed goose, or turkey. As in France, the table centerpiece is often the *Bûche de Noël* (recipe page 102), the decorated yule log cake eaten for dessert.

Tourtière (also Tourte)   Meat Pie

Yield: *serves 4 to 6*

2 tablespoons vegetable oil
1 onion, **finely chopped**
1 clove garlic, finely chopped, or ½ teaspoon garlic granules
2 pounds lean ground meat: pork, beef, fowl, or combination
½ cup finely chopped celery
2 boiled potatoes, **peeled** and mashed or 1 cup prepared instant mashed potatoes
1 teaspoon ground cinnamon
½ teaspoon ground cloves
salt and pepper to taste
double unbaked (9-inch) pie crusts, homemade (recipe page 108) or frozen prepared pie crusts, thawed
egg glaze

Equipment: Large skillet, mixing spoon, 9-inch pie pan, fork, sharp knife, **pastry brush**

Preheat oven to 400° F.

1. Heat oil in large skillet over medium-high heat. Add onion and garlic, and, stirring constantly, fry until soft, about 3 minutes. Reduce heat to medium, add ground meat and celery, and, stirring frequently, cook about 20 minutes, or until meat is done. Remove from heat, and add mashed potatoes, cinnamon, cloves, and salt and pepper to taste; stir well.

2. Fill unbaked pie crust with meat mixture. Cover with top crust, and, using fork tines, crimp top and bottom edges together. Cut 6 or 8 steam vent slashes in top with a knife. Brush top with **egg glaze** using pastry brush.

3. Bake in oven 15 minutes. Reduce temperature to 350° F., and bake for 30 minutes more, or until golden.

To serve, let pie rest for at least 10 minutes before cutting into wedges.

The English Canadians like to keep up the Christmas traditions of their ancestors who came from England. The traditional holiday feast, called Christmas lunch, was the meal of "roast joint" (roast beef) with Yorkshire pudding. Today beef, somewhat of a luxury, is being replaced by less expensive turkey, pork, or goose, but the Yorkshire pudding is still included. For many, however, nothing can ever replace beef for Christmas, regardless of cost.

Roast Beef

Yield: *serves 6 to 8*
  4- to 5-pound cut of beef roast, sirloin tip, or
      top round
  3 tablespoons Dijon mustard

Equipment: Roasting pan, oven mitts, mixing spoon or **bulb baster**, meat thermometer, meat knife and cutting board

Preheat oven to 425° F.

1. Set beef in roasting pan, fat side up. Coat beef with mustard, place in oven, and roast for 20 minutes.

2. Lower oven temperature to 350°, and continue roasting to desired doneness, about 1½ hours, to medium, basting frequently using spoon or bulb baster. To test if meat is done, insert tip of meat thermometer in thickest part of meat. It should register 140° F. for rare, 160° F. for medium, and 170° F. for well done.

To serve, remove beef from roasting pan. Set aside pan drippings for following Yorkshire Pudding recipe. Allow beef to stand for 20 minutes on cutting board before slicing. Keep warm.

Yorkshire Pudding

Yield: *serves 6 to 8*
  1 cup all-purpose flour
  ¼ teaspoon baking powder
  ½ teaspoon salt
  2 eggs, beaten
  ¾ cup milk, at room temperature
  ½ cup water, at room temperature
  2 tablespoons pan drippings from roast beef
      (recipe precedes) or butter or margarine

Equipment: Flour **sifter**, medium mixing bowl, **whisk** or mixing spoon, **pastry brush** or wad of wax paper, 8- x 10-inch baking pan, oven mitts, heat-proof work surface

1. **Sift** flour, baking powder, and salt into medium mixing bowl. Make a well in the center, add eggs, and mix well with whisk or spoon. Add milk and water, and beat to a smooth batter. Set aside for 1 hour.

Preheat oven to 400° F.

2. Using pastry brush or wad of wax paper, coat baking pan with pan drippings, butter, or margarine. Wearing oven mitts, put empty pan in oven for about 5 minutes to heat. Remove pan from oven, and place on heat-proof work surface. Pour batter into warm pan and spread evenly.

3. Bake in oven for 20 minutes. Reduce oven to 350° F., and continue baking until pudding is puffy and golden, about 30 minutes more.

*Serve the pudding while warm, cut into squares with roast beef. **Degrease** remaining pan drippings, heat through, and serve in separate bowl to spoon over roast and pudding.*

In English homes, baking is an important part of the Christmas holiday ritual. English Canadians retain the practice of preparing breads, cookies, pies, and cakes to have ready for the family and guests, among them Christmas pudding with lemon hard sauce (recipe page 106) and *spritz* (recipe page 114).

The following inexpensive English dessert is a good way of using up stale bread.

Manchester Tart

Yield: *serves 8*

1 (9-inch) unbaked pie crust, homemade (recipe page 108) or frozen, thawed
4 tablespoons raspberry jam
2 cups white bread crumbs
1 ¼ cups milk
2 tablespoons melted butter
2 tablespoons granulated sugar
3 **eggs, separated**
¾ cup confectioners' sugar

Equipment: Pie pan, work surface, tablespoon, medium mixing bowl, mixing spoon, rubber **spatula**, small mixing bowl, egg beater or electric mixer, oven mitts

Preheat oven to 400° F.

1. Put unbaked pie crust in pie pan on work surface and spread the jam over the bottom. Set aside.

2. In medium mixing bowl, use mixing spoon to stir bread crumbs, milk, melted butter, granulated sugar, and egg yolks until well blended. Pour the mixture over the jam.

3. Bake in oven for 30 minutes. Remove from oven. Reduce oven heat to 300° F.

4. In small mixing bowl, use egg beater or electric mixer to beat egg whites until stiff. Beating constantly, add confectioners' sugar, a little at a time. Spread meringue evenly over the top of pie. Bake in oven until meringue turns light golden brown, about 5 minutes.

To serve, cool to warm and cut into wedges.

For the children and those not busy in the kitchen, a classic Canadian Christmas afternoon is spent sledding, skating, or skiing. Returning home and enjoying a hot holiday beverage like *glögg* (recipe follows) is a delightful treat.

Glögg   Hot Holiday Beverage

Yield: *serves 8*

8 cups cranberry-apple juice cocktail (available at all supermarkets)
6 cups apple juice
2 cinnamon sticks or 2 teaspoons ground cinnamon
1 teaspoon ground cloves
sugar to taste

Equipment: Large saucepan, mixing spoon, ladle

Pour cranberry-apple juice and apple juice in saucepan. Add cinnamon, cloves, and sugar to taste, stir, and cook over medium-low heat for about 1 hour. At serving time, cover and keep warm over low heat.

Serve hot, ladled into heat-proof mugs.

United States

Independence Day, July 4

In many countries of the world, the most important national holiday is Independence Day. Independence Day celebrations are usually festive affairs complete with parades, brass bands, marching soldiers, speeches, and elaborate fireworks.

On July 4, 1776, the Declaration of Independence was signed in Philadelphia by 56 delegates, all of whom risked death for treason if the Revolution failed. Today, these men are still celebrated for their remarkable commitment to independence. The Fourth of July is a day for American-style feasting including backyard barbecues and picnics in the park or at the beach. Americans cook a wide range of foods from a simple meal of hot dogs and beans to a Texas barbecue or a New England clambake. Many regions have slightly different cooking traditions, but the most important thing is to keep it cool and simple.

A July Fourth favorite is corn on the cob. The fresher the corn, the better it will taste. Keep corn refrigerated and unshucked until just before cooking.

Corn on the Cob

Yield: *serves 6 to 8*
   10 to 12 ears of corn
   water, as needed
   butter or margarine, for serving
   salt and pepper to taste, for serving

Equipment: Large saucepan with cover, metal tongs

1. Remove husks and silk from each ear, and rinse them under cold running water.

2. Fill large saucepan about half full with water. Bring water to a boil over high heat. Using tongs, carefully drop corn into water, making sure each cob is completely submerged. Bring water back to boiling for 1 minute, cover, and turn heat off. Leave the cover on the pan, and let corn sit in water 5 to 10 minutes (5 minutes for young ears, longer for mature corn).

3. Remove corn cobs from water, using metal tongs.

Serve with butter or margarine and salt and pepper to taste.

Cookies are fun to munch on while watching the parade or fireworks. These are easy to make, no-bake cookies.

Peanut Butter Cookies

Yield: *about 2 dozen*
   1 cup peanut butter chips
   1 cup chunky peanut butter
   4 cups cornflakes

Equipment: Medium saucepan, wooden mixing spoon, 8-inch square baking pan

1. In medium saucepan, melt peanut butter chips over low heat until smooth. Add peanut butter, and mix well.

2. Remove from heat and **fold in** cornflakes. Spread in 8-inch square baking pan and refrigerate until set, about 2 hours.

To serve, cut into 24 serving-size pieces.

Thanksgiving

Thanksgiving is a time for family reunions and bountiful feasts shared with others. For American children, it is a time to learn about their American heritage, the legend of the Pilgrims, and the story of Thanksgiving.

Today's Thanksgiving is a blend of three Pilgrim traditions: rejoicing after a successful harvest, based on ancient English harvest festivals; the Puritans' solemn religious ritual combining prayer and feasting; and the celebration of the Pilgrims' landing, known as Forefathers' Day.

The story of the Pilgrims is one of courage and survival for the men and women who left their homeland in search of a better life. They sought to escape religious persecution and economic problems by immigrating to America in 1620. Thus, in the autumn of 1621, after a year of sickness and scarcity, their labors were rewarded with a bountiful harvest. The Pilgrims gave thanks with a feast and prayer in the English tradition they knew so well. They invited neighboring Indians, who had helped them through their ordeal, to join in their three-day celebration.

It was Abraham Lincoln who declared Thanksgiving Day to be an official national holiday in 1863.

This salad recipe is taken from an original 1591 cookbook brought to America by the Pilgrims. Boiled Salad was called *boyled sallet.*

Boiled Salad

Yield: *serves 6*

3 pounds fresh spinach, **blanched,** or 2 (10 ounces each) boxes frozen chopped spinach, thawed

¼ cup butter or margarine

½ cup seedless raisins or dried currants, soaked in warm water 10 minutes and drained

$^1/_3$ cup vinegar

1 tablespoon brown sugar

salt and pepper to taste

Equipment: **Colander,** large skillet, mixing spoon

1. Chop spinach, if necessary, and drain in colander.

2. Melt butter or margarine in large skillet over medium-high heat. Add raisins or currants, vinegar, and brown sugar, stir, and cook for 3 minutes to blend flavors. Add spinach and salt and

pepper to taste; toss to coat well. Cook to heat through, about 3 minutes, tossing frequently.

Serve as a side dish with Thanksgiving turkey.

Cranberries are an important part of the Thanksgiving feast. The Pilgrims gave the cranberry its name, "crane berry," because its pink blossom and drooping head looked like the head of a crane. Indians and Pilgrims used cranberries for food, cloth dye, and medicinal purposes.

Fresh Cranberry Relish

Yield: *about 4 cups*

1 pound cranberries, fresh or frozen, thawed and **finely chopped**

1 large, seedless orange, with the skin on and finely chopped

2 cups sugar

1 cup drained, crushed canned pineapple

Equipment: Medium mixing bowl with cover, wooden mixing spoon

In medium mixing bowl, mix cranberries, orange, sugar, and pineapple. Cover and refrigerate for at least two days before serving.

Serve as a relish with turkey. Relish freezes well.

Corn, native to America, was unknown to the Pilgrims; the Indians taught them how to grow it, and it was eaten at the first Thanksgiving. Today corn remains a symbolic reminder of the feast and the friendship of Indians.

Indian Corn Pudding
(also called "Hasty Pudding")

Yield: *serves 6 to 8*

3 cups milk

¼ cup cornmeal

¼ cup sugar

½ teaspoon *each* salt, ground ginger, and ground cinnamon

⅛ teaspoon baking soda

¼ cup dark molasses

1 cup frozen whipped topping, thawed, for serving

½ teaspoon ground nutmeg, for **garnish**

Equipment: Medium saucepan, wooden mixing spoon, buttered or nonstick 1-quart casserole, oven mitts

Preheat oven to 275° F.

1. In medium saucepan, cook 2 cups milk over low heat until small bubbles appear around edges, about 3 minutes. Add cornmeal, a little at a time, stirring constantly until well blended. Stirring frequently, cook for about 15 minutes, or until thickened. Remove from heat.

2. Add sugar, salt, ginger, cinnamon, baking soda, remaining 1 cup milk, and molasses; stir well. Pour pudding batter into buttered or nonstick 1-quart casserole.

3. Bake in oven for 2 hours, or until set.

Serve warm with dollop of whipped topping, and sprinkle each serving with nutmeg.

Traditionally, the Thanksgiving feast ends with pumpkin pie.

Pumpkin Pie

Yield: *serves 8 to 10*

1½ cups canned solid-pack pumpkin

3 eggs, beaten

1 cup sour cream

½ cup heavy cream

½ cup unsulphured molasses

1 teaspoon *each* ground ginger, ground allspice, and ground cinnamon

9-inch unbaked pie crust, homemade (recipe page 108) or frozen, thawed

Equipment: Large mixing bowl, mixing spoon, rubber **spatula**, 9-inch pie pan, aluminum foil, baking sheet, oven mitts

Preheat oven to 400° F.

1. In large mixing bowl, mix pumpkin, eggs, sour cream, heavy cream, molasses, ginger, allspice, and cinnamon. Pour pumpkin mixture into pie crust and place on foil-covered baking sheet.

3. Bake in oven for 20 minutes. Reduce heat to 325° F., and continue baking for about 30 minutes, or until pie is set but slightly wobbly in the center.

Serve at room temperature, cut into wedges.

Kwanzaa
December 26 to New Year's Day

Black Americans have played a vital part in American history. It is important to recognize the role they have had in making freedom, for all people, a cherished right.

At the height of the Civil Rights movement in 1966, a Californian by the name of Maulana (Ron) Karenga organized a cultural observance for Black Americans. He called it *Kwanzaa,* which means "first fruits of the harvest" in Swahili, the language used by most East Africans. Kwanzaa begins on December 26th, ends on New Year's Day, and is observed by millions of Black Americans; Mr. Karenga wants the rituals to continue for generations to come.

In many large cities, one day of *Kwanzaa* is devoted to showcasing Black culture with dances, music, readings, and remembrances. Some communities organize a lavish feast, the *Kwanzaa Karamu,* for which only authentic African, Caribbean, and South American dishes are prepared. Most of the recipes in the African, Latin American, and Caribbean sections of this book can be prepared for *Kwanzaa*.

Eating the same food ancestors ate is one way children can assimilate their culture. Cornmeal mush was all that most slaves had to eat. This recipe is from an old Southern cookbook printed in 1929, called *Mandy's Favorite Louisiana Recipes*.

Cornmeal Mush

Yield: *serves 4*

2 cups stone-ground white or yellow cornmeal
½ cup hot water
1 cup milk
1 teaspoon baking powder
1 egg, beaten
1 tablespoon sugar or corn syrup
salt to taste
sugar, for serving
4 tablespoons butter, more if necessary
milk or light cream, for serving

Equipment: Medium mixing bowl, wooden mixing spoon, medium cast iron or nonstick skillet, metal **spatula**

1. Put cornmeal in medium mixing bowl. Add hot water, and mix well. Add milk, baking powder, egg, sugar or corn syrup, and salt to taste; mix well.

2. Melt butter in medium cast iron or nonstick skillet over high heat. Add cornmeal mixture, and, using a spatula, spread it out to cover bottom of pan. Reduce heat to medium, and let a bottom crust form. As the crust forms, use the spatula to keep turning sections of the mush over to brown it all over.

Serve as a dessert with sugar, milk, or light cream.

One-pot stews were made with whatever the hard-working plantation slaves could grow, catch, or kill. Years ago in the South along the Gulf of Mexico, the bayous and estuaries were full of shrimp, crayfish, crab, and fish. Shrimp were so plentiful that they could be scooped up by the bucket, using hand nets.

This recipe is a typical Southern dish that can be served for *Kwanzaa Karamu*; any size shrimp can be used.

Jambalaya   Ham with Rice

Yield: *serves 4 to 6*

4 slices bacon, **coarsely chopped**
1 large onion, coarsely chopped
3 cloves garlic, **finely chopped**, or 1 teaspoon garlic granules
2 green peppers, **cored**, **seeded**, and cut in chunks
1 cup raw rice
1 (16- to 20-ounce) can stewed tomatoes
3½ cups chicken broth, homemade (recipe page 52) or canned
1 cup coarsely chopped cooked smoked ham
1 pound headless shrimp, **peeled** and **deveined**
salt and pepper to taste
liquid red pepper sauce, to taste

Equipment: **Dutch oven** or large saucepan with cover, mixing spoon

1. Heat bacon in Dutch oven or large saucepan over medium-high heat until **rendered,** about 3 minutes. Add onion, garlic, and green peppers, and, stirring frequently, fry until soft, about 3 minutes. Add rice, stir, and cook for 3 minutes.

2. Add tomatoes, chicken broth, and ham, and stir well. Bring to a boil, and then reduce heat to simmer. Cover and cook for 15 minutes. Add shrimp, salt and pepper to taste, and red pepper to taste; stir well. Cover and cook over low heat for 10 minutes, or until shrimp are **opaque** white and rice is tender.

Serve from the cooking pot with crusty bread for sopping.

Combining peanut butter with jelly is an American favorite all children seem to enjoy. During *Kwanzaa* make a batch of cookies described below for family and friends, and while everyone is munching, tell them that peanut butter is made from groundnuts and that we have the African slaves to thank for this delicious treat.

In the early 1500s the Portuguese brought the peanut to West Africa where it was soon established as a crop in Senegal and Gambia, still two of the world's largest peanut-producing countries. From West Africa to Tanzania and Mozambique in East Africa, peanut butter is added to meat and vegetable stews, cornmeal, beans, spinach, and squash.

Quick and Easy Peanut Butter and Jelly Cookies

Yield: *makes about 25 cookies*
  1 cup peanut butter, either plain or chunky
  1 cup sugar
  1 egg, beaten
  ½ cup your favorite jam or jelly, more or less, for **garnish**

Equipment: Medium mixing bowl, wooden mixing spoon, ungreased or nonstick cookie sheet, oven mitts

Preheat oven to 350° F.

1. In medium mixing bowl, mix peanut butter, sugar, and egg until well blended.

2. Form dough into ping-pong-size balls and place 1 inch apart on cookie sheet. Flatten slightly, and, using your finger or handle of wooden spoon, poke a dimple into the top of each cookie.

3. Bake in oven for about 25 minutes, or until light brown around the edges and firm to the touch.

4. When cooled to room temperature, fill each dimple with ¼ teaspoon of your favorite jam, for garnish.

Serve as a sweet snack with a glass of milk.

Cinco de Mayo
Texas and Southwestern United States

A regional celebration among Mexican Americans in Texas and other Southwestern communities is *El Cinco de Mayo*, on May 5. It is the anniversary of the Mexicans' victorious battle over the French in 1867, who had invaded and conquered Mexico in 1864 and had placed their French emperor, named Maximilian, on the throne. The Mexican army under General Ignacio Zaragoza defeated the French, even though the Mexicans suffered heavy losses. The military victory in itself was not so important. It was more of a moral victory, symbolizing the eventual defeat of French intervention. Throughout Mexico, every year, there is a reenactment of the battle, and the performance is called *La Batalla del Cinco de Mayo*, "The Battle of the Fifth of May."

Celebrating *Cinco de Mayo* gives Mexican American communities in the United States a chance to celebrate their heritage with huge *fiestas* (celebrations), colorful parades with mariachi bands (Mexican musicians), traditional Mexican folk dancers, vendors selling pottery, weaving, and assorted art work, as well as a great fireworks display in the evening.

The fiestas include plenty of food and beverage booths with *quesadillas* (recipe follows later in this section) and *sopa de tortilla* (recipe follows), made with *tortillas* (recipe page 249). *Nogada* (recipe page 248) and *tamales* (recipe page 251) are also served as part of the festivities.

Sopa de Tortilla   Tortilla Soup

Yield: *serves 4*

2 (6-inch each) corn tortillas, homemade (recipe page 249) or commercial (available at most supermarkets)

4 tablespoons vegetable oil

4 cups chicken broth, homemade (recipe page 52) or canned

4 tablespoons **finely chopped** onion

6 tablespoons tomato paste

2 tablespoons finely chopped fresh **cilantro** or 1 teaspoon dried **coriander** (cilantro)

½ cup shredded Monterey Jack cheese, for **garnish**

Equipment: Knife, work surface, baking sheet, paper towels, medium skillet, tongs or metal **spatula**, medium saucepan, mixing spoon

1. Cut tortillas into ¼-inch strips. Cover baking sheet with paper towels. Heat oil in medium skillet over medium-high heat. Add tortillas strips, and fry, turning frequently, until crisp and lightly browned, about 3 minutes. Drain on paper towels and keep warm.

2. Pour broth into medium saucepan. Add onion, stir, and cook over medium heat for about 15 minutes until onion is soft. Add tomato paste and fresh cilantro or dried coriander, stir, and cook for 5 minutes.

To serve, divide tortilla strips equally between 4 individual soup bowls, fill with broth mixture, and sprinkle with cheese.

Quesadillas are grilled sandwiches using tortillas instead of bread.

Quesadillas   Tortilla Sandwiches

Yield: *serves 3 to 4*

1 tablespoon vegetable oil

3 tablespoons *each* **finely shredded** or chopped yellow squash, zucchini (**cored** and **seeded**), red bell pepper, onion, and carrots

2 to 4 tablespoons water or chicken broth

salt and pepper to taste

½ cup shredded Monterey Jack cheese

6 (6½-inch) flour tortillas

1 tablespoon butter or margarine, more or less as needed

Equipment: **Grater** or knife, large skillet, mixing spoon, work surface, metal **spatula**

1. Prepare filling: Heat oil in large skillet over medium-high heat. Add squash, zucchini, red bell pepper, onion, and carrots, and stir-fry for about 3 minutes, until soft. Add 2 tablespoons water or chicken broth, and simmer for 5 minutes, mixing frequently. If mixture is too dry and sticks, add remaining 2 tablespoons water or broth; mix well. Add salt and pepper to taste; mix well.

2. Place 3 tortillas side by side on work surface. Cover each tortilla equally with cooked vegetables and sprinkle equally with shredded cheese. Make into sandwiches by covering each filled tortilla with one of the 3 remaining tortillas.

3. Grill *quesadillas*: Melt 1 tablespoon butter or margarine in large skillet over medium heat. Place 1 quesadilla sandwich in pan, and gently press down, using back of metal spatula. Add more butter or margarine, as needed. Fry until golden brown and cheese melts, about 3 to 5 minutes on each side. Keep warm until ready to serve.

To serve, cut each into 4 wedges. To eat, pick up with your fingers.

Mardi Gras
New Orleans and Louisiana

In New Orleans and southern Louisiana, Mardi Gras begins with the Twelfth-Night Reveler's Ball and comes to a close at the final ball on Mardi Gras night. Mardi Gras is the last fling or celebration most Catholics enjoy before heading into the 40 days of Lent, and it is very similar to the Carnival celebrations held throughout Latin America and other Catholic countries. The celebrations include parades with fantastic floats, costumed and masked dancers, many marching bands, and Mardi Gras beads, which are thrown from the floats.

The traditional Creole food, such as red beans and rice (recipe follows later in this section), *jambalaya* (recipe page 265), and king cake (recipe follows), are part of the Mardi Gras celebration.

The tradition of king cakes began with the celebration of Epiphany centuries ago. Epiphany, which was also sometimes called "Little Christmas" or the Twelfth Night of Christmas, was a time for exchanging gifts and feasting. Epiphany is celebrated on January 6 and honors the coming of the Wise Men bearing gifts to the Christ child twelve days after his birth (Christmas Day). In European countries Twelfth Night was celebrated with a special cake baked for the occasion. The king cake was made to honor the three kings. Today the traditions continue. The Europeans hide a bean inside their cake, and the person finding it must portray one of the kings. Latin Americans put a small figure inside the cake representing the Christ child. It is said the finder will have a year of good fortune and is obligated to host the next Mardi Gras party.

Louisiana adopted the tradition, and king cakes have become part of Mardi Gras. King cake parties continue from the twelfth day of Christmas up to Fat Tuesday, Mardi Gras day. Louisiana king cakes are baked with a figure inside representing the Christ child. The finder of the figure is obligated to host the next Mardi Gras party. King cakes were originally a simple ring of dough with little decorations; the New Orleans-style king cake is brightly decorated with Mardi Gras colors—gold, purple, and green. It is sprinkled with colored sugar and pieces of glazed fruit.

King Cake

Yield: *serves 8 to 10*
  2 cups all-purpose flour
  ¼ cup sugar
  1 package active dry yeast
  ½ cup milk
  ¼ cup butter or margarine
  3 eggs, at room temperature
  ½ cup *each* mixed candied fruits and raisins
  foil-wrapped symbolic toy figure that is heat-proof (optional)
  colored sugar sprinkles, for **garnish**

Equipment: Large mixing bowl, small saucepan, mixing spoon or electric mixer, kitchen towel, greased 10-inch **tube pan,** oven mitts

1. In large mixing bowl, combine ¾ cup flour, sugar, and dry yeast.

2. Pour milk into small saucepan. Add butter or margarine, and heat until lukewarm (butter or margarine does not need to melt).

3. Gradually add milk mixture to flour mixture in large bowl, and beat, using mixing spoon or electric mixer, until well blended, about 2 minutes. Add eggs, one at a time, beating well after each addition. Add ½ cup flour, or enough flour to make a thick batter, and beat for about 2 minutes. Add remaining ¾ cup flour and beat well for another 2 minutes. Cover with kitchen towel, and set in warm place until bubbly, about 1 hour.

Preheat oven to 350° F.

4. Using mixing spoon, fold candied fruit and raisins into batter. Pour batter into greased 10-inch tube pan and poke foil-wrapped, heat-proof toy into batter.

5. Bake in oven for about 40 minutes, or until golden brown.

Cool to warm and sprinkle with colored sugar sprinkles, for garnish.

For many years the standard wash day Monday supper among the Cajun, Arcadian, and Creole people living in Louisiana was red beans and rice. Red beans and rice are part of the New Orleans cooking heritage and are traditionally eaten during Mardi Gras.

New Orleans Red Beans and Rice

Yield: *serves 4 to 6*

 2 tablespoons vegetable oil
 ½ cup **finely chopped** onions
 ½ cup finely chopped celery
 1 green bell pepper, **cored, seeded,** and finely chopped
 3 cloves garlic, finely chopped, or 1 teaspoon garlic granules
 2 cans (about 12 ounces each) red beans, including liquid (available at most supermarkets)
 ¼ teaspoon ground red pepper, more or less to taste
 salt and pepper to taste
 4 to 6 cups cooked rice (keep warm, for serving)

Equipment: **Dutch oven** or medium saucepan with cover, mixing spoon, potato masher

1. Heat oil in Dutch oven or medium saucepan over medium-high heat. Add onions, celery, green pepper, and garlic, and, stirring constantly, fry until onions are soft, about 3 minutes.

2. Add beans with liquid from can and ¼ teaspoon ground red pepper (more or less to taste), and stir. Cover and cook, stirring occasionally, for 15 minutes.

3. Using potato masher or back of mixing spoon, coarsely mash beans and continue to cook, uncovered, over low heat until thickened, about 20 minutes. Add salt and pepper to taste; stir well.

To serve, spoon bean mixture over rice in individual soup bowls.

Oktoberfest
German-Americans

In the United States, there are some German settlements that keep alive the tradition of holding the popular Munich festival, the *Oktoberfest*, in the fall of the year. Few communities, however, do it better than the Germans in Wisconsin.

The Munich *Oktoberfest* lasts for 16 days in late September and early October. It began in 1810, to celebrate the marriage of Crown Prince Ludwig of Bavaria.

At the Munich festival it is the tradition to spit-roast whole oxen over open fires, as well as whole chickens, fish, and tons of *bratwurst* (recipe follows). For the children, there are tables of sweets, among them *lebkuchen* (recipe page 117).

At a regional Octoberfest in the United States there are the oom-pa-pa bands, costumed folk dancers, and singing. Everyone has a *gemütliche* (wonderful) time, eating, drinking, and singing old German songs; most evenings end with fireworks.

Bratwurst   German Sausage

Yield: *serves 6*

 1½ pounds coarsely ground lean pork
 ¼ pound finely ground fatty pork
 1 teaspoon ground sage
 1 teaspoon ground cloves
 ½ teaspoon rosemary
 salt and pepper to taste
 6 hard rolls, for serving
 2 tablespoons mustard, for **garnish**

Equipment: Medium mixing bowl with cover, mixing spoon, wax paper, work surface, large skillet, large metal **spatula**

1. Put ground pork, sage, cloves, rosemary, and salt and pepper to taste in medium mixing bowl,

and stir well. Cover and refrigerate for flavors to ripen overnight.

2. Using wet, clean hands, form the meat into 6 balls, put on wax-paper-covered work surface, and press into patties.

3. Fry patties in large skillet over medium-high heat, for about 8 minutes on each side, until well done. Keep warm, and continue frying in batches.

To serve bratwurst, *make a sandwich on a hard roll and spread with mustard, for garnish.*

Chinese American New Year
San Francisco and other large cities

It has been the custom for generations of Chinese immigrants to settle within a certain section of large American cities, which became known as "Chinatowns." Within the American Chinatowns, there are grocery, drug, and clothing stores; bakeries; tea houses; and restaurants filled with foods and products familiar to the Chinese people, allowing the community to maintain the Chinese culture and way of life.

The Chinese Americans keep ancient traditions alive, such as celebrating the Chinese New Year. The Chinese New Year falls sometime between January and February, depending on the Chinese calendar. The celebration begins with a new moon and ends two weeks later with the Feast of Lanterns when the moon is full. The elaborate festivities are accompanied by loud noises made by banging on gongs, cymbals, and the constant shooting of firecrackers to keep away evil spirits. Chinese firecrackers are always red; the traditional color of good omens. The highlight of the celebration is the dragon parade. (The golden dragon is one of the four divine creatures of the Chinese. The others are the unicorn, the phoenix, and the tortoise, and they all are supposed to dispel the bad spirits of ancient times.)

For the Chinese American New Year, the house must be cleaned and all debts paid. One is not supposed to use sharp instruments, because they will cut away good fortune, nor wash one's hair, because according to legend, it will drown luck.

The New Year's feast would include *jo pien san wei*, spring rolls, and New Year's rice (see recipes under China). The only dessert most Chinese like is fruit, and the following recipe is a popular combination.

Litchi Nut Fruit Mixture

Yield: *serves 6 to 8*

1 (10-ounce) can seedless litchi nuts, drained (available at some supermarkets and all Asian food stores)

2 kiwis, **peeled** and thinly sliced

1 cup seedless green grapes

1 cup canned pineapple chunks, drained

½ cantaloupe, seeded, peeled, and cut into ¼-inch chunks

Equipment: Medium mixing bowl, mixing spoon

In medium mixing bowl, combine litchi nuts, kiwis, grapes, pineapple chunks, and cantaloupe chunks; toss gently and refrigerate until ready to serve.

To serve, spoon into individual dessert bowls.

Festival of San Gennaro
New York City

Between the years 1880 and 1910, there was a large influx of Italian immigrants who came to America, mostly from the southern and central regions of the country, among them the Sicily, Calabria, Campani, and Abruzzi regions. A large number of immigrants settled in one area of New York City that became known as "Little Italy."

Every year in "Little Italy" the descendants of relatives who came from Naples hold the Festival of San Gennaro, in honor of the patron saint of Naples (Gennaro is also known as St. Januarius). The celebration is held for 11 days in September, beginning with religious processions and solemn masses, and continuing with music, dancing in the streets, games of chance, and every kind of traditional Italian food imaginable.

There are booths selling pizzas, sausage, Italian ice cream, *uova tonnate* (recipe page 94), and sweets of every description, among them *torta mandorla* (recipe follows) and fruitcake pizza cookies (recipe follows).

Torta mandorla develops a fuller flavor if made a day ahead. This recipe is from Isle of Capri.

Torta Mandorla   Almond Torte

Yield: *serves 8 to 10*

¾ cup butter or margarine, at room temperature, more as needed

1 tablespoon all-purpose flour, for preparing pan

7 **egg yolks**

1 cup sugar

2 cups **finely ground** almonds

1 cup melted semi-sweet chocolate squares or chips

¼ cup confectioners' sugar, for **garnish**

Equipment: 8-inch **springform pan**, scissors, wax paper, medium mixing bowl, mixing spoon or electric mixer, rubber **spatula**, oven mitts, toothpick

1. Set oven rack so that it sits in the lower half of oven. Preheat oven to 350° F.

2. Prepare springform pan: Cut a circle of wax paper to fit smoothly over bottom of pan. Using 1 tablespoon butter or margarine, lightly grease pan

bottom, cover with wax paper, and then grease wax paper and sides of pan. Sprinkle with 1 tablespoon flour and shake off excess.

3. In medium mixing bowl, use mixing spoon or electric mixer to mix egg yolks and sugar until creamy. Add ¾ cup butter or margarine, and mix until smooth. Add almonds and melted chocolate, and mix about 3 minutes. The batter will be dense, not fluffy. Using spatula, transfer batter to prepared springform pan.

4. Bake in lower half of oven for about 45 minutes, until set. Cool to room temperature.

To serve, remove sides of pan, invert cake onto serving platter, and pull off wax paper. Sprinkle with confectioners' sugar and cut into wedges.

Fruitcake Pizza Cookies

Yield: *about 26 pieces*

2 cups all-purpose flour

½ teaspoon salt

½ cup cold butter or margarine, **coarsely chopped**

1½ cups sugar

3 eggs

3 tablespoons light cream

1 cup *each* seedless raisins, chopped dates, chopped candied fruit, and chopped walnuts, almonds, or pecans

juice of 2 lemons

Equipment: Large mixing bowl, mixing spoon, small mixing bowl, mixing spoon, 4 (6-inch size) greased or nonstick pizza pans, medium mixing bowl, oven mitts

Preheat oven to 350° F.

1. In large mixing bowl, mix flour and salt. Add chunks of butter or margarine, and, using clean fingers, blend until mixture resembles coarse crumbs. Add 1 cup sugar, and blend well with fingers until mixture resembles fine crumbs.

2. In small mixing bowl, mix 1 egg and cream. Add to flour mixture, and, using your hands, form into smooth dough. Divide dough into 4 balls. Pat each out to cover bottom of 4 greased or nonstick 6-inch pizza pans.

3. Bake in oven for 20 minutes, until set.

4. Prepare topping: In medium mixing bowl, mix remaining ½ cup sugar, 2 eggs, raisins, dates, candied fruit, nuts, and lemon juice until well blended. Spread evenly over baked dough. Return to oven and continue baking for about 20 minutes. Remove from oven and, while still warm, cut each into 6 or 8 wedges.

Serve as sweet snack. Refrigerate in airtight container.

Index

by Ty Koontz

Breads (*continued*)
cheese, Georgian *(khachapuri)*, 143
Christmas, Italian *(panettone)*, 94–95
corn, Romanian bread of gold *(mamaliga de aur)*, 81
corn *(sopa paraguaya)*, 231
cornmeal cakes *(mealie-meal)*, 16
of the dead *(pan de muerto)*, 255
dumplings, bread *(houskové knedliky)*, 87
Easter bread, Greek *(lambropsoma)*, 76
flat, Arab *(kimaje)*, 69
flat, coconut, Sri Lankan *(rotis)*, 163
flat, cornmeal (tortillas), 249–50
flat, Ethiopian *(injera)*, 8
flat, Indian *(paratha)*, 161
fried pillows *(sopapillas)*, 245
fried, sweet potato *(bammies)*, 204–05
fritters, banana *(buñuelos de plátano)*, 243
fritters, black-eyed pea *(acarajé)*, 229–30
fritters, corn, 214
kneading, xxvi
Lucia buns *(lussekatter)*, 124–25
matzo meal cakes, fried *(boobelach)*, 53
nut and potato cake *(bolo polana)*, 10–11
pancakes, potato *(latkes)*, 54–55
pizza, Armenian *(lahmajoun)*, 145
pudding, chocolate *(capirotada)*, 242
pudding, Indonesian *(kueh prol nanas)*, 192
pudding, South American *(capritoda)*, 235
pudding, sweet apple bread, 134
punching down, xxvii–xxviii
rusk, buttermilk *(karringmelkbeskuit)*, 14–15
sweet, Pakistani *(shahi tukra)*, 158–59
Turkish rings *(simi)*, 63–64
unleavened *(matzo)*, 52

Breaking of the Fast. *See Eid al-Fitr*
Broth. *See* Soups and stews
Brown Sauce, 185
Browned-Flour Soup *(Mehlsuppe)*, 91–92
Brussels sprouts, chestnuts and, 107–08
Bstila (Chicken Pie), 42–43
Bûche de Noël (Yule Log Cake), 73, 101–03
Buckwheat Noodles in Broth *(Toshi Koshi Soba)*, 180
Buddhism, 150
calendar, xxxiv
Bulb baster, xxiii
Bulgaria, 79–80
Khliah Raiska Ptitsa (Bird-of-Paradise Bread), 80
Tarator (Yogurt Walnut Soup), 79
Bulgogi (Korean Barbecued Beef), 177–78
Bulgur
pilaf *(bulgur pilavi)*, 65
salad *(tabbouleh)*, 59
Bulgur Pilavi (Cracked Wheat Pilaf), 65
Bullas (Caribbean Christmas Cookies), 215–16
Buñuelos de Plátano (Banana Fritters), 243
Buñuelos (Fried Pastry), 252–53
Burkina Faso, 36–37
African Greens in Peanut Sauce, 37
Groundnut Cookies (Peanut Cookies), 37
Groundnut Truffles (Peanut Candy), 37
Burma. *See* Myanmar (Burma)
Burundi. *See* Rwanda/Burundi
Butter
clarified Indian *(ghee)*, 160
ghee rice, 163–64
peanut, 36
peanut butter cookies, 262
Butter cookies
Armenian *(shakarishee)*, 146
Hungarian *(pogacsa)*, 86–87
Butter Festival, 134–35
Buttermilk rusk *(karringmelkbeskuit)*, 14–15

Cabbage
and bacon, 15–16
braised red cabbage *(rodkaal)*, 120–21
pickled *(kimchi)*, 178

salad, pineapple and cabbage, 195–96
soup, Laotian *(keng kalampi)*, 173
Cacik (Turkish Cucumber Salad), 65–66
Cakes. *See also* Breads
almond *(bolo de amêndoa)*, 98
almond torte *(torte mandorla)*, 271
almond, with lemon syrup *(basboosa)*, 49–50
apple, Bavarian *(apfelkuchen)*, 90
coconut loaf, 215
cornmeal *(mealie-meal)*, 16
with cream of coconut *(bien me sabe de coco)*, 238–39
crullers, May Day *(tippaleipa)*, 127–28
date bars *(mescouta)*, 44
Easter *(kulich)*, 135–36
fruitcake, boiled, 113
King, 268
matzo meal, fried *(boobelach)*, 53
Mother Monsen's *(Mor Monsen's kaker)*, 123
nut and potato *(bolo polana)*, 10–11
orange, 217–18
plum pudding ice cream cake, 199
potato, crusty *(rösti)*, 92
potato, Ecuadorian *(llapingachos)*, 234
pound, Scandinavian *(sandkake)*, 118–19
rice, golden *(kateh)*, 62
Sicilian *(cassata alla Siciliana)*, 95–96
spice, Caribbean, 206
sponge, cream filled *(chajá)*, 225
sponge, fried *(torrijas)*, 246–47
sponge, Passover lemon, 54
upside down, 197
Yule log *(Bûche de Noël)*, 101–03
Calabaza Enmielada (Honeyed Squash), 244–45
Calendars
Buddhist, xxxiv
Chinese, xxxiv
Christian, xxxii
Gregorian, xxxii
Hebrew, xxxii–xxxiii
Hindu, xxxiii
Islamic, xxxiii